Martin Heidegger's Path of Thinking

Contemporary Studies in Philosophy and the Human Sciences

Series editor: John Sallis
Associate editor: Hugh J. Silverman

Published

* Robert Bernasconi: **The Question of Language in Heidegger's History of Being**
  Peter Caws: **Structuralism**
  Mikel Dufrenne: **In the Presence of the Sensuous**
* John Llewelyn: **Beyond Metaphysics?**
  Louis Marin: **Utopics: Spatial Play**
* Graeme Nicholson: **Seeing and Reading**
* Otto Pöggeler: **Martin Heidegger's Path of Thinking**
* Charles E. Scott: **The Language of Difference**
  Jacques Taminiaux: **Dialectic and Difference**
  David Wood: **The Deconstruction of Time**

Forthcoming

James W. Bernauer: **Michel Foucault's Force of Flight**

* Also available in paperback

Martin Heidegger's Path of Thinking

Otto Pöggeler

translated by
Daniel Magurshak
and
Sigmund Barber

HUMANITIES PRESS INTERNATIONAL, INC.
Atlantic Highlands, NJ

Originally published as Der Denkweg Martin Heideggers,
©1963   Neske Publishers

First published in 1987 by
Humanities Press International, Inc.,
Atlantic Highlands, NJ 07716

Reprinted 1989

Paperback edition first published 1989

Reprinted 1990

©1987, 1989 by Humanities Press International, Inc.

Library of Congress Cataloging-in-Publication Data

Poggeler, Otto.
    Martin Heidegger's path of thinking.

    (Contemporary studies in philosophy and the human
sciences)
    Translation of: Der Denkweg Martin Heideggers.
    Bibliography: p.
    Includes index
    1. Heidegger, Martin, 1889—1976.   I. Title.
II. Series.
B3279.H49P613   1987   193   85-27152
ISBN 0-391-03367-0
ISBN 0-391-03616-5 (PBK.)

PRINTED IN THE UNITED STATES OF AMERICA

Contents

Preface   vii
Preface to the American Edition   ix
Introduction   1

1. The Entrance into Metaphysics   9

2. Metaphysics and History   17
     Dilthey and Modern Historical Thought   19
     The Factical Experience of Life in the Christian Faith   24

3. Fundamental Ontology as the Grounding of Metaphysics   33
     The Fundamental Analysis of Dasein   38
     Dasein and Temporality   44
     Time and Being   47

4. Phenomenology—Transcendental Philosophy—
     Metaphysics   51
     Transcendental and Hermeneutical Phenomenology   51
     Transcendental Philosophy and Metaphysics   62

5. Going Back to the Ground of Metaphysics   69
     Truth and Freedom   71
     On the Essence of Truth   75

6. Metaphysics as History   79
     Plato's Theory of Truth   79
     Nietzsche as the Turning Point   82
     Metaphysics as the History of Being   107

7. The Overcoming of Metaphysics   115
     Identity, Difference, Ground   117
     The Transformation of Thinking   131

8. The Other Beginning   153
     The First Beginning of Thinking   158
     The Seminality of Art   167
     Hölderlin and the Other Beginning   174

9. The Freeing Toward What Is One's Own   191
      Insight into What Is   193
      The World as Fourfold   200

10. The Question of Saying   217
      The Way Toward Language   218
      The Topology of Being   227

Appendix   243
Notes   247
Afterword to the Second Edition   259
Index   289

PREFACE

A year after the first English translation of *Sein und Zeit* appeared in English, Otto Pöggeler's *Der Denkweg Martin Heideggers* was published. Among those whose imaginations were captured by Heidegger's thinking and who learned German to experience his ways, this book became something of a find. It became known as perhaps the most comprehensive, most accurate overview of Heidegger's thinking available in any language. Its focus on the origins of Heidegger's ways, the sense of his new concepts, and the transformation of these concepts as his questioning unfolded provided much impetus to the still growing wave of international Heideggerian scholarship. Yet for whatever reasons, the book which has been translated into several languages has not appeared in English until now, even though many recognized English-speaking Heidegger scholars acknowledge *Der Denkweg* as perhaps the single most helpful introduction to Heidegger's enterprise that is available.

Over twenty years has passed since this book appeared in German. In that time, the English-speaking world has contributed volumes of excellent scholarship to the understanding of Heidegger's thinking. The philosophical scene has also changed significantly since then in ways familiar to all. Nonetheless, it is a testimony to the quality of this book that in 1983 a second, unrevised German edition was published, and that Humanities Press has undertaken to make it available in English.

The book provides its own introduction in Professor Pöggeler's preface to what he calls the "American edition." It also enters into the contemporary discussion about Heidegger in the new "Afterword to the Second Edition." Hence, only a few translator's comments are necessary.

The quixotic aim of all translators guided this effort: to render the German text as faithfully as possible into the clearest English without distorting the sense of the work. The difficulties that Heidegger's work presents to the translator are by now common knowledge, and the plethora of available translations of key terms is a mixed blessing. We did not aim at breaking new ground. We considered the possibilities, both tried and untried, for key concepts and then decided upon what seemed best to us. The choice may often be controversial. We have also decided to leave all references to the German editions of Heidegger's writings as they are. This allows the reader to check the translation against the original discussion of whatever is at issue. The system of referencing followed by Pöggeler throughout the text usually is as follows. In his initial reference to the work, he provides the reader with the title; afterwards, if reference has been made to no other work in the meantime, he provides only a page number. If reference to other works has occurred, he uses an abbreviation for the previously mentioned work along with the page number. The slight variations in this method which can be found pose no serious problems for the reader. The index of works at the end of the text gives a key to these abbreviations; it also correlates the German texts with available English translations. As a service to the reader, the marginal pagination provides easy access to the original German text.

A note about the term *Denkweg*. The best translation for this term is "way of thinking" in the sense of the "course" or "path" that thinking takes. The crucial connotations of journeying, being underway, and travelling which accrue to "way" must not be overlooked, for Pöggeler, following Heidegger, returns to them again and again. "Way," however, can also mean "method" or "manner" in English, as in the "way things are done," but this latter sense fails to capture the richness of *Denkweg*. Thus in contexts where "way" could be understood as method, we have translated it as "path." We speak, depending on context, of Martin Heidegger's way or path of thinking.

As in any effort of this magnitude, much thanking is in order. A fellowship from the Alexander von Humboldt-Stiftung made possible, among other things, my personal acquaintance with Professor Pöggeler and the first translation of the work. In addition, both Grinnell College and Carthage College have provided funds to help defray the costs of this enterprise. Special thanks must go to Dr. Michael Heim, our reader, for his invaluable suggestions, and to Professor John Sallis, our editor and my mentor-friend, for his constant encouragement from start to finish. We must also acknowledge the boundless yet finite patience of Humanities Press. Finally, we must acknowledge the patience, love, and encouragement of Trudy and Judi as we labored for what seemed to be years in travelling this way; one's own way is never merely one's own.

DAN MAGURSHAK

Carthage College
October 31, 1984

PREFACE TO THE AMERICAN EDITION

In 1952, Ludwig Landgrebe published a much used little book entitled *Philosophie der Gegenwart*. This pupil of Husserl and Heidegger was shaped by the philosophical situation of 1929. At the end of the twenties the late Scheler consistently travelled his own new ways, and Helmut Plessner's philosophizing, founded in anthropology and biology, assisted the reification of the phenomenological approach. At the same time, Heidegger became the prominent partner of the Dilthey school in its conversation with phenomenology. Since 1929, however, Heidegger's continuation of the phenomenological movement proved to be a revolt against Husserl. After World War II, when Ludwig Landgrebe entered the discussions from the time of the world economic crisis, the catastrophe of the National Socialist struggle for world domination had finally destroyed the old Europe. The erroneous ways which had been taken appeared to necessitate a "turning" of thinking which had to reach back beyond Hegel, Marx, and Kierkegaard and to transform Western thought in its entirety. In France, the philosophy of existence, simultaneously attributed to both Jaspers and the Heidegger of *Sein und Zeit*, was honed through Sartre's effort to Existentialism; at the same time, the new adoption of Hegel and his followers led to the task of mediating between the transcendental philosophy which arose from Husserl's reflection upon the crises of the European sciences and historical experience. Landgrebe believed in a convergence of the different ways; that is, Husserl and Heidegger appeared to work toward the same new philosophy—a "departure from Cartesianism." Man's radical reflection upon himself was to lead to that "turning" by which Heidegger sought to dismantle all subjectivism and highhandedness of thinking. Husserl's phenomenological approach, Dilthey's humanistic approach, the speculative tradition, the abolition of philosophy in Marx and Kierkegaard, and the new establishment of philosophy in the phenomenology of things did not stand next to each other without any unity; they were led to the one philosophical reflection in a situation in which humanity is in crisis.

This summing up of contemporary philosophizing was certainly typical and symptomatic of the fifties. Characteristically, Landgrebe's small book appeared in English but under the restrictive title, *Major Problems in Contemporary European Philosophy* (New York, Frederick Ungar Publishing Co., 1966). Whoever used the book as an access to philosophy could read with surprise a review in a British journal or hear the same judgement by an American professor that this small volume represents a curious conception of philosophy, a continental European straying towards senselessness and absurdities. What was expressed could not stand up to analytic philosophy as it was established in a many voiced yet coherent endeavor, since Peirce and Russell had turned away from the Idealistic tradition and the Anglo-Saxon philosophers had united with the Vienna school. Yet in the present book, notes 36, 43, and 55 point out that this rift between the phenomenological movement and analytic philosophy or so-called logical positivism had been bridged long ago. Oskar Becker, along with Heidegger, Husserl's assistant in the early Freiburg years, had worked out not only a philosophy of mathematics and the outline of a philosophy of aesthetics, but he also, with his contributions to modal logic, for example (e.g., in constant examination of the works of Prior), had combined ontological deliberations about the concept of possibility, phenomenological analyses, and mathematical logic. The phenomenological tradition is destroyed if one does not see the scope which Husserl gave to it through the conscious effort of his assistants in various fields of endeavor. This scope may not be shortened to a philosophizing which turns to explanations which have previously occurred in the history of metaphysics or which bases its own way of speaking to a large extent upon the quotations of poets, which tends toward essayism. Note 55 of this book also refers to an early work of Karl-Otto Apel: *Sprache und Wahrheit in der gegenwärtigen Situation der Philosophie.* The title itself expresses the conviction that the problem of truth—precisely in a philosophy with ontological intentions—is not to be linked epistemologically with the problem of consciousness, but rather more concretely in a hermeneutical turn with the problem of language in the broad sense of the word. According to the subtitle, the essay is "a consideration apropos the completion of the neo-positivistic philosophy of language in the semiotics of Charles Morris." It combines the analytic-pragmatic approach of Morris with Vico's *Neue Wissenschaft* and the notion of topic, as well as with Heidegger's thinking as it developed in the so-called turning and in reflection on the history of Being. Apel's approach, at first carried out against the mood of his surroundings, culminated in the large portrait *Der Denkweg von Charles Sanders Peirce*; viewed systematically, he demanded a *Transformation der Philosophie.* With that the task had been set. Heidegger, and indeed the philosophical tradition which followed Husserl and Dilthey, were to be placed in terms of the guiding motifs of thought into the larger context of that philosophizing as it developed in our century from the leading impulses of the time in the Western and Eastern parts of the world.

The present book puts Heidegger's way to *Sein und Zeit* into the phenomenological movement as "hermeneutical phenomenology"; later I used the name "hermeneutical philosophy" for the philosophizing that developed under the impetus of Dilthey and Heidegger. In the summer of

1923 Heidegger wanted to lecture about logic. Since the scholastic philosopher used the term logic, Heidegger chose the title "ontology" for the course catalogue. On the blackboard and in the course itself, he spoke of the "hermeneutics of facticity." In his essay on Novalis, Dilthey had spoken of "historical facticity" as the point of departure for the Christian religion; nonetheless, this facticity is inserted into dogmas and ideas. In the significant section 58 of the first book of *Ideen zu einer reinen Phänomenologie und phänomenologischen Philosophie*, Husserl had wanted to exclude the transcendence of God from phenomenological consideration, while he had spoken about the "facticity" of that constituting consciousness which is crystallized as "pure" consciousness in phenomenological reduction. Not the "fact in general" but rather "the fact as source" forces the question about the ground for this facticity "into infinite possibilities and actualities of value"; still, ground here does not mean ground in the sense of a real cause (material-causal). Metaphysical questions are raised when Husserl considers that "marvelous teleology" which makes pure consciousness correspond with factical consciousness and the fact of the real world. Yet Dilthey as well as Nietzsche combined the limit of the metaphysical approach with the delimitation of the principle of ground or the guide of causality. In his famous correspondence with Dilthey, Husserl, of course, belittled the "historical-factical" as "example" in his alignment with "the *pure* ideal"; thus he could require an *a priori* "which as such is in no way limited by anthropologically historical facticities" (June-July, 1911). In contrast with this, Heidegger, in his early Freiburg lectures, grasped the phenomenological regress to origin as the regress to the factical life which is historical. With respect to this life, the well-known principle *Individuum est ineffabile* may have value; nonetheless, this talk of inexpressibility may not prevent a hermeneutical conceptualization from initiating one to life and its individualization (as Heidegger called for it in his review of Jaspers' *Psychologie der Weltanschauungen*). Thus hermeneutical phenomenology, as *Sein und Zeit* says repeatedly, becomes an "interpreting" which can open up facticity as an impenetrable ground only in multifaceted efforts from a specific, historical, hermeneutical situation. This interpreting must repeatedly stand the test as hermeneutics in the understanding of concrete scientific work or in the clarification of praxis; it thereby turns upon understanding Dasein, changing it if the occasion arises.

If Heidegger differentiated his hermeneutical phenomenology from Husserl's transcendental phenomenology and finally dissociated himself from Husserl, then this differentiation and dissociation refer back to the creative protest against Hegel. In Hegel, a new sensibility for history was ultimately played out by a metaphysical position which this sensibility was to have supported. Thus Hegel could conclude his phenomenology of sensory certainty by indicating that what the utterly individual means [*meinen*] remains "inexpressible." The achievement of meaning must also be "experienced" and clarified; nonetheless, according to Hegel, in its isolation it remains as that which is "untrue, unreasonable, merely intended." In the first note to the expositions regarding being, nothing, and becoming from the *Wissenschaft der Logik*, Hegel critiques the statement "*Ex nihilo nihil fit*," yet also criticizes Kant's critique of the ontological proof for the existence of God. Hegel acknowledges that everything finite is reciprocally related to something else and here quotes the ("basically tautological") assertion of metaphysics: that if one tiny particle in the world would be destroyed, the whole universe would collapse. (Proceeding from this statement, Sartre then asserts in the "conclusion" of *L' etre et le néant* that a "hole" in Being arises with the for-itself; Being is divided into in-itself and for-itself.) Nonetheless, Hegel insists that we must distinguish pure being in its interconnection with nothing and becoming from that being which is attributed to a specific being [*Daseienden*]; it makes a difference to my wallet whether a hundred thalers are in there or not. I cannot use this talk of specific being or non-being with respect to the universe. In the first edition of the initial book on the *Wissenschaft der Logik*, Hegel still formulates this in a precarious yet significant manner: if things are taken together in their totality "then the specific being which relates itself to others also vanishes, for there will be no more other for the universe, and there is no difference whether something is or is not." In post-Idealistic philosophy, this position became untenable. Since in *Sein und Zeit* Heidegger proceeded from being-in-the-world and took this as a facticity which is to be disclosed historically or simultaneously as "existence," he had to justify the approach of his hermeneutical phenomenology by a new discussion of the principle of ground or of identity, difference [*Differenz*], and ground in contrast with the metaphysical approaches. Phenomenology and Dilthey's approach as well became mere variations of the tradition where the tradition is not radically investigated. Around 1929, when Heidegger responded to the crisis of the age with such probing questioning, he gave up titles such as phenomenology and hermeneutics in order to establish all the more securely the matter at issue. Although at that time Georg Misch initiated the Dilthey school's examination of phenomenology and, above all, of Heidegger, in these years of radical determinations they never achieved an actual discussion, something which until today has remained a *desideratum*. (For details, cf. my introduction to Wilhelm Dilthey: *Das Wesen der Philosophie*. Hamburg, 1984.)

In 1960 Hans Georg Gadamer spoke of his main work, *Wahrheit und*

Methode, in its subtitle as the "basic features of a philosophical hermeneutics." Heidegger had provided the decisive impetus for placing into
question the philosophical tradition and its trust in reason on the basis of
the experiences of our time through a critical adoption of the metaphysical
tradition but also through a critique of the reciprocity among the enlight-
enment, romantic, and historical ways to history. Dilthey's context of
effects became an open history of actuality in which we always stand, and
the hermeneutic which interprets this history of effects moved into the
center of philosophizing. Still, was a hermeneutical philosophy already
provided with such a philosophical hermeneutic? Rather, did not the
danger exist that a single manner of interpreting the experience of truth
became the medium of all other ways? Oskar Becker protested against
such a "pan-hermeneutic." If one asks about the accomplishment of
mathematics, one must distinguish this accomplishment from understanding and not classify it in terms of understanding, but rather contrast
it antagonistically with understanding. Understanding has a living relation [*Lebensbezug*] to that which is understood; in order to restore the
disturbed living relation upon a higher plane, understanding must step
out of the hermeneutical circle, and with regard to its comprehension of
the particular, examine its preconception of the totality of what is to be
understood and thus differentiate it. One also works in the natural
sciences in this way, for example, in describing the well-known plant
kingdom. Nonetheless, explanation [*Erklärung*] stands opposed to such
description and understanding. For example, we explain and interpret a
throwing action with the help of mathematics in that we put it together
out of linearly uniform inertial movement and a uniformly accelerated fall.
We thereby presuppose that it is clear what "inertia" and "fall" are.
However, in more difficult explanations and interpretations we can no
longer accept this clarity as given; nonetheless, we still try to give our
formulas consistency in order to confirm them through an experiment. In
this activity, the living relation to the matter at hand is not only differentiated but has been fundamentally broken off (although every experiment,
to be sure, can again be placed into the totality of life and thus also be
"understood" in a higher sense). According to Becker, one may not grasp
explanation and interpretation of this type as a modification of understanding, but rather must antagonistically or "complementarily" oppose
this "mantic" as something other than what is "hermeneutical." (Cf. my
essay "*Hermeneutische und mantische Phänomenologie*" in the anthology which I
have edited, *Heidegger: Perspektiven zur Deutung seines Werks*. Köln-Berlin,
1969. pp. 321–357.)

Is not mathematical interpretation close to the conception of the
aesthetic forms of art, although art is often considered the domain of

hermeneutics? Becker asks whether we place art hermeneutically into the history of the truth of life, or whether we must rather proceed from the fact that since Kant, aesthetics has won an autonomy in the manner that mathematics became pure mathematics among the Greeks. Regarding this, Becker notes that the region of the unconscious, with its "instinctive desires," stands perpendicular to factical historical life like mathematics and in a certain sense like forms of speech of what is aesthetic; the unconscious therefore demands something other than a hermeneutical interpretation which permits the language of the unconscious to be totally wrapped up in the spirit which historically individualizes itself. The different spheres each have their "principles"; nonetheless it remains open whether these principles can be presented clearly and justified in a conclusive manner. Instead, they must be grasped as "hypotheses" which must hold true when the structure of the aforementioned spheres is disclosed. Yet for this reason, Husserl's demand that philosophy must become "strict science" can no longer be held—not even in the sense that the scientific illumination of life is given out as the regulative principle for an endless process. Even with this commitment to a regulative principle, the individualization of life, which at least composes a side of life, still comes up short. According to the young Heidegger's hermeneutical phenomenology, philosophy must throw "torches" into the scientific enterprise. In his later years, Becker added that it must also actually burn, and at that time—in the memorable years in Freiburg immediately after the First World War — it did "burn."

Can one not call a philosophy whose hypotheses must first be proven in concrete philosophical work a "hermeneutical" one in its entirety, bound in the hermeneutical circle? In this sense I used the title *Hermeneutische Philosophie* in 1972 for an anthology, and again in 1983, I took up the introduction to this volume in the book *Heidegger und die hermeneutische Philosophie*. Against this usage one can certainly argue that the clarification of that which hermeneutics performs and the difference between what is hermeneutical and what is mantical could not itself be hermeneutical. In fact, one must take the adjective "hermeneutical" in the title "hermeneutical philosophy" in a second sense, which is to be precisely differentiated from hermeneutics as an auxiliary science of jurisprudence and theology, but also from the philosophical hermeneutics which is concerned with understanding distinguished from explanation and interpretation. Beyond this, one must distinguish the various basic forms which became actualized in the development of hermeneutical philosophy. For example, in addition to the Dilthey school there was also the resurgence of practical philosophy as Joachim Ritter attempted it. While Heidegger and Gadamer seek to return to an integrated origin by passing through these divisions—for example, they refer to an art as festivity and celebration to distinguish what is aesthetic and what is cultic—Ritter, on the other hand, wants to hold onto the divisions between the aesthetic sphere and every-day life or even between state and society in Hegel's sense, as the differences of the "modern" world. Hermeneutical philosophy, as it has developed above all in continental Europe, must then be classified as a specific type of that philosophizing which is represented today throughout the entire world. With his works, Karl-Otto Apel added decisively to the fact that the continental-European tradition could understand itself as one way among others and thus could be classified in a comprehensive *Transformation der Philosophie*; yet perhaps precisely in Apel's later work the specific concerns of a hermeneutical philosophy were covered up all too much by the representations of an untransformed Hegelianism or the logical socialism of Peirce. In contrast, Paul Ricoeur in his substantial books tried to justify the hermeneutical concern in increasing measure against other orientations. Nonetheless, does not a Hegelianism foreign to the phenomenon remain Ricoeur's guide as well? The Mediterranean-European traditions—as formerly in Hegel—are to be brought together in such a way that they point to the convergence of philosophy and theology; in the discussion of Freud's epoch-making accomplishment, the uncon-scious is grasped as a becoming of spirit in the sense of Hegelian terminol-ogy, even though this unconscious could stand "perpendicular" to historical spirit. As far as Heidegger is concerned, he in fact did take up the motif of Hegelian phenomenology, as well as the mediation between reason and language in the sense of Hegel's meta-critique and Hum-boldt's science of language. Nonetheless, his thinking can hardly be grasped as the way from an existential philosophy to a Hegelian media-tion between reason and history or even as a stronger hermeneutically-oriented mediation of reason, history, and language. In my book, *Hegels Idee einer Phänomenologie des Geistes* (1973, cf. pp. 299ff.), I already pointed out that Heidegger takes up the mediation of metaphysics or transcenden-tal philosophy and historical experience only to leave it behind ultimately as a one-sided approach. Heidegger's later talk of destiny and appropria-tive event may no longer be understood in terms of history since history is indeed only one region among others.

To be sure, the present book characterizes Heidegger's way to *Sein und Zeit* as a "hermeneutical" phenomenology; nonetheless, the later works of Heidegger were represented as a "topology of Being." The concluding differentiation of explanation, elucidation, and emplacement takes expla-nation as a hasty metaphysical reduction, as the recovery of the alleged two substances of extension and thought or of nature and history. By means of elucidation, phenomenology then is to focus upon the things themselves, upon the independence of the logical in contrast with the psychical. Nonetheless, elucidation is not only bound up with an understanding; this understanding which can be "conceived" subjectively as a self-understanding is transformed with Heidegger's demand for a turning of thinking into the emplacement which conforms to the way of truth. If discussion of what is hermeneutical is traditionally coupled with understanding, then this discussion remains behind as characterizing Heidegger's early hermeneutical phenomenology, although not until the thirties do his works develop a concrete hermeneutic of the world with respect to the decisive spheres of art, politics, science, and technology. Only Heidegger's latest work explicitly takes up the indication from *Sein und Zeit* that understanding and state of mind are united in discourse (thus in Dilthey's "articulation"). Heidegger could thus conceive of his thinking as a thinking "on the way to language" and thereby as the "Saying" of an "abode."

Nonetheless, the present book also sets the discussion of a topology of Being in a context which Heidegger himself did not use; it is bound up with the idea of topic as it was developed, for example, by Vico. Vico had delimited philosophy from the preceding encompassing mythology and religion; yet he had thereby related mythology as philosophy back to the "discovery" of the guiding viewpoints within man's historical attempts to gain a position in the world (cf. my essay "Topik und Philosophie" in *Topik*, edited by D. Breuer and H. Schanze, München, 1981, pp. 95–123). This understanding of topology ties Heidegger's new impetus with a tradition which Heidegger does not heed or repel, that is, with rhetoric in which the notion of topic has its place. Rhetoric appears as the shadow which accompanied metaphysics and from which one can ask about the right and limits of the metaphysical tradition. In any case, so-called metaphysics is not taken as the one-dimensional dramatic history which leads from Anaximander to Nietzsche. This tradition contains many motifs and is therefore also capable of appropriating new initiatives, for example, from the Christian experience of the world or of integrating along with Vico the topical tradition into a new experience of history. Heidegger's search for first beginnings (in Parmenides and Heraclitus or after 1945, also in Lao Tse) proves to be a vision of history, still quasi-substantialistic, which disguises the actual occurrence. To be sure, it also appears doubtful whether philosophy can be obligated to complete reality by means of the adjective "hermeneutical." The hermeneutical tradition was decisively impressed by impulses from the reformation and romanticism; yet have these epochs been capable of representing the complete reality of human life upon this earth?

If even in spite of such misgivings the formation of a "hermeneutical" philosophy made use of Heidegger, then the present book prepared for this conception in that it understood Heidegger not only from his own texts but also from the impetus which he gave to Continental-European thought. Here one can mention the repeatedly renewed examination of the phenomenological tradition, then the discussion of the history of metaphysics in which the presence of the Greeks and of scholastic and idealistic philosophy was determined anew. Also to be mentioned is the attempt, along with Bultmann and in the examination of him, to take hold of the task of theology in a new way from the Old Testament or from Sophocles and Hölderlin. Finally, there is also the concrete development of the question as to how not only science and technology, but also art, "ethical" behavior, and politics belong to our world. Within analytic philosophy, extreme positions were developed which treated everything metaphysical and speculative in a radically restrictive way as a part of poetry or even music and tried to exclude it from philosophy. In a mirror-image reversal, Heidegger decided on behalf of the proximity of art and for a poetic thinking which articulates the decisive human concerns and which thereby opposes the allegedly universal "cybernetics" of "industrial society" (as formulated in Heidegger's Athens lecture of 1967, "Die Herkunft der Kunst und die Bestimmung des Denkens"). On the analytic side, it is no longer "hermeneutically" asked whether the radical restrictions are not themselves a piece of "metaphysics" in the bad sense of the word; on Heidegger's side, it is no longer clear how poetic thinking examines itself and stands the test in the concrete interpretation of the actual world. One must finally ask whether Heidegger brings art into view at all in the way that it belongs to our time. The brief reference to Celan's translation of Char in note 50 contains the conviction that poetry must be realized from the impulses of our time in ways different than those which Heidegger saw (cf. my book *Die Frage nach der Kunst. Von Hegel zu Heidegger*. Freiburg/ München, 1984).

When Heidegger's collection of essays and lectures, *Unterwegs zur Sprache*, appeared in 1959, it disappointed all those who had expected from Heidegger a guide for a philosophizing which follows the impulses of *Sein und Zeit* and the suggestion of a turning, yet which does so from the myriad ways of philosophizing in our time; from that time on philosophy in the German-speaking countries no longer sought its decisive impetus from Heidegger. Unexpectedly, however, Heidegger's late movements of thought found a new echo in France and Italy and indeed within a transformed philosophical situation. Emmanuel Levinas established the connection to French phenomenology in a confrontation with Sartre. It was no longer a matter of placing the individual in his self-relation into the totalizing circle of being-with-one-another; rather the relation of one person to another in his inaccessible otherness was to lead into the ethical dimension. Thus Heidegger's thinking was asked whether it did not—in spite of its protestations—merely repeat the metaphysics of identity and thereby the attempt to secure "mythically" (as the young Nietzsche had required) what is one's own and native through the myths surrounding it. It was precisely the publication of Heidegger's lectures about Nietzsche that brought Heidegger's thinking into France and Italy but into new contexts as well. The mediation of transcendental philosophy and history in connection with Hegel and Husserl's *Krisis* was no longer the main concern; the concern was rather an "ideological critical" one regarding a hermeneutics of suspicion in connection with Marx, Nietzsche, and Freud. Heidegger's "critique of logos" now came to stand next to Nietzsche. When Jacques Derrida tries to read the phenomenological texts anew, his leading words indicate that Heidegger's later works were appropriated but also subordinated to new alternatives. Since Cavailles and Lautmann, the tradition of French scientism received new weight with the question as to whether we do not find in mathematics structures which unfold out of themselves. Jacques Lacan translated Heidegger's essay about the logos of Heraclitus because he found in the unconscious a language which differentiates itself, and he wanted to reclaim Heidegger's considerations for the dethroning of the self-consciousness which determines itself from itself. In this way, the controversial situation of 1927 was revived, in which Husserl published in the same volume of his yearbook the hermeneutical phenomenology of *Sein und Zeit* and Becker's ontological investigations of mathematics. In 1970, Joseph J. Kockelmans and Theodore J. Kisiel brought together the work of Husserl, Weyl, Becker, Heidegger, Bachelard, Cavailles, and others in their anthology, *Phenomenology and the Natural Sciences*; Thomas Kuhn's breakthrough to a new way of raising the question in the history of science led to considerations regarding the extent to which there is "hermeneutics" even in the natural sciences. This way of elucidating the history of phenomenological philosophy from the things requires pursuit and discrimination; in any case after all these new tendencies, one can no longer represent the philosophy of the present by phenomenology, as was done in the fifties.

In America in the sixties, only marginal groups had anything to do with Heidegger. Heidegger was discussed first in small phenomenological circles and then finally in theological seminars and in the humanities. In the meantime, this situation has changed radically. Important translations of Heidegger's texts were made available. No longer do only uncertain notes from Heidegger's courses circulate, but many lecture courses have now been published. The history of phenomenological philosophizing has been newly elaborated in its entirety, and Heidegger received his place in this history; nonetheless, other philosophical currents took an interest in him as well. Regarding such changes in particular, one may not overlook the fact that American philosophizing has experienced a basically new orientation; no longer does it one-sidedly follow in conjunction with English philosophy the analytic and linguistic-analytic traditions. There is increased interest not only in phenomenological philosophy, but also in the presence of the Greeks in today's thinking (as it was emphasized again by the school of Leo Strauss). In addition there is a new interest in German Idealism as well as the regress to the original pragmatic approaches, above all, in Peirce. One cannot overlook the fact that this change in basic orientation goes with a change in the general situation and the spiritual atmosphere. In the last two decades, the United States of America has become more acutely aware of what it means to be a state with world political responsibility and difficult internal political problems. It is believed that by means of the new orientation one can find help in a philosophizing which goes beyond all too rigorous restrictions and which introduces speculative approaches into an encompassing historical reflection. Thus, in spite of all attempts at resistance, Hegel and Heidegger gained new attention. What became interesting was a philosophizing which belongs to a land long divided religiously and convulsed politically, a land which all the more sees itself compelled to metaphysical questions. French intellectuality also produced a new result which seeks to influence public life with radical positions and which maintains its closeness to literature.

In this new orientation, the principal task was to form an independent philosophy from the questions of our time. For the sake of this task, one must test the extent to which the questions are justified which Heidegger used to lead phenomenological philosophy, and the philosophical tradition in general, beyond itself. The present book (first published in German in 1963) follows the step-by-step development of Heidegger's questioning upon the way of his thinking; thus it may not be without significance for America's way to a reflection upon the task of philosophy today.

Introduction

When Martin Heidegger published the first part of *Sein und Zeit* in 1927, the thinking that had proceeded for so long in the seclusion of a university teacher's activity suddenly burst forth into the glaring light of publicity. It appeared that by means of *Sein und Zeit* Heidegger had advanced not only to the forefront of the phenomenological movement, to which he knew he belonged, but even to the vanguard of contemporary philosophers in general. In no way, however, did the influence of *Sein und Zeit* remain confined to the narrower philosophical circles; to a large extent it provided impetus for fundamental decisions. Some perceived that in it man's attempt to stand completely and solely on his own had at long last been radically accomplished, while others viewed it as an aid allowing man's discourse about God or even God's address to man to be heard in a new way. *Sein und Zeit* became a guidepost for many young inquiring individuals, if only that from it each learned to die "his own" death even in the darkness of revolutions and wars—on one side of the battlefield or the other.

In this turning to his work which, moreover, remained a fragment, Heidegger himself could see only a misunderstanding of his genuine concern. In his lecture course about Nietzsche's "single thought," about the notion of eternal recurrence, Heidegger sought to understand the fate of his own thinking as well. He constantly reiterated the "necessity" that the contemporaries and disciples of the thinker, who has an essential question, must misunderstand him (NI, 269, 288, 337f, 403f). As Nietzsche had been silent about his "single thought," so Heidegger was now silent about his. He knew as well as Nietzsche that "as soon as one communicates his knowledge, he no longer loves it well enough" (NI, 265f). Can a thinker, who is still on his way, who still seeks the way, speak about his way? Must not this speaking divert him from his sole task, from devoting himself totally to that which is to be thought? Furthermore, each direct communication of that which is thought can again lead to misunderstanding. What is thought is not taken as an indicator, as a signpost of a search for a way, but rather as a finished result and "understood" from the point of view of what is already known, that is to say, misunderstood.

The task at hand cannot be to combat these misunderstandings. How could it help to say that Heidegger was misunderstood—perhaps even that along the way he himself had temporarily misunderstood himself and his purpose? The decisive question is: What is the basis of this misinterpretation, that is, where does it originate? The "somnambulistic cer-

8

1

tainty" with which philosophy missed the "genuine and sole question" of *Sein und Zeit* was not, as Heidegger soon recognized, "a matter of mis-understanding a book, but rather of our abandonment by Being" (WiM, 19). To comprehend the source of our "abandonment," to seek the possibility of an egress, and thus to find a way to that which is to be thought, and to lead there as well, was now to be the task.

What Nietzsche wanted to achieve with the "bits and disguises" which he related about his "single thought," Heidegger also wished to accomplish by means of the essays, lectures, and lecture courses he published after the last war. His aim was "not to bring about complete comprehension, but rather to pave the way for a transformation of the fundamental mood," a change in the basic attunement, from which what must be said becomes gradually more comprehensible (NI, 269, 266). That which is truly to be thought lies "wrapped in silence" in these publications. To be sure, all thoughts lead toward that which must be thought, but nowhere is it directly addressed or articulated. Yet since readers in these stressful times questioned the utterances of the thinker in order to attain ultimate answers, these publications too were destined to be misunderstood—be it as a renewal of Western metaphysics' concern with Being or as an escape or flight into a new "mythology." Above all, it was believed that since one could not perceive the consistency of Heidegger's way, one had to ascertain and discuss a change in Heidegger's point of view.

An appreciation of Heidegger's thinking can be awakened only if the reader of Heidegger's writings is prepared to accept all that he or she reads as a step toward what has to be thought, something toward which Heidegger himself is under way. One would have to understand Heidegger's thinking *as a way*, but not as a way of many thoughts. It is rather a way which restricts itself to a single, solitary thought, one which the thinker hopes "will one day endure as a star in the firmament of the world. To head towards a single star, only this" (AED, 7). Thus, Heidegger has always understood his thinking as travelling along a way, as a being under way. At the end of the published portion of *Sein und Zeit*, he says that the strife with regard to Being has yet to be enkindled, but that such enkindling demands preparation; "toward this goal alone the present investigation is *under way*" (SuZ, 437). Twenty years later Heidegger writes that these statements are still valid. "Let us remain also in days to come on the way as wanderers into the neighborhood of Being" (PL, 93).

The way which Heidegger attempts to travel is a way leading into the neighborhood of Being. Being is the theme of the classical form of Western thought, metaphysics. As a way into the neighborhood of Being, Heidegger's thinking aspires to be nothing other than the attempt to follow the course of Western thought. By travelling this way Heidegger believes that he will surely experience the fact that Western metaphysics has never fully developed its question, the question of Being, and that it consequently has never arrived at its own ground. His aim is to search for this ground and to get an idea of, discover, and reclaim a field which had to remain unknown due to the dominance of metaphysics (HW, 194f). The way by which Western thought surpasses itself is the way which leads back into its neglected ground. The way which Heidegger travels achieves its compelling character by aiming to do nothing more than to bring to language in a verifiable manner these neglected presuppositions of previous thought.

That Western thinking can be taken as a way presupposes that it can be understood as a way at all. According to Heidegger's conception, every phase of metaphysics in fact does manifest part of a way "which the destiny of Being paves for itself in sudden epochs of the truth concerning beings" (HW, 193). But the way of this truth adapts itself to the all-encompassing occurrence of sense and truth which sustains Western thought and all other thought as well. The Western way originates from that "movement" [Bewegung, in the sense of making way] which is a releasing of ways whereby ways can first of all arise. Heidegger reminds us **10** that the word "Tao," the key term in the poetic thinking of Laotse, really means "way." "Perhaps there is concealed in the word 'way' or 'Tao' the mystery of all mysteries of thoughtful saying, that is, if we permit these terms to return to what is unspoken in them, and if we are capable of such permitting . . . Everything is way" (Sp, 198).

Yet, how can those who travel different ways converse with one another? How, for example, might the "unavoidable conversation" between the Western and the East Asian world be set into motion (VA, 47)? It is a question about which nothing can be decided beforehand. In attempting such a dialogue, this question must first of all be clarified as a question. Heidegger's *Aus einem Gespräch von der Sprache* [A Dialogue on Language], notes from a conversation with a Japanese guest, clearly demonstrates the difficulty of such a dialogue.

The task of an introduction to the thought of Martin Heidegger can only be to stake out guideposts which permit some of the stretches and turns of the way which Heidegger travels to become visible. The introduction must grasp Heidegger's attempts at thinking as steps upon a way and thus in a preliminary and provisional manner familiarize the reader with the field paths, timber tracks, and all the different ways which Heidegger travels. It must at the same time renounce from the outset any wish to convey the results of Heidegger's thinking or to bring his work to a *single* level, thus synthesizing it as a self-contained totality. This renunciation is called for, not because such a task cannot yet be carried out, or at least not in an introduction, but rather because it is in principle inappropriate to Heidegger's path of thinking. It can only disfigure that path and conceal what is most proper to Heidegger's intentions.

This introduction is to be a guide to Heidegger's path of thinking. As such it can perhaps do its part in providing the reader of Heidegger's writings with the possibility of appropriating Heidegger's path of thinking for his own. But if it is to accomplish this, the introduction has to confront the reader with the most decisive question of all, namely whether or not Western thought has yet attained the ground upon which it stands. For although this thought has left its mark on the face of the earth through sciences and technology, it must be asked whether or not it has become capable of advancing from its unique element toward the unique elements of the other great ways that truth occurs. For those to whom Heidegger's thought becomes visible as the possibility of a way, this thinking can become the impetus for travelling the way themselves, the way upon which they have always been, and for appropriating this way expressly as the way. Thus Heidegger's way becomes in turn a signpost along the way which each person must travel himself.

But if each must follow his own course, then an introduction cannot even aim "to bring anyone" to Heidegger's way of thinking; above all it cannot provide the first techniques for a thinking which wants to base itself securely "upon Heidegger's thinking" and from there "to think beyond it." What is primarily at issue is not *Heidegger's* thought, but rather the task envisioned by him, and since the points of departure are different, the way of one person can never simply be the way of another. If, however, the origin is different, then what will follow must also differ, since what follows is the origin now grasped explicitly. Whoever takes Heidegger's way as an available ground upon which to stand has already been *excluded from* this way as the way of a *thinker*. A thinker who is himself under way has no teaching to communicate which could merely be assimilated and passed along. As Heidegger says in the Foreword to *Vorträge und Aufsätze*, he can, as an author travelling the roads of thought, "at most only point the way without himself being a wise man in the sense of being a σοφός." He has nothing to express and nothing to communicate; he dare not even want to inspire, "because the inspired are already certain of their knowledge." With a bit of luck he can set the reader upon a way which he himself, the author, has scouted out in order to release, as an *auctor*, an *augere*, "a flourishing."

Moreover, Heidegger's thinking is inevitably misunderstood when one takes it as the way to something new as the most modern of things modern. The uniqueness of a thoughtful being under way lies precisely in the fact that it only points out that forgotten matter which has always

11

borne along all thinking. As such, this being under way produces nothing new and never progresses toward what has never been. On the contrary, in this thinking there is a step back; it is a regress to what has been, to **12** what has been unthought with respect to its origin; it is the way into the future. This way back, the unhurried return to where we have been all along, is certainly the most difficult. It is "infinitely more difficult" than the frenzied journeys of an advancing scientific-technological conscious- ness (Sp, 190). Because essential thinking travels a way peculiar to it, it avoids the scientific attentiveness to the most recent results and advances of research as well as the journalistic nose for what is currently modern and most modern. Those who *understand* the thought of a thinker are never those "who immediately busy themselves with the newly arising thought as a 'modern' one, for these are ones without a foundation, ones who feed themselves only with what is currently 'modern'. Those who genuinely understand are those who come from afar out of their own ground and foundation, who bring much with them in order to transform much." The first disciples, as Heidegger says with Nietzsche, "prove nothing *against* a theory" (NI, 404).

A way of thinking will alway shun the curiosity of those who want to know how it has been, and herein lies the greatest danger which threatens this introduction. It tries to comprehend Heidegger's work as steps upon a way of thinking so that his thinking can become an impetus for the reader himself to travel the way of thinking. However, the introduction could be taken as attempting a historical presentation, an "explanation" of the "development" of Heidegger's thinking. A presentation is not even possi- ble because sufficient sources and materials are not available. Aside from this fact, it is not at all the goal of this introduction to present Heidegger's thinking as something complete, to relegate it to the past, perhaps to discuss its future prospects as well, and thus to have done with it in this manner. As Heidegger says, "the desire to know and the craving for explanations will never bring us to thoughtful questioning. Invariably the desire to know is already the concealed arrogance of a self-consciousness which relies on fabricated reason and its reasonableness. *Wanting* to know does not *want* to relinquish hope in the face of that which is worthy of thought" (Sp, 100).

Certainly nothing historically inaccurate is to be said here; that is, nothing more is to be added to the many historical errors which have been disseminated regarding Heidegger. However, the goal of this intro- **13** duction is not a detailed, comprehensive historical presentation which relies on its correctness. Its aim, rather, is to guide us to the question of whether or not the manner in which Heidegger appropriates the course of Western thinking is required by this thinking. One ought to consider what

Heidegger's attempt at thinking contributes to the task of understanding our history so that we can come to terms with it. On the other hand, if in this context the discussion concerns Heidegger's relationship to Dilthey or Husserl, to Hellenism or Christianity, the question is not whether Heidegger interprets Dilthey in a historically accurate manner, or whether he does justice to Dilthey, Husserl, Hellenism, or Christianity. Such discussion should demonstrate only how Heidegger in each case brings the tradition onto the way of his thinking and how the tradition calls him to this way. Although the question as to whether Heidegger does "justice" to the tradition should be raised, its answer lies outside the projected goals of this introduction.

Finally, this introduction has to shield Heidegger's thinking from the craving of those who immediately grasp after definitive answers to questions of knowledge and faith—a grasping only too easily and too quickly encouraged by the unrest and need of our time. Heidegger's path of thinking certainly was molded by past decisions, by slowly awakening changes, and by sudden revolutions. Therefore one can ask, for example, about the relationship of the early Heidegger to Christian theology or about the relationship between his later work and the mythical-poetic *theologia* of Hölderlin. Heidegger's political decisions and his attempt to comprehend current events in world history may also be brought into question. One might also examine the "gnostic" characteristics in *Sein und Zeit* and ask about Heidegger's later attempt to return to an early age in which the "world" was still a "homeland," and thinking was situated in the neighborhood of myth and poetic speaking. Even the relation of Heidegger's thinking to contemporary phenomena such as "dialectical" theology or existential philosophy can be questioned. Such questioning habitually assesses Heidegger's relation to whatever is at issue with respect to an answer to the ultimate questions of thinking and faith. The question remains, however, whether such questioning comes before that

14   question which decides everything, which Heidegger's path of thinking confronts. In any case, this introduction has excluded questions of the former type; they can of course be properly raised only when the interrogators have come before what must be thought, toward which Heidegger is under way. When Heidegger's thinking is linked to contemporary or historical trends of immediate interest, this connection says at most only something about the wishes, desires, and opinions of those who point out the relationships. We would therefore do well if we were to refrain from relating Heidegger's thought to topical matters too quickly. We should rather open ourselves to the insight about how strange his thinking appears in our time and amidst current events. Such strangeness should not be bridged too hastily; first of all, it must gape in all its profundity.

As far as the answers to ultimate questions about knowledge or faith are concerned, Heidegger protests expressly against the fact that one imputes to thinking the "presumptuous claim of knowing the solution to the riddle and of bringing salvation." As a "perpetual learner," he himself wants only to scrutinize previous thinking for what has been unthought in it; thus, he will perhaps be able to discover in his own way the abode of the truth of Being as the site of a future activity of building and dwelling. "We can, however, prepare for dwelling in that abode only though the process of building. Such building may hardly already have in mind the construction of the house of God and the dwellings of mortals. One must be content with building the *way* . . ." (*Zur Seinsfrage*, 26, 41f).

How little the customary "scholarly preoccupation" with Heidegger enters the region of this thinker's question is unmistakably evident in its inability to leave Heidegger in peace, to leave him to the freedom of his way. The first requirement incumbent upon one who wants to "understand" Heidegger is this: one does not grasp after ultimate answers, prejudge, or evaluate, but rather first of all simply listens to the one question which Heidegger thinks through. Such listening does not increase knowledge, nor does it determine answers to ultimate questions. It could be, however, that simply by listening, one's own thinking is imperceptibly but fundamentally transformed. The composed thinking which expects nothing and wants nothing for itself but which is prepared to let itself be tested and transformed by a claim is perhaps alone capable of **15** experiencing what must be thought, that which has summoned Heidegger's thinking along its way.

This introduction would like to be a signpost for this way; in fact, it should be nothing but a signpost by which he who seeks a way can orient himself, but which remains behind for him who has already set out on the way. Perhaps it can allow Heidegger's way to become provisionally visible for some as possibly their own way; for others it can lead a step nearer to the decision not to travel this way. However it may be, it will suffice if this introduction to Martin Heidegger's thinking elucidates to some extent Heidegger's path of thinking as a whole in terms of what he once said in a conversation with a Japanese guest about a very specific stretch of the way: "I always followed only an obscure trace, but I did follow. The trace was a scarcely perceptible promise which bespoke a releasing into the open. It was at times dark and perplexing, sometimes flashing like a sudden insight which then again withdrew itself for a long time from every attempt to put it into language" (Sp, 137).

1

THE ENTRANCE INTO METAPHYSICS

Martin Heidegger's thought is enkindled by the question, *Tί τὸ ὄν*, what
is a being [*das Seiende*], a being in its Being [*Sein*]? In an incomparable and
exclusive way this is the leading question of Western metaphysics, and the
task of the "first science," metaphysics, is to grasp a being *as* a being, in its
Being. Pertinent to this task is Aristotle's thesis that "being is said in
many ways."[1]

This Aristotelian thesis stands as the motto for the dissertation of
Edmund Husserl's teacher Franz Brentano, the title of which reads: *Von
der mannigfachen Bedeutung des Seienden nach Aristoteles* [*Concerning the Manifold
Meaning of Being According to Aristotle*] (Freiburg-im-Breisgau, 1862). It
develops in detail how Aristotle seeks to grasp the manifold expressibility
of being, how he distinguishes among *ὄν κατὰ συμβεβηκό*s (the acci-
dents, *ens per accidens*), *ὄν ὡς ἀληθέ*s (being in the sense of the true, *ens
tanquam verum*), *ὄν δυνάμει καὶ ἐνεργείᾳ*] (being in terms of potentiality
and being in terms of actuality), and *ὄν κατὰ τὰ σχήματα τῶν
κατηγοριῶν* (being which is once more said in diverse ways, namely in
accordance with the multiplicity of categories). As Heidegger himself
reports, he was struck by the question which governs his thinking, the
question of Being, during the study of this writing in his final years at the
Gymnasium in the summer of 1907. Thus he was brought to the way of his
thinking (Sp, 92f).

In his dissertation, *Die Lehre vom Urteil im Psychologismus. Ein kristisch-
positiver Beitrag zur Logik* [*The Doctrine of Judgement in Psychologism, a Critical-
Positive Contribution to Logic*], Heidegger asks about a specific mode of
Being, about *ens tanquam verum*, about Being as being-true or sense [*Sinn*].
He grasps the reality of the logical as *sense which is valid*. Judgement is as
logical reality valid sense. Only because it is sense can it be nonsensical or
meaningless. Sense is valid for an object, and *every* being is an "object."
Sense is valid for an object if the object is specified, "determined," by a
meaning-content [*Bedeutungsgehalt*] and is thus recognized and becomes a
"true" object. This determination of the object occurs in judgement—
every judgement signifies, insofar as it is true, a cognition "and every
cognition is always a judgement" (98). Sense can be valid for an object

because the object, the *ens*, can stand in the mode of reality of the *verum*. "The old concept of truth, *adequatio rei et intellectus*, can be subsumed into the purely logical if one conceives of *res* as object and of *intellectus* as the determining meaning-content" (99).

With his dissertation, the young Heidegger engages in the "psychologism controversy" that marked his day. He wants to contribute his part to the realization that logical reality is radically different from psychical reality. Psychologism is reproached not only for misconstruing the object of logic, but also for not knowing it at all (87). Psychologism does not know the object of logic because it seeks this object in the psychical realm, wants to grasp it in its origin in the psychical, and thus does not distinguish the logical from the psychical, or at least it does not do so definitively enough. While the reality of the psychical is an activity which runs its course in time, "whatever has a character of temporally elapsing, of being active," remains "of necessity" alien to "the domain of purely logical theory" (90). Logical reality, sense, is a " 'static' phenomenon which stands beyond every development and change, and which consequently does not *become, come into* being, but rather is valid. It is something which in every case can be 'comprehended' by the subject who forms a judgement but which is never altered by means of this comprehending" (102).

Can it be demonstrated, contrary to psychologism, that the logical exists alongside the psychical as yet another entirely different reality? Regarding this question Heidegger remarks in principle that a being—the "objective" or "actual"—can "as such not be proven but rather at most only exhibited" (90). Sense as *one* of the modes of reality can no longer be derived from a higher genus, and the question about the sense of sense can no longer advance beyond a more precise description and paraphrase. "Perhaps we stand here confronting an ultimate, irreducible matter regarding which all further illumination is impossible and every further question necessarily comes to a standstill" (95). The question as to how the mode of reality of meaning, the *verum*, is articulated out of the Being of any being is faced with the ultimate and supreme task of philosophy, to sort the "entire domain of 'Being' into its different modes of reality" (108).

In his *Habilitationsschrift, Die Kategorien- und Bedeutungslehre des Duns Scotus* [*Duns Scotus' Doctrine of Categories and Meaning*],[2] Heidegger continues to ask about the place which the reality of sense occupies in the entire region of beings. He thinks in accordance with the "fact" "that meaning and sense adhere to words and word complexes (sentences)" (108). But however closely sentence and sense, word and meaning may be linked, they belong—and this Heidegger points out explicitly here—to different regions of reality. Sense and the "constituent parts" to be found therein, the meanings, are, over against real beings, a "world" in their own right. They retain their own reality even when they are brought to expression through language (108f, 111). The interpenetration of the two separate regions of meaning and word is grasped by means of the concept of sign. Linguistic constructions are signs of meanings, of sense; sense and meaning are then in turn "signs" of the objects for which they are valid. As formations laden with meaning and sense, linguistic constructions are signs of a peculiar sort. They are, as Husserl says, not directional signs but rather *significant* signs. They are "expressions" (114, 118). Meaning, sign, expression—with these concepts the young Heidegger seeks to grasp the unity of and the distinction between sense and language.

Language exhibits a "grammatically" conceivable order which is indicated by the parts of speech: noun, pronoun, verb, and so on. These parts of speech reflect the particular involvement that there is in connection with meaning. The peculiar character of this involvement is due to the formal determinations of the meaning, of the *modi significandi*. In these *modi* lies the "possible form of the arrangement of the concrete complexions of meaning" (144f). The forms of meaning must be forms for a matter; this matter is the *ens*, objectivity in general. The forms of meaning are based upon the possible formal determinations of the object; the *modi significandi* are based upon the *modi essendi* (134, 131). But the object must become known; that is, it must be the object of cognition and thereby stand in a *modus intelligendi* so that the *modi significandi* can be grasped on the basis of the *modi essendi*. Only by way of the *modus intelligendi* can the *modus essendi* determine the *modus significandi* (136ff). Determination of the object (*modus essendi*), determination of the knowledge of the object (*modus intelligendi*), **20** and determination of the meaning (*modus significandi*) correspond to one another. The parts of speech are then constituted by the forms of meaning. When the theory of meaning sets forth the *modi significandi*, it sketches out an *a priori* grammar to which all historically occurrent grammars must conform. Heidegger seeks to secure recognition for the idea of a "pure grammar" (149), also advocated by Husserl, in that he appropriates anew the speculative grammar of the medieval tract *de modis significandi*.

The question of how the object, sense or meaning, and the significant sign of language belong together leads to the ultimate and supreme problems of the "doctrine of categories." It asks about the *ens*, the Being of beings. It determines the *ens* as objectivity by means of the "category of categories." The *ens* as objectivity is an "ultimate" and "supreme" matter "beyond which there can be no further questioning." Its character of finality asserts itself in the transcendentals, those supreme and ultimate determinations of objectivity which are subordinate to no genus and about which "nothing more can be expressed." These transcendentals—such as *unum, verum, bonum*—are "convertible" with *ens* (24ff). In his *Habilitationsschrift* Heidegger shows how the different regions of the mathematical, the physical, the psychical, the metaphysical, and the logical can be attained by the specification of meaning of the *unum* and of the *verum*.

The doctrine of categories takes up the task of demarcating the "different regions of objects into confines categorically irreducible to one another." At the same time, it relates the "unfolding spheres" to "the ultimate categorical sphere of the objective (the transcendentals)" and thereby unites them (229ff). But the object is to be grasped categorically only as *known* object. "The category is the most general determination of an object. The object and objectivity have sense as such only *for* a subject. In this subject, objectivity is established through judgement. Accordingly, if one wants to grasp decisively the category as the determination *of the object*, then it must be brought into an essential relationship with the structure which establishes objectivity. Thus, it is no 'accident', but rather is grounded in the innermost core of the problem of categories that both in Aristotle as well as in Kant it emerges in some connection with predication, with judgement" (232). The problem of categories must be placed within the problem of judgement (the problem of knowledge) and the problem of the subject. More decisively than medieval thinking, recent "critical" thinking demands a return to the sphere of the problem regarding subjectivity. Thus, the doctrine of categories becomes a general theory of knowledge, that theory of the various forms of judgement formation which for the first time grounds the work of each particular science. Since the problem of judgement advances to the forefront, the "theory of the theoretical sense" can also carry the name "logic." "Logic" in this wider sense of the word then includes "the doctrine of the constituent parts of sense (*doctrine of meaning*), the doctrine with regard to the structure of sense (*doctrine of judgement*), and the doctrine of structural differentiations and their systematic forms (*doctrine of knowledge*)" (160). Therefore, metaphysics as *critical* metaphysics is logic, or viewed objectively, a doctrine of categories which is explicitly introduced into the problems of judgement and subject.

The final chapter which Heidegger subsequently attached to his *Habilitationsschrift* once again takes up the problem of categories in a fundamental way. The problem of knowledge—the question as to how sense can actually be valid for objects—receives in this final outlook a "metaphysical resolution" (232). By no means, says Heidegger, should the categories be reduced to mere functions of thought, and by no means should philosophy stop at exhibiting the structural multiplicity of the merely logical. The "transcendental" philosophizing which must be taken beyond the opposition between realism and idealism results precisely from the fact that all cognition is cognition about the *object* (233). One must, therefore, not only question logical sense with regard to its structures, but also make it problematic according to its "ontical meaning," "Only then will it be possible to have a satisfactory solution to the question of how 'unreal', 'transcendental' sense guarantees us true reality and objectivity" (236). The question about the logical mode of reality leads up to a context which is "translogical." "Philosophy," says Heidegger, "cannot in the long run dispense with its genuine optics, *metaphysics*." A "metaphysical-teleological" interpretation assigns sense to consciousness, sense as that which is originally unique to consciousness. Thus, consciousness is conceived of as the "active mind" (*lebendiger Geist*), and the mind is brought into relation with its "metaphysical origin" from which alone "Being" can be a "being-true" (*Wahr-Sein*). Consequently, what the Middle Ages knew as the "transcendent original relation of the soul to God" is thought anew (235f, 239f). **22**

If consciousness is grasped as active mind, then it must also be realized that the "epistemological subject does not explain the metaphysically most significant sense of mind, let alone its full complexity." The active mind is essentially *historical* spirit (*historischer Geist*). "History and its cultural-philosophical-teleological interpretation must become an element for the problem of categories, an element which determines meaning . . ." (237f). The highest metaphysical problems provide a historical perspective. Naturally Heidegger still incorporates history in the philosophical taxonomy in such a way that he associates it as value-formation with time and change; however, he associates the validation of value, which philosophy comprehends, with eternity and absoluteness (240). On the basis of this distinction Heidegger can pursue the history of philosophy as "the history of problems," with reference to the continual recurrence of the same problems. In fact, at the beginning of the *Habilitationsschrift* he states that, due to the "constancy of human nature," philosophical problems repeated themselves in history; time as a "historical" category is, "as it were, eliminated" in the history of problems (4f).

If spirit grasps its history, if it elevates the formation of value to the comprehended validity of value, then it achieves "a continually increasing means for the active comprehension of the absolute spirit of God" (238). The essence of God is here thought in terms of an eternity which is contrasted with the temporal character of the world. A saying of Meister Eckhart which Heidegger gave as a motto to his *Habilitation* lecture, "The Concept of Time in the Science of History," aims at the distinction between time and eternity: "Time is that which changes and diversifies; eternity simply endures."

Heidegger's first works resolve the question about the manifold **23** expressibility of Being, about the distinction and breakdown of the regions of reality, how this expressibility had presented itself in the question about the peculiarity of the *verum*. This resolution is accomplished by means of a metaphysical-teleological interpretation of consciousness which corresponds to a philosophical-teleological interpretation of cultural history. The question about the unity of Being in its manifold expressibility appears to be silenced once again by metaphysical determinations which are ultimately founded by speculative theology.[3]

By means of his own work upon the problems, Heidegger seeks to appropriate anew what has been thought in Western metaphysics. He takes up Aristotle's question about the manifold ways in which Being can be expressed. He assimilates medieval thought, and indeed with its entire burden of tension. In the *Habilitationsschrift* he promises both a complete presentation of medieval logic as well as a philosophical interpretation of Eckhart's mysticism (16, 232 note). The conclusion of this writing refers to Hegel: "The philosophy of the active mind, of the productive love, of the reverent indwelling of God [*verehrende Gottinnigkeit*], is faced with the great task of a fundamental confrontation with the system of a historical *Weltanschauung*. This philosophy whose most general aims, particularly a doctrine of categories led by its fundamental tendencies, could only be hinted at, confronts a system prodigious in abundance, depth, wealth of experience, and conceptualization, which as such has subsumed all previous fundamental philosophical leitmotivs. In other words, it must come to terms with *Hegel*" (241). The young Heidegger comes to Hegel not so much through the then incipient neo-Hegelianism and its methodological-epistemological problematic, but rather by means of the speculative theology of the Tübingen school of Catholic theology (Möhler, Kuhn, Staudenmaier).

As far as the philosophical tendencies at the beginning of our century are concerned, the young Heidegger believed he could find decisive help for his own work in the transcendental-logical Kant interpretation of the Marburg and the Southwest German schools. Rickert is the teacher; the *Habilitationsschrift* is dedicated to him: "To him," Heidegger says in the foreword of his dissertation, "I am indebted for the vision and understanding of modern logical problems." Then it is mainly Emil Lask to whom Heidegger refers again and again. Apart from the Neo-Kantian beginning, the phenomenology of Edmund Husserl becomes decisively significant for Heidegger. In his inaugural address before the Heidelberg Academy of the Sciences, Heidegger says: "Since 1909 I have tried, of course without the proper guidance, to delve into Husserl's logical investigations. Through the seminar exercises with Rickert, I became acquainted with the writings of Emil Lask, who, mediating between both, also tried to attend to the Greek thinkers."

His dissertation, "Die Lehre vom Urteil im Psychologismus," is in essence "phenomenological," quite apart from the fact whether the author considers himself to be of the phenomenological school or not. It is essential for phenomenology that it no longer traces one state of affairs back to another in order to "explain" the former; rather, by means of clarification it lays hold of the matter in question according to its character. The decisive example of the application of the phenomenological method became the dispute with psychologism in the domain of logic. In his *Logische Untersuchungen* [*Logical Investigations*], Husserl pointed out that psychologism explains away the genuinely logical when it sets out to grasp it from its genesis in the psychical. In his dissertation Heidegger polemically carries this thought through as he opposes various representatives of "psychologism"; in doing so he finds support in the transcendental-logical interpretation of Kant and in Husserl. Those in Marburg and the Southwest German School who rejected a psychological interpretation of Kant have "vigorously paved the way for the knowledge of the logical as such." Natorp could say correctly of the Marburg Neo-Kantians that there simply was not very much left for them to learn from Husserl's *Logische Untersuchungen*. "However," says Heidegger, "Husserl's fundamental investigations which were quite successfully formulated, are precisely those which broke the psychologistic spell and paved the way for a clarification of logic and its tasks" (1f).

Husserl's idea of an *a priori*, pure grammar is a guiding notion in Heidegger's *Habilitationsschrift*. Heidegger refers again and again directly to Husserl's phenomenology. He expresses the matters to be discussed in "phenomenological terminology," even if only tentatively (130). He can also point out that in the "scholastic mode of thought" moments of "phenomenological observation" lie concealed in spite of metaphysical inclusions, "perhaps most strongly in it than anywhere else" (11).

25

After the First World War, Heidegger became Husserl's assistant (Husserl had been called to Freiburg in 1916). Thus closer collaboration was achieved. On the basis of the complete orientation of his work in phenomenology, Heidegger could seize the possibility of a way for his thinking. Henceforth, and for ten years thereafter, he gave his lectures and his works the title "phenomenology." Heidegger's thinking was "transcendental" not only through the connection with Neo-Kantianism but still more substantially through the predominant interest in the *ens tanquam verum*. Consequently, he had to view phenomenology too as transcendental. The question was, how could Heidegger bring his (soon to be called "hermeneutic") interest in history into accord with the phenomenological method? In keeping with the metaphysical orientation of his thinking he had to bring transcendental phenomenology into the service of the question of Being, to grasp phenomenology as "ontology". But phenomenology strives to be a philosophical method which by looking at the matter at hand leaves behind all "metaphysical" presuppositions. Thus, an intense tension had to result from Heidegger's attempt to appropriate anew the questions of metaphysics: Could metaphysical problems be settled in a new way on the basis of phenomenology? Could phenomenology be made more profound by returning to the questions of metaphysics?

Metaphysics, this classical form of Western thinking, was called into question not only by the new beginnings of phenomenology but also by anti-metaphysical thinkers. Even while Heidegger immersed himself in transcendental philosophy and phenomenology in order to be able to settle metaphysical questions, thinkers who aspired to overthrow "metaphysics" influenced his thinking. In his inaugural address at Heidelberg, Heidegger reports: "In 1908 I found my way to Hölderlin by means of a *Reclam* volume of his poems which is still available today . . . What the stimulating years between 1910 and 1914 brought cannot be duly stated, but can only be intimated by a selective enumeration: the second, doubly **26**   enlarged edition of Nietzsche's 'Will to Power', the translation of the works of Kierkegaard and Dostoevsky, the emerging interest in Hegel and Schelling, Rilke's writings and Trakl's poems, and Dilthey's 'collected works'." Names like Kierkegaard and Nietzsche designate the forces which unmask the impotency of the reigning school at that time, which place into question the entire metaphysical orientation of Western thinking and which were to reveal the profundity of the convulsions whose catastrophic consequences became visible even abroad in the First World War and also in the revolutions and wars which followed thereafter.

2

METAPHYSICS AND HISTORY

If we move from Heidegger's first publications to the lecture courses he gave *after* the First World War—approximately to the lecture course on selected problems of pure phenomenology given in the winter semester of 1919–20—an entirely new point of departure manifests itself. The discussion about Being which may be in different modes of reality and which may be grasped in its unity only through ultimate metaphysical principles has vanished. Factical life, life in its actuality, now comes into question.

The "self-sufficiency" of this factical life is asserted. Life answers its questions only in its own language; it understands itself. Expression, appearance, and testimony belong to it. "Sense" is not a world unto itself which would have to be grasped as static and resting in itself; sense is rather that which is inherent in factical life and which must be grasped from life according to its structure. This life in its actuality is a context of significance. Of course, significance can be levelled through the human tendency toward reification [*Verdinglichung*] or "objectification"—in fact, the tendency toward objectification has often been put forth in modern philosophy as the idea of scientific knowledge itself—nevertheless, objectification must be conceived of as the "de-vivifying" [*Entlebung*] of life. Thus, life is deprived of its "life," its "tendentious" structure, and the relations of significance of its world. Life, which in its actuality takes place in contexts of significance, exists in "situations." A sense of performance, a sense of content, and a sense of relationship comprise the structure of the situation. In factical life, the sense of performance dominates. The performance of life itself comes before the orientation toward "contents." Life derives its fundamental sense when it grasps itself in its performance; in this way, though, it understands itself as "historical" life (intrinsically historical) and is on the way to its origin.

Like Husserl, Heidegger also pursues "phenomenology" as the science of origins. The sense of phenomenology, as Heidegger understands it, is the self-interpretation of factical life, which grasps itself in its primordiality when it understands itself as historical. Heidegger roots phenomenological philosophy and research in the understanding of factical life, but in doing so he does not turn back to that psychologism against which he had struggled in his first works. That is, amidst the life which is the topic of discussion, man is not to be understood as a determinate being to which another being is to be referred, from which the other being is to be explained in its Being. The factical historical life is "origin" in the sense of the transcendental I; however, if the discourse is to turn to the transcendental I, then the transcendental-philosophical orientation toward the schema "material object-subject" must be abolished and the ineluctability of intuition vis-à-vis the reference to the "constitutive" I must be put forward. Self-possession, which is what really matters in life, is not the possession of an isolated subject and certainly not the possession of the I as an object; it is, rather, the process of winning and losing a certain familiarity of life with itself, whereby life is a living-in-the-world. Life lives itself into the world; life is not the I from which the bridge to things would still have to be constructed; it has always been a living in the world.

Properly understood, Hegelian philosophy, Dilthey, and above all, the primordially Christian experience of life all point out that factical life is historical. But has Western philosophy, that is, has metaphysics as the theory of Being been capable of seeing this facticity and historicality of life? For the young Heidegger, who had taken up the question of Being and whose thinking now began with factical-historical life, the question had to be asked whether metaphysics had after all done any justice to factical life. Was not metaphysics still accompanied, as by its own shadow, by a metaphysically not quite comprehensible belief and an anti-metaphysical thinking? Heidegger's questioning came under the influence of those thinkers who ventured the assault upon the Western tradition in its entirety. Of course, it was still to be a decade before Nietzsche's radical attack on the Platonic-Christian tradition and before Hölderlin's poetic-mythical saying became decisive for Heidegger. First Heidegger took the initiative which originated with the thinking of Wilhelm Dilthey and from witnesses of faith such as Kierkegaard. Dilthey's work, which did not become evident in its complete range and depth of profundity until the publication of his *Gesammelten Schriften*, raised the question of whether or not metaphysical thinking should be abandoned, since it had never done justice to full historical life. Kierkegaard's call for a discernment of spirits and his struggle to undo an almost two-thousand-year-old falsification of the Christian faith began to question whether thinking was capable at all of reaching into those depths of life into which faith leads.

Of course Heidegger's early Freiburg lecture courses deal not only with Dilthey and Paul, Augustine, Luther, and Kierkegaard, but also, and to a greater degree, with Aristotle. The lecture courses from Heidegger's Marburg years (1923–1928) concern the ontological tradition from Plato to Thomas Aquinas, and up to Kant. This does not mean, however, that Heidegger wants to solidify the interpretation of factical life into a new

Scholasticism, to bring it back to the rigid concepts of Being which have been handed down. On the contrary, Heidegger seeks to escape a danger here. The interpretation of factical life could fall prey to the traditional theory of Being precisely by the fact that it lets this theory stand as an unsurmounted antithesis and is thereby governed by it in a hidden way after all. The interpretation of factical life has to question anew the traditional mode of conceptualization from the ground up. The theory of Being, or ontology, must also become a problem once again in terms of the interpretation of factical life, the hermeneutic of facticity. In 1923 Heidegger lectured on *Ontologie oder Hermeneutik der Faktizität* [*Ontology or the Hermeneutic of Facticity*].

What follows will show—while rigorously restricting the definitive way of stating the question—how Heidegger became acquainted with the experience of history through thinkers like Dilthey and the life-experience of the Christian faith so that he would then include this experience in the theory of Being of metaphysics, which was once again to be decided upon.

DILTHEY AND MODERN HISTORICAL THOUGHT   **30**

In his *Habilitation* address, *Der Zeitbegriff in der Geschichtswissenschaft*, Heidegger makes a distinction between natural science and historical science by contrasting the concept of time of the one science with that of the other. In physics time becomes a simply ordered progression of points in time. One instant differs from the other only by means of its location measured from an initial point. The flow of time is frozen and solidified into a homogeneous arrangement of locations; it becomes a graduated scale, a parameter. But in historical science, time is no measurable, homogeneous progression. On the contrary, the times of history differ qualitatively from one another without it being possible to determine by some law how they follow one another. "The qualitative nature of the historical concept of time signifies nothing other than the concentration . . . (crystalization, of . . .) of an objectification of life given in history" (187). Even at the onset of chronology (for example, such and such a year after the founding of Rome, after the birth of Christ) the principle of historical concept-formation, the qualitative determination, the "relation of value" [*Wertbeziehung*], becomes evident.

When Heidegger tries to separate natural science and historical science in this way, he takes up an attempt which Wilhelm Windelband and Heinrich Rickert had started. Nevertheless, the question remains as to whether history comes into view primordially enough when one wants to do what Heidegger attempts to do here; that is, if while keeping in mind the "reality" of historical science, one wants to ground science in a scientific-theoretical manner by going back to its fundamental concepts and their formation, and to contrast this science with natural science. Can history be delimited as a determinate, specific region by philosophy, or does reflection upon history belong to the founding of philosophy itself? Does traditional conceptualization suffice for the determination of what history is, or must this conceptualization be revised when thinking demonstrates that reflection upon history belongs to the founding of philosophy itself? Does the traditional, metaphysical mode of conception, the "ontological" beginning of Western thinking, perhaps disguise history in its primordiality? Wilhelm Dilthey ventured into these questions; he thereby decisively led the question about history beyond the neo-Kantian approach. In a strong move against the all-determining center, Heidegger tried to appropriate Dilthey's work, so that in *Sein und Zeit* he could finally say in retrospect that the analysis of the problem of history which he accomplished in this study "grew out of the appropriation of Dilthey's work" (397).

Heidegger takes Dilthey seriously not only as the great historian, which he had always been esteemed as, but also as a thinker who is concerned with the founding of philosophy. Dilthey, as it says in *Sein und Zeit*, is more than "the 'sensitive' interpreter of intellectual history, especially literary history, who 'also' strives to distinguish between the natural sciences and the sciences of man. He thereby assigns to the history of these sciences and to 'psychology' a distinctive role, letting the whole become blurred in a relativistic 'philosophy of life'." The diversity of the approaches which permeate and intersect one another in Dilthey's work should no longer disguise the core of this thinking: "What looks like disunity and uncertain, haphazard 'experimenting' is the elemental restlessness toward the one goal: to understand life philosophically and to secure a hermeneutical basis for this understanding from 'life itself'" (397f).

As Heidegger goes on to say, Dilthey, "taking into account contemporary discussions," certainly had his own research forced one-sidedly into the field of the theory of science, but this direction was not central for his work. In fact, Dilthey at first understood his work as a "critique of historical reason." This critique, as an epistemological or transcendental-philosophical deepening of the work of the particular sciences, as a founding of the sciences of man, was to be placed on a par with the Kantian critique which is grasped as founding only the natural sciences. Thus Dilthey concerned himself with neo-Kantian endeavors, that is, with extending the Kantian critical concept of nature through a critical concept of history as well. Dilthey saw himself obliged to legitimize his attempt by means of a far-reaching historical reflection. In the *Einleitung in die Geistes-*

wissenschaften [*Introduction to the Sciences of Man*], he portrayed the "domination and decline" of metaphysics, yet he thereby attempted to furnish evidence that metaphysics had not somehow become lost, but rather that it had been broken up by the research efforts of the particular sciences. In Dilthey's opinion, there still remained the task of founding the work of the particular sciences through a transcendental-philosophical, "epistemological" reflection. The second, unfinished volume of Dilthey's *Introduction* or *Kritik der historischen Vernunft* [*Critique of Historical Reason*] was therefore supposed to bear the title: *The State of the Sciences of Experience and Epistemology. The Contemporary Problem of the Sciences of Man.*[1]

Dilthey's critique of historical reason is the critique of "man's capacity to know himself and the society and history he created"; it is based on an "epistemological founding for the sciences of man."[5] Dilthey's attempt to lay the foundation, a "logic" of the sciens of man, nevertheless, changes into the question about historical life itself from which humanistic work arises as well; it changes into an analysis of the transcendental I which is now no longer a "bloodless" consciousness, but rather a full, essentially historical "life." Along these lines, Count Paul Yorck of Wartenburg grasped with complete clarity the critique of historical reason. The Count was Dilthey's philosophical partner in conversations and correspondence, and their exchange of letters was published in 1923. Heidegger refers to Yorck when in *Sein und Zeit* he sets up the task of appropriating Dilthey's work. Heidegger is resolved "to foster the spirit of Count Yorck in order to serve the work of Dilthey" (SuZ 404).

Yorck achieves, as Heidegger notes, clear insight into the fundamental character of history; however, he does this not exactly "from the object of historical observation in a scientific-theoretic manner," but rather "from the knowledge of the character of Being of human *Dasein* itself." Heidegger quotes Yorck's statement: "The fact that the total psychophysical datum lives rather than *is* is the germinal point of historicality, and a self-reflection which is directed not toward an abstract I but rather toward the fullness of my self will find me historically determined, just as physics knows me as cosmically determined. Just as I am nature, I am history . . ." (401). Heidegger remarks that in this statement Yorck takes the "is," Being, as being-present-at-hand and contrasts the ontical as the present-at-hand with the historical as life. Such a contrast, however, "is only the reflection of the unbroken domination of traditional ontology, which, originating from the ancient way of formulating the question of Being, fixes the ontological problematic within fundamental strictures" (403). Only the "present-at-hand" of "Nature," and not the life of history, is adequately grasped by ancient ontology. But the task now is not merely to contrast the historical with the present-at-hand or "ontical"—as Yorck does—but rather to make the sense of Being problematic again, and metaphysics along with it. In this way one obtains an "idea" of Being which encompasses the "ontical" and the historical.

Only when Being itself again becomes a problem can historical thinking be grounded in its primordiality. Heidegger thinks that the modern discipline of history has not forged ahead toward such a grounding, but rather has remained closely dominated by the inadequate notion of Being handed down by classical antiquity. He quotes with approval Count Yorck's controversial judgement of Ranke: "Ranke is a great eyepiece for whom what has disappeared can never become an *actuality*" (400). Ranke does not grasp history in its actuality because he does not enter into it as into a context of effects; he believes, rather, that as an "objective" historian he can and must "present" history absolutely. One can in any case see and present the "present-at-hand" by means of a lens or an eyepiece, but the history which occurs vanishes in its unique reality when it is merely "presented." Certainly the historical school also knew that it is not possible to grasp history solely by means of knowledge which presents material and combines it in a judgemental manner. It precisely demanded empathy with what is irreducibly individual and complete.[6] The question remains as to whether the historical sense for the individual is not merely added superficially to the traditional rationality of knowledge, so that this task of grounding the experience of history in a primordially unified thinking is missed. Heidegger says that the historical school did in fact fail in this task with the following statement of Count Yorck: "*That school was not a historical one at all*, but rather an antiquarian one construing things aesthetically at a time when the great dominant activity was that of mechanistic construction. Therefore, what it contributed methodologically, to the method of rationality, was just a general feeling" (400).

A historical cognition that only presents history, and that additionally projects itself into the *individuum ineffabile*, cannot do justice to history's unique reality. Hence, alongside this thinking which objectifies and thus transforms history into a mere past, there stands a revolutionary action which seeks to grasp the future and to master history. Count Yorck, and Heidegger along with him, suggest this connection: "The 'scientists' stand in contrast to the forces of the time like the overly cultivated French society of the revolutionary movement—here as there formalism, the cult of the form. Determinations of relationship are the last word of wisdom. Naturally, such a direction of thought has, I suppose, its own as yet unwritten history. The groundlessness of such thinking and of the belief in such thinking—epistemologically considered, a metaphysical attitude—is a historical product." In blunt terms, "'modern man', that is, man since the Renaissance, is ready to be buried" (400f).

34

Dilthey has led the thinking of the historical school to self-reflection, but the limits of that school remain also his own. Already in his early lecture courses Heidegger pointed out that Dilthey did indeed experience the context of history as a system of interconnections, but in accordance with his humanistic ideas and his aesthetic manner he views this context only from a neutral and external perspective. In *Sein und Zeit*, Heidegger advances his critique a step further by proceeding in a fundamental, "ontological" manner: Dilthey has merely left behind metaphysical-representational thinking which is oriented toward beings as present-at-hand but has not overcome it on its own basis. The question about Being itself was not taken over primordially. Thus, that which Dilthey set up in opposition to the present-at-hand, "life," was left in "ontological indifference" (209). The limits of Dilthey's "problematic and those of the conceptualization with which it had to be verbalized" become apparent in his fundamental concept, "life." These are the limits of that metaphysical way of formulating the question, which was precisely what Dilthey had wanted to avoid (46ff).[7]

But if recent historical thinking, from which Dilthey started out, remains inadequate, and if "modern man" is ready to be buried anyway, then from where is thinking, which prepares to take up the question of Being and history, going to receive its decisive impetus? *Sein und Zeit* gives no direct, or at best, an indirect answer to this question. Nevertheless, Heidegger's early lecture courses show that it was the primordial Christian belief which directed Heidegger to the decisive questions.

Count Yorck also saw that the task for thinking was to profit from what Christian faith had experienced. He wrote to Dilthey: "Dogmatics was the attempt at an ontology of the higher life, the historical life. Christian Dogmatics had to be this contradiction-ridden expression of an intellectual struggle for life because the Christian religion is life's highest form of vitality." Dilthey had to consider as his own the task of exhibiting "the universal value for life" that all dogmas have "for every human vitality." As he saw it, the Christian dogmas are "untenable in their restriction to the facts of Christian history"; however, in their "universal sense" they signify "the ultimate vital contents of all history."[8] Count Yorck reawakened in Dilthey a concern which originally belonged to his way of thinking. Dilthey had, of course, begun as a theologian and with theological works. In 1860 at the age of 27, he summed up his life as follows: ". . . my vocation is to grasp the innermost essence *of the religious life in history* and to provide a moving portrayal of it in our time, a time which is concerned exclusively with the state and with science."[9]

When Dilthey moved from theology toward a thinking which made history central to his questions, he adhered to a way which modern

35

thinking has travelled repeatedly. Not only Hamann, but also Herder and
Hegel began their way with "biblical meditations." Even Heidegger still
keeps to this way. Heidegger began upon his way influenced by a theology
which was convinced more and more that it was now valid to experience
in a completely new way the Christian faith in its primordiality, and this
after centuries, indeed after millennia of obfuscation of the primordial
Christian faith through both philosophy and theology. Witnesses of faith
like Luther and Kierkegaard upheld this notion, and they of all people
were most like the young Heidegger in this respect. Heidegger's relationship to modern historical thinking raised by Dilthey to philosophical
self-reflection is from the outset surpassed by his regard for another, more
primordial historical thinking. The experience of history, manifested by
primordial Christian faith, preceded the modern form of historical thinking.

THE FACTICAL EXPERIENCE OF LIFE IN THE CHRISTIAN
FAITH

In his Freiburg lecture course, *Einführung in die Phänomenologie der
Religion* [*Introduction to the Phenomenology of Religion*] (Winter Semester,
1920–21), Heidegger referred to the "factical experience of life" as it is
expressed in the letters of the Apostle Paul. Heidegger considers the
passage from the fourth and fifth chapters of the first letter to the Thessalonians (4, 13ff), in which Paul speaks of the hope upon which the Christian's life is based, the hope in the second coming of Christ. About this
advent, the "future" of the Lord, Paul says: "But it is not necessary to
write you, beloved brothers, about times and hours; for you yourselves
certainly know that the day of the Lord will come like a thief in the night."
Paul, as Heidegger points out, gives no date for the second coming; he
even explicitly refuses to name a date. For example, the second coming is
not to be pinned down by the millennium of the Chiliasts; Paul speaks only of
its "suddenness." He does not use "chronological" but rather "chairological" characteristics. The *chairos* [a time reckoned according to significant
events rather than by some scientific standard of measurement, e.g., the birth
of Christ—*trans.*] places it on the razor's edge in the decision.
Chairological characteristics do not reckon with and master time; rather
they place one into the threat of the future. They belong in life's history of
performance which cannot be objectified. The second coming can also not
be characterized by means of substantive moments. To be sure, history
can also be described in terms of its subject matter, as the history of

contents, ideas, styles, etc., as the history of "objective Spirit." (Hegel even tried to grasp the appearance of Christ in terms of its substantive sense, as the revelation of the profundity of substance or idea.) However, according to Heidegger, the primordial Christian experience of life is precisely for that reason a factical and historical one, an experience of life in its actuality, because it sees life's dominant structure in the significance of performance rather than in the significance of contents. If man tries by means of chronological computations or content-oriented characterizations to define the inaccessible event which suddenly bursts upon the scene, the event upon which his life is based, he then eliminates that which should determine his life as the always inaccessible and replaces it with the secured, the accessible. In this way, however, he deceives himself about life's actuality. Paul writes: "For when they will say, 'there is peace, there is no danger', perdition will rapidly descend upon them as pain befalls a pregnant wife, and they will not escape." Heidegger's thinking continued to rest upon the supposition that the thinking which computes time and turns toward accessible "objective" contents, thereby disguising for itself its relation to the inaccessible future, will not escape ruin.

In his lecture course on the phenomenology of religion, Heidegger considered yet another passage from Paul's letters, the one in the Second Letter to the Corinthians (12, 1–10) which discusses the meaning of the pneumatic-mystical charisma. That is to say, it is about the theme of "the thorn in the flesh," which Kierkegaard also dealt with so thoroughly. In this passage Paul says that he will not brag about himself in the same manner as a mystic could who was carried off into the third heaven all the way to paradise. Were he to boast, he would in fact only be telling the truth; however, he was given a thorn, a spur in the flesh, in order that he not appear presumptuous because of profound revelations. He was given an "angel of Satan" who strikes him with fists. He prayed to the Lord three times for this angel of Satan to leave him be. But the Lord said: "Be content with my grace; for my strength is powerful in the weak." For that reason, the Apostle wants to boast first of all about his weakness, if at all, and not about revelations and visions. Concerning this report of the Apostle, Heidegger points out that turning toward the facticity of life rests precisely in the appropriation of weakness and the renunciation of content-oriented visions, apocalypses, and pride in a special blessing.

The primordial Christian faith experiences life in its actuality. As the early Heidegger says, it is to be found in the factical experience of life; that is, it is itself this experience of life. However, the factical experience of life is "historical" [*historisch*]; it understands life "historically" [*geschichtlich*]. It lives not only in time, but lives time itself. By reflecting upon primordial

Christian religiosity as the model of factical life-experience, Heidegger obtains the guiding concepts which present the structure of factical life or, as Heidegger says later, of "factical existence."

Since according to the view of the early Heidegger, primordial Christian religion is factical life-experience, it needs only to be "explicated." In later history, however, this life-experience is no longer kept up in its purity. To be sure, thinkers such as Augustine, the medieval mystics, Luther, and Kierkegaard recover this experience in spite of all the distortions; nevertheless, it is permeated by a metaphysical conceptualization which ultimately remains inadequate to this experience. In the case of Augustine the factical experience of life is distorted by Neoplatonic concepts. Therefore, Augustine may not only be explicated; he must also be destroyed. The interpretation must grasp through the concepts at the experience which is truly at the core in order to free this experience from the inadequate concepts by which it is expressed.

In his lecture course *Augustinus und der Neuplatonismus* (Summer semester, 1921), Heidegger showed by means of the tenth book of the *Confessions* how Augustine thinks from the factical experience of life. Augustine grasps the blissful life not in terms of content but rather in terms of performance. The decisive question is how the blessed life is appropriated in the will. As Augustine says in the twenty-third chapter of the aforementioned books, men want to be blissful, and yet they do not want it strongly enough to be able to achieve truly that which they would like. They can find the blissful life only where it is to be found, in God. Men, however, in whom the flesh strongly protests against the spirit, hit upon what for them is proximally attainable and are satisfied with it. They do not want the blissful life in God as earnestly as is necessary for it to be attained. The blissful life is joy in the truth, and therefore men love truth. But they love in it only the light and hate the judgement it contains. They love the truth which reveals itself but hate the truth which reveals them—the truth which strikes back at men, which is self-knowledge and which demands performance. However, the truth veils itself from that man who in his insolence would like to remain concealed himself while everything else is revealed to him. In these interpretations of the blissful life and of truth, Augustine's performance-oriented tendency is clear throughout; the factical life-experience is characterized through the predominance of the performance-oriented tendency over against the orientation toward contents.

Augustine's mode of conceptualization, however, is not always oriented to factical life. The *fruitio Dei* as Augustine conceives of it Neoplatonically simply opposes the having of a self. According to Heidegger, both of these elements do not grow from the same root but rather grew together from without. The conceptualization taken up by Augustine distorts the experience which is to be expressed in it. Thus arises the problem of "Augustine and Neoplatonism."

Augustine appropriates from Neoplatonism the notion that being good and being beautiful belong to Being, that they can be "enjoyed." In the *fruitio Dei* God is enjoyed as the *summum bonum*, and he alone may be enjoyed. As in Neoplatonism, a distinction is made between visible and invisible things; visible things are only to be used (*uti*) for other ends; invisible things alone are to be enjoyed (*frui*). The *perversio*, the "subversion of values," lies in the fact that what is only to be used and exploited is enjoyed, and what is to be enjoyed is used for other purposes. However, Heidegger sees what must be destroyed already in the fact that an order of value is established at all, that God is valued as *bonum* and is compared to other good as *summum*. A quietism accompanies the valuing and esteeming which extricates itself from factical life and seeks God as the "rest" (in accordance with Augustine's saying, "*Inquietum est cor nostrum, donec requiescat in te*"). To be sure, Augustine lives and thinks starting from the unrest belonging to factical life; nevertheless, in the quietism of the *fruitio Dei* which stems from Neoplatonism he misses the factical life-experience of primordial Christianity and becomes untrue to himself.

Augustine believed that one could understand the thoughts of Platonism as *coniecturae*, as inquiring projections upon the truth of the Christian message. The rest of the patristic and scholastic tradition went further than he in this view. Does not the Apostle Paul say in his letter to the Romans (I, 20) that God's invisible nature, his eternal strength and divinity could be seen in his works, in his creation? Through this statement patristics and scholasticism saw their appropriation of Greek metaphysical thinking legitimized, since this thinking does indeed proceed from God's creation to God himself. In contrast, Martin Luther tried to show that this interpretation of the Pauline statement was a fundamental misunderstanding. For this reason, Heidegger referred to Luther in his lecture course on Augustine and Neoplatonism and indeed to the theses of the 1518 Heidelberg Disputation. These were still not well known in 1921, but in the meantime have received notice to a great extent through the introduction of "dialectical theology." In the nineteenth and twentieth theses, Luther says that *he* who perceives and understands God's invisible nature through his works cannot rightly be called a theologian; rather, the theologian is one who grasps the visible aspect of God's nature and who has turned toward the world as portrayed in the Cross and the Passion. In Romans (I, 22), the apostle labels as foolish precisely those who seek to understand God's nature from his works. Luther points to the remarks of the first letter to the Corinthians (I, 20ff) in which Paul says that God

40

makes those who believe in him blessed through foolish sermons. Since the world through its wisdom has not known God in his wisdom, God has transformed the wisdom of this world into foolishness. In the 1949 introduction to *Was ist Metaphysik*, Heidegger still refers the theologians to these remarks of the Apostle (WiM, 20).

In the Heidelberg theses for disputation, Luther goes on to say that the "theologian of God's glory"—he who desires to know God's invisible nature, his strength and glory by his visible works—calls the bad good and the good bad. In accordance with its essence, metaphysical-theological speculation wants to be a theodicy, a justification of God. It must look away precisely from that wherein God has actually acted, from the Passion and the Cross. Luther therefore states that the wisdom which is to allow God's invisible nature to be seen in his works swells up and makes one blind and unrepentant. In his "Theology of the Cross" Luther thus retrieves the "factical life-experience" of primordial Christianity. Such Christianity renounces all visions and revelations, above all even the visions of metaphysics, and by appropriating weakness plumbs the depths of the factical, the essentially "historical" life. Luther's pure *listening* to the word of salvation, his theology of the Cross and his discourse about justification through faith alone—"This Lutheran hearing in its terrifying consequence is for the philosopher what is strangest, most peculiar, and what existentially hardly intimates a language" (Jaspers)—existentially pointed to a language for Heidegger, and Heideggers's attempt to renew metaphysical thinking went through the extreme counterposition to meta-physics and the sharpest attack upon it. Of course it is only the *young* Luther, according to the conception of the early Heidegger, who again primordially understands the Christian faith against all concealments of tradition. The later Luther, in Heidegger's opinion, again fell prey to tradition and with Melanchthon fostered a new scholasticising.

But why is metaphysical conceptualization insufficient for the experi-ence of life in its actuality? It disguises the fact that what matters for factical life is the non-objectifiable performance, and that this perfor-mance is "historical." Heidegger saw himself continually led to the insight that every attempt to find acceptance in the language of metaphysics for a particular concern of a different nature must succumb to the constraint which proceeds from this language. For example, if the experience of God is interpreted as *fruitio Dei*, if God is "enjoyed" as the "rest" of the heart, then it is forced out of the unrest of the factical-historical life and fixed in the vitality that is most its own. To be sure, it does not immediately become the merely presented, dead God, but the development toward this endpoint is ushered in, actually forcibly brought about, when metaphysi-cal conceptualization is taken up. Heidegger later drew attention to the consequence of the fact that the man who values and enjoys God will at some point—thanks to Nietzsche—by revaluating all values raise his hand against the merely presented God who is removed to a quiescent dead eternity and "kill" this God already long "dead."

But wherein lies the actual failure of that thinking which we character- **42** ize here summarily enough as "metaphysics" (taken from the linguistic usage of Heidegger's later works)? It lies in the fact that—and this knowledge was for Heidegger the decisive step on the way to *Sein und Zeit*—metaphysical thinking thinks Being as a constant being-present-at-hand and thus cannot do justice to the temporality of factical life's performance. Since its earliest beginnings metaphysical thinking is oriented to seeing. Therefore, Being signifies even for Augustine, for example, constant being-in-view and thereby being-present-at-hand or constant presence.[10] In the *fruitio Dei* as the *beatitudo hominis* the *frui* means a *praesto habere* (Hw 338); consequently the Being of God is also conceived on the basis of a constant being-in-view, except that here the *inner* eye of the heart is meant rather than those eyes which take an interest in various "external" distractions. Because Being is thought as being-in-view, Augustine is no more able to think about his great discovery, time, in its unique essence, in its Being, than is Aristotle or Hegel, Schelling or Nietzsche. Using Aristotle's words almost *verbatim*, Augustine says that time which cannot be brought into view as constant presence (as "Being") "*et est et non est*" (WhD, 41). Since in its primordiality time cannot be read from that which is in view and which thereby is merely "in" time, it enters into a distinctive relationship with soul and with mind. (At the end of the published portion of *Sein und Zeit*, Heidegger presents an exemplary description of Hegel's struggling with this relationship.) In spite of this relationship, metaphysical thinking does not succeed in conceptualizing primordially the factical, historical experience of life. The thinking which is oriented to sight aims at that which can be presented and thus misses the irreducibly temporal-historical realization which temporalizes time.

Heidegger opposes the conceptualization and the metaphysical presuppositions which occur in the works of Augustine and other theologians; nonetheless, he can make the "factical life-experience" of these theologians fruitful for his own work. Augustine, as *Sein und Zeit* points out, saw the remarkable priority which vision has for human knowledge. He conceived of the desire-to-know, eagerness for knowledge or curiosity, as *concupiscentia oculorum*, as the desire to see, and recognized in it a characteristic tendency of the Being of everydayness in general. In curiosity, one **43** thing and then again something new is taken in its mere "appearance" as something which is in view or present-at-hand. Curiosity wants to see "not in order to understand what is seen, which means to approach it in its Being, but rather *only* in order to see." It is drawn from one thing to another, but does not allow itself to be seriously affected by anything. It uproots man's being-in-the-world in that it lets him lose himself among beings. However, the fact that the philosophy born of the Greeks grasps knowledge in general as "the desire to see" finds expression only in the ultimate honing of this curiosity. According to Parmenides the seeing of intuitive perception discovers Being. "Primordial and genuine truth lies in pure intuition. This thesis has henceforward remained the basis of Western philosophy. The Hegelian dialectic starts from this thesis and is possible only on its ground" (170ff). As Heidegger later showed, this tendency to understand knowledge as a seeing comes to a close in the blinking of Nietzsche's last human beings. However, it does so also in the violence with which becoming is to be established in the eternal recurrence as a Being.

Augustine shows further that in anxiety factical existence is extricated from the throng of beings and is cast back upon the fact that it itself is and has to be. This anxiety is not fear of this or that being, but genuine anxiety about being-in-the-world itself—not *timor servilis*, as fear of the bondage which flees the punishing God and shudders before transitory trials and tribulations, but rather *timor castus*, as genuine fear of God lasting into eternity (cf. note 190). Anxiety is ultimately anxiety about death: "The anthropology worked out in Christian theology—*futurae vitae*—has always seen death as part of the interpretation of "life" (249, note I). "Dying," as Luther says in the twenty-fourth of the aforementioned theses, "means sensing death as being present." In the extremity of its being-toward-death, in essential anxiety, factical existence, as it is developed in *Sein und Zeit*, can perceive the decisive call to its conscience (272). In going through anxiety, seen as Augustinian anthropology has seen it (note 199), knowledge becomes care; it is torn away from that which lies externally in view and is grounded in an understanding which concerns its capacity for understanding. Within knowing, priority is taken away from seeing, but along with it the ontological priority of the present-at-hand is also abolished, a priority which corresponds to the noetic priority of pure intuition (147).

In the Christian faith "factical life" is experienced as the place of that "clearing" in which knowledge as seeing first of all becomes possible. This clearing is truth in that primordiality according to which it belongs to the actuality and historicality of life. (Heidegger takes up the traditional discourse about the clearing and the *lumen naturale*: SuZ, 133, 170, 350.) The Christian faith discovers not only truth but the world in its primordiality as well. It is discovered as the "How" in which beings as a whole show themselves historically (G 24ff). This experience of truth and world, however, has never been grounded in thought; instead it has been consistently disguised by means of an inadequate conceptualization. The apprehension of truth, for example, as it is expressed in the Augustinian and the medieval light-oriented theories, finds room for its unfolding in the region of a concept of truth which lets its own origin lie in oblivion. Knowledge understood as seeing presupposes the clearing in which it is realized without meditating upon the essence of this clearing (VA, 252). The factical life-experience of the Christian faith has not been able to wrest itself away from inadequate metaphysical conceptualization. Thus Augustine, Luther, and Kierkegaard offer more an "ontical" than an "ontological" instruction; they saw decisive matters in an "ontical" manner, but they would not have been able to arrive at an adequate "ontological" conceptualization. They therefore "edify all the more compellingly," where they speak with the "least degree of conceptualization" (SuZ, note 190). Since "ontologically" they are dominated by ancient philosophy, there is often more to learn from their "edifying" writings than from the "theoretical" ones (235 note).

When Heidegger raises a problem like "Augustine and Neoplatonism," he does not try to make distinctions with the philological affectation that interests only the historian, nor is his relation to Augustine an opportunity for antiquarian research edified by a self-evident store of tradition. On the contrary, those decisions which Western thinking has formed are again brought up for a decision by means of a theme such as "Augustine and Neoplatonism" (or also "Kierkegaard and Hegel"). The example of Augustine shows that the metaphysical approach cannot be supplemented by adding or correcting this or that so that it would be able to satisfy questions about the realization of factical existence or about the divinity of God. There is a mistake rooted in this approach which cannot be annulled through a critique of merely isolated particulars. One must therefore ask whether metaphysical thinking has uncovered its ground at all. In order to build upon its fundamental presupposition, namely that thinking is seeing and that Being is being-in-view or constant presence, did it not allow this presupposition to remain as something unthought and as something not linguistically expressed any further? If the answer is yes, then must not the metaphysical question of Being be taken up again where Aristotle and Plato left it unsurmounted?

45

3

FUNDAMENTAL ONTOLOGY AS THE GROUNDING OF METAPHYSICS

At the beginning of Heidegger's path of thinking stands the leading question of metaphysics: What is a being? How is a being to be grasped in its Being? If a being in its Being can be expressed in many ways, then how can one think of the unity of the manifold meanings of "Being"? The question about the unity in the multiplicity of Being must become urgent precisely when the traditional metaphysical-theological determinations, by means of which Heidegger still reduced this question to silence in his first works, come to nothing. This happens because suspicion is aroused that the God of Philosophy is not at all the living God of faith and that metaphysical theology is not the final answer to the questions of thinking.

Adverting to factical life does not leave behind the question of Being. This advertence may at first be a moving away from metaphysical "speculations"—still this departure must for its own part become questionable. Can the interpretation of factical life even travel a way apart from the metaphysical doctrine of Being? Must it not fall prey to this doctrine and the experience of Being developed therein if it simply lets this experience be and stand next to itself as an unsurmounted antithesis? Did not Dilthey's thinking remain determined by metaphysical presuppositions precisely because he let his fundamental concept of "life" stand in "ontological indifference," because he left behind the metaphysical doctrine of Being without again making problematic the judgements by which it became what it is? Did not a similar fate befall the factical life-experience of the Christian faith?

The shortcoming of metaphysics—this was Heidegger's decisive insight—is that it conceives of thinking as a "seeing" and of Being as a constant being-in-view, a constant presence; thus it cannot ascertain the realization of factical-historical life itself which cannot be brought to a standstill. Indeed, do not facticity and historicity perhaps stand behind all metaphysics as what has been forgotten? If metaphysics thinks Being as constant presence, does it not then conceive of it from a specific mode of time, the present? Does the judgement about the sense of Being occur in a region which in its essence is "time"? Does time belong to the sense of Being, and is this time what is unthought and forgotten in metaphysics?

If this equation, Being is constant presence, is no longer accepted as a matter of course, then the question about the sense of Being can emerge as the question about Being and time. The area in which thinking accomplishes the transition from beings to Being, the transcendental horizon for the determination of Being as Being, is now examined with respect to its essence. The ground for the manifold expressibility of Being becomes problematic with regard to the manner of its being the ground. Thus another question, the question about the sense of Being itself, is placed before the question about the manifold expressibility of Being. The metaphysical doctrine of Being, ontology, is grounded in a fundamental-ontological manner by the question about the sense of Being which functions as the ground for every possible meaning of Being.

Sein und Zeit develops the question as to how time belongs to the sense of Being. *Sein und Zeit* attempts to recover through thinking that which has remained unthought, the forgotten ground of metaphysics upon which everything that has been thought certainly rested. Thus it is appropriate that the prologue to this work is the question from the beginning of metaphysical thinking: what the expression "being" actually means. Regarding this question from the *Sophist*—that Platonic dialogue which Heidegger exhaustively interpreted during his Marburg teaching years— Heidegger notes that today we not only have no answer to this question but we do not even feel the need for such questioning. Therefore, the question about the sense of Being must not only be raised once again, but first of all an understanding for this question must be awakened (SuZ 1).

The introduction to *Sein und Zeit* thus provides an "exposition of the question about the sense of Being." The first section shows that the question of Being—the battle of the Titans over Being, as it says in the *Sophist*—occupied Plato and Aristotle in their research; later, however, the question fell into oblivion. Not only did it fall into oblivion, but neglecting to raise this question was expressly sanctioned by a philosophical dogma which evolved on the basis of the Greek attempts at interpreting Being. This dogma says that Being is the most general, emptiest, and therefore undefinable concept; it is nonetheless still self-evident. The second section shows that we always maintain an average and vague understanding of Being, but we can give no answer to the clearly formulated question about the sense of Being, nor can we even develop the question adequately.

The question about the sense of Being must be raised again, because it has belonged to metaphysical thinking from the beginning as what has been unthought. But above all the question must be raised anew from those essential grounds in which the "venerableness" of its origin is rooted. Thus, in the third section Heidegger develops the "ontological priority of the question of Being." "Ontology" is now the name for the question about the Being of beings. Heidegger points out that the movement into which the sciences have fallen presses for a revision of the fundamental concepts and thereby demands primordial, ontological questioning. By such questioning, Plato, Aristotle, and even Kant developed a "productive logic" which does not merely lag behind the sciences (like the Neo-Kantian, theoretical-scientific reflection), but rather "springs ahead as it were into a definite region of Being. Thus it discloses this region in its state of Being for the first time and makes the structures obtained in this fashion available to the positive sciences as transparent instructions for inquiry" (10). Ontology aims at an "*a priori* condition for the possibility" of the sciences, "which investigate a being as such and such a being and thereby has always moved within an understanding of Being." On the other hand the question of Being aims at "the condition for the possibility of the ontologies themselves which precede and ground the ontical sciences." (Consequently the question of Being does not ask about the Being of the various regions of beings and about the manifold expressibility of Being in general; rather it asks about the unity of "Being" within this multiplicity, about the *sense* of Being.) If ontology as the question about the Being of beings does not question the ground upon which it stands, the sense of Being itself, and does not become grounded in a "fundamental ontology" by means of this question, it remains "naive and opaque." In fact it "is then fundamentally blind and reverses its ownmost intentions." Fundamental ontology, understood as the question, "what do we really **49** mean by this expression 'Being'," is placed before ontology ("the doctrine of categories") as the "genealogy of the various possible modes of Being." (11).

In the fourth section, Heidegger shows that if the question of Being is to be raised, then within the ontical or among beings an entirely determinate being has priority. This being is man, insofar as he is "Dasein." Dasein is distinguished from other beings in that it does not simply occur among other beings; rather, this Being is at issue for Dasein in its Being. Dasein—and Dasein alone!—has a relationship to Being and therefore an understanding of Being. It is intrinsically that which understands Being, ontological; however, this being ontological may not even be an expressly appropriated and developed understanding but rather an undeveloped, "pre-ontological" understanding of Being.

To have a relationship to Being means (according to Kierkegaard) to have existence, to be determined by existence. Heidegger calls the Being or "essence" of Dasein "existence" (12, 42). If Dasein is questioned about its Being, then the structures of existence are sought. Heidegger calls these structures existentials. He distinguishes them from categories which he now conceives of as the determinations of the Being of beings which lack the character of Dasein (44). The existential analytic seeks (ontologically) to expose the structures of Being of existence. In this way it distinguishes itself from existen*tiell* understanding for which the formal structures are not or are not primarily at issue, but which is concerned with settling the concrete question of existence "through existing itself." This question, whether existence grasps or misses itself in its concrete possibilities, can only be decided by each Dasein itself; it is not an "ontological" but rather an "ontical" matter (12).

How does the question about the Being of Dasein, the existential analytic, belong to the working out of the question of Being? Dasein is that being which raises the question of Being and which therefore must be made transparent in its Being if this question is to be worked out. In addition, the priority of Dasein over other beings is to be grasped more fundamentally. This priority is threefold: 1) Dasein has an ontical priority—it is distinguished from all other beings in that it is defined by a relationship to Being, by existence; 2) on the basis of being defined by existence it is intrinsically ontological; it understands Being, and thus has an "ontological" priority; 3) on the basis of its understanding of Being, it understands its own Being and the Being of the beings which lack the character of Dasein; thus it is the ontico-ontological condition for the possibility of all ontologies. "The *fundamental ontology*, from which all others can first of all arise, must therefore be sought in the *existential analytic of Dasein*" (13). On the other hand, it is true that the existential analytic can only work if it knows what existentiality is. It must understand the constitution of *Being* of existence, and it must thereby already have an idea of Being in general. "Thus the possibility of realizing the analytic of Dasein also depends on working out beforehand the question about the sense of Being in general" (13).

The analytic of existence is to expose the horizon within which Being as Being is understood at all (sec. 5). This happens in three steps. Being-in-the-world, being-in-a-context-of-significance, is exhibited as the fundamental structure of Dasein in its everydayness and averageness (of "life" in its "facticity"). It is then shown that this being-in-the-world is essentially temporal and historical (that "factical life" is "historical"). Time is then to be understood in terms of the temporality of Dasein, how it belongs to the sense of Being itself, how it consequently determines that horizon in which Being as Being is understood. Time should not function as the "criterion for the separation of regions of Being"—as it still did in Heidegger's *Habilitation* lecture—but it should rather be shown as belonging to the sense of Being itself. It is to be shown both "that the central

50

problematic of all ontology is rooted in the properly seen and properly explicated phenomenon of time, and also how it is so rooted" (18). The first part of *Sein und Zeit* which accomplishes the three aforementioned steps bears the title: "The Interpretation of Dasein in terms of Temporality and the Explication of Time as the Transcendental Horizon for the Question about Being." It is divided into three divisions: "1. The Preparatory Fundamental Analysis of Dasein. 2. Dasein and Temporality. 3. Time and Being" (39).

However, must Being be grasped "from time" at all? Is the assertion that time belongs to the sense of Being and that the way to time leads across the temporality of factical existence not an arbitrary hypothesis, a "new standpoint" whose right remains to be shown? That which is "new," says Heidegger, is of no consequence. What matters much more is that what is thought "is *old* enough to learn to grasp the possibilities made available by the 'ancients'" (19). If Dasein is essentially historical, then all research—as a possibility of this Dasein—is also historical; only in recapitulating tradition does the question of Being achieve its "true concretion" (26). For this reason, historical recapitulation of the ontological tradition belongs to the "systematic" development of fundamental ontology. This recapitulation is "destruction," an exposing of the primordial experiences and the secret prejudices of the traditional interpretation of Being. Fundamental ontology and the destruction of the history of ontology together form "the twofold task in the working out of the question of Being" (15).

The destruction of the history of ontology must show how traditional ontology has passed on to thinking the question of Being, even though this ontology has not expressly raised the question about the sense of Being. Ontology asks about the Being of beings. It is oriented in its questioning toward those beings which it finds in the world and can bring into view. The Being of every being, even the Being of man, of Dasein, is understood in terms of a being which is present-at-hand and presentable. The ontology born of the Greeks is proof "that Dasein understands itself and Being in general in terms of the 'world'" (21f). When in modern times "subject," "spirit," "person" move into the center of questioning, they are understood in their Being by an ontology oriented to the being which is presentable and present-at-hand. The "categorial inventory of traditional ontology" is also transferred "with corresponding formalizations and purely negative limitations" to the subject, the spirit, the person (22). The Being of the "subject" and the sense of Being in general are not questioned again in a primordial fashion. On the contrary it adheres to the prejudice whereby thinking is understood in terms of seeing and Being in general as being-in-view. "The λέγειν itself, or rather the νοεῖν—the

51

52 simple perception of something present-at-hand in its pure presence-at-hand which *Parmenides* had already taken as a model for the interpretation of Being—has the temporal structure of the pure 'making present' of something. The being which shows itself in it and for it and which is understood as the genuine being is therefore interpreted with regard to the present [*Gegen-wart*]; it is conceived as presence ($o\dot{v}\sigma\acute{\iota}\alpha$) [*Anwesenheit*]" (25f).

If Being is grasped as being-in-view or presence, then it is interpreted with regard to a definite temporal mode, the present (25). In the Greek interpretation of Being, time functions as a guide even though this interpretation may have no explicit knowledge of this guide. That is, the Greek interpretation remains "without knowledge, even without an understanding of the fundamental ontological function of time, and without any insight into the reason for the possibility of this function. On the contrary, time itself is taken as one being among others, and by using the horizon for an understanding of Being which is implicitly, and naively, oriented to time this interpretation attempts to conceive of it in its structure of Being" (26). The Greeks gather what Being is from that being which is in the world and thereby *in* time. In accordance with this understanding of Being, they think the Being of time itself. Consequently thinking never poses the question about time itself, the question about time as it belongs to the sense of Being, about time as "temporality" (19).

Heidegger takes up this question about Being and time as it has been handed over by tradition as an unasked question and, using this as his point of departure, he once more brings to a head the Western interpretation of Being in its "fundamentally decisive" phases. The second part of *Sein und Zeit* was to provide the "main features of a phenomenological destruction of the history of ontology with the problematic of temporality as a guide" (39). Heidegger wanted to go back to Aristotle by way of Kant and Descartes. Kant sees the connection between time and the "I think," but shrinks back from it. He adopts the ontological position of Descartes who determines the "I think," the *cogito*, according to medieval and therefore Greek ontology and thus does not comprehend it in its primordial, temporal essence. The primordiality of time remains concealed in

53 metaphysics—Aristotle's essay on time is the way of "discriminating the phenomenal basis and the limits of ancient ontology" (23ff, 40).

Now it is time to retrace the individual steps of *Sein und Zeit*.

THE FUNDAMENTAL ANALYSIS OF DASEIN

The first division of the first part of *Sein und Zeit* is a preparatory analysis which is to uncover the fundamental structure of everyday, average Dasein. Being-in-the-world is presented as this fundamental structure, analyzed according to its various moments and finally grasped in its unity as care.

Being-in-the-world does not mean to occur in the so-called "world," in the totality of beings just as other things do. The being-in of being-in-the-world signifies rather "dwelling alongside," "being familiar with" (SuZ 54). Dasein is being-in-the-world; that is to say, it "is" its world; it is from out of a familiarity with the world. Just as it is not an object which occurs in the "world," in the totality of beings, neither is it a worldless subject from which one would have to build a bridge to the "world," something that has been tried time and again since Descartes. On the contrary, as being-in-the-world Dasein has always been alongside things. Since it has always been alongside things, it has also been with others. It is not an I which would first of all have to establish a relationship to others but rather one which exists primarily in Being-with-others.

Heidegger does not grasp ,the world in which Dasein exists as the totality of beings, but rather as the manner [*das Wie*] in which beings as a whole can show themselves. In the sense of this concept of world, Dasein "is in" the world; worldhood belongs to it. The world in which Dasein factically is, however, is always a definite world. "Worldhood itself can be modified according to the respective structural wholes of particular 'worlds', but includes in itself the *a priori* character of worldhood in general" (65).

The world of Dasein in its everydayness, the "natural" world, is the "environment." The being which we meet every day is not some displaced something "present-at-hand" but rather something "ready-to-hand," a "piece of equipment," with which it has a definite involvement. The piece of equipment serves some purpose; one piece refers to another and thus has a "meaning." The sum of the contexts of reference and of significance **54** is the world as environment. It is anchored in that ultimate "for-the-sake-of" which is Dasein itself. Existence which in its Being is concerned with this Being makes the "for-the-sake-of" possible and thereby grounds the worldhood of the world in the existential character of Dasein.

To be sure, the world is not merely environment; nonetheless, environmentality offers the first decisive clue to the structure of the world. If one experiences the world as existence does, in terms of the context of reference and of significance, then one can think of it as the region of an *occurrence* of sense. The being which achieves its Being from this occurrence is not the "present-at-hand" of a remote seeing but rather the "ready-to-hand" of a praxis. If thinking experiences the world in terms of the environment, then with regard to that which is fundamental it opposes the traditional philosophical orientation. Thinking usually orients itself toward presenting an exhibitable being; from a "theoretical" perspective it understands itself as seeing and presenting, and it understands the being as the present-at-hand which is available for presentation. All of this together, the "totality" of the present-at-hand as it is supposed to be for a consciousness which oversees everything, is then regarded as the "world." Consequently, "a *skipping over* of the phenomenon of worldhood" (as it is first manifested in environmentality) accompanies "the failure to recognize Being-in-the-world as the constitution of Dasein." "Instead," as Heidegger in *Sein und Zeit* explains the basic tendency of the "previous ontology, one tries to interpret the world in terms of nature, that is, from the Being of beings which are present-at-hand within the world, but which have yet to be discovered." Nature is comprehended only insofar as it is "present-at-hand." It is "a limiting case of the Being of the possible beings within the world," in which the worldhood of the world just does not show itself. Thus, the knowledge of nature as present-at-hand "is characterized by a definite removal of its worldhood from the world" (65).

Even "at its beginning, and explicitly in the case of *Parmenides*, the ontological tradition which is decisive for us" skips over the phenomenon of the world and continues to do so. The being within the world, first of all found in "nature," replaces the neglected phenomenon as the theme (100). In the course of this development, the extension of natural things becomes for Descartes the fundamental determination of the world. He finds in a "mathematical" cognition the mode of access to the Being of the world—not out of a preference for mathematics, but rather because thinking as a "seeing" has always been oriented toward the constantly present-at-hand, and mathematics above all knows what is always there, what remains constant and outlives all change (SuZ, 96. Cf. also *Die Frage nach dem Ding*, 52ff). Even then one will continue to remain on the ground of Cartesian ontology if one regards being present-at-hand or being extended merely as a "fundamental stratum" upon which one can erect other strata up to specific qualities such as beauty, usefulness, etc. In contrast to the solely reactive attempt to complete the Cartesian analysis of the world aided by the phenomenon of value, Heidegger notes: "Adding on value predicates cannot in the least offer any new insight into the Being of goods, but will merely presuppose once more that their mode of Being is pure presence-at-hand . . ." (SuZ 99).

Although Descartes takes extension as the most comprehensible matter, Heidegger himself tries to root the extension of the thing as a derived phenomenon, in the spatiality of Dasein and thus in the aroundness [*das Umhafte*] of the environment (sec. 22f). If the worldhood of the world is won back, then knowledge can no longer be understood merely as representing a constant *present-at-hand*; it must rather be measured against the circumspection of practical concern; it must see itself in the world's *relationships of involvement* [*Bewandtnisbezüge*] and contexts of reference [*Ver-*

55

weisungszusammenhänge]. With that, the priority that pure seeing had in knowledge "since the beginnings of Greek ontology until today" (358) is annulled.

The Being-in of Being-in-the-world expressly became the theme for analysis after Heidegger showed that Being-in-the-world is not only concern, Being alongside beings within the world, but also care-for-others, being-with others, and only in this manner the care for oneself of Being-oneself. Dasein is a Being-in-the-world in that it has always been "thrown" into the world, but has taken over this thrownness in the "projection" and has "articulated" the thrown projection as an articulated totality of meaning. Thrownness (facticity), projection (existence), and articulation are each disclosed in attunement (state-of-mind), in understanding, and in discourse.

The fact that Dasein exists is not based upon a free projection of itself; rather Dasein has always been delivered over to its "that it is." It has been "thrown" among beings. Thrownness is the "facticity" of Dasein, but this facticity is distinguished essentially from the actual occurrence of a present-at-hand. It is the facticity of Dasein's being delivered over to itself (56, 135). Dasein is factical; that is, it "finds" itself in the midst of beings as a whole. This finding oneself among beings always occurs in a completely determined "how" as the state-of-mind of being-in-the-*world*. It is attuned to this how in one "mood" or another, each state-of-mind, or attunement discloses the facticity of being-in-the-world, that being-in-the-world is at all, that I am and these things are, that I can be ready for things and that they can matter to me. **56**

Dasein is "delivered over" to its thrownness only insofar as it is "projection." It is characterized equiprimordially by "existentiality" as well as by facticity. It is existence in the narrower sense of the word, the self-projecting potentiality-for-Being (Heidegger characterizes existence in the wider sense as the *totality* of factical existence). As potentiality-for-Being or understanding, Dasein is "primarily a Being-possible." The possibilities which it has are not added as the not-yet-actual to an already present-at-hand. The Being-possible of Dasein is not at all to be characterized as that which is not yet actual and has never been necessary, because it would then be thought of as the modality of the present-at-hand and not as the potentiality-for-Being of existence (143). Sight is based on potentiality-for-Being as understanding; in this sight, Dasein becomes transparent to itself as Being-in-the-world, as the "circumspection of concern," as the "considerateness of care-for-others," and as the "sight of Being as such for the sake of which Dasein in each case is as it is." The sight which belongs to the understanding of Dasein is the basis upon which knowledge can be grasped as seeing (146f).

Every understanding is a state-of-mind. Thrownness has always given definite possibilities to the projection of understanding and has deprived it of certain other possibilities. Thus the thrown projection articulates for itself an articulated totality of meaning. With respect to language as a distinctive manner of articulation, Heidegger calls this articulation "discourse" (sec. 34).

57   The understanding which has a state-of-mind and which articulates itself comprises the disclosedness of Dasein, the Being-in-the-truth of existence as primordial truth (sec. 44). In this being-in-the-truth, beings lacking the character of Dasein can be discovered, and beings with the character of Dasein can disclose themselves. Any being which has been understood and is in the truth has "sense." "Sense is an existential structure of Dasein, not a property which adheres to a being, lies 'behind' it, or 'hovers' somewhere as an 'in-between region'." (151). In his dissertation (94), Heidegger had said that Lotze, led by the problem of the mode of reality of the Platonic Ideas, had found "validity" to be the decisive designation for the mode of being of sense. Later Heidegger analyzes "validity" as an "iridescent concept," a "linguistic idol." The alleged "irreducible 'primordial phenomenon'" owes the role that it plays, so it is said, simply to its ontological unclarity (SuZ 155f). *Sein und Zeit* bases sense on the movement and disclosedness of Dasein as Being-in-the-world. Sense is not a "static phenomenon," but more "the upon-which" of the *projection* which is structured by means of fore-having, foresight, and preconception. "Something becomes intelligible as something" on the basis of the upon-which of the projection which has a state-of-mind. That is to say, something emerges into its truth as that which has sense (151). The place of truth and the guide for the understanding of beings as beings is, according to the traditional conception, the assertion, the judgement. In the assertion, however, something is taken as something only if a Being-present-at-hand can be ascertained in it, and if thinking, when it acquires the corresponding view, can always return to it. The thinking which asserts and judges posits beings as present-at-hand, and the world which is primarily a context of significance of the ready-to-hand is reduced to a context of the present-at-hand. Understanding, which interprets itself *circumspectively* and, in an open, practical mode, moves in the world as a context of significance, changes into a purely theoretical attitude. If on the contrary, as Heidegger attempts to show (sec. 33), assertion and judgement are founded on the circumspective interpretation of understanding, then it becomes problematic to take the theory of judgement as the *authentic* place of truth. The analysis of sense, as the ontology of Dasein undertakes to do it, confronts the question as to whether the paths of thinking can be exhausted by

means of the traditional logic, whether the language of thinking can be **58**
understood on the basis of a logic-oriented grammar. Is traditional logic
capable of grasping the movement of sense, or is it merely the logic of the
present-at-hand (129)? Can logic-oriented grammar conceive of language
as the articulation of the primordial disclosedness of being-in-the-world,
or must it be "liberated" from logic (165f)? Heidegger rejects on principle
his own attempt to solve the question of logic and grammar in his
dissertation and in his *Habilitationsschrift*. This attempt, which takes Being
and sense as something static, rests upon an unfounded metaphysical
thesis.

The Being-in of Being-in-the-world is articulated thrown projection. If
we conceive of projection as a Being-ahead-of-oneself in possibilities,
Being-thrown as Being-already-in-the-world [*Schon-sein-in-der-Welt*], and
articulation as the articulation of Being-alongside-beings-within-the-
world [*des Seins-bei-innerweltlich-Seiendem*] as well as Being-with-one-
another [*des Mit-seins-mit-anderen*], then Dasein is in accordance with its
Being as being-in-the-world an ahead-of-itself-being-already-in-the world
as being-alongside-beings-occurring-within-the-world in being-with-one-
another (sec. 41). "Care" is what Heidegger calls this Being of Dasein
grasped in its multifaceted unity.

Care is the fundamental structure of Dasein just as it is encountered at
first and most often in its everyday environment. Although the sense of the
Being of Dasein (its "essense") announces itself in care, it still remains
concealed because Dasein in its averageness and everydayness tends to
deny itself its authentic Being; thus it tends not to arrive at the sense of
this Being. Precisely for that reason Dasein does not usually see the
authentic sense of its being-in-the-world immediately, because it is "first
of all and for the most part taken by its world" and absorbed in it (113).
To be "thrown" alongside beings and into Being-with others is part of
Dasein; as long as it is at all, it remains "in the throw." It is whirled
around into this daze by that which is in the world and which intrudes as
the self-evident Dasein-with of others. Thus, Dasein provides "itself with
the constant temptation to fall" (177).

Heidegger has forcefully pointed out how Dasein "falls prey to" the
beings one encounters within the world. The result is that Dasein understands itself and Being in general in terms of the beings which can be **59**
encountered. Dasein does not live at all as itself, but rather as "one" lives;
life "is lived" by means of the "dictatorship" of the One [*das Man*] (sec.
27). In its state-of-mind or attunement it does not usually pay attention to
the fact "that" it is; rather, Dasein turns away from the That of its
Being-in-the-world and attends only to what occurs in this Being-in-the-
world. It fears this or that, but this is not the authentic anxiety in which

the That of Being-in-the-world does come into question (sec. 30, sec. 40).[11] Discourse does not allow an authentic disclosedness of Being-in-the-world but instead becomes "idle talk" which remains an "ambiguity" (sec. 35, sec. 37). While Dasein succumbs to the temptation to fall prey to the so-called "world" and thereby to forget Being-in-the-world itself, it sinks into inauthenticity. However, the fact that it can sink at all shows that Dasein can be modified in its very Being; that is to say, it can be inauthentic but also authentic. Only in authenticity will Dasein be able to understand the sense of its Being.

DASEIN AND TEMPORALITY

In the second division of the first part of *Sein und Zeit, Dasein and Temporality*, Heidegger attempts to throw into relief the sense of Dasein's Being, to understand Dasein primordially in its Being.

If Dasein is characterized as care through being-ahead-of-oneself and therefore is always not yet something, then the question remains whether Dasein is to be comprehended in its totality at all. Heidegger points out how Being in the anticipation of death is always "whole," but certainly not "whole" in the sense of the Being-whole of something present-at-hand. In this anticipation, the manner in which Dasein is factical existence is more sharply delineated. Dasein is, as understanding or potentiality-for-being, possibility, but it is authentically this possibility only when it constantly anticipates the extreme, unsurpassable possibility. This extreme possibility is death. The anticipation of death heightens the possibility, which Dasein is, to its extreme limit where it becomes boundless impossibility, namely, the impossibility of any existing as a definite potentiality-for-being. The possibility of Dasein as a potentiality-for-being arises from a final impossibility which is not a possibility for any manner of potentiality-for-being. "Existence" is based on "facticity."

Conscience attests to the fact that Dasein can be itself in an *authentic* manner. By the "call" of conscience, Dasein calls itself forth into its unique potentiality-for-being, into "resoluteness" [*Entschlossenheit*]. It is thereby understood that Dasein is "guilty." This "Being-guilty" does not indicate moral guilt, but is meant in an entirely formal manner as "Being-the-basis for a Being which is determined by a not—that is, as *Being-the-basis of a nullity*" (283). In the first place, this nullity arises from the fact that Dasein has not itself thrown the thrownness which is its basis, and yet it must accept this thrownness. Dasein is not master of its Being; its possibilities stem from an ultimate impossibility. By accepting its thrownness, Dasein must as itself be that basis which it did not lay by itself, but which it must rather always accept as pre-given. It has been "*set free*" from this basis *not through* itself, but rather *to* itself, in order to be *as this basis*" (284f). Dasein knows itself to be determined by a nothing. What sense this nothing has and how it might even belong to Being itself are questions which Heidegger still leaves open (285f).

The concept of guilt in *Sein und Zeit*, when it is understood properly, does not accentuate a "night view" of Dasein. On the contrary, it is part of the attempt at a final "grounding" of thinking in which thinking "presupposes" for itself the nothing and in the nothing presupposes Being as the "basis" of itself. Schelling undertook this attempt in a similar, yet speculative-metaphysical manner when, after the *Untersuchungen über das Wesen der menschlichen Freiheit* [*Investigations of the Essence of Human Freedom*], he once more wanted to overtake Hegel's metaphysics by means of a grounding with a more profound beginning.[12] Heidegger's analysis of being guilty as being-the-basis of a nullity, nevertheless, has another side by which this analysis is also drawn from that thinking attempted later by Schelling under the name of a "positive philosophy."

Dasein is not only *generally* null because of its thrownness but also null because of its *concrete* projection, that is to say, insofar as the latter is a choice which can choose one alternative only by rejecting the other. Thrownness has always delimited an area of what is open to choice. The "One" believes that this area can be taken as self-evident, but only the **61** resoluteness called forth by conscience *discovers* the given possibilities *as* factical. It discloses the there [*Da*] of Dasein, which has always been closed by the irresoluteness of the "One," as "situation." Dasein as thrown projection discovers its being-in-the-position (its potentiality-for-being) as a being-in-a-position, as being-in-the-situation. The resoluteness of Da-sein is always circumscribed situationally and consequently characterized by a not in this second sense as well (298ff). Resolute existence is certain of the truth of its resoluteness only because it wrests this truth from the untruth of the "One" and does not forget the situated character of this truth. Existence may not stubbornly insist upon the truth of a given situation, but must keep itself open for either possible withdrawal or resolute repetition. Da-sein in its authenticity knows that the truth in which it stands has a location, and in this sense it has its "there" (307f).

By continually anticipating death, Dasein is always complete, and it is authentic in that it follows the call of conscience in its resoluteness. In its authenticity, care is anticipatory resoluteness. As the ahead-of-itself-which-already-exists-in-the-world, it is a being-futural which anticipates death, but which in so doing comes back upon itself and resolutely takes upon itself the "guilt" of already-being-in-the-world. In the resolute anticipation of death, Dasein returns from its futurity to its having-been, and thus it is authentically that which it always has been. Only as the futural having-been is Dasein the present, and only as such can it make present what it encounters in the situation. "Coming back to itself futurally, resoluteness brings itself into the situation as it makes present. The past as having-been arises out of the future in such a way that the future which has been (better yet, which is as having-been) releases the present from itself. This unified phenomenon which appears as the future which has-been and makes-present we call *Temporality*." Temporality reveals itself as "the sense of authentic care" (326). If Dasein understands the sense of its Being, then in an authentic manner it can be what it is.

If temporality is emphasized as the sense of care, then the individual moments which constitute care must also be understood in terms of
62 temporality. The analysis therefore returns once again to the everyday, average Dasein and shows how the future is predominant in understanding, how the past as having-been dominates in the state-of-mind, etc. Above all, however, temporality itself must be grasped in its primordial essence. Thus as the temporalization of temporality, it is historicality. To be historical means to have a destiny, to anticipate death, to let oneself be thrown back upon the factical There and its finitude, to surrender to traditional possibilities, and thus to exist "in an insightful moment" [*augenblicklich*] for one's own time (385). But Dasein is only the temporalization of time and thus is in an insightful moment, as "historical," as "establishing a world," in that it exists alongside beings as *factical* existence already in the world.

Alongside historicality stands within-time-ness. It is understood not as the temporalization of time but is rather oriented to the being in time and thereby certainly bypasses time in its primordiality. Within-time-ness is not the futural temporalization of time in an insightful moment which is as having-been, but rather exists as awaiting beings still not present in time, as retaining the past, and as making the present-at-hand present. It is the making-present which awaits or retains, or, in its irresoluteness, a making-present which does not await and forgets. As such it is so lost to the present that it can no longer "bring together" "time"—past, future, and present (336ff, 409f).

The everydayness and inauthenticity of Dasein must be understood as within-time-ness. In this within-time-ness, Dasein thinks of that which is in time and thereby forgets the temporalization of time itself. Within-time-ness is the temporality of everydayness, the temporality of the "vulgar" concept of time. Since within-time-ness also "stems" from Dasein's temporality and is "equiprimordial" with historicality (377), the inauthenticity of Dasein also receives a certain justification. Discussion about inauthenticity is not a moral evaluation but simply evidence of a manner of being which irrevocably belongs to Dasein. Inauthenticity is not at all something that could be left behind by Dasein. Dasein can be authentic only if it repeatedly tears itself away from its inauthenticity, which is thereby taken for granted, and if it continually lifts itself out of mere within-time-ness toward the temporalization of time itself.

If the inauthenticity of Dasein is understood as a within-time-ness **63** which irrevocably belongs to Dasein, then one can also answer the question as to why the metaphysical tradition has not thought time in its primordiality. In accordance with Dasein's fundamental tendency, traditional ontology hits upon the being which occurs in time and thereby misses the temporalization of time itself. It thinks the Being of beings in terms of beings in time and then thinks about time on the basis of the understanding of Being thus achieved. Thus it thinks time as a series of "existing" or occurring points in time, or at least through negation it remains oriented toward this understanding of time when it brings time, which simply is not to be encountered, into a "distinctive relationship" with soul and spirit (427). Even Kierkegaard, who no doubt "saw the *existentiell* phenomenon of the insightful moment most penetratingly," proceeds from the traditional understanding of time as within-time-ness when he seeks to determine the moment with the help of "now" and "eternity," in other words with the help of time as a series of now-points and of eternity as atemporality (338). However, the Christian experience of faith and the historical experience of Dilthey and Yorck give impetus to the attempt to conceptualize in an ontologically primordial manner Being-in-the-world as historicality, as the temporalization of time itself.

TIME AND BEING

In the first division of *Sein und Zeit*, Dasein is understood as Being-in-the-world and as care; in the second division, care is understood in its authenticity, and the sense of Dasein's Being as temporality. However, these two divisions serve only to prepare for the task which is set for the third division, to think the temporalness of the sense of Being. As it is developed in the second paragraph of the introduction, the goal of the questioning is the sense of Being. All questioning, as stated there, asks about something, namely about what is *sought after*. It asks about the sought after in that it examines something and has the latter as its *object of examination*. It determines what is asked of that which is examined in terms of what is to be found out by the asking. "That which is asked about, lies then, as that which is really intended, in what is asked. It is through this that the inquiry attains its goal" (5).

64　　In the question of Being, Being is that which is asked about. The objects of examination are beings and from among them one distinctive being, Dasein. That which is asked about is the sense of Being. The first and second divisions of *Sein und Zeit* provide an analysis of what is examined (Dasein), but purely for the sake of what is asked about (Being). Still, the investigation in these divisions does not yet arrive at that which is to be discovered by the inquiry (not yet to the sense of Being). The investigation does not yet achieve its goal. Thus, the end of the second division states that the exposition of Dasein's ontological constitution is "only a *way*," for the "goal" is the working out of the question of Being in general (436). After temporality has been grasped as the sense of the Being of Dasein, the decisive step still remains to be taken—to bring to thinking from this temporality the temporality of every understanding of Being, the temporalness of the sense of Being. For this reason Heidegger asks in the last sentences of the second division of *Sein und Zeit* how a "disclosing understanding of Being according to Dasein is even possible." Dasein understands Being; however, Dasein's primordial ontological constitution is temporality. "Therefore, a primordial mode of the temporalization of ecstatic temporality must itself enable the ecstatic projection of Being in general. How is this temporalizing mode of temporality to be interpreted? Does a way lead from primordial *time* to the sense of *Being*? Does *time* itself manifest itself as the horizon of *Being*?" Consequently one must also ask about "*time* and *Being*."

　　The sentences quoted above not only concluded the second division of the first part of *Sein und Zeit*, but they in fact bring the published portion of that work to an abrupt end. *Sein und Zeit* remained a fragment; the investigation which was set into motion did not reach its goal in this work. Heidegger failed in his attempt to bring the metaphysical theory of Being back to its ground by means of a fundamental ontology. In the third division, Heidegger attempted to grasp Dasein's temporality in the unity of its ecstasies (future, past as having-been, present) in order to be able to interpret Dasein's temporality as the temporality of the understanding of Being. This attempt, however, was made in vain. The problem of space arose once more. Can the spatiality of Dasein, the clearing away of space,

65　be "grounded" in temporality, indeed, in the inauthentic temporality of making present? Has the "ontological sense" of the "coupling" of space and time already been realized in such grounding (368)? Furthermore, the decisive question remained: How is the understanding of Being the "transcendental horizon of the question about Being" (39)? How is transcendence, the ascent beyond beings to Being, to be grasped at all? How do Dasein's temporality and time as the transcendental horizon of the question about Being belong together? What does transcendental mean here? In addition, are Dasein's understanding of Being and the sense of Being (the transcendental horizon) simply to be equated, or how do they belong together? Heidegger says that "sense is that wherein the intelligibility of something maintains itself" (151). Therefore, the sense of Being is that in which the intelligibility of Being maintains itself. But how do the intelligibility of Being and the understanding of Being belong together? Heidegger writes: "But the exposition of the horizon in which something like Being becomes intelligible at all is equivalent to explaining the possibility of understanding Being in general, an understanding which itself belongs to the constitution of the being which we call Dasein" (231). How is the equivalence expressed here to be thought?

The goal toward which *Sein und Zeit* is underway, time as the transcendental horizon of the question about Being, is not a hereafter which lies far beyond the traveled way. It is rather that which the investigation has always carried with it from its very basis. It is "presupposed" in accordance with the being-ahead-of-itself of Dasein which grasps itself from out of its future. The investigation moves in that "hermeneutical circle" which has a positive sense because it corresponds to the mode of Being of the understanding Dasein (153). *Sein und Zeit* already presupposes an "idea" of Being since the idea of existentiality, the differences between authenticity and inauthenticity, between being-present-at-hand and being-ready-to-hand, etc., can be understood only in the horizon of this idea (13, 313f). On the other hand the sense of Being should first of all be brought into question through the clarification of Dasein's mode of Being, through the difference between authenticity and inauthenticity, and so forth! The course of *Sein und Zeit* is not a linear advance proceeding directly to the distant goal, but rather a going back and forth, the traversing of a cirle.

Throughout *Sein und Zeit*, Heidegger notes that the train of thought moves in a circle. He says, for example, that not until later can the method of proceeding be settled definitively. The more than provisional development of the idea of phenomenology, ontology and science, and the new determination of logos are postponed until later (357, 230, 357, 160). Many things, the discussions of language and of the connection between space and time, for example, are put aside for later (349, 368). The "as" in taking-something-as-something and, therefore, the difference between presence-at-hand and readiness-to-hand is to be further developed later (333, 351, 360, 436f), and everydayness is later to be understood more deeply (372). In fact, many a question can not be clarified until later.

Such is the case with questions about Western thinking's forgetfulness of the world, about the connection between Being and truth, and about the "Being" of time (100, 357, 406). The entire existential analysis demands a "renewed repetition within the scope of the fundamental discussion of the concept of Being" (333, 436).

But why does fundamental ontology not arrive at the basis upon which it already stands, at the sense of Being, so that it too, because of this failure, is unable to ground the metaphysical doctrine of Being? In retrospect, Heidegger said that in working out the third division of *Sein und Zeit*, thinking was not able to succeed "with the help of the language of metaphysics" (PL 72). Which language, then, does *Sein und Zeit* generally speak? To what extent is this language metaphysical?

4

PHENOMENOLOGY—
TRANSCENDENTAL
PHILOSOPHY—METAPHYSICS

Heidegger dedicated *Sein und Zeit* to Husserl because the investigations which this book provides became possible only "on the basis which *E. Husserl* had laid." Phenomenology burst forth with Husserl's *Logical Investigations*, and the method of *Sein und Zeit's* investigations was also phenomenological. Heidegger explains what phenomenology is—at least provisionally—in the introduction to *Sein und Zeit*. He does not want to follow phenomenology as an existing, "actual" philosophical "movement," but rather to apprehend phenomenology as a "possibility" (SuZ 38, cf. Sp 92). Thus the question arises: What is phenomenology? What is phenomenology in the specific sense that Heidegger gives it? If Husserl's phenomenology is a "transcendental" one at the stage at which Heidegger begins, then one must ask not only about phenomenology in general, but also what "transcendental" means. What is transcendental philosophy in Husserl's sense, and what is it in the sense of the more original form it took for Kant? And if, according to Heidegger's later insight, the phenomenological investigations of *Sein und Zeit* still speak a "metaphysical" language, then it remains to be asked: to what extent are phenomenology and transcendental philosophy "metaphysics"?

TRANSCENDENTAL AND HERMENEUTICAL PHENOMENOLOGY

For Husserl, phenomenology means above all the demand to go to the things themselves. The "phenomena" are to be brought into clear view and described impartially without any metaphysical presuppositions. What is given should not be explained away; for example, logical phenomena are not to be "explained" as psychological phenomena by means of a "psychologistic" reinterpretation. Phenomenology is the impartial description of the phenomena; it is "descriptive."

If one explicates that aspect of a phenomenon which remains invariable in all its variations, one then grasps the essence, the *eidos* of the phenomenon. Through this reduction to the *eidos*, the "eidetic reduction," descriptive phenomenology becomes eidetic. Thus it becomes "ontology," since ontology seeks the essence or the Being of beings.

In "phenomenological" or "transcendental" reduction, the phenomenon is grasped as "phenomenon," as the sort of thing which is given to consciousness. All statements which transcend this being-given are not taken into consideration, for example, the statement that the given is actual in an empirically discoverable manner. Consequently, one goes back to the transcendental consciousness in whose acts a being is constituted *as* a being. In the transcendental reduction, the essential contents which are laid out by means of the eidetic reduction become the guides for returning to the accomplishments of consciousness which correspond to them. According to the conviction of transcendental phenomenology, being-directed toward objects, the "intentional" relation, is not something which somehow comes into contact with objects from outside. It is rather the case that in this relation the object is constituted *as* object, the being as being. Not only is the nonhuman being so constituted, but also man as he understands himself as one being among others, as a being in the "world." Husserl's final works grasp this transcendental constitution as the life of an absolute I.

During his years of teaching at Göttingen, Husserl was able to gather a large following around descriptive and eidetic (ontological) phenomenology. However, when he completed his move toward transcendental phenomenology, most of the "phenomenologists" and "ontologists" who belonged to the Göttingen school were unable to see this step as the consequence of the phenomenological approach. Husserl, now widely known as the head of a large school, became increasingly alone in his philosophizing. He found only a few individuals who agreed with his approach and who he believed could be considered his students. Moreover, the transcendental approach led to difficulties. When Husserl was called to Freiburg in 1916, his transcendental phenomenology was in a crisis, out of which his later work, the return to the absolute I, was to develop gradually in a lonely labor of thought.

69

In his *Habilitationschrift*, Heidegger appears to be attracted to the way which Husserl traveled from the *Logische Untersuchungen* (1900–01) to the *Ideen zu einer reinen Phänomenologie und phänomenologischen Philosophie* (1913), and he appears ready himself to take the step from Neo-Kantian transcendental philosophy to transcendental phenomenology. However, the courses which Heidegger gave after the First World War show that he did not follow the way to the transcendental and absolute I. In fact, Heidegger even shrank back from the *Ideas* and preferred to base his phenomenological exercises on the *Logische Untersuchungen*, which by then Husserl no longer held in particularly high esteem (Sp 90). In the lecture course from the winter semester of 1919–20, Heidegger begins with "factical life." Can this point of departure actually still be called phenomenological at all? As the positivism of Avenarius and Mach already did in its fashion, phenomenology sees as its task the attainment of a "natural concept of the world" (SuZ 52). That world in which we have always moved about— even when we philosophize—is to be grasped philosophically and not to be "explained" or attributed to something else in such a way that it vanishes as the "natural world" from which one does indeed proceed. If one understands the task of phenomenology in this manner, then by beginning with "factical life" Heidegger does nothing but radically carry out the phenomenological approach.

With this approach, in fact, Heidegger expresses his misgivings about Husserl's way of developing phenomenology in his first lecture courses after the First World War. Phenomenology does not have to start from "intuition," in the sense of an intuition of "objects," but rather from "understanding." The "description" should not be grasped as the description of the objective, of a being as a thing, but rather must be guided by understanding. Phenomenology's knowledge of essence is grasped one-sidedly when it is understood as eidetic knowledge, that is, if essence is equated with genus and is supposed to be apprehended in a generalizing universalization. "Transcendental" knowledge stands in danger of a refined naturalism; one proceeds from an object considered as a thing back to a subject, but from the outset this procedure bypasses life in its facticity, life in the context of significance of the world. In understanding, on the other hand, the notion of essence receives a sense other than "eidos," and Heidegger replaces the transcendental I with life in its actuality. This "factical" life is life in a world. Ultimately "historical," it "understands" itself "historically." Thus, history becomes the guide for phenomenological research.

Like Husserl, the young Heidegger considers phenomenology to be the science of origins, science with a "radical" tendency. However, the way to the origin is now the way from life in its facticity to life in its historicality. Phenomenological philosophizing is traveling along with life. To be sure, if phenomenological intuition is understood as a "perception" ("seeing") of objects as things and if phenomenological reduction is interpreted as the return to a constitutive consciousness from just such an understanding of knowledge, then of course traveling along with life must be rejected, cancelled in the reduction. Yet if one begins with "understanding," then philosophy is in its own way a concern that life discover its origin and not fall away from it. Nevertheless, philosophizing does not mean forming a "world view." Philosophizing does not at all secure definite answers—it

70

is not a leap onto the secure shore but a leap into an unsteady boat. In addition, philosophy is not simply a science; the particular sciences build upon definite presuppositions whereas philosophy must question these very presuppositions and thus throw "firebrands" into all scientific-theoretical work.

Heidegger bases phenomenology on the "understanding" of factical life, on the "hermeneutic of facticity." Thus, phenomenology becomes "hermeneutical phenomenology." Heidegger was familiar with the term "hermeneutics" from his theological studies; he found it again in Dilthey who also became acquainted with it through theological studies, especially in his work with Schleiermacher. Hermeneutics is "a science which deals with the goals, ways, and rules of the interpretation of literary works," above all the science dealing with the interpretation of the book of books, the Bible. In the wider sense, hermeneutics is the "theory and methodology for every type of interpretation, e.g., even for works of the fine arts" (Sp 96f). If "hermeneutical" is used as an adjective for "phenomenology," then it takes on a still wider, more essential sense. It does not mean then, "as is usually the case, the methodology of interpretation, but rather interpretation itself" (Sp 120). Yet, even this determination is still insufficient. In hermeneutical phenomenology, hermeneutics means "neither the theory of the art of interpretation nor interpretation itself but rather the attempt to determine in the first place the essence of interpretation from that which is hermeneutical" (Sp 97f). That which is most originally hermeneutical, in terms of which interpreting is to be thought first, is indicated by the root of the word "hermeneutical," that is, by the Greek verb which means "to bring tidings." Consequently, the hermeneutical signifies "initially not interpretation but prior to that the bringing of news and tidings." "Hermeneutical" phenomenology is concerned with the bringing news about the Being of beings, but in such a way that Being itself appears (Sp 121f). In the words of *Sein und Zeit*, phenomenology becomes "hermeneutical" when it takes its point of departure from the fact that Dasein understands Being. Dasein is intrinsically hermeneutical because its own Being and the sense of Being in general become manifest; in fact, upon this basis the Being of every being is made known (SuZ 37).

Since hermeneutical phenomenology seeks to proceed from the question about the sense of Being *of Dasein* to the question of the sense of Being, the "primary sense" of hermeneutics is that of an "analytic of the existentiality of existence" (SuZ 38). Because Heidegger determines the sense of Being of Husserl's transcendental I as a factical existence intrinsically hermeneutical, Husserl's *transcendental* phenomenology becomes for Heidegger *hermeneutical* phenomenology. The hermeneutically understood "transcendental knowledge" is both the question about the sense of

Dasein's Being and about the sense of Being; it is therefore "ontological," a disclosure of Being. The transcendence of Dasein is certainly distinctive, **72** insofar as Being is at issue for Dasein in transcendence, in going beyond beings to Being, and to the extent that in Dasein's transcendence "there lies the possibility and necessity of the most radical *individualization*." Nonetheless, just as in the scholastic theory of transcendence, Being is specified as the utterly "*transcendens*." "Being and the structure of Being lie beyond every being and every possible existing determination of a being" (SuZ 38). The analytic of the transcendental *I*, that is, of the existentiality of existence, remains in the service of a hermeneutics which is ultimately concerned with the question about the sense of Being in general and which is in this sense ontological.

Heidegger reproaches Dilthey, Scheler, and Husserl (SuZ 46ff), but also Kant and Descartes (24f), indeed, all of metaphysics, theology, and science (48ff) with the fact that they never expressly developed the question about the sense of the Being of Dasein, of the subjectivity of the subject and of the transcendental I. Due to the influence of traditional ontology, Dasein's sense of Being is conceptualized positively or negatively in terms of being-present-at-hand; hence, the necessity for asking in a new, original manner about the sense of Being was not perceived at all. To be sure, Husserl's transcendental phenomenology does not grasp the sense of Being of the transcendental I as being-present-at-hand, but rather as not-being-present-at-hand, a determination opposed to the traditional interpretation of Being. It is thereby conceived solely in a negative rather than in a positive way (47f). The being which is present-at-hand is grounded in the constituting activity of a transcendental I. Since Being remains determined as being-present-at-hand, and even though the transcendental I is not a being, is never merely present-at-hand, Husserl cannot call transcendental phenomenology ontology. Ontology, the question about the Being of beings, can only provide the guidelines for constitutive transcendental phenomenology. It remains inferior to and superior to transcendental phenomenology which asks about the constitution of the Being of beings in the transcendental I, an I which lacks the existence of a thing and is not present-at-hand. In contrast, Heidegger's hermeneutical phenomenology is ontological because it asks about the sense of *Being* of the transcendental I in a positive way. Because it does so, it cannot take Being as being-present-at-hand because it must raise anew the question about the sense of Being.

Phenomenology, which for Heidegger as well directs one "to the things **73** themselves," means to keep away all unproven presuppositions. Heidegger grasps the phenomenon as that which shows itself in itself, as that which is manifest, and he understands the λέγειν in the λόγος of phenom*ology* as making manifest, as letting something be seen from itself. Phenomenology then means: "to let that which shows itself be seen from itself as it shows itself by itself" (SuZ 34). What must expressly be allowed to be seen, to be exhibited, is not the beings which obtrude but rather that which is concealed and covered, the Being of beings and the sense of Being. As an exhibition of the Being of beings and of its sense, hermeneutical phenomenology is ontology. Phenomenology is the methodological, ontology the substantive designation for the same thing. "Philosophy is universal phenomenological ontology which takes its point of departure from the hermeneutics of Dasein; the latter as the analytic of *existence*, has secured the end of the guiding thread for all philosophical questioning at the point from which it *arises* and to which it *returns*" (SuZ 38, 436). The hermeneutical phenomenology of *Sein und Zeit* seeks to find *fundamental* ontology in the existential analytic so as to arrive at the question about the sense of Being through the question about Dasein's sense of Being. In this way it is to ground anew the theory of Being. Nonetheless, the questioning pursued in *Sein und Zeit* does not achieve its aim. Therefore, the published portion of *Sein und Zeit* provides only the fundamentals of an initial and provisional (more indirect than direct) critique of Husserl's phenomenology.

Heidegger replaced the transcendental I with Dasein. Dasein is not an I which constitutes every being while itself lacking the characteristics of a being. Rather, its sense of Being is positively determined as "factical existence" and thereby set apart from every other being. Existence is being-in-the-world, and indeed a factical having-always-been in the world alongside beings and with others. This facticity cannot be dissolved into the constituting accomplishments of a subject; the disclosure of this facticity (of being-thrown) is equiprimordial with the self-disclosing projection, understanding. The "state-of-mind" as the disclosure of facticity says to Dasein that it has always been in the world. The speculative idealism of Fichte, Schelling, and Hegel—but in his own way even Husserl—interprets this state-of-mind—under the rubric "sentience"— as the bottommost level of knowledge and thus puts it in a comprehensive context. On this level, the I should find itself limited "from without" without being able to see the boundary of this limitation as self-imposed. The I may falsely attribute the stimulation of sensation to a not-I; it may not see that the accomplishments of subjectivity basically construct the world. If state-of-mind is grasped as a basic structure of being-in-the-world, this idealistic interpretation of sensation is short-circuited and of course the realistic account of sensation is also corrected. The evidence of state-of-mind reminds one that even "pure theory," even science has a state-of-mind or is "attuned" so that even it does not grasp things in their

74

pure and neutral "in itself." Rather it comprehends them within the Being-in-the-world, which understands as having a state-of-mind and in which the "constituting accomplishments" are primordially united with having-always-been alongside things.[13]

Being-in-the-world means to be in an "environment" and ultimately in a historical world. Dasein is concerned about its being-in-the-world, and it does not see only the present-at-hand, but also deals with the ready-to-hand. It shudders in anxiety, and in the anticipation of death it comes to its most extreme possibility. It lets itself be affected by the call of conscience and takes over its destiny. The transcendental I, on the other hand, is totally different. Husserl's analyses show (if we may here disregard the later analyses), even in the style of his description, that the transcendental I is a pure seeing which apparently never has to die, which needs its body at most when it must step away from its desk to be able to see a thing from different sides and thus to describe it adequately. Husserl strictly committed phenomenological philosophizers to the use of the eyes, that is, to acknowledge no traditional principles, no presuppositions, but rather to say only that which allows itself to be exhibited in intuition. In his "hermeneutical" phenomenology Heidegger questions for the first time whether the equation of thinking and the use of the eyes, of thinking and representational seeing, and thereby of essence and *eidos* ("view"), is merely a presupposition which has been developed in the history of thought, whether the "phenomenologist" was possible only on the basis of this history. Is not intentional analysis merely a special case of the one-sidedly "theoretical" attitude of Western thinking? Does not this theoretical attitude, the seeing of a view, of an idea, become possible only when Dasein is removed from the world, when the significant features of the world are levelled out, when being-ready-to-hand turns into mere being-present-at-hand (SuZ 356ff)? Must not the *intentio* of intentional analysis be rooted in the "biased" structure, in the tension of factical existence? When Husserl grasps intentional analysis as a "making present," does he not then point to the task of grounding intentionality in the *full* ecstatic temporality of Dasein and of not orienting it one-sidedly to the temporal mode of the present (SuZ 363 note)? Dasein can get hold of itself in its full temporality only in the *accomplishment* of its factical existence (cf. SuZ 48), but not in terms of its "contents." As that which itself accomplishes cognition, Dasein can no longer be fixed in an idea, eidetically reduced, so that it then can get back its facticity as a colorless realization. If Husserl pointed out to Heidegger that "facticity" itself is an *eidos*, then the presupposition which lies therein, that every "essence" or "Being" is an *eidos*, is to be rejected. In *Sein und Zeit*, Heidegger grounds the "intuition of essence" in the understanding of factical existence; however, he

75

wants to reserve final judgement about the type of phenomenological seeing until—and this is not yet accomplished in the published part of *Sein und Zeit*—"the explicit concepts of Being and the structure of Being are achieved, as which only phenomena in the phenomenological sense can develop" (SuZ 147).

If it is shown that Dasein is factical existence, "historical," then one cannot avoid the insight that the question about Being "is itself historical in character" (SuZ 20). Phenomenological-ontological investigation can therefore touch ground only there where it has always stood, in history. The investigation must attempt to press vigorously toward the origin of the history which determines it and to free this origin from all concealments; this is done so as to question history anew and thus to be able to "repeat it." For this reason, Heidegger's plan for *Sein und Zeit* sets a second, more "historical" destructive part next to the first, a more "systematic" one. Fundamentally this is not a matter of the coexistence of two parts, but rather one of an interlacing. The first part is, therefore, already interspersed with destructive demonstrations, and consequently the second part is to make visible a task which is to be comprehended "systematically." Finally, as Heidegger says along with Count Yorck, the difference between systematization and history, "with respect to the inner historicity of self-consciousness," is "methodologically inadequate" and "incorrect according to its essence" (SuZ 401f). Insofar as Heidegger grasps phenomenological investigation as historical, he denies the possibility of what Husserl demands, the possibility of a radical new beginning from the matters themselves. To be sure, even for Husserl, beginning in a radically new fashion has its limits. Certain men, because of certain properties, can be "blind" to certain phenomena. Since the capacity for "seeing" is limited in some individuals, phenomenology is from the outset the work of an entire "school." In contrast, phenomenological research has, according to Heidegger, an inner, irremovable limit in the historicality of the understanding. The tradition formulates the question, and the view on the phenomena opens up only from the respective situation.

In certain statements of Max Scheler's phenomenology, Heidegger finds support for the attempt to root the phenomenological "intuition of essence" in understanding the state-of-mind of Dasein as being-in-the-world. Scheler started not with cognition interpreted as seeing or representing, but rather from the emotional life. Referring to emotional phenomena such as love, hatred, and shame, he not only made these phenomena objects of knowledge, but also asked how knowledge is grounded in them. "In taking up the impetus of Augustine and Pascal," he "directed the problematic to the foundational interconnection between 'representational' acts and those which 'take an interest' " (SuZ 139).

Scheler refused to begin with the isolated subject (116), and within phenomenology he provided and showed the strongest impetus toward working out the ethical problematic, namely, that beings confront us primarily as having value (cf. 99). Heidegger must nonetheless point out that these statements allow the ontological foundations to remain "in the dark" (139). In his later work, Scheler sought to comprehend man's world of meaning, to conceive of the central questions of philosophy as those of philosophical anthropology (cf. K 189f). Heidegger was so interested in Scheler's attempt that, after Scheler's death, he wanted to work on the publication of his posthumous work, a publication which unfortunately did not then come about. Nonetheless, in contrast to Scheler's disparate approaches, which contained an abundance of concrete knowledge, and in contrast to the speculations proceeding in the traditional metaphysical possibilities, Heidegger first asked how the question about man pertains to the question about Being at all, and thereby to the attempt at a primordial repetition of metaphysical thinking. It is no accident that Heidegger's book on Kant, which takes this question a step further, is dedicated to Scheler's memory.

In 1927 there came still another collaboration and dispute with Husserl. At that time Husserl tried to explain what phenomenology is for the *Encyclopedia Britannica*. Heidegger collaborated in this attempt and used the opportunity "to characterize the fundamental tendency of 'Being and Time' within the transcendental problem."[14] He sees that he and Husserl both agree that the totality of discoverable beings, the "world," cannot be explained in its "transcendental constitution" "by going back to a being with the same type of Being." For Heidegger, however, the place of the transcendental has "in no way the mode of Being of such a being." Rather, one must grasp the type of Being of the constituting being in a positive manner, namely, as the mode of Being of factical existence. This means that the sense of Being in general must again become problematic. Since Husserl does not question anew the sense of Being, but rather accepts it traditionally as being-present-at-hand, he can give only a negative characterization of the mode of Being of the transcendental I. He thus arrives at the questionable distinction, a distinction explicitly criticized by Heidegger, between the "pure I" as the place of transcendental constitution and the human I. What Husserl grasps as "transcendental constitution" Heidegger comprehends as "a central possibility of the existence of the factical self. This, the concrete man, is as such, a being, never a 'real worldly fact', because man is never merely present-at-hand, but rather exists." Factical existence is psychological as well as physical; only on the "basis of the concrete totality of men" are the "one-sided" considerations of physiology and pure psychology possible. When Husserl abstracts pure psychology from the somatic and makes it the propaedeutic to phenomenology, he misses the concrete totality of man in an opaque Cartesianism. Factical existence, because it is factical, is always in a world. Therefore, in contrast to Husserl, Heidegger asks: "Does not a world in general belong to the essense of the pure *ego?*" One must question anew not only the mode of Being of existence, but also the mode of Being of the being, alongside which existence has always been factical. "The problem of Being is therefore universally related to that which constitutes and that which is constituted." Thus, the question of Being as Parmenides first saw it stands at the beginning of the draft edited by Heidegger. On the basis of the question of Being, both the recent and the Husserlian approaches from consciousness, already present in antiquity, become problematic: "Is this turning of one's gaze from beings to consciousness accidental, or is it demanded by the distinctiveness of that which Philosophy has constantly sought as its field of problems under the name of Being?" Still, Husserl did not appropriate the reference to the question of Being in the final draft of his article; in other words, he did not make the modern approach from consciousness problematic on the basis of the question of Being. ·

Hermeneutical phenomenology asks about Dasein's sense of Being in order to be able to question anew the sense of Being in general. In the published part of *Sein und Zeit* Heidegger determines the meaning of Dasein's Being. In doing so, he can appropriate the initiatives of Dilthey's "hermeneutical" thinking and above all those of "hermeneutical" theology as well. Yet, Heidegger wants to develop his hermeneutics so close to the traditional, metaphysical theory of Being, that he assigns to the ἑρμηνεύειν of Dasein the task of letting the sense of Being be manifest with its own Being and the Being of nonhuman beings (SuZ 37). If phenomenology becomes hermeneutic, then it must be related back to the leading question of Western thinking, the question of Being. The title "hermeneutical phenomenology" therefore denotes neither a "direction" within an existing phenomenological "school" nor certainly any "new" direction; instead, it attempts "to think the essence of phenomenology more primordially so that in this way it can direct it back expressly to its relationship to Western philosophy" (Sp 95). If phenomenology is more primordially directed back to Western thinking, then the task becomes to confront this thinking rather than Husserl's phenomenology, to confront the origin rather than that which arises from it. *Was ist Metaphysik?*, the address which marks Heidegger's succession to Husserl's Freiburg position, represents his departure from phenomenology. At the beginning of the Freiburg period this term still stands as a mark of respect to the *genius loci*, but later it no longer appears in the title of Heidegger's lectures and work.

Husserl was unable to see Heidegger's attempt to explicate Dasein's sense of Being positively as the "transcendental I" and thus to allow the sense of Being in general to become problematic. He assessed Heidegger's attempt as "existence-philosophy"—in accordance with the common interpretation of *Sein und Zeit* prevalent at the time—and reproached it by saying that it did not understand the "ascent from the mundane subjectivity (of man) to transcendental subjectivity"; consequently it did not understand the transcendental reduction.[15] Husserl's marginal notes to *Sein und Zeit* and to Heidegger's book on Kant show that he classified Heidegger with naturalism and objectivism and—with Scheler and Dilthey—with the anthropological tendency: "Heidegger transposes or transfers the constitutively phenomenological clarification of all regions of beings and of the universals, of the total region, world, into anthropology . . . " From then on, Husserl saw this "anthropologism" as his real opponent.[16]

Husserl viewed Heidegger's transformation of phenomenology into anthropology, this "modern" existence-philosophy, together with every anthropologism and historical relativism, as sinking in the crisis of modern times, a crisis whose overcoming became ever more the central question of his thinking. Yet, perhaps it is Husserl's tragedy that his overcoming of the crisis of modern times ultimately just repeats once more the way of modern metaphysics. The genuine tragedy of Husserl would then not lie in the injustice which was inflicted upon him for political reasons, nor even in the fact that both the earlier and the later disciples whom he had helped in breaking through into a new freedom of thought did not follow his path of thinking. Husserl's deeper tragedy would be that he who had spoken in favor of the things themselves and against all metaphysical constructions ultimately repeated the way of modern metaphysical systems; he did not even realize that he did not see through the presuppositions which had become transparent. When Heidegger attempts to make questionable those metaphysical decisions which still determine even Husserl's thinking, he then serves the *matter* of phenomenology in a manner entirely different from those who simply carry "phenomenological" research further or else take Husserl's work historically and value it as the work of a "classical" philosopher. Such thinkers do not carry out Husserl's only wish: that from the turn toward matter one build further upon the basis laid by him.[17]

80

TRANSCENDENTAL PHILOSOPHY AND METAPHYSICS

In the published portion of *Sein und Zeit*, the "existential analytic" is not yet grounded on the basis from which it arises, on the expressly unfolded sense of Being. Dasein's manner of Being is delimited, but the question remains open as to how the *veritas transcendentalis* of hermeneutics announces the sense of Being, how transcendental philosophy is ontology and thereby repeats metaphysics' way of raising questions. Is it at all possible to grasp transcendental philosophy as the disclosure of Being and therefore as metaphysics? Heidegger no longer develops this question by discussing Husserl, but instead turns to other thinkers, to Kant first of all.

The first sentence of his book on Kant clearly states what the reflection upon Kant sets out to accomplish: "The following investigation undertakes to interpret Kant's *Kritik der reinen Vernunft* as laying the foundation of metaphysics in order to bring into view the problem of metaphysics as one of fundamental ontology." If Kant is to be seen as a metaphysician, then this explanation must be fundamentally different from Neo-Kantianism's proffered explanation of him. In Neo-Kantianism, Kant's work appears as epistemology; his "Critique" is interpreted as a "theory of experience" or indeed as the "theory of the positive sciences" (K 25). One presupposes science as a fact, and then its justification is sought after. Kant's concept of beings is thereby grasped as the bare concept of nature, which must then also be expanded by means of a critical concept of history or culture. The issue regarding the unity out of which the sciences of nature and culture separate themselves remains more or less open. By drawing the cultural sciences into its attempt at justification, Neo-Kantianism approaches Hegel more and more; however, unlike Hegel, it does not unite the justification of the sciences within a unity which dialectically unfolds itself.

From the beginning, Heidegger takes Kant's *Kritik der reinen Vernunft* not as a theory of mathematical-physical experience, but rather as questioning the inner possibility of ontology (of general metaphysics as the necessary preparation for specialized metaphysics). Kant's *Kritik* is not limited to the question concerning a critical concept of nature which would then be supplemented by a critical concept of history; it is, rather, led back to the leading question of metaphysics: (τί τὸ ὄν), what is a being? The transcendental I is interpreted in terms of its temporality; it is grasped as existence and as being-in-the-world. Thus, one is to find the point of departure for a thinking of time as that horizon in which the question, "what is a being?" can be primordially unfolded. Only on this basis of developing the "metaphysical" problematic in this manner can one then ask about the sciences, about particular regions of Being, such as nature and history, and even about the sense of discourse concerning the "*a priori*." Heidegger senses in Neo-Kantianism the absence of this primordial grounding of the questions. Thus in a review of Cassirer, for example, he says: "One can first of all doubt with good reason whether Cassirer's interpretation, or indeed the Neo-Kantian epistemological interpretation of what Kant means by the 'Copernican Revolution' goes to the core of the transcendental problematic as an ontological one in its essential possibilities. Aside from this, does the *Kritik der reinen Vernunft* allow itself simply to be 'expanded' to 'a critique of culture?' Is it then so certain or indeed most highly questionable whether the foundations for Kant's unique transcendental interpretation of 'nature' are already explicitly exhibited and justified? What about the always unavoidable ontological formulation of the make up and mode of Being of that which is indeterminately enough referred to sometimes as 'consciousness', sometimes as 'life', 'spirit', 'reason' . . .?" Heidegger's fundamental-ontological question about the "subjectivity" of the "subject" ends up in a renewal of the question of Being. In such a renewal, what matters for philosophy is not a "rich" consciousness, proficient in all the sciences, but rather that the need for fundamental questions which have remained unresolved since antiquity again bursts forth. (Discussion of *Ernst Cassirer: Philosophie der Symbolischen Formen, 2. Teil,* 1925 1007f, 1011f.)

Does the fundamental, still unresolved question about Being appear in Kant's thinking? Can Kant's thinking be grasped as metaphysics, metaphysics grounded in a fundamental ontology? According to Kant, metaphysics belongs to the "nature" of man. As an ontological analytic of man's "nature," fundamental ontology prepares the foundation for metaphysics; it is consequently that which is required to "make" metaphysics "possible." The idea of fundamental ontology as laying the ground of metaphysics must be proved in an interpretation of the *Kritik der reinen Vernunft*, because laying the ground of metaphysics can never happen from nothing; it occurs "rather in the strength and lack of strength of a tradition which sketches out for it the possible approaches." If metaphysics belongs to the nature of man, then, as Heidegger interprets Kant's thought, it "exists factically" with man, that is, it has "always developed in some form." A foundation of metaphysics must base itself upon the "tradition contained within itself" and repeat the task in a different way which was already undertaken (K 14).

Metaphysics (ontology in the wider sense of the word) asks about the Being of beings. At some point it will actually ask about a being *as* being or about a being as such, and thus it is general metaphysics (ontology in the narrower sense of the word, in the sense of eighteenth-century school metaphysics). Still questions are raised not only about those features

82

which are to be traced to any being, to a being as such, but also about the
83 Being which makes a particular, specific being what it is. Thus it is special
metaphysics. Indeed metaphysics from the beginning has asked about the
being as being only in such a way as to determine *beings in totality* in terms
of a pre-eminent being—the supreme or the divine being. As in the
Christian faith where God was understood as the *creator* of *man* and the
world, theological metaphysics was divided into the three parts of the
traditional *metaphysica specialis* (natural theology, psychology, and cosmol-
ogy).

Metaphysics asks about beings as such and in totality. It seeks to
ground the manifestation of the being—the ontic truth—in the disclosedness of the being's constitution of Being, of its ontological truth. The
question about the possibility of ontic knowledge is attributed to the
question about the possibility of that which enables ontic knowledge, to
the question about the possibility of ontological knowledge. Kant's
"Copernican Revolution" means nothing more than leading the question
about the possibility of ontic knowledge back to the question concerning
the possibility of ontology itself. Thus for the first time since Plato and
Aristotle, ontology, and thereby metaphysics, became problematic once
again in the thought of Kant (K 21).

Metaphysics' question of Being becomes problematic in the "Copernican Revolution" within a "transcendentally philosophical" formulation of
the question. Kant calls that knowledge transcendental which concerns
itself not only with beings, with objects, "but rather with our mode of
knowledge of objects insofar as this is to be possible *a priori.*" Transcendental knowledge is ontological knowledge (*a priori* synthesis according to
Kant). "Consequently transcendental knowledge does not investigate
beings themselves, but rather the possibility of the precedent understanding of Being, which means at the same time the ontological constitution
of beings. It concerns the going-beyond (transcendence) of pure reason
toward beings so that experience can now first of all take the measure of
them as possible objects. To make the possibility of ontology problematic
means to ask about the possibility, that is, about the essence of this
transcendence belonging to the understanding of Being, to philosophize
transcendentally" (24f). To the extent that "pure reason" knows the
84 principles *a priori*, and that ontological knowledge or *a priori* synthesis is
but a judging about these principles, and insofar as pure reason must be
delimited in its essence and separated from its misuse, then transcendental philosophy as the question about the possibility of ontology is the
critique of pure reason (23).

In the *Kritik der reinen Vernunft* Kant develops the essential unity of
transcendence by asking repeatedly and variously about the unity of

thinking and intuition. According to Heidegger, the transcendental imagination finally shows itself as the root from which thinking and intuition grow.[18] Nonetheless, Kant turns back in the face of the decisive step, thinking the transcendental imagination as primordial time. Had Kant taken this step, then he would have accomplished that movement of philosophizing "which reveals the breakdown of the foundation of metaphysics and thereby the abyss of metaphysics" (194). Kant calls pure thinking, the I, "permanent" and "abiding"; he describes time in the same way. He thinks—like metaphysics in general—in terms of the permanent and abiding presence, but he does not think this presence in accordance with its complete temporal character (174). Time is pushed away even further into the other moment of transcendence, in intuition. The pure I is "in accordance with the generally dominant interpretation set over against all temporality and all time" (157).

What *Sein und Zeit* asserted remains valid: Kant does not grasp the transcendental I as factical, essentially temporal existence; although it is really not to be thought of as "substance," it is nonetheless still thought of as "substantial," that is, as something abiding, unchanging, and constant, as something "which has always been present at hand" (SuZ 320f). Thus, Kant makes the same fundamental omission as Descartes who did not explain in primordial fashion the sense of Being of the *sum* in *cogito sum*, but rather interpreted it in terms of traditional metaphysics. He thereby concurs with the failure of ancient ontology, which was incapable of thinking about time in its primordiality (SuZ 23ff). In his book on Kant, Heidegger attempts to put forth the "unsaid" in Kant's thinking, to exhibit time, as it belongs to the transcendence of the understanding of Being, as a problem (K 182).

In *Sein und Zeit* Heidegger reproaches Kant further for not having established transcendence primordially enough as being-in-the-world, as **85** a being-already alongside things. "Kant did not see the phenomenon of the world . . . " (SuZ 321). Thus he believed that he still had to prove the reality of the external world. Because of this he did not depart from the "Cartesian approach of an isolated, present subject" (SuZ 204f). In Heidegger's book on Kant, this problem of the world appears as the question about the unity of ontological and ontic knowledge, as the question about the enabling of empirical truth by means of transcendental truth. According to Heidegger, transcendence holds open a horizon which first makes possible the view of beings which lets the Being of beings become perceptible. Kant grasps this horizon in terms of the "X" of the transcendental object which is not a being but which is indeed "something," namely, the horizon for beings and their Being (K 114f). Heidegger's book on Kant does not pursue the question as to whether Kant was capable of developing "being the horizon for . . . " primordially enough as world.

Kant's incapacity to let the primordiality of time and world become visible is rooted in metaphysics which forgets both time and world. Kant is significant because his transcendental philosophy has made time as well as world (horizon) questionable once again; thus through him metaphysics has become a problem. Making metaphysics problematic must be carried out as a primordial repetition of metaphysics; thus it can appear as an overtaking and surpassing of metaphysics. Kant therefore describes the kind of investigation begun in his *Kritik der reinen Vernunft* as "the metaphysics of metaphysics" (cf. K 208). If ontology is grasped as the question about the Being of beings and thereby as the center of metaphysics, then the metaphysics of metaphysics is the founding of ontology, fundamental ontology. In his book on Kant, Heidegger calls this fundamental ontology the "metaphysics of Dasein."

The metaphysics of Dasein seeks the essential unity of transcendence in imagination and its temporality. Consequently, this metaphysics asks about man, but not like anthropology, which takes man as one (even if distinctive) being among others, and certainly not like anthropologism which places every being before man and toward him and explains it in **86**   terms of him. The metaphysics of Dasein asks rather how the question, "what is man?" indeed belongs to metaphysical questioning. It asks how the question about man and the question about Being belong together.

The question of Being asks about the Being of beings. In this question there lies the more primordial question about Being as such. It is evident that Being is said in many ways, for example, as what-something-is, as that-it-is, and being-true. The unity of these modes of articulation of Being can be discerned only if one raises the question about Being as such. But this question is driven back to an even more primordial question: "On what basis is something like Being with all its rich articulations and relations to be grasped at all?" (K 203). Access to this "where" from which Being as such is to be grasped is sought through the interpretation of man's understanding of Being. This understanding is not merely a property of man. Rather, man is man only on the basis of the understanding of Being. Thus he is the "there, by whose Being the disclosive breakthrough into the realm of beings occurs." (206). With this "breakthrough" both the being which man himself is, as well as that which he is not, can become manifest. The metaphysics of Dasein does not mean metaphysics about Dasein, but rather "the metaphysics which necessarily happens *as Dasein*," the question about the Being of beings and about Being as such which occurs from the there of Being (208). Being-there

[*Da-sein*] becomes the basis of metaphysics, and since Dasein is this foundation, and because the disclosure of the constitution of its Being is ontology, the metaphysics of Dasein is also called fundamental ontology. But this fundamental ontology (as existential analytic) is "only the first step of the metaphysics of Dasein" (209). It exposes both Dasein's need of Being, which lies in oblivion, as well as the temporality of this needfulness (210). It thus points to the genuinely "fundamental-ontological" sense of the question about time, to the task of thinking in terms of Dasein's temporality that time in whose horizon metaphysics has established Being as "persistence in presence" (216f).

In his book on Kant, Heidegger hints only briefly as to what complexities the metaphysics of Dasein must encounter in this further step of thinking the temporality of the sense of Being. Metaphysics which *occurs* as Dasein has a "fate" which keeps it "bound to the concealed occurrence of metaphysics in Dasein itself" (208f). The interpretation of historicality carried out by *Sein und Zeit* is to yield a preliminary notion of the mode of Being of this occurrence (218). If this occurrence itself comes into view, then the thought becomes inescapable that the interpretation of the *Kritik der reinen Vernunft* oriented toward fundamental ontology intensifies the problematic of grounding metaphysics but "stops at the decisive point." Not even once does the interpretation turn toward the transcendental dialectic which in Kant's work follows the transcendental aesthetic and analytic. Heidegger asks whether this dialectic is not to be conceived primordially from an essence of truth to which untruth as nonessence belongs. Does the essence of truth conceived of in this way refer to that occurrence which is the occurrence of metaphysics (221f)?

Does the reflection upon Kant induce Heidegger's thinking to take the decisive step from Dasein's temporality to the time which belongs to the sense of Being itself? Or does the reference to Kant bind Heidegger's thinking even more to that "metaphysical" language which is spoken by *Sein und Zeit* but which, according to Heidegger's later insight, hindered the aforementioned step? In any case his Kant book shows what the introduction to *Sein und Zeit* already expressed: that questioning about Being forces "itself constantly before the possibility of disclosing a still more primordial, more universal horizon" "from which the answer to the question, what is called 'Being'? could be drawn" (SuZ 26f). Might it not be the case that one must conceive the truth from which the transcendental dialectic of the *Kritik der reinen Vernunft* is to be explained as the basis out of which all metaphysics arises, out of which alone the analytic of Dasein can also be accomplished?

5

GOING BACK TO THE GROUND OF METAPHYSICS

Heidegger asks about the unity of Being in its manifold expressibility and, for the sake of this question, about the sense of Being. The traditional manner of considering Being (namely as constant presence or present-ness) leads to the all-pervading opinion that time belongs essentially to the sense of Being. Heidegger tries to think the temporal character of the sense of Being from the temporality of factical existence. He therefore conceives of the transcendental I as factical existence, and asks about the time which belongs to the "I think." Since, in the working out of the problematic of temporality, of the temporal character of the sense of Being, since in the third division of the first part of *Sein und Zeit*, Heidegger is not successful, he now attempts to broach the question about the sense of Being or the "transcendental horizon" of every understanding of Being independent of the problem of temporality. Thus he asks: What is transcendence, going beyond beings, the "meta" of metaphysics? What indeed is metaphysics? How is the transcendental horizon to be thought as the sense of Being? Instead of "sense of Being" Heidegger now says "truth of Being." "'Sense of Being' and 'truth of Being' are the same" (WiM 18, VWW 26). Thus one must still ask: How is the essence of truth, the truth of Being itself, to be conceived?

    Already in his first works Heidegger asks about the *ens tanquam verum*. He appropriates that metaphysical view according to which being-true is one of the ways of articulating Being. For the Greeks, and then in various ways for metaphysics in general, truth is "discoveredness." If a being is taken as a being, then it is taken in its Being, but as it "is" "in truth." Being and truth (discoveredness) mean the same; the Being of the being is its discoveredness, its truth: *ens et verum convertuntur*.

    In the metaphysical relation between Being and truth, Being is thought of as constant presence just as truth is thought of as that which is constantly present for knowledge, or, in terms of knowing, as a measure of the constantly present. A decisive impetus was necessary so that Heidegger could come upon the way of questioning back behind this coining of the "essence" of Being and truth. This impetus came above all from Christian theology. Within it, in spite of all foreign influences from metaphysical thinking, an understanding of truth has a lasting effect which we already find in Jewish belief. In Hebrew truth is related to time and history. To the word-family of truth (*'emunah*) belong words like supporting, being carried, doorpost, attendant of a child, educator, stability, perseverence, reliability, and *loyalty*. "Show me," Jacob entreats his son Joseph as the time of death draws near, "goodwill and truth (faithfulness), and do not bury me in Egypt"—not in the foreign land, but rather in the land of the fathers (I Moses 47, 29). From *'emunah* comes the prayer ending "Amen"; when the Greek Bible does not translate Amen with ἀληθῶς, it says γένοιτο. In the Jewish and Christian faiths truth is faithfulness which must be maintained throughout the changing history which is to be endured. Truth and faithfulness which keep in mind, which do not forget the once sealed bond and which in such recollection know that they owe thanksgiving, belong together.[19]

Western philosophy and theology are the constantly renewed confrontation between Greek metaphysical and Judeo-Christian concepts of truth. In this confrontation the non-metaphysical concept of truth becomes entangled in metaphysical conceptualization, for example, when Kierkegaard interprets essential truth as "subjectivity" and thereby utilizes concepts which lead back through many revisions and negations to Greek concepts.

Heidegger endeavors to get out of this entanglement by working out anew the question of Being and truth in a primordial way. In this attempt, Being is no longer conceived of as constant presence, and truth is no longer thought of as interchangeable with Being conceived in this manner. Being true is no longer one of the modes of articulation of that Being which does not remain unquestioned with regard to its unity in the multiplicity of these modes. Rather, the *unity* of Being in its multifaceted expressibility is interrogated, and thus about the sense, the truth of Being. The sense or the truth of Being is to be brought up as the basis upon which the question about Being and about the multiplicity of its modes of articulation has always stood. The presupposition that Being is constant presence also rests upon this basis in a not yet visible manner. Consequently, the question about Being and truth is no longer merely ontology but rather fundamental ontology, no longer only metaphysics, but rather "the metaphysics of metaphysics." It is, as Heidegger explained in an introduction to *Was ist Metaphysik?*, printed in 1949, the "going-back to the ground of metaphysics."

TRUTH AND FREEDOM

In *Sein und Zeit* Heidegger seeks the foundation for the theory of Being by raising the question about the sense of Being with Dasein's understanding of Being as a point of departure. In the published sections, the question about Being and truth is not yet developed (SuZ 357), but it comes into view in a provisional way as the question about the connection of Dasein, disclosedness, and truth (sec 44). Being—the discoveredness of what a being is in truth—and truth stand in a "primordial connection," "go together" (SuZ 213), are "equiprimordial" (230). They are disclosed in the Dasein which understands Being. "'There is' Being—not beings— only insofar as truth is. And there *is* truth only insofar as and as long as Dasein is" (230).

If truth is understood in terms of its disclosedness in Dasein, then the traditional concept of truth is led back to its unthought presuppositions. Traditionally, truth is defined as the correspondence of a judgement with its object. Since this conception leads to difficulties, Heidegger asks how a cognition is shown to be true. It can be shown to be true only when it is "discovering." The *"being-true (truth)"* of the statement must be understood as *"being-discovering"* (218). This being-discovering is grounded in the disclosedness of Dasein. Truth as correspondence must be understood more primordially in terms of the being-discovering of disclosedness, and it must be derived from this disclosedness. In turn, the discoveredness which belongs to disclosedness is preserved in what is expressed. The expressed is then taken as present-at-hand and is thus related to that being with regard to which the discoveredness is discoveredness. In this way discoveredness becomes the correspondence between two present-at-hand beings (*intellectus* and *res*). If Dasein is grasped as being-in-the-world which has always been alongside beings, then the interpretation of truth (that is, the disclosedness of Being-in-the-world) as a relation between two present-at-hand beings is averted from the outset.

As the disclosedness of Dasein in its authenticity, truth is the "truth of existence" (221). It is characterized by thrownness and projection but in such a way, as Heidegger points out only briefly in *Sein und Zeit*, that it is also characterized by anticipatory resoluteness and thereby historicality. Since factical existence is always authentic and inauthentic at the same time, Dasein is, "because it is intrinsically falling" also always in untruth in accordance with its ontological constitution. A being shows itself in its discoveredness, but at the same time it remains disguised and concealed; it is in the mode of semblance (222). Dasein, disclosed in its there, maintains itself equiprimordially in truth as well as in untruth (298).

Being factical, thrownness, is inescapable for truth as the truth of factical existence. Dasein must presuppose truth, for disclosedness or truth necessarily belongs to Dasein. Yet in this presupposing, Dasein does not presuppose something demonstrable; it rather projects itself upon its own insurpassable being-factical. The "skeptic" cannot be refuted insofar as the necessity of the existence of Dasein and truth cannot be demonstrated to him. Yet insofar as he is a radical skeptic, he does not need to be refuted at all because he extinguishes Dasein and truth along with it in the despair of suicide. "Truth does not allow itself to be demonstrated in its necessity because Dasein cannot be submitted as proof for itself" (229). Truth and Dasein are factical; that is, they cannot be grounded in a *causa sui* or in an absolute subject, and the question about the why of truth receives no answer. "In itself it is incomprehensible why beings should be *discovered*, why *truth* and *Dasein* must be" (228). Truth is ἀλήθεια, uncon-cealment, which must be torn away from an ultimately insurpassable concealment (219, 222).

At the highest level which the published portion of *Sein und Zeit* attains, Dasein's being-factical shows itself as the basis of a nullity. One conse-quently reflects upon the essence of truth as the disclosedness of factical existence, the essence of ἀλήθεια, when the nothing of this nullity be-comes problematic. The essay *Vom Wesen des Grundes* and the lecture, *Was ist Metaphysik?*, take up the task already set forth in *Sein und Zeit* (285): to ask about the ontological sense of the nullifying of the existential nullity and in general about the ontological essence of the nothing. *Was ist Metaphysik?* asks about the nothing and *Vom Wesen des Grundes* inquires into the ontological difference. "The Nothing is the not of beings and thus Being experienced in terms of beings. The ontological difference is the not between beings and Being . . . The former negating not of the nothing and the latter negating not of the difference are indeed not one and the same, but the same in the sense of what belongs together in the essencing of the Being of beings" (G 5).

The essay *Vom Wesen des Grundes* starts with the idea that traditionally Being, truth, and ground (reason) belong together; being-*true* is com-prehended as *being*-in-truth (G 16), and truth is explicated as an explana-tory combining [*auseinanderlegendes Verknüpfen*] whose agreement is an agreement on the basis [*Grund*] of . . . (11f). With respect to truth, one must distinguish between the revealedness of Being (ontological truth) and the manifestness of beings (ontical truth). Ontological and ontical truth belong together intrinsically on the basis of their relation to the difference between Being and beings, to the ontological difference (15). The ontological difference is held open by Dasein which as an under-standing of Being relates to beings, and thus distinguishes Being and

92

beings. Heidegger calls this differentiating the going beyond beings toward Being, the "transcendence" of Dasein. The question about ground leads to the question about truth, the question about truth to the question about the ontological difference, the question about the ontological difference to the question about the transcendence of Dasein.

The transcendence of Dasein is that going beyond each and every being which has somehow always occurred. It is a going beyond from which Dasein can first of all return to things, to other Daseins, and to itself in an authentic manner, and from which the question about Dasein's possible relationship can first be raised. Transcendence, the going beyond the totality of beings, occurs toward the world and is therefore being-in-the-world. World is not the totality of beings, but rather this totality in which Dasein has always found itself, understood in the how of its manifestness, in ever-differing degrees by means of an anticipating-enveloping understanding. "World as totality 'is' not a being but rather that from which Dasein *directs itself towards* the beings to which it relates in the manner in which it can do so" (37). Thus the world is joined together with the for-the-sake-of-itself which Dasein exists as. It is the "world-forming" surpassing of being, transcendence as being-in-the-world, which first grants beings an entrance to the world so that they can become manifest as themselves. Transcendence is, therefore, the primal occurrence, primordial history itself (39). It must be grasped as freedom, for freedom contrasts itself with a "for-the-sake-of-itself" and thus lets the world hold sway.

Freedom as letting the world hold sway is the origin of ground in general. It is "to ground," namely: 1. as founding or endowing (as the projection of the for-the-sake-of-which, as understanding); 2. as the laying hold of ground (as infatuated with beings, state-of-mind); and 3. as the giving reasons for (articulation or classification, discourse). As the threefold yet unified grounding, freedom is being-the-ground, the origin of ground, the "ground of ground." Yet, it is finite, "thrown." That it is at all or that it occurs as transcendence is not a matter of freedom. As the ground of ground, it is the ground's staying away for its proper being-the-ground, the abyss [*Abgrund*].

Being, ground, and truth must be grasped from out of freedom's abysmal being-the-ground. There is Being only in being-the-ground of transcendence; "ground" is primordially a transcendental, essential character of Being itself, and only because of this can it give the principle of ground as a principle regarding beings. From this belonging-together of Being and ground, the question about truth must be asked in a primordial manner. The "transcendental" grounding—the articulation of the world which is there only together with founding and laying-hold-of-the-

94 ground—is the ontological truth which, as the revelation of Being and of the constitution of Being, precedes every becoming-manifest of beings (the ontical truth) (48f).

Does the essay *Vom Wesen des Grundes* already arrive at the primordially asked question about Being and Truth when it differentiates ontological and ontic truth, when it establishes ontological truth as enabling ontic truth? Or must the essence of truth be thought of more primordially than occurs in this differentiation? And is this the case because transcendence is the ground of ground only as the abyss, because non-essence belongs to the essence of ground in such a way that perhaps the non-essence of truth must also belong to its essence? The essay gives us no answer to this question.

Was ist Metaphysik? grasps transcendence, the realization of the ontological difference, as the heart of metaphysics. The step beyond (*meta*) beings is understood as the being-held-out into the Nothing. The Nothing reveals itself in essential anxiety as the nihilation of every being. In anxiety, all beings slip away, yet by means of this nihilation (not annihilation) they can show themselves in the utter strangeness of the fact that they are and that it is not the case that they are not. Nihilation takes away from Dasein beings as self-evident, familiar, and at one's disposal in order to give these beings back to it in the strangeness of "Being" which stimulates "wonder." The Nothing of nihilation thus enables the manifestation of beings *as* beings and thereby the realization of transcendence, the "metaphysical" going beyond, which goes beyond beings in order to be able to receive them back as that which has become manifest in its Being.

In essential anxiety, Dasein lets itself go into the Nothing and thus shudders in asking, "Why is there anything at all rather than Nothing?" This question stands at the end of *Was ist Metaphysik?* as the "fundamental question of metaphysics" which itself forcefully obtains the Nothing. In the *Einführung in die Metaphysik*, a lecture course given in 1935, Heidegger considers this question. This question is indeed the fundamental question of metaphysics, and it is also expressly asked in metaphysics (e.g., by Leibniz, cf. WiM 21ff, N II, 446ff). Nonetheless, when metaphysics questions in this manner, it goes back to a supreme being as the basis of all beings. Thus it neither thinks Being in itself, nor does it allude with the **95** sense or the truth of Being; rather, it bases every being on a supreme being without the sense of Being in general expressly becoming a problem. Insofar as Heidegger takes up " . . . and not rather Nothing" into the question, he subjects every being to this question and bars the way to a supreme being which is not to be questioned. He bends the question "why?" back upon the question about the sense or the truth of Being. This question is presupposed as the basic question of the leading question of metaphysics: "What is a being?" (Of course, as a mere introduction, the *Einführung in die Metaphysik*, rather than developing this question, passes over to the preliminary question: whether in metaphysics and in our language in general Being is thought in accordance with its entire wealth, whether metaphysical distinctions such as "Being and becoming," "Being and appearance," "Being and thinking," "Being and should," do not define Being in an inappropriate manner, namely, in terms of the equation: Being is constant presence.)

The question, "Why is there anything at all rather than nothing?" is metaphysics' fundamental question because it once more questions the heart of metaphysics—the manifestness of beings and transcendence as the holding open of this manifestness—and also makes its "essence" questionable again. Thus the basis of metaphysics, the sense or the truth of Being, comes before thinking. Metaphysics—the going out beyond beings, transcendence as primordial history in which beings as beings are manifest—"is the basic occurrence in Dasein," "is Dasein itself." But Dasein is, as the essay *Vom Wesen des Grundes* has shown, the *abysmal* ground. From there metaphysical thinking receives its gravest concern: "Because the truth of metaphysics dwells in this abysmal ground, the possibility of the deepest errancy constantly lurks in its immediate vicinity" (WiM 41).

How does error belong to the truth? How does—this question occurs at the end of Heidegger's Kant book—the non-essence of the transcendental appearance belong to the essense of truth? How does non-essence belong to the essence of truth at all? Does it belong, as abysmalness belongs, to Dasein's being-the-ground? If being the ground of the nullity, of the "guilt" of resolute existence, is understood as abysmalness, does not then abysmalness compel existence to the further step of releasing itself from **96** out of being-the-ground in its abyss in order to experience truth in accordance with its essense and non-essence, in order to experience the "essence" of truth?

ON THE ESSENCE OF TRUTH

In his lecture *Vom Wesen der Wahrheit* Heidegger starts with the old as well as current determination that truth is the correspondence of a statement with a state of affairs. Truth is therefore thought of as the correctness of a correspondence. But how, asks Heidegger, does the approximation of the statement to a state of affairs come about? The statement puts forth a state of affairs *just as* it is. It presents, it places something over against us. "As that which is so placed, what stands in contrast must traverse an open opposition and thereby still remain standing in itself as the thing and show itself as something constant. This appearing of the thing in traversing the opposition occurs within an opening whose openness is not first of all created by presenting, but which is rather received and appropriated only as a realm of relations" (VWW 11). In presenting—or in another accomplishment of truth such as acting or working—that conduct is accomplished in the open region and thereby adheres to that which is manifest, to that which is "present" or "is." Only in the standing open of conduct can something manifest become the standard for a conceptual approximation. The standing open must first of all assign its standard, the guideline for the correctness, and thus be instructed in the correctness of a correspondence. In other words, the standing open must become *free* to take on an obligatory guideline; it must be *free* to accept what is manifest in the open. This becoming free and being free is the essence of freedom. It thereby becomes evident that "The essence of truth is freedom" (12).

The lecture *Vom Wesen der Wahrheit* retraces those steps which *Sein und Zeit* and the essay *Vom Wesen des Grundes* have already taken. Truth, understood as the correctness of a correspondence, is reduced to resolute existence which is now grasped as freedom. *Vom Wesen der Wahrheit* then goes one step further. It interprets freedom as setting oneself free for what is manifest in the open, as "letting the being be" (14), and thus as immersion into the open of unconcealment and of what is unconcealed in it. The unconcealment is preserved by the immersion which is the self-exposing, ek-sistent admission into unconcealment. Freedom is the basis of the inner possibility of truth as the correctness of a correspondence, but this is so only "because it receives its own essence from the more primordial essence of the sole essential truth," from truth as unconcealment (14).[20]

Since freedom was grasped as the *abysmal* ground in *Vom Wesen des Grundes*, freedom's letting-oneself-into the truth as unconcealment must rediscover the abyss in truth, the staying away of the ground in grounding. The staying away of the ground shows itself in the essence of truth as the non-essence of untruth. Non-essence is not thought of here as the distortion of the universality of an essence grasped in the Platonic sense; nor is untruth thought of as the distortion of truth (correctness). Non-essence means a non-presence in the essence (to be thought verbally), a holding oneself back and in this sense the "pre-essential essence" (20). The untruth is truth holding itself back. Truth opens itself up only as unconcealment in that it holds itself back as concealment. The non-essence of truth, concealment, which belongs to the center and origin of the essence of unconcealment, is the "mystery." The mystery is not a riddle which can one day be solved, nor is it that which is simply closed

97

up, which is of absolutely no concern to us. Finally, it is not one mystery among others, but rather the one and only mystery, the concealment upon whose basis the unconcealment of beings as a whole and as such exists.

It belongs to the essence of concealment that it conceals itself and thereby sinks away into oblivion. The self-concealing concealment allows man to stand alongside the ordinary and the available, alongside the products of his activity. Nonetheless, at best concealment announces itself as what is unclarified and questionable in the ordinary or as the boundary of knowledge. If it is considered only in this manner, it has, as the *fundamental occurrence* in truth, already sunk into oblivion. Man, who, in accordance with his essence, ek-sists into the truth as unconcealment, insists; that is, he sticks obstinately to that "which beings open in themselves offer as they offer it from themselves" (21). He believes that he is able to create for himself the measures for his presenting and acting, and he forgets that every provision is based upon the concealment of unconcealment which is not at one's disposal. Thus he is in errancy which, as counter-essence, belongs to the non-essence in the essence of truth. Because errancy belongs to the essence of truth, no one escapes it. Error is bound up with *every* truth; it "extends from the most pedestrian slip-up and miscalculating to going astray and losing one's way in essential attitudes and decisions." In incorrect judgement and false knowledge, it shows itself only in the "most superficial manner" (22). Errancy is simultaneous with revealing—the unveiling of the truth of beings as such—and with concealment, the concealment of beings as a whole, that is, of the self-concealing of the concealment in unconcealment. In errancy appearance becomes powerful; it leads man to cover up and to disguise beings (17).

98

The decisive experience of thinking is that there exists a distinctive errancy, "the question about the *Being* of beings which is essentially misleading in its ambiguity and has therefore not been mastered." It is the question which has been understood since Plato as philosophy and then as metaphysics (23). Metaphysics insists upon the manifestation of beings, which is granted to itself, and thereby allows Being itself to sink away into oblivion. If from the errancy of this questioning thinking asks about Being, about mystery as the non-essence of truth, then it seeks to bring the question about Being out of its obstinate fixing upon the already granted but ungrounded openness. To common opinion (*doxa*), talk about the non-essence of truth may appear to be a paradox, but for the "initiated" "the 'non' of the incipient non-essence of truth as untruth points to the not-yet-experienced region of the truth of Being (and not just of beings)" (20).

Vom Wesen der Wahrheit leads to this question about the truth of Being.

Through the course of its development it is to show that this question is posed historically, "that the essence of truth is not the empty 'universality' of an 'abstract' generality. It is rather the self-concealing singularity of the unique history of the unveiling of the 'sense' of what we call Being and what we have been accustomed to consider for some time now only as the totality of beings" (25). The question about the essence of truth must turn toward the question about the truth of essence, the truth of the erring-fateful Being that presences. The question about truth, considered first (in *Vom Wesen des Grundes*) independently of the problem of "temporality" (that is, of the temporal character of the sense of Being), essentially develops into the question about the truth of Being, that is, how it is timely and fateful, "temporal" (SuZ 19). Already in the original plan, *Vom Wesen der Wahrheit* was to be supplemented by a lecture entitled *Von der Wahrheit des Wesens*. But this lecture was not completed (VWW 26). The question about Being and truth was not yet a point of focus. One first had to clarify the manner in which the question was to be raised at all. For this reason it was necessary to experience the singular errancy into which thinking had fallen, the error of metaphysics, *as* error. Thinking had to insert itself into metaphysics as that history about which the judgement is still outstanding.

6

METAPHYSICS AS HISTORY

If thinking does not merely suppose that time belongs to the region of the **100** sense or truth of Being, that is, if it rather experiences the temporal and historical character of the truth of Being, and if it inserts itself into the history of this truth, then going back into the ground of metaphysics becomes the intrinsically historical recovering of an ungrounded ground. The question of Being is unfolded in grappling with that thinking which historically determines our own, in grappling with metaphysics' thinking about Being. Metaphysics is experienced as the truth in which beings are thought as beings, their Being, but in which Being itself is not expressly experienced as Being, that is, from its truth. The question about the truth of Being becomes the question of a historical reflection. Therefore, along with *Vom Wesen der Wahrheit*, 1930–31, Heidegger begins to develop the question about *Platons Lehre von der Wahrheit* (we have a later version of the working out of this question which was first published in 1942). What began with Plato—metaphysics as the errancy of the questioning about Being—comes to an end, according to Heidegger's experience, with Nietzsche. It is completed in such a way that its essential possibilities are exhausted. It must therefore either be pursued further without question or placed into question in an entirely new way. Thus Nietzsche's thinking becomes decisive as the fulfillment and the end of metaphysics. Yet with Plato and Nietzsche metaphysics in general stands in question. It is a "problem" in that it is that history of Being about which the judgement is still lacking.

PLATO'S THEORY OF TRUTH

During the working out of *Sein und Zeit*, Heidegger interpreted Plato's *Sophist*; he could thus formulate the task of a new questioning about Being with a statement from this dialogue. In the course of developing the **101** question about the truth of Being, Heidegger, in explicating the parable of the cave from Plato's *Republic*, showed that the "unsaid" in Plato's thinking which determines the "said" is an alteration of the essence of truth. This alteration not only impressed itself upon later Greek thinking, but has also remained current "as the long established and, therefore, still fixed all-pervasive, fundamental reality of the world history of the earth, a world history which rolls on into its newest modernity" (PL 50).

It seems that Plato's parable of the cave does not deal with truth at all but rather with education. It shows how man must attain certain levels of an ascent if he wants to come out of the enclosure of his accustomed abode, the cave, and arrive at the open region of the light. He must accustom himself to each of the different levels, secure the fundamental direction of his striving in some attitude, and develop this attitude into a stable conduct. He must "form" himself, wring educational formation out of formlessness. In the case of his teacher Socrates, Plato had experienced that this struggling is a battle of life and death. The different levels which man attains in his self-education are differentiated respectively according to how they manifest beings, e.g., as the shadow of a copy, as the copy, as the reflection of beings, and as the being itself.[21] A being shows itself in the various levels of its unconcealment, but the unconcealed is the true. Consequently education seeks to free man for turning toward the uncon-cealed as the true. The essence of education, understood as liberation, as the way out of the chains and the cave and into the open air, is grounded in the essence of truth. Thus the parable of the cave indeed deals with education, but actually with truth.

Already in *Vom Wesen der Wahrheit* Heidegger showed how freedom is grounded in truth as unconcealedness. Now he seeks to grasp the fact that immediately after the beginning of Western thinking, the essence of truth is transformed, and the deliverance toward freedom, education, draws all attention to itself. Primordially experienced, truth is unconcealment. There can be a parable of the cave only there where the truth is thought in terms of the contest between unconcealment and concealment. Plato as well thinks of the truth in terms of unconcealment when he clarifies its essence in a cave parable. But Plato turns his attention not to the counteraction between concealment and unconcealment, but rather to unconcealment as mere "unconcealment," as mere revealing. "To be sure, unconcealment is named in its various stages, but it is considered only in terms of how it makes what appears accessible in its appearance (εἶδος) and how it makes visible this showing of itself (ἰδέα)" (PL 34). The consideration is for the idea which, as appearance, releases the view into the present and thus allows what is present (the being as that which appears) to be present in its permanence, in the visible aspect of its existence, and in this sense in its "Being." The idea, which is nonetheless the idea only on the basis of unconcealment, refers no longer to any concealment. If the essence of truth is understood in terms of the idea,

102

then truth surrenders the basic feature of unconcealment, the relation to concealment.

The idea is no longer subordinate to unconcealment; in service to the unconcealed, it no longer merely brings this unconcealed to appearance. It is rather the case that the appearance of the idea determines that which may be called "unconcealedness" within this appearance and solely in reference to it. The unconcealed is now what is accessible within the appearance of the idea (PL 46). Access to the unconcealed is opened and held open through a perceiving which, as a relation to the idea, is now a "seeing" in a distinctive sense. By means of education, this seeing must qualify itself to correctly measure up to the idea. Now it all comes down to the correctness ($\dot{o}\varrho\theta\acute{o}\tau\eta\varsigma$) of the perception of the idea. Thus there is a shift within the center of gravity in the essence of truth. Truth is no longer unconcealment as a basic feature of the beings themselves, but rather the correctness of perceiving and thus a characteristic of human conduct toward beings (PL 42). Truth turns into correctness from unconcealment. Correctness as the correspondence of knowing with a state of affairs (as $\dot{o}\mu o\acute{\iota}\omega\sigma\iota\varsigma$, *adaequatio*) is secured in knowledge, be it in human knowledge or else—as in the Middle Ages above all—in divine knowledge. Thus in recent times truth can become the certainty into which thinking brings itself, and when Nietzsche finally grasps the truth as a necessary type of error, he is still thinking truth in terms of the correctness which has become certainty.

103

Because Plato brings truth under the yoke of the idea, thinking becomes "philosophy," a knowing-one's-way, which is intrinsically an intimacy with and a special liking for the ideas which grant the unconcealed. Philosophy becomes what Plato had already called it; it becomes "metaphysics," a transcendence of shadowy beings toward the Being of beings. Since within the preference for the ideas and the transcendence toward Being there is a demand for correct measuring up to the ideas or to Being, the truth of Being itself—unconcealedness—sinks into oblivion, while "education" as the concern for the correctness of measuring up receives distinction. "Humanism," the concern about man, arises together with philosophy and metaphysics. This humanism places man—the individual or the community—in a "metaphysical, fundamental framework of beings" in order to free him for himself and his possibilities and to secure him in self-certainty. This liberation and assurance can happen in the most varied ways, "as the coining of the 'moral' attitude, the salvation of the immortal soul, the development of creative powers, the cultivation of reason, the fostering of personality, the awakening of the public spirit, the cultivation of the body, or as suitable combination of some or of all these 'humanisms'" (PL 49f). Thinking always circles around man; above all he is the concern, and everything is delivered up to him.

The transformation of the essence of truth, as it occurs in Plato's thought, is the presupposition for philosophy, metaphysics, and humanism, and in this sense for our very own present age. Heidegger is concerned with the limit and the hidden origin of this present essence when he points to what in Plato sinks into oblivion and then remains forgotten, the truth of Being. The work on *Platons Lehre von der Wahrheit* provides no image of Plato. It does not explicate the basic features of Plato's thinking, nor does it demonstrate the right and wrong of the Platonic theory of ideas. Even though Plato incorrectly brings truth in general under the yoke of the idea, it may nevertheless be the case that within limited spheres (for example, in the question about the essence), thinking rightfully, that is, from the phenomenon, thinks toward the idea, to a being which constantly makes present insofar as there is unconcealedness at all. In no way does Heidegger bring the entire Platonic theory of ideas into view. Had he wanted to attempt this, he would have had to show, for example, how the later Plato introduced "movement" or "life" into the realm of ideas in a new way. Heidegger's interpretation of the parable of the cave disregards all these questions and intentionally focuses upon only one matter, upon the change in the essence of truth which begins in Plato's thinking and which determines all of Western thought. However, *Sein und Zeit* is also determined by this change when it *first* sets out to liberate man for his unique freedom so that it can experience what previous thought has forgotten, the truth of Being. Above all, Heidegger's reflection on Plato is also a reflection upon his own point of departure. Therefore, Heidegger can place the *Brief über den Humanismus* alongside his work on Plato's theory of truth; he attempts to free his own intellectual approach from the metaphysical and humanistic, "anthropological" misinterpretation, and to have this attempt be seen as the way to the truth of Being itself.

NIETZSCHE AS THE TURNING POINT

The analysis of the "basic constitution of historicality" found in *Sein und Zeit* says that resolute Dasein hands to itself the possibilities it has inherited; that is, it grasps the heritage as possibility from out of Being free for its own death and thus comes into the "simplicity of its fate." The authentic repetition of a possibility of existence which has been, "that Dasein chooses its heroes for itself," is grounded in anticipatory resoluteness. Only from the fidelity to one's own fate can there arise the fidelity to what has been as that which can be repeated (SuZ 385). From such fidelity, Heidegger chooses Nietzsche as his hero in the repetition of the question of Being as the question of metaphysics. He does not "choose" this hero for himself, if by choosing one still thinks of a subjective arbitrariness; rather upon a definite stretch of his path of thinking he encounters Nietzsche as the thinker who hands down that which is to be thought.

Already in his *Habilitationsschrift* (4) Heidegger provided a reference to **105** Nietzsche. Nietzsche, "in his relentlessly austere thinking and imaginative skill at presentation," defined all philosophy from subjectivity with the formula "the drive that philosophizes." Heidegger had heard Rickert's lectures on Nietzsche. Thus Heidegger came into close contact with Nietzsche very early, even though his relationship to Nietzsche remained oriented to the question of value; thus his view was obstructed. Then, *Sein und Zeit*, at an important point in the analysis of historicity (396f), provided a reference to Nietzsche's *Zweite Unzeitgemässe Betrachtung* [*Second Untimely Meditation*]. Still, Nietzsche became decisive for Heidegger only in the years immediately following the appearance of *Sein und Zeit*. How Nietzsche became decisive is shown by Heidegger's next public reference to him. The rector's address of 1933 about the *Selbstbehauptung der deutschen Universität* stated: "And if indeed our unique Dasein itself stands before a great journey, if what Friedrich Nietzsche, the last German philosopher who passionately seeks God, says is true: 'God is dead'—if we must put into practice this abandonment of contemporary man in the midst of beings . . ." Nietzsche's phrase "God is dead" speaks of the truth of beings as a whole; it says that the ground in which this truth was grounded has lost the strength to ground. If one accepts this phrase, then what began with Plato comes to an end, the grounding of the truth of beings in a pre-eminently existing or highest being. If, like Nietzsche, one puts into practice God's abandonment of contemporary man in the midst of beings, then neither does there remain any longer that support based on a non-metaphysical theology, as *Sein und Zeit* still had it to the extent that this work opposed no less than it consigned Augustine, Pascal, and Kierkegaard to metaphysics and suggested Luther for a renewal of theology (SuZ 10). Because Nietzsche in his radical manner experiences the "death of God," the emasculation of the most pre-eminently existing being, he pushes to the extreme the question about Being as the truth of beings and about the sense of Being; his thinking calls for a decision regarding this question.

Heidegger does not want to provide a "portrait of Nietzsche"; he disregards Nietzsche as a person as well as his work insofar as it is conceived of as the expression and result of the person or of the age (NI, **106**

474). "The name of the thinker stands as the title for *the matter* of his thinking" (NI, 9), the name Nietzsche as the title for the determination of the question of Being. This matter, the question of Being, requires the highest pinnacle of thinking. Nietzsche is not regarded as the "existing" thinker whose testimony is supposed to arouse but not to be taken as binding. In such a relation to Nietzsche—for instance, as Jaspers represents him—one cannot, for example, think Nietzsche's decisive doctrine of eternal recurrence in accordance with its content nor as the consequence of the metaphysical beginning of thought; this is so because the appeal to what is incomprehensible and existentiell cancelled from the outset the binding nature of what is expressed (NI, 32). The confrontation with Nietzsche should clarify in precisely *which* manner there is a binding "truth of the concept" in the question of Being. It should become apparent that in its own way Nietzsche's thinking "is no less *weighty* and rigorous than the thinking of Aristotle" (Hw 230).

Since Heidegger, in his confrontation with Nietzsche, is concerned with settling the question about Being, he must forego all that previously stood in the foreground of the turn toward Nietzsche: letting oneself be stimulated and aroused, the sharpening of one's view for psychological and moral phenomena, cultural criticism and cultural propaganda, the struggle of world views with, against, and around Nietzsche. Heidegger can learn little from the previous literature about Nietzsche because he approaches Nietzsche with a raising of the question that is entirely different from the accustomed one. He conducts his examination of Nietzsche in those years when Nietzsche was temporarily and in part claimed for the National-Socialist world view; and thus when the grossest misuse of Nietzsche's thought was being carried out, Heidegger tries to lead the way out of this abuse, indeed out of every mere use of Nietzsche's thought—and for what thinker or poet of our time would Nietzsche not be the stimulator or adversary, the great watershed? He does so in that he asks how the struggle of world views, or, as Nietzsche says, the struggle for the domination of the earth in the name of philosophical fundamental doctrines, has come about at all. Are the decisions to which Nietzsche challenges our time the decisions which really matter? Or is it necessary to arrive first at a decision about the space in which the "for" and "against Nietzsche" operate? Since Heidegger raises the question of Being in his examination of Nietzsche, he thinks ahead to the following question: is man, as Nietzsche and metaphysics instruct him, to set himself up as lord of the earth, or is he to forego the mere mastery of the totality of beings and the struggle, thought out by Nietzsche, for domination of the world in favor of a decision for another relation to the totality of beings (cf. NII, 262).

107

Nietzsche thinks of what the metaphysical tradition calls the Being of beings as the eternally recurrent will to power. Through the course of thought [*Gedanken-Gang*] leading to the will to power, Nietzsche "lays a course" into the "history of Being," "into the still untraversed regions of future decisions" (NI, 475). Heidegger finds the transcript for the ways of this way of thought not in Nietzsche's published works, but rather in the posthumous notes. The posthumous notes are Nietzsche's "genuine philosophy" while the published works of Nietzsche remain "always a foreground" (NI, 17). Not until 1880 to 1883 does Nietzsche find himself; the subsequent years are aimed at working out the "main work" which never took on a final form. "During this time when Nietzsche was at his height the truth of beings as such wants to become expressed in language. One course of action replaces the other. One after the other reveals the framework of what the thinker wants to say. First the 'eternal recurrence' is the main title, then 'the will to power', then 'the transvaluation of values'. Where the one title recedes, it appears as the title for the concluding piece of the whole, or as the subtitle of the main heading" (NII, 259; 124f). According to Heidegger, Nietzsche attains greatest clarity and calm in his thinking in the years 1887–88, shortly before his breakdown; Heidegger therefore favors notes from this time (NI, 486; II, 44). Indeed Heidegger believes that Nietzsche's last so-called "development" "leaves behind all he overcame on the path of his thinking" (NI, 618). However, shortly before his plunge into insanity, a singular uneasiness comes over Nietzsche. In the last writings he no longer waits for the slow maturation of his work; he attempts to prove himself and to make his position in the world obvious (NI, 17). But these last writings, the "outcry" of Nietzsche, are not those upon which Heidegger finds support.

108

The posthumous notes, Nietzsche's "genuine philosophy," were edited —at least in part—in a work which was entitled *Der Wille zur Macht*—in accordance with a plan of Nietzsche that was merely one specific plan among others. In his lectures, Heidegger becomes more and more critical about this "work" which, as presented, is not Nietzsche's work but rather a patching together of Nietzsche's texts for which the editors are responsible (NI, 17f, 327ff, 412ff; NII 42f). As he worked on Nietzsche, Heidegger had been appointed to the commission for the historical-critical publication of Nietzsche's works, and he had taken it upon himself as a special task to contribute his part to a proper edition of the posthumous notes. However, following a conflict with the then public authorities, he withdrew from this commission. Work on the new edition of Nietzsche's posthumous notes, interrupted by the war, has not yet been adequately taken up again.

In light of this, an attempt to show the unity of Nietzsche's course of thought encounters the greatest difficulties. The one who attempts to follow Heidegger's difficult attempt at interpretation encounters the further difficulty that Heidegger himself is still "under way," that the lectures and essays cannot be put on one level and thus be worked out. For example, in the rector's address of 1933 which contained the first decisive public reference to Nietzsche, Heidegger demands nothing more decisive than the "willing," which intrinsically allows the essential, that which matters, to come "to power." Yet in the first Nietzsche lecture he believes that one can interpret the "creation" of the "superman" as "preparing for readiness for the gods, the yes to Being" (NI, 254). However, Heidegger's examination of Nietzsche finally comes to the experience that precisely the will and its wanting to create, as it becomes dominant in modern times, hinder an experience of the truth of Being and thereby obstruct being open for what is essential, indeed the divine. His examination of Nietzsche as the determination about settling the question of Being is also a decision about Heidegger's thinking, a way upon which Heidegger works off definite presuppositions which determined his thinking.

109

If the examination of Nietzsche becomes decisive for the question of Being, then an entirely foreign theme, the theme of Being, appears to be forced upon Nietzsche's thinking. In fact, Heidegger is not concerned with following Nietzsche's conception of himself. The question which Heidegger develops is rather the question of how Nietzsche fits in the tradition of Western thinking, how his thinking is determined by this tradition, and how it in turn determines the tradition, whether Nietzsche expressly experiences and knows this or not. Heidegger subordinates his reflection on Nietzsche to the all-embracing presupposition that the Western tradition gathers and is brought to completion in Nietzsche's thinking in accordance with a consideration that is decisive for us in this time of transition. In this way, the examination of Nietzsche becomes an examination of previous Western thought in general. This examination must follow Nietzsche's thinking "into its effective power rather than into its weak aspects," but it does so "in order that we ourselves become free for the highest effort of thought" by means of the examination (NI, 13). We must not allow ourselves to be misled by the fact that Nietzsche sometimes expresses his concern in the inadequate language of his time; we must rather think what is said back into the totality of the Western tradition and thus bring it up for decision. Whoever tries to accomplish this task must confine himself to what is most essential. "Yet in all of this it remains crucial to hear Nietzsche himself, to question with him, through him, *and thus at the same time against him*, but *for* the one single, common, innermost matter of Western philosophy" (NI, 33).

Heidegger grasps the matter of Western thinking under the name "Being." As "metaphysics," Western thinking brings Being into the discussion as the truth of beings. Nietzsche's thinking is also metaphysics, not metaphysics as a definite, philosophical discipline, but rather metaphysics as the truth about beings. Nietzsche's thinking is the metaphysics of our age. This metaphysics thinks out in advance the main features of the age in which the struggle for the domination of the earth is carried out **110** and takes part in this struggle itself. Heidegger's examination of Nietzsche has a proximate as well as a distant goal: the proximate goal is the representation of the inner unity which Nietzsche's metaphysical fundamental position has as the fundamental position of our age; the distant goal is the development of the question as to whether the highest conflict to be waged is the metaphysical struggle for domination of the earth, or whether our history can find another beginning which is no longer metaphysical (NII, 261f).

Consequently what matters first of all is to comprehend Nietzsche's thinking as an intrinsically unified metaphysics, as the truth about beings, but thus to understand Nietzsche's metaphysical fundamental position as the consequence of Western metaphysical thinking and thereby as that thinking which permits the essential features of our age to be seen. In his first lecture course on Nietzsche, Heidegger grasps the uniformity of Nietzsche's metaphysical fundamental position as the unity of the thoughts of the will to power, eternal recurrence, and revaluation (NI, 25). Later the thought of revaluation is articulated into the notions of truth as evaluation or justice, of nihilism as the history of evaluation and revaluation, and of the superman as the one who accomplishes the revaluation (NII, 40, 257ff, cf. also the articulation of a fundamental metaphysical position in accordance with only four respects: NII, 137). Heidegger grounds the unfolding of Nietzsche's metaphysical fundamental position according to its necessity in the essence of metaphysics in general. Metaphysics is the truth of beings as such and in totality. It asks *what* a being is—Nietzsche specifies the will to power as the being-ness of a being. It brings to language that the totality of beings is and how it is—according to Nietzsche the totality of beings is in the manner of the eternal recurrence of the same. Metaphysics brings beings into their unconcealment or truth—the essence of truth, as Nietzsche thinks it, is justice. This truth has a history—according to Nietzsche this history is nihilism. This history demands a mankind which provides the decision regarding it—Nietzsche's superman (NII, 257ff). Each of the *five fundamental thoughts of Nietzsche* is first of all to be exhibited here in its own right, but always in reference to the totality by which it is determined.

111   1. The *will to power* is for Nietzsche the fundamental characteristic of
life and that means of Being. This will does not want power as something
other, as the goal which lies outside of itself; it is rather will as power. If
the will becomes will to power, it is not then given a new goal (in power),
but rather that which is commonly understood as will becomes altered in
its essence (NI, 52). The willing of the will is no longer thought of as
wishing or striving, but as a commanding which empowers itself with
respect to itself. As command the will is the accomplishment of having
oneself at one's own disposal. Power is the preservation and enhancement
of power; it *steadies* itself toward itself and secures itself in itself in order to
be able to surpass itself again and again. As the empowering toward the
overpowering of itself, power is constantly underway to itself and is,
therefore, the Being of beings as a becoming (NII, 263ff).

In the language of *Sein und Zeit*, the will to power is "resoluteness"
which does not encapsulate itself in the resolving ego, but rather stands in
the totality of beings (NI, 59). In willing, or even in not willing, will to
power brings beings to light, "and indeed into a light which is first kindled
by means of willing itself" (NI, 63). Just as strongly as Heidegger
accentuates the character of willing and command, he emphasizes that
side in the will to power in accordance with which this will is non-will.
The will itself cannot be willed since all willing is already will. Will is the
attuned (thrown) resoluteness (with a state-of-mind). It is just as much a
command and "being lord over . . ." which reaches beyond itself as it is
emotion—the blindly stimulating shock, passion—the sweeping away
which reaches out into the expanse of beings, and the unity of emotion and
passion, feeling—the attunement which is unclosedness for beings and
thereby also for itself (NI, 59, 64, 71).

When Nietzsche grasps the will to power in terms of command,
emotion, passion, and feeling, does he not then understand the Being of
beings (will to power) in terms of a certain being (man)? Certainly
Nietzsche travels in a circle here, but never in such a way that he
(directly) utilizes philosophically the results of a definite science (I, 54f).
The will to power is nothing which could be conceived of psycho-
logically—for instance, even as one faculty of the soul among others;
112   rather the projection of beings upon their Being, will to power, is a
metaphysical projection. And when Nietzsche wants to grasp psychology as
"the morphology and the theory of development of the will to power"
(NII, 60ff, 263f), then he does not undermine metaphysics psychologi-
cally, but rather takes—and this is what must genuinely be grasped—
something other than the customary psychology as metaphysics, as the
truth about beings.

But does Nietzsche not proceed arbitrarily when he addresses the Being of beings as will to power? Heidegger points out that the great modern philosophers from Leibniz to Schelling have found the "most basic Being" in willing (NI, 44f). And if Nietzsche grasps the power in will to power as strength, as being mighty and as being-at-work, as being-out-beyond-oneself, and as coming-toward-oneself, then he follows the course which Aristotle and the thinkers before Aristotle have already travelled: in his metaphysics, Aristotle deals with δύναμις, ἐνέργεια, and ἐντελέχεια as the highest determinations of Being (NI, 78f). The attempt to determine the Being of beings as will to power is so little an arbitrary one that perhaps it even has a consequence. We will still have to ask about this consequence when we try to think along with Heidegger about the unity of Nietzsche's fundamental thoughts.

2. In will to power, Nietzsche thinks beings as such, beings in their Being. In the *thought of the eternal recurrence of the same*, Nietzsche thinks the manner in which the totality of beings is, the manner in which the Being of beings is as Being: the totality of beings comes back eternally into itself. The will to power, the Being of beings as constantly becoming, is no longer drawn toward a goal lying beyond it, but neither is it thought of as aimlessly advancing and subsiding becoming; rather, as the eternally recurrent becoming, it is brought to a stand and placed upon itself. The thought of eternal recurrence stands so little in simple opposition to the theory of will to power that the latter does not come to completion until the thought of recurrence.

If the theory of will to power is proof of an "ultimate fact to which we descend," then the thought of the eternal recurrence is the "thought of thoughts," the "most weighty thought" (NI, 417, 274, 276). This most weighty thought is portrayed by Nietzsche as a course of proof. Nietzsche, **113** so it appears, thinks of the world in its total character and he thinks of it as force. He thinks of this force as finite and limited so that for him the totality of the world itself also remains finite. The totality of the world is nonetheless not an equilibrium of force, but rather a constant becoming. The becoming, the movement of the finite world, runs its course in a time which—unlike space—is actual and unlimited. In this endless time the movement of the world must run back into itself, because it achieves no state of equilibrium. (If this state were at all achievable, then it must have been achieved already in the endless time of the past.) The becoming which runs back into itself is eternal recurrence. It could be avoided only if an anticipatory purpose and a fixing of an aim would have excluded it. Nietzsche, however, excludes such intentions and goal-setting insofar as he thinks of the world as "chaos" and thereby disallows in advance any ordering will of a creator (NI, 341ff, 369ff).[22]

Nietzsche's course of proof, Heidegger says, is not that of natural science because natural science as science presupposes precisely what Nietzsche places in question, the concepts of force, finitude, becoming, space, time, and so forth (NI, 371ff). This course of proof in accordance with its unique essence is not that of natural science nor even a course of proof at all. Here one does not "arrive logically at the principle of eternal recurrence from previously established propositions about the nature of the world"; rather, these propositions first become proposable at all through the development of a metaphysical projection. "What sets itself up representationally as proof is only the revelation of positions which are co-posited, indeed, necessarily co-posited in the projection of the totality of beings upon Being as eternally recurring in the same" (NI, 377). This development of projection can never be the calculation or exploration of projection, but rather the "leap" into the "riddle" of the totality of beings and thus an "experiment" with truth (NI, 289f). Since the thought of eternal recurrence was hardly computed and arrived at from previously secured propositions, it in fact had to "come" to Nietzsche at a completely specific time and place, in August of 1881, 6000 feet beyond man and time, before a mighty, pyramidal, towering block of stone in Engadin. The thought came—as all great thoughts—only "because it—unimagined-ly—was prepared for and sustained through a long labor." It demanded the resolute devotion of a thinking which could not discuss its decisive thought because the former was to be the abode of the latter's unfolding (NI, 263f).

114

The truth of the thought of eternal recurrence can "never directly be proven or be demonstrated" in its actuality by facts because the return cannot be read off from beings at all. The thought of eternal recurrence grasps the how of the totality of beings, and there cannot be a man who would place before himself the totality of beings and who as a spectator would read something from it. "Consequently, what is thought in this thought is never given as a present-at-hand, individual reality, but only as one possibility" (NI, 392). The thought of recurrence can only be thought if the leap into the totality of beings grasps it as possibility. As the thought of a possibility, this thought requires that it be appropriated in freedom, and it is not thought at all if the thinker reckons up the totality of beings in terms of eternal recurrence and thereby forgets his freedom. We therefore go astray if we set eternal recurrence conceived as a necessity opposite freedom and thus force the thought of recurrence into the traditional schema of opposition, "necessity-freedom" (NI, 395ff). As the thought of a possibility which claims to be appropriated in freedom, the thought of recurrence requires a "thinking from out of the moment." The recurrence and its eternal character require that they be grasped in the moment as the authentic temporalizing of time; they are only for one "who does not remain a spectator, but who *is himself* the moment" (NI, 311). The moment in which eternity is at stake is not representable as a point in time; thus the recurrence cannot be calculated chronologically. Between the one recurrence and the other there lies no time at all insofar as time is regarded as calculable and presentable. "It passes as quickly as a lightning bolt, even though living creatures measure it according to billions of years and could not even measure it" (cf. NI, 399f). The moment is the decision upon which everything depends. Nietzsche thinks the thought of recurrence as the "crisis" in which European history changes as the history of nihilism. Nihilism is "the event of the disappearance of all **115** consequence from everything," and only that thinking which puts "an end to the concealment and masking of this event" can find new importance in the thought of eternal recurrence (NI, 421). The idea of the return is thought only if it is thought as a "counter-thought" to nihilism, and experienced as the decision about Western history (NI, 434, 446f).

By means of penetrating images, Nietzsche has delimited the thinking of eternal recurrence from that thinking which does not think out of freedom, the moment, and decision. He introduced (in the *Fröhliche Wissenschaft*) the thought as a possibility with which a demon tempts man (cf. NI, 270). Tragedy begins with the thinking of this thought (NI, 278ff), that tragic way upon which the hero comes to himself only by his downfall. This way is the way of Zarathustra who only in the most serious illness learned to say yes to the fact that everything, even that which is most contemptible, suffering, evil, and destruction, all recur, stand eternally in themselves (NI, 312, 315). Zarathustra leaves behind the dwarf who indeed thinks the return but not as the moment (NI, 292ff). Zarathustra sees through the song of the animals. "Everything passes, everything comes back; the wheel of Being" rolls eternally as does a song of a barrel organ and lyre. He must also put up with the animals, who merely look at everything and do not think out of decision, as well as with their song, this perversion of the thought of recurrence. The recurrence can be thought only by the young shepherd into whose throat a black snake—the gloomy monotony and pointlessness of nihilism—crawled and who cannot become free of this snake without biting off its head. The thought of recurrence is only this bite, this decision about the history of nihilism (NI, 445).

Heidegger's portrayal of the doctrine of the eternal recurrence is determined by the conviction which governs everything; that is, in this theory *what* is taught recedes in significance behind *how* it is taught (NI, 332). The how is decisive because the thought of the eternal return is separated

116 from its inversion only by the "smallest gap," which is the most difficult to bridge precisely because it has not opened up enough. The animals use the same words as Zarathustra in their barrel-organ song, which is passed off so often as Nietzsche's own theory, and yet these words are in truth only "rainbows and illusory bridges between what remains forever apart" (NI, 307). Actually, in the theory of the eternal return the phrase "everything is the same" can have two meanings. It can mean that every moment is of no consequence because everything indeed returns; there is no freedom and no decision since everything necessarily returns. Yet it can also mean that everything returns, that every moment is a matter of supreme decision, the decision for eternity, and nothing, therefore, is inconsequent. Heidegger's interpretation of the theory of return has to be distinguished not only from an interpretation capable of thinking this theory only as the dwarf in "Zarathustra" does, and therefore not at all (NI, 295), but also from an interpretation devoted to Nietzsche's theory of eternal return because it believes it has experienced that whatever can happen is without purpose, goal, or sense.

In the theory of return, the how is therefore more decisive than the what because man must first still transform himself into that man or superman who is capable of thinking this theory (NI, 284). Not until one finds the "how" will the "what" also come to the fore; beyond the "how" the "what" changes the man who thinks the thought of return. "With respect to this thought, *what* is to be thought strikes back at the thinker by means of *how* it is to be thought and presses him hard; again, it does this only to draw him into that which is to be thought" (NI, 447). (Heidegger's words here correspond directly to Augustine's statements about truth; indeed Heidegger's interpretation of the theory of the eternal return of the same generally calls to mind directly and repeatedly his earlier statements about Christian hope for the moment of Christ's return.) The thought of the return therefore strikes back at the thinker and draws him into what is to be thought, because this thought is a "metaphysical thought," a thought about the totality of beings (NI, 448). As a metaphysical thought, it opposes and thereby also relates to Plato's theory, that the totality of beings has its essence in the ideas, as well as to the biblical, Judeo-Christian conception of the "world" as creation (NI, 257). Does not Nietzsche himself ask whether the ring which comprises eternal return is a **117** *circulus vitiosus deus* (NI, 320f)? Does not Heidegger correctly use a statement of Nietzsche about God and world as the guiding thought for his lecture *Die ewige Wiederkehr des Gleichen* [*The Eternal Recurrence of the Same*] (NI, 255, 472f)? To be sure, the thought of eternal recurrence is the *counter*-thought against Platonism which pushes the idea out beyond beings and thereby beyond human willing as that which intrinsically is; it is also the *counter*-thought against the Judeo-Christian belief which places beings in the hand of God and thus removes them beyond human reach. In recurrence, nothing other returns than will to power itself; this stands on its own in that it wills itself as eternally recurring. But if Nietzsche thinks of will to power as permanent, as what steadies itself toward itself, then is not his way of thinking still similar to metaphysics, which takes Being as constant presence?

3. The question arises as to how Nietzsche in general thinks Being as the *truth* about beings. Nietzsche thinks what is true in truth, but for him, as for Plato, this is what is *"truthful,"* the steadfast being, as it is only for thinking cognition. Yet in contrast to the knowledge of truth, Nietzsche proposes art as another way to accomplish the openness of beings and, thereby, "truth" in a broader sense. *Art and knowledge* are two ways in which will to power as the Being of beings is the *truth* about beings.

Nietzsche asks about art at a time in which the Western philosophy of art came to completion in Hegel's theory of the end of art, at a time which actually lacks a great art laying down a standard binding upon all. To be sure, there are still artworks which have a certain compellingness for particular classes of people. In addition, there is still artistic activity, but it no longer stands in the service of a great self-reflection on the part of Dasein as it did with Herder and Winkelmann; this activity rather more and more becomes a special branch of knowledge (NI, 107). There is also Richard Wagner's attempt once more to represent an "absolute" in a "total work of art." "However, the absolute is now experienced only as the purely indeterminate, as complete disintegration into pure feeling, the sinking floating in nothing" (NI, 104). Nietzsche, at first passionately interested in Wagner's great endeavor, soon realized that Wagnerian music lacked style, that in it a pseudo-Christianity was mixed with fervent love and rapture. Thus Nietzsche had to begin the quarrel with Wagner for the sake of the matter of art.   **118**

For Nietzsche, art is something exalted and decisive. Art is the counter-movement to the movement of nihilism which continues to embrace philosophy, morality, and religion. Art can be this countermovement because it is the most transparent form of will to power, and because it gives a view of will to power as the Being of beings. Art, grasped in terms of the artist, is the fundamental occurrence in every being, namely, the occurrence of creation and self-creation; thus it is will to power. The artist who produces the works of "fine art" is an artist only in a particular, narrow sense. As a creator, the man of will to power is, in general, an artist (NI, 82ff).

Nietzsche grasps art "aesthetically," that is, in terms of the artist, of man and his perceiving. He thinks of aesthetics "physiologically" by taking sensuality and the body as a guide. He specifies "intoxication" as the basic aesthetic state, the feeling of strength and fullness, the feeling in oneself of will to power. What is beautiful, that which "we value and honor as the model of our nature, determines intoxication as attunement" (NI, 132).[23] It is so little a seething and boiling of feeling and a sinking into experience that creation, the fundamental state of intoxication, is characterized by order, limit, control—by what Nietzsche calls form in the conceptual language of aesthetics (NI, 139, 95f). The desire for the ordered is a fundamental condition of embodying life. Intoxication and beauty, creation and form submit to the unity of the "grand style" which is a form of life as will to power (NI, 143, 162).

How can art thought in a physiological aesthetic of intoxication, and thus of sensibility and the body, be a countermovement against nihilism? For Nietzsche, nihilism is the "Platonism" which finds what is true in the transcendental idea, an idea which shows itself to knowledge only when the latter has freed itself from sensibility. The application of the transcendental idea as the true being slanders embodying life; it weakens and empties it and is, therefore, nihilism. Consequently, the countermovement against nihilism must be an inversion of Platonism. Art thought in terms of sensibility offers the possibility of such a reversal, a saving of embodying life. Art opposes "truth," and Nietzsche speaks about a discrepancy between art and truth which gives rise to dismay. For the reversal of Platonism, which is not to be mere positivism but rather the decision about nihilism, he suggests the principle: art is worth more than the truth (NI, 166f).

In Platonism, as Plato himself develops it in the *Republic*, art is subordinate to truth, the transcendental idea. Consequently, truth is worth more than art. In the *Phaedrus*, Plato also thinks the relationship of truth and beauty as a schism. Beauty stands in conflict with truth because it illuminates on the level of the senses (of the sensuous), whereas truth does so on a supersensible level. Yet this discord is one that brings happiness since beauty corresponds with what is true in that it can also manifest Being, show Being precisely in the sensuous (NI, 227f).[24] In the reversal of Platonism, the happy discord between truth and art becomes one that stimulates dismay. The "apparent world" of art is placed above the "true world" of knowledge. The true world is "abolished"—but does not the "apparent world" thereby also fall? Nietzsche himself speaks in this way (NI, 240), but he thereby simply announces that his reversal of Platonism is really an unscrewing of thinking out of Platonism. Nietzsche does not simply want to eliminate the transcendental world; he flatly demands an ever greater spiritualization. He wants to eliminate only the "misinterpretation and the denouncement of the sensuous" as well as the "overdoing of the transcendental." He does not simply want to reverse the Platonic order of precedence of the sensuous and transcendental but rather to think it anew (NI, 242).

Nietzsche finds the fundamental actuality in the sensible. It is the genuine reality to which the transcendental, namely, as appearance, also belongs. Reality is intrinsically "perspectival." Every living thing is open to another; that is, it has an angle of vision in accordance with which it interprets in terms of its own life everything that it encounters. "This **120** perspective and its region of vision mark out what in general confronts the organism and what does not. For example, the lizard hears the slightest rustle in the grass, but it does not hear a pistol shot discharged in its closest proximity" (NI, 244). Appearance belongs to the perspectival life in a double sense. In the first place, appearance is the solidification of one of the several perspectives in life which contest with one another. Such solidification of a perspective produces what is permanent, the "true world," "Being" in the Platonic sense. As the solidification of *one* of life's many perspectives, appearance is mere "semblance." As mere semblance, what is true, Being, is error, but nonetheless a necessary error since solidification and making permanent is necessary for life if it is not to slip away. In the second place, appearance belongs to life as the transfiguration and the exaltation of life, as that "shining forth" of new possibilities as produced by art, the genuine "metaphysical" activity of life. To be sure, the appearance of art as appearance is also mere semblance because it must also establish a definite possibility of the transfiguration of life (NII, 317). Still, art as transfiguration and exaltation of life is more life-enhancing than truth, the mere making permanent as semblance. Thus art is "worth more" than truth. Within the one reality of life, truth and art separate from one another as the fixing of appearance as mere semblance and as the exaltation and the transfiguration of life as the shining forth of truth "to be created."

In his lecture, *Der Wille zur Macht als Erkenntnis*, Heidegger shows along with Nietzsche how Western metaphysics takes non-sensuous thinking, representation, placing-into-view, and thus the providing of a constant semblance as the guide for the interpretation of beings as beings. Reason becomes the court of judgement about beings. It determines that only that which can be represented as constant presence ought to be counted as being (NI, 496, 530f). Yet in no way is it now established that the totality of beings is in its Being a constant presence. Rather, Western man has "at the same time displaced this which matters in his life out into the 'world', into the 'totality', because somehow what matters to him first and last is constancy, endurance, and eternity" (NI, 545).

121   Nietzsche takes this crystallization of a "true world" back into the life
which posits it. Truth is useful for life, it is an asset for it, a necessary
condition insofar as life must stabilize itself so that it does not melt away.
If the totality of beings is "chaos," embodying life, then knowledge as
holding-as-true is the "schematizing" of chaos in accordance with a
"practical need." Out of life's need not to succumb to its pressure and to
have Being in its becoming, the praxis of the accomplishment of life must
fix life in schemata ("categories") and thus differentiate Being and becoming. As the stabilizing of becoming into Being, truth is a necessary
asset, even if only a necessary error, since it is not, like art, in harmony
with life as chaos and becoming. Nietzsche so little opposes the sciences
that he even demonstrates the necessity of their manner of knowing (NI,
581).

       According to Nietzsche, the true as stabilized life arises not from
adaptation to something present-at-hand, something fixed in itself, but
rather from the command which life as will to power gives itself. Knowledge is for Nietzsche no longer the setting-forth of a being upon its Being
as its "in-itself," but rather setting-forth. Life establishes itself in the
"framing" of a "form" (NI, 576, 607ff). Thus, unlike Aristotle, Nietzsche
does not interpret the principle of contradiction as a principle of "Being"
which could not simultaneously both be and not be, but rather as a
command which life gives to itself out of an inner need (NI, 602ff).

       If Nietzsche abolished the "true world" of Platonism, if he as well
brought his thinking out of the mere reversal of Platonism, in other words,
if every orientation to a "true" world, present-at-hand, and "in-itself"
falls away, what then will become of the essence of truth—"truth" taken
here in a wider sense as the truth of art and the truth of knowledge? Will to
power instructs itself in the conditions for every holding-as-true of knowledge as well as for the possibilities of transfiguring life through art. The
will roots art and truth in its empowering-itself-toward-itself and its
overpowering-of-itself. Except for itself, the will to power can find no
measure and no guide which could justify its knowledge and the creation
122   of its art; consequently, will to power is the vindication and justice for
itself, and this justice is "the basis of the necessity and the possibility of
every type of harmony between man and chaos whether this harmony is
the higher one of art or the equally necessary one of knowledge" (NI,
647f); ("equally necessary" was inadvertently omitted in the printed
text). Nietzsche himself certainly never thought the essence of truth in
terms of justice; despite this, Heidegger believes that he is following
Nietzsche's course of thought when he interprets Nietzsche's understanding of the essence of the truth in terms of Nietzsche's thought about
justice. Justice, as Nietzsche thinks it, is certainly not the justice which

appeals to a law present-at-hand in itself. This justice is rather the justice of the "immoralist" who forbids himself the appeal to a "true world" existing in itself, an appeal which has become hypocrisy, and thus believes himself to be "beyond good and evil" (NI, 626ff). The justice of will to power instructs itself in the conditions. Thus it is "building," establishing the direction and law for what is to be true in the future. Consequently it is also exclusionary, even "destructive," as it surpasses previous fixing of standards. It is then, finally, the "highest representative of life itself." Life, which is will to power and wants nothing but itself, represents itself in justice; it portrays itself and focuses everything back upon itself and is, therefore, in its truth.

If Nietzsche thinks truth as justice, does he then still hold to the course of the Western notion of truth? He brings this notion of truth to its extreme consequence. The fact that truth can be thought of as justice presupposes that the primordial essence of truth, its essence as unconcealment, was forgotten at the beginning of Western philosophy in favor of truth as an accurate measure. In modern times, truth as correctness changed into truth as the certainty in which representational thinking secures itself. For Descartes, Leibniz, Kant, and Hegel, truth as self-certainty became in increasing measure the justification which thought brings to completion in the presence of itself. It was not by accident that at the beginning of the modern age the question about the certainty of salvation became the question of justification (Hw 225f). Nietzsche pushes the metaphysical, recently transformed essence of truth to extremes; thus he finally conceals the original essence of truth, unconcealment. Nevertheless he still lays claim to an essential movement of the obstructed and concealed unconcealment when he interprets art in terms of the shining forth which transfigures and surpasses (NII, 318). At the same time he brings back in his manner something else from the Heraclitean concept of truth when he seeks to unmask the truth of knowledge, the making permanent, as error and illusion.

123

4. Nietzsche has experienced the history of the transformation of truth about beings, but not as something which one could establish and report with the equanimity of the historian. It is rather that history—as the history of nihilism—which demands an ultimate decision from us or destroys us. Nihilism is the history in which it becomes evident that it is of no use to find what, as having the most being and as authentically "true," determines all beings. Nihilism is, as Nietzsche says, the "devaluing" of the "highest values." According to Nietzsche's experience, this nihilism dominates not only his century, but is rather the fundamental characteristic, indeed the lawfulness and logic of all of Western history. It will even

determine the next centuries. The devaluation of traditional values is not the first sign of nihilism. Nihilism is already present when values are fixed at all as the "in itself" of beings, when Platonism takes a transcendental, other world as the measure of the sensuous and of this world so that the latter (life) are devalued. Insofar as Christianity devalues this-worldly existence as a "valley of tears," as the mere passage to a beyond, it is, as a "Platonism for the people," also nihilism. (Nietzsche grasps Christianity as that world-political determination which has formed Western history. Whether his experience at all encompasses what is Christian in New Testament faith, which is indeed to be distinguished from "Christianity," need not be gone into here [cf. Hw 202f].) To the extent that the name "God" is also the name for the metaphysical-transcendental, Nietzsche can express the consequence of nihilism in the phrase: "God is dead" (NII, 33f, Hw 193ff).

124　　The decision which Nietzsche demands with respect to nihilism is the "revaluation of values." This revaluation does not simply put new values in the place of old ones. According to Nietzsche, Platonic-Christian thinking is not in the wrong because it establishes values, but rather because it mistakenly puts these values in a region of the in-itself; thus in its powerlessness toward power, it does not grasp the values as the establishing of values of will to power (NII, 82, 89, 117, 121). If new values are put in place of old values, if the moral law, the authority of reason, progress, the happiness of the greatest number, culture or civilization, step into God's place, this in no way shatters the basic Platonic-Christian framework "in accordance with which a positing of goals reaching into the transcendental dominates sensuous, earthly life" (Hw 203, 208). A time of transition dawdles about in different forms of "incomplete nihilism"; thus it averts the seriousness of the decision as Nietzsche requires it—that decision to think in another manner of the place of the positing of values, to take values back into value-positing will to power.

How does Nietzsche even come to understand the history of the truth of the totality of beings in terms of valuation and revaluation, to understand metaphysics morally? Plato thinks the Being of beings as ἰδέα; he finds the fundamental character of the idea, the idea of ideas, in ἀγαθόν, in making something capable. "The essence of the ἰδέα is to make something capable, that is, to enable a being as such so that it presences in the unconcealed" (NII, 225f). If Being is conceived of as idea, then it comes to have the character of enabling and conditioning. Yet it is in no way already thought of as "value," either in terms of powerlessness toward value-positing will to power or in terms of power toward power. Being as ἰδέα is rather thought of in terms of the Φύσις which holds sway, which produces unconcealedness and thus lets being be a being in the ἰδέα. However, through the interpretation of Being as idea, the emphasis in the essence of truth shifts from unconcealedness to the accomplishment of this unconcealedness, to the thinking which seeks to measure up to the idea. Truth becomes the correctness of the thinking which catches sight of the idea, and thinking—be it divine thinking or, in modern times, finally human thinking—becomes the place where truth is decided. Consequently, the previous theory of ideas becomes the *a priori*, which always belongs to thinking as the representing of a being as a being. The idea changes from the condition of the possibility of experience itself as well as of the objects of experience to that condition which enables man to represent beings as beings (Kant) (and that now means objects as objects). In the representing and delivering of objects, willing holds sway as the essence of representing, and if representing unconditionally enables itself toward itself, it reveals itself as will to power. The Being of beings, the idea which makes capable, the condition of the possibility of the experience of objects now becomes value. Value is the viewpoint which is posited by will to power in order that this will can aim at something, in order that it can account and value, in order that it can empower itself toward itself and overpower itself. There are values in the genuine sense of this word only in the epoch of will to power (NII, 48, 98), and only in the "revaluation of values" is value grasped *as value*, that is, from will to power as power toward power (NII, 282). When Nietzsche characterizes Being, and that means the truth of beings, as value, he brings to light what has been sketched out in metaphysics since its beginning, that Being as the enabling of beings must come to be at the disposal of representation (NII, 222, 226f). Yet on the other hand, Nietzsche buries everything contained in metaphysical thinking which does not comply with the determination of Being as value. The equation of ἀγαΘόν and value levels the decisions of the history of metaphysics. It overlooks the way of access which lies between Plato and Nietzsche, and that is the history of metaphysics (NII, 226). It does not allow the earlier fundamental metaphysical positions to get a hearing in their truth (NII, 111). Whether the Being of beings ought to be thought of as value at all, and that means ultimately as the value-positing will to power, and whether all history may be interpreted in terms of will to power is a question of the decision about the history of truth; it is, thereby, also a question about the truth of the position which thinking occupies in this history (NII, 115).

5. This history of truth is in each case accomplished by a specifically determined humanity. For Nietzsche, the one who decides about this history is *the superman*. This superman surpasses the previous man; he

125

126

turns against the previous man who, as *animal rationale*, had his essence in *rationalitas*, in "thought" as "reason." If reason is the guide for the interpretation of beings as beings since the beginning of metaphysics, it is only in the modern age that it becomes the court of justice about every being. That which is constantly present in every presencing, the *subjectum*, is in the modern age no longer something which is present from itself, to which thinking must measure itself, but rather is this thinking itself, "subjectivity." In the modern era man, and he alone, is distinguished with the name "subject." One certainly cannot deny that the nonhuman being is of itself, but man is posited as that ground which guarantees the truth, the openness of beings *as* beings. The Being of beings is now representability; a being is object for a subject, that which stands opposed. Truth is the certainty into which thinking brings itself by going through doubt and "methodically" securing the true for itself. Heidegger emphatically points out that man in antiquity could not yet play the role which he receives in the modern era. In the well-known saying of the Greek sophist Protagoras, man is not posited as the measure of all things; it is rather presupposed that Being is presencing into unconcealment. Man is consequently only the measure in accordance with which that which presences and is unconcealed from itself is confined to the nearest presencing. He is this measure without the farthest being excluded and without man pretending to a decision about the presence and absence of that which is farthest (NII, 140, 172).

The certainty which characterizes truth in the modern age is also prepared for by the fact that the Christian faith directs man's concern to the certainty of his salvation, and as Luther orients faith toward justification, he also cofounds the modern age (NII, 421ff, 142ff, Hw 226). The modern age nevertheless understands itself as the history of liberation *from* medieval bonds; consequently, it forces the Christian faith ever more compellingly out of the arena of world-historical decisions. However, the Christian certainty of salvation may also prepare the self-certainty of the modern age—the modern age could then only be understood as an age of "secularization" if one were mindful about which world, which century here becomes "secularized" (NII, 146, 321).

The subjectivity which in modern times becomes the *fundamentum inconcussum veritatis* as *ego cogito* is first conceived of, and in fact Kant still thinks about it in this manner, as being conditioned by another, the divine being. Leibniz shows that thinking as placing-before-oneself and placing-toward-oneself is just as much representation (*perceptio*) as it is striving and willing (*appetitus*); he also shows that representing and striving belong together in a unity whose fundamental characteristic is force (*vis*), in terms of which force is thought of as the Being of beings, the reality of the

127

real (NII, 429ff). Hegel brings this knowing-willing subjectivity to completion in the unconditioned. What conditions the truth of every being is now no longer thought of as conditioned itself. The polemic which Nietzsche directs against Descartes should not deceive one into thinking that Nietzsche completes the way which began with Descartes. Nietzsche exhausts the last possibilities of subjectivity brought to completion in the unconditioned in that he reverses subjectivity by no longer taking *rationality* or reason but rather the *animalitas* of the *animal rationale*, the body, as the first guide of the interpretation of beings. In the *animalitas* of the "blond beast," the excessiveness of instinct is the higher element, whereas reason is only the lower albeit necessary stabilizing and fixing of becoming (NII, 190f, 300ff).

The converted and thereby complete, unconditioned subjectivity requires the superman for its accomplishment. The Being of beings is no longer the idea as that perspective which needs the vision of man. Now the Being of beings is the idea as the "form" of a humanity (cf. VA 123, Hw 288, *Zur Seinsfrage* 15ff). Man—previously the undetermined animal—is determined by Nietzsche in the form, the "type" of the superman. In this superman the will to power wills nothing but itself; thus the superman is not to be characterized by any specific goal of its willing since all of these goals are already surpassed by the will willing *itself*. Because the superman must side with the type which he is, the thought of "breeding" now becomes necessary, since Being is thought of as the form of a humanity (NII, 309).

In will to power, the superman conquers previous man's powerlessness   **128**
toward power. He achieves will to power as the Being of beings. Does he not thereby take the place of God? Whoever says that man takes the place of God in the "superman" certainly thinks of God's essence as not very divine. Man, who cannot reach the essential region of God, can only bring himself in relation to a place which *corresponds* to the abode of God. This is done by the superman who thinks of himself as the one who realizes will to power as the Being of beings (Hw 235f). In this manner the superman appears to replace God and the gods, and does not Nietzsche himself say, "All gods are dead; now we want the superman to live!"—? Yet, nonetheless, in his rector's address of 1933, Heidegger speaks of Nietzsche as the last German philosopher passionately *seeking God*. Perhaps God is dead in accordance with Nietzsche's experience because the previous man misappropriated him, thought of him only in a small way in accordance with man's own smallness. Perhaps this previous God was deprived of his power "because he was a 'misconception' of the man who denies life and himself" (NI, 254). But then in this case the Yes to Being, which the superman says, could be preparation for readiness for the gods (NI, 254).

In this sense Heidegger places Nietzsche's saying at the head of his first Nietzsche lecture: "Nearly two millennia and not a single new God!" In this sense he explains Nietzsche's alleged atheism as a knowing silence about God and even the discourse of God's death as a cry for God (NI, II, 255, 471; Hw 246f). The God which Nietzsche seeks is—this Heidegger only intimates—the God of will to power eternally willing itself, life and death at once, the God Dionysos (NI, 468).

If one asks about the unity of that which Nietzsche thinks in the five basic expressions, "will to power," "eternal recurrence," "justice," "nihilism," and "superman," then the *unifying character* of this unity is already in question. Can Nietzsche's thinking still be measured against the systems as they emerged before him, or is Nietzsche's "aphoristic" work the denial of every system? Is this either-or even insufficient because it moves in an inadequate alternative, only in what is conventional (NI, 485; NII 460)? The unity of these fundamental expressions lies in the fact that they, as "metaphysical" expressions, say only one thing: the word about the truth of the totality of beings as it is spoken at a definite abode in the history of truth. The individual words say this word in that they, speaking historically in each case, push the history of metaphysics to extremes. The unity of these fundamental expressions can therefore be thought—Nietzsche may or may not have seen this himself—only in terms of the decision about metaphysics as the history of the truth about beings.

In no case may one try to gain by force the unifying character of Nietzsche's thought by pushing one of his fundamental thoughts into the background in favor of another. It will not do, for example, to eliminate the thought of eternal recurrence in favor of the thought of will to power as Baumler does, or not to take this thought seriously as a substantive question as happens in Jaspers' work (NI, 29ff). To think the interconnection of these two thoughts is the first and most difficult task in reflecting upon Nietzsche's thought.

Nietzsche thought of eternal recurrence earlier than he thought of will to power, because the thought of recurrence is *"substantively* earlier, that is, more anticipatory" (NII, 10). The thought of eternal recurrence of the same being pushes to extremes the guiding projection of Western metaphysics, that Being is constant presence. What is is eternally identical with itself and therefore permanent. When pushed to extremes, the thought that Being is constant presence requires the thought of will to power. If Being is thought of as constantly presencing and thus as always present, it then comes to be at the disposal of the thinking corresponding to it. Indeed, Being is perhaps thought of only as constant presence because thinking as representing something permanent has always been the guide for the projection of Being, even if it is concealed at first. Being is

129

thought of as constant presence *in order that* it be at thinking's disposal. If man stands into wanting-to-dispose-of, then the Being of beings becomes—in modern thinking—the representedness of objects. The will must ultimately reveal itself as the essential element in representing taken as the placing-before-oneself and placing-toward-oneself. Nietzsche draws only the final consequence out of the metaphysical, recently transformed approach when he thinks of Being—the *subjectum*, which is constantly present in every being and is thus the basis for everything—as subjectivity brought to completion in the unconditioned, as will to power. This subjectivity becomes that which it is in its consistently modern manner—namely, what constantly presences and lies at the root; that is, it wills itself as eternally recurring and thus secures itself in constant presence. The thought of eternal recurrence and the thought of will to power, each in its own way, think the same.

130

  Both of these thoughts think the same thing to such an extent that there is scarcely a basis upon which to differentiate them. In his first lecture, Heidegger characterizes the theory of will to power as a statement about Being, the basic character of beings, but the thought of recurrence as an answer to the question about the "sense," the character of this Being itself (NI, 26f). Later he takes the theory of will to power as an answer to the question about the constitution, the what-it-is of a being, a being *as such*, and the thought of recurrence as the answer to the question about the that-it-is, about the how of the totality of beings (NI, 463f; NII, 14ff). In Platonic thinking, the that-it-is belongs necessarily to the what of a being, to the constant presence of the idea. Aristotle, and in another way, the Judeo-Christian thought of creation, allow the problematic of that-it-is to step forward more distinctly so that finally what-it-is appears as the possible and that which enables, while that-it-is appears as the actual and that which brings to realization. If Nietzsche thinks will to power, the what-it-is of a being, as that which enables, as the condition for the totality of beings to be in the manner of eternal recurrence, then will to power is "in this conditionality simultaneously the authentic and single that of the organism, that is, of the totality of beings" (NII, 16f). Thus Nietzsche can speak of will to power as an ultimate "fact." The difference between what-it-is and that-it-is, the essential origin of which remains unthought, vanishes in the conversion of metaphysics as Nietzsche attempts it.

  Insofar as Nietzsche thinks the sameness of will to power and recurrence in this manner, he throws metaphysics into its shallow non-essence. In the crassest way he makes it appear that will and its will to dispose of—concealed at least—always hold sway where Being is self-evidently taken as constant presence and where the presentness of this presence is not reflected upon further. To the extent that Nietzsche thinks

131

the essence of Being, thought metaphysically, as the permanence of presence in terms of will to power which wills only itself in the eternal recurrence of the same, he conceives of this essence of Being "in its inescapable, involved completion" (NII, 11). Presentness in the constant presence of Being can no longer be a problem where the will itself appropriates the presentness in willing eternal recurrence. If presentness can no longer be a problem, then every trail to the question of *Sein und Zeit* and thereby to the question about the truth of Being is wiped out. Nietzsche thinks truth not as the truth of Being, but rather as the truth which Being (will to power at one with eternal recurrence) conveys about beings. Nietzsche thus thinks of truth consistently metaphysically, and in modern fashion as the justice in which will to power instructs itself in its evaluations. Nietzsche also thinks nihilism, the history of truth, only in terms of the flattened non-essence of truth, that is, from valuing and revaluing and therefore in terms of the equation: Being is value. The superman who accomplishes this history is in truth only the last man of metaphysics, the *animal rationale* who brings forth his *animalitas* and *brutalitas*.

Still, does Nietzsche himself not understand his thinking as the reversal of Platonic, that is, metaphysical thinking? Certainly Nietzsche thinks against Platonism in the revaluation of values insofar as Platonism devalues that which becomes and the sensuous in favor of something non-sensuous. Nonetheless, Nietzsche thinks against Platonism only from within Platonism. He pushes the error of Platonism, taking Being self-evidently as the constant presence at thought's disposal, to extremes without showing a sense for the primordial matter which Platonic thinking contains. Nietzsche's reversal of Platonism brings Platonism only to "blind obduracy and shallowness"; now there exists only the one level of will to power which empowers itself toward itself and endures (NII, 22f). Nietzsche intends to save "becoming" and thereby "life" over against dead "Being"; but in doing so he first brings this becoming entirely under **132** the domination of Being as the constant, self-sufficient presence only in order to establish the supremacy of becoming (NII, 18f). It is a completely misleading opinion to think that in his thinking Nietzsche fetches back "Being" and "becoming" as Parmenides and Heraclitus think them at the beginning of Western thought. To be sure, Nietzsche thinks of Being and becoming, but within the metaphysical approach; he is familiar with the beginning of Western thought only in its metaphysical deformity. Nietzsche's preference for the tragic age of the Greeks is a preference for the supposed "personalities" of this age and not for the matter of this time (NI, 464ff; NII, 12; Hw 296ff). In his reversal of Platonism, Nietzsche includes Platonism, that is, metaphysics, in its superficial non-essence and thus excludes every genuine beginning.

Insofar as Nietzsche pushes Platonism to its extremes and thereby reverses it, he exhausts the last possibilities of Platonic-metaphysical thinking. He is, therefore, the last metaphysician—the last thinker who can carry out a primordially metaphysical project and not merely use the components of metaphysical thinking to outfit a world view in the so-called "resurrection" of metaphysics (NII, 201). As the last metaphysician, however, Nietzsche is the thinker who thinks out in advance the fundamental characteristics of the present and the coming age. "Even if Nietzsche is no longer even known by name, that which his thinking had to think will dominate" (NI, 479). Nietzsche's time, the consummate modern age, is the age of the forgetfulness of sense or of the truth of Being driven to its limits and of the decisive reaching out for the totality of beings, the age of "perfect senselessness." Beings appear as capable of being made and that which, in the narrower sense of the word, is not capable of being made is given over to experience. "The act of making" and "experience" confirm each other; in them there appears the will which as will to power wills nothing but itself (NII, 20ff; *Beiträge*). Perhaps the enthusiasm for will to power still disguises the fact that this will to power is nothing other than the naked will toward willing. Perhaps this will toward willing is even more adequately interpreted by Ernst Jünger than by Nietzsche himself when the former, on the basis of Nietzsche's metaphysical perspective, interprets it as "total mobilization" as it is brought about by the "worker" (VA 81; Hw 258; NII, 21; *Zur Seinsfrage*). Basically, however, Nietzsche has thought ahead of our age so that **133** Heidegger can understand not only our age from Nietzsche, but also Nietzsche's fundamental expressions from the slogans of the age of "total mobilization," "total war," and the elimination of the difference between war and peace. For example, Heidegger can find proof in the war of propaganda that truth today is actually as Nietzsche conceives of it: the "justice" of will to power which commands its truth for itself as necessary illusions (NI, 538, 627; NII, 198; WhD 31f). Indeed, Heidegger believes he can presume that the "superman" exists here and there even if he is invisible to the public. This superman is certainly not man grown to abnormal size but rather that man who wills what is, as standing "eternally" in itself, and who dispenses with the "masquerade" which morally cleans up emotional states and differentiates between good and evil (WhD 26; NII, 332).

Nietzsche is the thinker who, as the last metaphysical thinker, foresees the fundamental characteristics of our time. For Heidegger, however, the issue is not only who Nietzsche is, but above all, "who he *will be*" (NI, 473). If Nietzsche pushes metaphysics to the limits of its non-essence, then can his thinking not decide for us whether we can even pursue the metaphysical approach any further? Being as the truth of beings is an issue for every metaphysical thinker. But Nietzsche could place the unique issue before us: whether we continue to raise only the question about the Being of beings as metaphysics does, or whether we are to take this question as merely the leading question and develop it into the "fundamental question" about Being itself and its truth (NI, 26, 80, 454ff; II, 260). Without having willed it or even having merely known about it, Nietzsche raises the ultimate issue, the issue "between the supremacy of beings and the dominion of Being" (NI, 476). Allowing Nietzsche's metaphysical basis to become visible is only the "proximate goal" of the reflection on Nietzsche. The most distant goal to which this proximate goal is subordinate is the question as to what in fact a metaphysical basis is, what metaphysics is, whence metaphysics finds its way to its essence (NII, 261f). The most distant goal deals with working out the "basic question" about the truth of Being itself.

In his work on Nietzsche, Heidegger gives few suggestions for this question about the truth of Being itself; thus the point from which Heidegger conducts his examination of Nietzsche remains hidden in this work. Still, Heidegger does not isolate Nietzsche's metaphysics in itself; rather, Nietzsche's metaphysics is to become visible as the end of metaphysics and thereby as the need to raise again the leading question of metaphysics, the question of Being. However, Heidegger only skims over the questions in which the one question about the truth of Being unfolds: the question about the belonging together, about the identity of Being and man, the question concerning the difference between Being and beings, the question about the basis upon which this difference is based, and the question about the manifold meaning of Being (NII 203ff., 240ff, 246ff). Nietzsche himself does not relate to these questions. For Heidegger, to be sure, Nietzsche is as the thinker of our age the closest while he remains the farthest regarding the question about the truth of Being, the thinker who disguises this question. It becomes evident how far Nietzsche's thinking is from the thinking which Heidegger attempts when we take a short comparative look at the respective questioning of Nietzsche and Heidegger. If Nietzsche thinks of will to power as the ultimate fact, Heidegger asks about the truth of will to power and of every determination of Being; he asks whether the totality of beings is basically always will to power or whether it shows itself only at a specific time, at the end of the modern age, in the light of will to power. Where Nietzsche thinks of will to power as the eternal recurrence of the same, Heidegger asks about the horizon of time in which determinations such as "constant presentness" and "eternal recurrence" can be thought. If Nietzsche asks about the truth of art in order to bring will to power as the Being of beings into view, Heidegger asks about the origin of the work of art in order to get beyond the metaphysical determination of truth as the openness of beings to the question about that truth from which an openness of beings can first actually show itself, and so forth.

As the closest and the farthest, Nietzsche raises the following issue: Is the modern age which is coming to an end self-evident, or is it rather the need for overcoming metaphysics insofar as it is the completion of metaphysics, the final age? Is the modern age, as it endures in self-solidification or else drives on toward a sudden catastrophe, the questionless age not worthy of further questioning, or is it the counterposition and counterplay to another beginning which gains its originality from the insistence in the truth of Being (NI, 470, 480; II, 27ff)? In passing through Nietzsche's thinking, the "problem" of metaphysics, and thereby the problem of Western thought, becomes ripe for decision. Metaphysics becomes that history about which the decision is still lacking.

135

METAPHYSICS AS THE HISTORY OF BEING

If Nietzsche's thinking determines metaphysics, then metaphysics becomes that history which already at its beginning, in Plato's thought, forgot the basis upon which it stood—the truth of Being itself—which must therefore drift with fatal consequence to its completion and its end in the metaphysics of will to power. If metaphysics is experienced in this manner, then it is no longer the history of truth in general, but rather that history in which thinking thinks Being as the truth of beings. Yet in keeping with its entire approach, the truth of Being itself must be left unthought.

Metaphysics thinks of beings in their Being. It interrogates the beings of the various regions regarding their Being. It thinks of beings in general in accordance with the fundamental characteristics of their Being, differentiating, for example, what-it-is and that-it-is. In the theory of transcendentals, it portrays Being according to the various aspects which it offers as Being, for instance, as being-true. It inserts man into the history which Being has as the truth of beings. It thinks of the totality of beings in accordance with its Being, thinks of this Being Platonically as *ἰδέα*, recently as the representability of objects, and finally as will to power. Thus metaphysics is the theory of the Being of beings, ontology. This ontology posits a self-evident constant presence as the fundamental feature of Being. Beings can be grounded in Being, which is constantly   **136** present and is therefore at one's disposal. However, Being also requires the grounding for itself so that it can be the Being which constantly has presence. Thus metaphysics seeks that being which in a specific way fulfills the demand for being constantly present. The self-sufficient, divine being, Θεῖον, meets this requirement. Metaphysics is, therefore, not only ontology, the foundation of beings in Being, but also theology, the foundation of Being is a supreme being, in Θεῖον. Because it grounds at all, it is a -logy. It is therefore onto-theo-logy (NII, 344ff; ID 35ff). After will to power has finally wrung itself out as the Being of beings, then it will no longer permit itself to be grounded by means of another being; instead, it will create the foundation for itself in that it wills itself as eternally recurring and thus as the self-sufficient constancy of making present and absent. Will to power grounds itself in itself and thus has itself at its disposal as the ultimate ground of all that is. It is only in keeping with the basic onto-theological feature of metaphysical thought when Nietzsche even still gives the name of a god, Dionysos, to the will to power which wills itself as eternal.

Metaphysics grounds beings in Being and Being in a supreme being. Beings are determined with respect to their Being, but Being is not interrogated solely with respect to its truth. Instead, it is thought of in terms of the most real being which, for its part, is determined according to the truth of Being. At the same time metaphysics gives this truth no further consideration. It does not hold Being and beings apart in such a way that Being in its truth could become a problem. According to this truth, Being is taken self-evidently as constant presencing. The projection of Being upon the permanence of presencing, a projection questioned no further, is the "background" from which particular basic metaphysical positions come forth without this projection. However, "they speak back unhesitatingly into this background" (NII, 8). Because metaphysics does not allow the projection of Being in terms of constant presence to become a problem, it also cannot think of an ontological difference like that between that-it-is and what-it-is in accordance with its essential origin and therefore in terms of its limits. As Heidegger tries to show, the difference between that-it-is and what-it-is is established if Being is constant presencing and thus if it appears in the respectiveness of presencing, in the that-it-is, and in the ever similar appearance of that which presences, in the what-it-is (NII, 399f). If the statement that Being means constant presencing becomes questionable, then one must also ask how wide the circle of beings is upon which the distinction between that-it-is and what-it-is can be used. In his thinking Heidegger proceeded from the fact that there are limits to this distinction, for example, it is not applicable to factical existence, to historical man.

In accordance with its theory of transcendentals, metaphysics, according to its fundamental presuppositions, must think being-true as convertible with a Being which constantly presences, as the openness of that which constantly presences and is thereby at one's disposal. The history of truth comes to a standstill in that a "basic insight" and "basic theory" are achieved. Man understands himself by grasping this ultimate basic insight. Thus truth is at the disposal of man and if not at his disposal, then at the disposal of a god who is thought in a completely specific way. As it says in Plato's *Republic* (597), God created only *one* idea for each thing, the *one* constant Being, because he did *not* want to be a creator of something unique and non-recurring but rather of a true being, that is, of that which constantly presences in its Being (NI, 213f). The question is whether we may think of God in this way.

Metaphysical thinking believes that every being can defer to an ultimate ground. Yet if man thinks in this way, certain consequences follow: first, he puts himself outside of his own essence to which the historical future, which is not at human disposal, belongs; second, inexhaustible nature which proceeds from itself and returns again into its fullness becomes the object of representing and becomes some inventory merely at one's disposal; and third, man becomes, as Nietzsche expresses it, the "murderer of God": the divine is not permitted its divinity if it is posited before man and toward him as what constantly presences and therefore as available. Metaphysics disguises beings and their Being in that it thinks of them. Its greatness lies in the fact that it tries to think of beings in their Being and opens the thinking of Being to something divine and self-sufficient. Its shortcoming lies in the fact that it does not make Being questionable with respect to its truth but takes Being instead as constant **138** presencing without further thought; consequently, Being is characterized as at one's disposal, and the thinking which grounds becomes the disposing of the grounds and the ultimate basis.

The reaching out toward beings which places them at one's disposal has today become "the struggle for domination of the earth," that is, the struggle to have the earth at one's disposal as the collection of available beings and to establish that humanity which is capable of taking charge of this disposal. Eighty years ago, Nietzsche wrote: "The time is coming when the struggle for the earth's domination will be waged,—it will be waged in the name of *fundamental philosophical doctrines*" (NII, 260ff, 333). The time of this struggle has in fact arrived, but is it being waged in the name of fundamental philosophical doctrines? In part it is being waged explicitly in the name of such doctrines, but it is perhaps being waged most forcefully in their names where philosophy, and surely metaphysics, are no longer discussed, but where the metaphysical tendency to secure and provide an ultimate basis for beings is being pushed to extremes, and where without any reflection upon what is being done, a permanently present Being, a supreme principle, is set above history as the goal which controls this history.

Those who wage this struggle must experience the fact that the goals which are posited ideologically as continually obligatory will soon become null and implausible. The experience of this becoming null, in other words, being affected by nihilism, in each case then tries for the positing of another goal, for a new "affirmation," a new courage to "be." Yet, as Heidegger thinks, perhaps nihilism offers another chance. Perhaps an essential experience of nihilism requires us to think of the Nothing not merely as the counterpart to the elevation of a determinate being, not merely as the becoming-null of this or that goal, but rather as belonging to Being itself. The Nothing would thus be experienced, as Heidegger says, as the "veil of Being" (NII, 353f)—as that veil which shows us Being by withdrawing it from us, and as that veil which therefore makes it impossible to grasp greedily at a permanently present and available Being as the basis of all beings. If the Nothing, to which man belongs through being-toward-death, would be thought of as belonging to Being, then Being itself would show itself in its truth as the current history which is not at one's disposal. From this history one could then think about how Being determines the truth about beings and how it can be powerful or null as the Being of beings (as "value," as Nietzsche says). The question about nihilism would take on an entirely new dimension insofar as one would think of it in terms of the history of the truth of Being and, therefore, as "concerned with the history of Being."

139

Nietzsche experiences nihilism as the logic of Western history and tries to overcome it. Thus Nietzsche thinks of beings as beings, in their Being. He thinks of Being as value, experiences the devaluation of the highest values, and demands revaluation. Nietzsche experiences the Nothing which determines the experience of nihilism only as the Nothing of Being taken as the being-ness of beings. He does not experience the actual Nothing, the Nothing belonging to Being itself and to its truth. Nietzsche's experience of nihilism and his overcoming of nihilism concern only inauthentic nihilism and in genuine nihilism they falter. This authentic nihilism is that history which shows that there is no use in pursuing Being itself, the truth of Being. Nietzsche shares this authentic nihilism with metaphysics in general. Metaphysics as a whole is nihilism because it does not think of the truth of Being. Plato's metaphysics is no less nihilistic than Nietzsche's; it is only that the essence of nihilism, which comes to appearance in Nietzsche's work, still remains concealed in Plato's metaphysics (NII, 343).

In metaphysics beings emerge *as* beings; they step into the openness of their Being while the truth of Being itself is left out. Being comes to presence as the unconcealedness of beings, but the unconcealedness of this unconcealedness, the "essence" of Being itself (the manner in which it comes to presence), does not come to thought. Being itself fails to appear; as this failure to appear it "is" in metaphysics. Being withdraws its truth from thinking. It withdraws as Being itself in that it remains in view only as the Being of beings (NII, 353ff). Metaphysics has its abode and its stay in the truth of Being in that this truth fails to appear in it and is forgotten **140** in favor of Being as the mere truth of beings. To be sure, even this failure to appear is still left out, and this forgetting itself sinks into oblivion. Metaphysics does not experience what is unique to its essence; it does not experience the failure to appear of the truth of Being as its abode and its place in the history of truth. To the extent that Nietzsche seeks to overcome metaphysics as nihilism but does not experience what is unique to metaphysics and to nihilism, he finally plunges thinking into the inauthenticity of metaphysics. Because the final possibilities of metaphysics are exhausted in its reversal, it is completed in its non-essence, in authentic nihilism as the forgetting of the truth of Being itself.

This completion of metaphysics in nihilism as its non-essence can provide the impetus to experience the self-leveling non-essence of metaphysics as non-essence, as the not-essencing and failure to appear of the truth of Being, and thus no longer to omit this failure to appear of the truth of Being itself. The failure to appear, the concealing, the "Nothing" is thought as belonging to the truth of Being. The truth of Being is experienced as a history in which this truth always conceals and also preserves itself. The essencing (to be thought verbally) of metaphysics is experienced as the history of this concealing and preserving but thus as the "history of the mystery of the promise of Being itself" (NII, 370). Nihilism is the need to determine whether this promise is heard as promise. The need for this decision is not merely a human need, but rather the need of Being itself, which needs man in order to be able to find its way into its truth. But in this way this need is the "danger" that for man it will not become the need that it is; rather that man will instead settle down in an apparent lack of need and will forget Being itself in favor of dominating beings (NII, 391).

Only if the "essence" of metaphysics—the history of the failure to appear of the truth of Being itself—is expressly experienced in this danger and is no longer omitted will thinking enter the open air of the truth of Being (NII, 397). A thinking that thinks "in terms of the history of Being" therefore takes over the task of setting metaphysics back into its essence, into its place, and within its limits, to think it expressly as the "history of **141** Being." Metaphysics has its place in the history of Being in that it takes

Being self-evidently as a constant presencing without, however, experiencing the truth of Being itself, from which Being as presencing is first of all to be thought. Since metaphysics still leaves out the failure to appear of the truth of Being, it can carry along its abode and its stay in the history of Being only as the forgotten. The individual metaphysical thinkers also do not consider that they are situated in the abode of metaphysics when they characterize constantly present Being as the idea or the representability of objects or the will to power. Only a thinking which can experience metaphysics as a specific history of Being from the experience of the truth of Being itself can discuss the abode of metaphysics and the abodes of individual metaphysical thinkers.

This thinking "in terms of the history of Being" ought not merely reconstruct what was thought in metaphysics. It must rather attempt to penetrate into what is unthought in metaphysical thinking. It must not simply take the particular, fundamental, metaphysical positions as various way of asking the leading metaphysical question, but it must set these metaphysical projections back into the history of truth by means of an inquiry into the fundamental question. One must clearly differentiate between the guiding question and the fundamental question, the question about Being as the truth of beings and the question about the truth of Being itself. Nietzsche, for example, answers the question of the Being of beings by saying that Being is life, and life is will to power. He answers the leading question of Western thought by putting forth will to power as the truth about beings. However, Nietzsche does not develop the leading question into the fundamental question which asks: What is this Being itself in its truth? Is this Being distinguished by the character of constant presence so that beings are basically always will to power even when this will is actualized only as powerlessness toward power? Or is it that this Being is not distinguished throughout by constant presence, that the experience of beings in light of will to power as the Being of beings belongs in an entirely specific and limited history, that Being has the character of historicality? Thus, like every

142   metaphysical thinker, Nietzsche also takes his truth to be convertible with a constantly present Being and thereby the ultimate and basically only truth. To be sure, the theory of will to power is for Nietzsche an "experiment" with the truth, but in this experiment will to power is not posited as the consistently modern and therefore historically situated interpretation of the Being of beings, but rather as an insight into an ultimate "fact." Naturally, Nietzsche sees that will to power was not always recognized and acknowledged as the ultimate fact. Nonetheless, he explains the behavior of the Platonic and Christian man who sets a god above himself as a powerlessness toward power which is basically nothing but disguised will to power. The metaphysical insight into permanent Being as the truth of beings wants to provide in each case an ultimate basis which grounds everything, a basic insight and a basic theory. The thinking which is after a basic insight is incapable of seeing the way in which the truth of Being itself "is" (NII, 335).

The reflection upon metaphysics in terms of the history of Being does not intend "to refute" the metaphysical thinkers even if this reflection provisionally shunts aside the question about what beings genuinely are in their Being in favor of the question as to whether the previous manner of asking about the Being of beings, the metaphysical manner, does not forget the basis upon which it stands, the truth of Being itself. The thinking about the history of Being takes metaphysics back into its concealed essence, into the history of the truth of Being itself, and is thus "remembrance of metaphysics" (NII, 481ff); as this remembrance it is, however, an "overcoming" of the essence of metaphysics into the truth of Being itself.

7

THE OVERCOMING OF
METAPHYSICS

In attempting to think the truth of Being itself by going back to the ground   **143**
of metaphysics, Heidegger experiences metaphysics as a history whose
ground remains concealed and obscured. Going back to the ground of
metaphysics therefore becomes necessary for its overcoming. Overcoming
metaphysics means that thinking renounces that metaphysical approach
which takes Being self-evidently as constant presencing and which does
not ask about the truth of Being. In order to be able to overcome the
metaphysical approach, thinking must turn toward what is unthought in
that which metaphysics thinks, toward the temporal character of presence
and thereby to the temporalness of the sense or the truth of Being. By
means of this turning, thinking finds its way into the "essence" of
metaphysics, which is to be thought verbally as the history of the failure to
appear and the oblivion of the truth of Being. This failure and this
oblivion must be experienced in their positive sense as belonging to the
truth of Being which is unconcealment, an existing-together of revealing
and concealing. Overcoming metaphysics as turning toward the
"essence" of metaphysics is thereby an encircling or entwining of what is
thought of in metaphysics (unconcealment as it was granted to metaphysics) by what is unthought (what remained concealed), a setting of Being
as the truth about beings back into the history of the truth of Being itself.
So it is only in the overcoming of metaphysics that "the abiding truth"
turns back "expressly to the apparently repudiated metaphysics as its now
appropriated *essence*" (*Zur Seinsfrage* 35). Overcoming metaphysics is
overcoming into that seminal element which supports metaphysical
thinking, but which is not discussed there (NII, 481).

The transition to the thinking of Being itself or of the truth of Being—of
Seyn as Heidegger wrote occasionally to distinguish Being itself from Being   **144**
as the mere truth of beings—occurs upon the way of reflecting upon what
is unthought in metaphysics. According to the *Beiträge zur Philosophie*,
"transitional thinking as *historical* reflection" accomplishes the grounding
projection of the truth of Being [*Seyn*]. This work carries the simple title
Beiträge [*Contributions*] because as an attempt to experience the truth of
Being, it is a "transition"—not the course away from metaphysics, but

rather the regress into its ground and thus the overcoming of metaphysics to that seminal element which was forgotten and obscured in metaphysics, and which is now to be drawn back in "another beginning," in the transition to the founding of the truth of Being itself. "What is said is asked and thought in the 'pass' of the first and other beginning to one another. This occurs out of Being [*Seyn*] 'being heard' in the need of the abandonment of Being for the 'leap' into Being. Such a leap goes toward the 'grounding' of the truth of Being as preparation for 'what is to come', 'the last god'." The first beginning of Western thought, which runs its course in metaphysics, demands that it be grounded in its forgotten seminality; thus it becomes the pass to the other beginning. Yet Leibniz's monadology, Kant's transcendental approach, Schelling's question of freedom, Hegel's phenomenology are also passes insofar as one rethinks them in terms of Dasein as the There, the abode of the truth of Being. Even the "manipulative" thinking which has advanced into the most extreme oblivion of Being is precisely what can allow the oblivion of Being to become a need, can make an issue of it and thus can allow Being [*Seyn*] to be "heard." The experience of the truth of Being cannot at all be achieved by continuously advancing from previous thought to the bases of previous thought, but only by leaping away into the abyss of the occurrence of this truth, only in the "leap." The question thus arises as to how there can be discourse about a "grounding" of the truth of Being at all and how perhaps something binding and divine can address man from this truth. If transitional thinking experiences the truth of Being as the current history not at one's disposal, then one can address this truth as "event." That work which bears the public title *Beiträge zur Philosophie* has *Vom Ereignis* as its essential heading.

145   Event refers to Being [*Seyn*] as the current occurrence of a truth which is not at one's command, a truth which needs man's thinking and is thus "identical" with him, which lets beings be seen in their Being historically, and which therefore tears open the "difference" between Being and beings. This difference is the "basis" for metaphysical thought about Being. How Heidegger tries to find the transition into the truth of Being is to be developed here, guided by the metaphysical-logical foundational terms: identity, difference, and ground. In this connection I proceed from talks that were published later, and from lectures, although these often speak only suggestively since they express to a wider public what was thought earlier. (I must not consider the fact that in these talks and lectures Heidegger occasionally provides designations which belong only in the steps of thinking to be dealt with later—for example, when he understands technology in terms of "enframing.") In a second section I shall then ask how Heidegger, by means of getting over metaphysics, also

wrests himself from the metaphysical presuppositions of his own thinking and thus finds the way to that which is seminal and his own—not the way to all-determining ultimate answers, but rather the way to that provisional questioning in which thinking from out of the event occurs: "A projection of the presencing of Being [*Seyn*] as *event* must be ventured because we are not acquainted with the task of our history" (*Beiträge*).

IDENTITY, DIFFERENCE, GROUND

If we take a being *as* being, then we take it in the *identity* in which it stands with itself. The principle of identity, A is A, counts as a law of thought, and if it did not make its claim, there would be no science. If "the sameness of its object was not guaranteed in advance" for science, then it could not be what it is (ID 17). The principle of identity is therefore a law of thinking because it is a law of Being; as the law of thinking and of Being, it thus decides how a being *as* being may appear in the sphere where it applies; it may appear as what is identical with itself. Insofar as the identical is to appear as the identical, as what is to agree with itself, identity always demands agreement; it is, therefore, "unity." Identity or unity belongs to every being as such; it is a basic feature in Being itself. **146**

If I accomplish the agreement in which a being is taken as itself, then I take a being as being, for example, man as man, and thus I take a being in its Being or in its truth. The "as" in the phrase "being as being" refers to the Being or the truth of a being, but at the same time it demands thinking. A being could not emerge as the being which it is nor could it come into its Being or into its truth if it were not "thought" (in a very broad sense of this word) of as that which it is. The identity of a being with itself refers to another "identity," to the belonging together of Being and thinking, Being and man. A being can appear in the identity which it has with itself when it is thought of in its Being, that is, when the identity of Being and thinking occurs. Identity in the second sense of the word is no longer a basic feature of Being; Being is rather a basic feature of this identity. Being, together with thinking, belongs to this identity (ID 19). This other sense of the word "identity" is not arbitrary, but suggested by the matter at issue. Moreover it is current—for example, Schelling speaks of an identity in duplicity as subject-object which originally occurs only in self-consciousness.[25]

Metaphysics expressed the belonging together of Being and thinking in that it thought of a being as convertible with the true; a being, as true, has an intrinsic relationship to thought. Heidegger also begins with the opinion that "in accordance with the unconcealment of Being the relation of Being to man's essence belongs indeed to Being itself." Heidegger makes *problematic* the belonging together of Being and thought (or man), as it is seen in metaphysics (WiM 13, WhD 73f). As he says in keeping with metaphysical trains of thought, man is indeed a being among others, but he is in his *essence* only when as Dasein or as thinker he is open to Being, "understands" Being, "conforms to Being." In his essence man belongs to Being; he is assigned to it. But Being is not a "being-in-itself" answerable only to itself, freed of any relation to man, the all-encompassing into which man is merely integrated. Being—as presencing, absencing and self-withdrawing—is rather nothing but the relationship to Dasein or thinking, to the essence of man. Being comes to presence and endures only because as claim, call, and behest it approaches man and needs his listening. Because Being as presencing is the open space of a clearing (the truth of beings), it needs man's thinking as the standing open toward Being and the holding open of Being. Being appropriates man. Certainly Being and man do not first stand on their own and then have to be brought into a relation "dialectically"; rather only by being assigned to one another are they as belonging together.

Traditional "metaphysical" thinking thinks the belonging together of Being and thought in a specific manner, and this manner never would have become problematic. A being is taken as a being, that is, in its unity with itself, in its Being and in its truth. Being is thereby self-evidently thought of as *constant*, presencing without negation, the unity (identity) as being-identical with itself which is constantly the same. Being as constant presencing and thus as the ground of beings becomes something at the disposal of thinking and ultimately the representability of objects; indeed, it becomes the deliveredness of a mere reserve, it becomes feasible in the sense of a universal technology. At the same time, man, the *animal rationale*, is used for representing and delivering over, for "work" as what determines his form. Because Being gives itself into man's hands as "something feasible," it thus seems to man that he encounters—as Werner Heisenberg has said—only himself (VA 34f). But the technology which produces this appearance is not a mere creation of man. Being is challenged to reveal itself as feasible by the history into which it has fallen, and man is challenged to posit Being as feasible. Being and man are assigned to one another in that appropriative event which reveals the "world" as the "technical" world (ID 25ff, *Zur Seinsfrage*, 27). Still, technical and indeed metaphysical thinking do not understand technology and metaphysics as appropriative event, as a definite destining of the truth about beings. They do not think of the togetherness of Being and man as a belonging-to-one-another because the manner in which Being and man are assigned to one another does not become problematic for them (PL 65).

If the manner in which metaphysics and technology provide the truth   **148**
about beings is questioned "in terms of the history of Being," then
metaphysics and technology "pass along" to us an experience of it and
become a "prelude" to what is called the "event of appropriation"
(ID 28f). The experience of the event of appropriation is "the abruptness
of the unbridged entrance" into that belonging which historically yields
the to-one-another of man and Being and thereby produces the metaphysical and technological constellation of both. This experience is the
"leap" into an abyss—namely, into that which is abysmal in the history of
the truth of Being itself (ID 24, 32). This leap springs away from man
insofar as he is thought of as *animal rationale* by the thinking which has the
ultimate ground at its disposal; it also loops away from Being to the extent
that it is taken self-evidently as constant presencing and thereby as the
ground at one's disposal (ID 24). In this leap one does not merely ask
about the horizon of time from which presence is determined; the equation, Being is constant presence, along with its different modifications, is
also experienced as appropriative event. Thus the possibility of overcoming metaphysics as well as universal technology in a more original
occurring of truth becomes visible (ID 29). This overcoming finds its
"escort" in seminal Western thought, in the statement of Parmenides
about the sameness of thinking and Being, and in the manner that
Heraclitus portrays the unity of Φύσις and λόγος. In the regress to this
seminal element, the metaphysical determinations of Being and thinking
are to be shaken violently (E 88ff). This overcoming goes back over the
way of Western thought which led from Parmenides to Nietzsche and to
technology (cf. WhD).

For a thinking which experiences the history of Being as the need for a
decision, and thus conforms itself to the history of the truth of Being, the
sameness of Being and thinking shows itself as appropriative event. The
truth of Being "is," that is, as an experience possible today it comes to
presence as that appropriative event in which the Being of beings, and the
thinking as standing open to this Being, are historically appropriated to
one another. The truth of Being is the history of this appropriating. It
grants the sameness of Being and thinking and thereby the truth about
beings; however, it does so only historically and without putting it at one's
disposal because, as unconcealment, it "is" only on the basis of concealment,
as the struggle between revealing and concealing. Thinking is "used" in   **149**
order that Being can be the truth about beings, but for thinking, Being is
not at its disposal as the representable, deliverable, or indeed producable;
for Being is the revealing of beings only on the basis of an enduring
concealment. If thinking cares for this concealment as the mystery of the
truth of Being, then it can only conform to the history of this truth and

never have it at its disposal. To be able to preserve and care for the concealment, it must transform itself, and surrender its previous, representing nature which disposes of everything. No longer may it hand over to itself only the Being of beings; instead, it must experience from out of the appropriative event the constellation of Being and openness toward Being (ID 32). If it is experienced from out of the appropriative event of its truth, Being can no longer be taken self-evidently as *constant* presencing and therefore as a ground at one's disposal, since it is presencing only together with absencing within the history of its truth. How Being is the Being of beings becomes a question when the difference between Being and beings becomes a problem.

If we differentiate one being from another, then we bring *the difference* between the one and the other to light. But we can differentiate between beings only if we grasp beings each *as* beings and differentiate the beings in some way with respect to Being. The ontological difference, the distinction between a being and its Being in which a being first emerges as a being, lies ahead of the ontical difference as the distinction of one being from another. The differentiation of a being from its Being constitutes the essence of metaphysics, its *meta*, the stepping beyond beings toward Being. Yet metaphysics turns the original differentiation between Being and beings into the difference between what-it-is and that-it-is; the true world of the permanent what-it-is is distinguished from the apparent world of the vanishing and transitory that-it-is. Consequently the unity of being-Being is destroyed (NII, 488, 399ff). Even when what-it-is as that which enables and conditions is taken back into the reality of that-it-is, being-Being is not experienced in its unity. The representing-delivering thinking which lends permanence is a uniting of the possible to which the experience of the actual-factical must still be added. When Heidegger (first in *Vom Wesen des Grundes*) makes the "ontological difference" problematic, he then attempts to take the metaphysical difference between Being (what-it-is) and beings (that-it-is) back to a more seminal differentiation (NII, 209f).

The difference, considered as difference, is the matter of thinking, because Being is the matter of thinking. Being is the Being of beings, and beings are the beings of Being. Being and beings each appear in their own way from out the difference (ID 43, 59ff). Being and beings are the same; in the differentiation between Being and beings, this sameness (the Being of beings, beings in their Being) is united only expressly in the unity with itself. Being is not something other than beings; if it were something else, then it would indeed be a being—and the ontological difference would be turned into the merely ontic. Being is the Being of beings; it comes to presence in the manner of the transition to beings; it is, as tradition says,

150

purely and simply *transcendens*, that overwhelming which reveals a being as a being. A being is a being of Being; it is not without Being, but rather, always an arriving in the unconcealed of Being, a self-concealing in it, arrival and presencing (ID 62). Being as revealing overwhelming and a being as self-concealing arrival come to presence from out of the difference. This difference does not place two different things next to one another, but rather opens a being in its Being, unites it into sameness with itself, bears this sameness out. "The Difference between Being and beings is, as the difference between overwhelming and arrival, the *revealing-concealing carrying out* of both" (ID 63).

In metaphysical thought, the difference has been carried out in a completely determinate way. The difference between Being and beings is thought from going beyond what is present (a being) toward constant presencing (Being). Being thereby becomes the ground in which a being is grounded. In order to be able to be constantly presencing Being, this Being, which "is" only as the grounding of beings, must for its part be grounded in that being which fulfills in a special way the demand for constant presence. This being which establishes beings is the most real of beings, the divine. Thus Being grounds beings, and the most real being establishes Being. The settlement of the difference is the "circling around one another of Being and beings" (ID 68), is the settlement which *grounds*. This settlement which grounds is different in Aristotle than it is in Nietzsche, different in Hegel than in the technical world; nonetheless as the "universal" in metaphysics, grounding determines the character of metaphysics; it determines it as ontotheology.

151

Heidegger conceives of the metaphysical carrying out of the difference in a way that metaphysics itself never thinks of, namely, *as* carrying out [*Austrag*], as a determinate, historical essence of carrying out. He thereby places this carrying out into question. Stepping back into that which is unthought in metaphysics, he asks about the essential origin of the difference. Metaphysical carrying out of the difference thus becomes the mere "outskirts" of the essence of the difference (ID 46, 61f, 65). Seminal Western thought is most likely to show a trace toward the essential origin of the difference, of the "twofold" (cf. Heidegger's Parmenides interpretations: VA 140ff, WhD 130ff), but it may be that the basic ontotheological character of metaphysics may already be seen in pre-metaphysical thinking, as Heidegger intimates with a reference to Heraclitus' fragment 32 (ID 67).

Heidegger only hints at the extent to which the difference "stems from" the essence of identity: "In the carrying out, the clearing of the covering up which conceals itself holds sway, and this holding sway grants the away-from and toward-one-another of the overwhelming and the arrival"

(ID 63). What holds sway in carrying out is the truth of Being itself as unconcealment and thus as the event of appropriation. The differentiation between Being and beings "is seminally the essencing of Being itself whose beginningness is the appropriative event" (NII, 489). The carrying out of the difference opens the sameness of Being and thought to the differentiation of Being and beings, so that beings as beings can come into the unconcealed of their Being before thinking. Only the belonging together of Being and thinking lets a being be a being without the being becoming disposable for thinking; still the being takes shelter in a Being to whose truth concealing belongs, just as revealing and being revealed do. If the carrying out of the difference is to be able to stem from identity as the event of appropriation, then Being may no longer be taken self-evidently and exclusively as constant presencing and thereby as disposable ground, the mere being-revealed of a being. At the same time, carrying out may no longer be grasped as grounding and establishing in a manner subject to no further reflection. The question about identity and difference forces one to think through the question about ground in a new way.

152

The *Satz vom Grund* states that nothing is without ground. One thing is based on the other, and everything has its ground. Moreover, there are different ways of grounding, for example, ground as cause,—e.g., thrust as causing the movement of a ball—and the reason that a perception is true. It is precisely the principle of ground that demands that the different ways of grounding be distinguished from one another. The "recently much discussed argument about the type and range of the validity of the principle of causality" does not refute the principle of ground; rather, this argument has its "ground and footing" in the fact that the contestants all stand under the claim of the principle of ground (SvG 99). The principle of ground states how a being as a being shows itself to thought; thus this principle concerning every being is the basic principle of thought. As this basic principle, it is in fact the ground of all principles insofar as a principle is valid only *on the basis* of the legitimacy of the connection between subject and predicate. Since the principle of ground states how a being is *as* a being, and therefore is for our thinking, it makes a statement about the Being of beings. It presupposes that Being is basic [*grundartig*], at the bottom of everything [*grundhaft*]. We should not hear the principle with only the usual accentuation, *nothing* is *without* ground. We must also listen to another accent: nothing *is* without *Ground*. Thus it grants to the "is," to Being, a grounding character (SvG 90ff, 204f).

Already Dilthey noted[26] that metaphysics had reached its formal conclusion when Leibniz laid down the principle of ground or sufficient reason. From out of the experience of history and freedom, Dilthey protested against the all-encompassing necessary context which this principle demands. In the fifteenth chapter of the *Geburt der Tragödie*, the young Nietzsche spoke of a "tragic" world view against the "exalted metaphysical illusion" which became known in this principle. In the name of historical or tragic life, the "metaphysical positions of cognition," "Socratism," and "Platonism" are rejected in the principle of ground. When Heidegger brings the principle of ground up for discussion as a principle which says something about Being and its sense, then he makes metaphysics problematic from metaphysics itself.

153

A thinking which asks about the principle of ground as a principle of Being must pay attention to how seminal Greek thinking thought about Being, as presencing, abiding and enduring, lying before one in unconcealment. To this Being belongs λόγος which is simultaneously a saying as a letting-lie-before, and the exhibition upon which what lies before lies; in short, it is the "ground." The belonging-together of Being and ground is thus discussed, but it is not experienced *as such* (SvG 177ff). The way in which φύσις and λόγος, Being and ground, belong to one another does not become a problem. Being conceals the truth about itself and lets the presupposition, which is thought about no further, to dominate, namely, that Being is *constant* presencing and in this sense the ground of beings. Ground appears "in the form of ἀρχαί, αἰτίαι, *rationes, causae*, principles, causes, and the rational arguments. In its withdrawal, Being leaves behind these forms of ground which nevertheless remain unknown with respect to their origin (SvG 183f). When Plato thinks of Being as idea and thus secures it in the character of constant presence (Plato's thought does not exhaust itself in this securing!), he then brings the belonging-togetherness of Being and ground up for discussion by grasping the basic character of Being, the idea of ideas, as ἀγαθόν, as enabling it so that Being is intrinsically "causal," "grounding." Causing, conditioning, and enabling are then consolidated as the character of Being in that Christian theology brings the will of God into play as the cause which conditions everything. Similarly, in Roman thinking it is ἐνέργεια—being brought forth into the open—in terms of effecting and making. Thus ἐνέργεια becomes *actualitas*, which is essentially *causalitas* (NII, 410ff).

If Being is thought of as constant presencing and thus as the "ground" of beings, then it is at thinking's disposal—either for the thinking will of God or else for the representing and willing of man as soon as beings are delivered to man. The ground, which the one who thinks has at his disposal, is the ground to be delivered over. The ground to be delivered over must at the same time be sufficient ground—that is, sufficient for being able to secure in its stand being as object. The permanence of the object must be secured through the completeness of the grounds to be delivered over, the *perfectio* of the conditions of the possibility of the object

154

(SvG 64). It is Leibniz who ends the "incubation period" of the principle of ground in that he formulates this principle and thereby brings into the discussion expressly what has always been suggested in thinking. He gives the reaching for ground its modern form in that he thinks the ground as the sufficient ground to be handed over. In his own way, Kant then meets the demand of the principle of ground, not so much because he argues with Wolff and Baumgarten about the principle of ground or with Hume about cause and effect, but rather because he provides in his critiques the conditions for the possibility, ordered as the sufficient ground to be delivered over *a priori*, by which nature and freedom can be. *Ratio* is not only the name for the ground itself, but also for the delivering of the grounds, reason. Modern thinking represents something as something, and thus imputes that what is represented has a sufficient ground to be delivered over. It relies upon this ground (*ratio*) and is, therefore, reason as calculating thinking (*ratio* in another sense of this word). In the double meaning of *ratio*, the sameness of Being as ground and of thinking as the delivering over of the ground is concealed (SvG 174, 127).

If thinking seeks a final account, it finds it in the god which is the ground of itself, *causa sui*. If this god loses its binding force, if it is, as Nietzsche expressed it, "dead," then the "world" still remains and in it man remains the field of a singular reaching out for the sufficient grounds to be delivered over. The reckoning with beings by means of seizing the grounds is accomplished by science which today permeates all of life. If, as Heidegger says, Schopenhauer already named as the mother of science the why which is asked by the principle of ground,[27] then science and research are grounded upon this principle (SvG 49f, 201), and technology rests upon them. The perfection of technology corresponds to scientific perfection in the completeness of the grounds to be delivered over. This perfection has released atomic energy so that our age today, in the East and in the West, calls itself the Atomic Age. It is defined by the natural energy to be delivered over, and perhaps justifiably so: "For the rest which still exists and which one still calls culture: theater, art, film, and radio, but also literature and philosophy, indeed even faith and religion, all of this everywhere only limps behind what names the age the Atomic Age" (SvG, 58). If the energies are released, then correct use must be secured. Work on safeguarding life, which must be secured constantly, needs information. Man is informed by means of information not only about supply and demand; he is also "formed." Language is dragged into technology and becomes the instrument of information. Consequently, computers and large computer installations become possible along with the information medium of the illustrated newspaper (SvG 58). A phenomenon such as "abstract art" also has its legitimate function in the realm of the technical-scientific world

155

construction (SvG 41, 66). All regions of today's life conform to the demand of the principle of the sufficient ground which is to be delivered over. Leibniz, who formulated the principle of ground, profoundly determined the metaphysics of German Idealism and thereby that dialectic which today has world-political significance. He not only accomplished this feat, but he is also the co-creator of modern mathematical thought, the father of logistics and cybernetics, as well as the inventor of life insurance (SvG, 202). The principle of ground points to the innermost character of modern times. It determines our times all the more the more self-evident and inconspicuous its domination becomes. "Thus it is today" (SvG 197).

When Leibniz formulated the principle of ground, Being appeared to arrive at the truth about itself. But something else happened: the truth of Being withdrew itself more decisively because the question did not awaken whether Being and ground ought to be thought together as they are thought together, namely, as constant presencing and as deliverable ground. The more strongly the principle of ground determines the thinking and activity of man, the less this question appears to be able to be heard. Perhaps this question can nevertheless be heard today since the apparently contradictory is happening, namely, that the unleashing of the demand for the delivering up of the grounds of beings, the omnipotence of technological production and delivery, robs man of every natural ground and basis, of everything which is native to him. If we men are so constituted "that what belongs to us shines forth for us only in the privation of what we have lost," then we could learn to glimpse the essence of Being in the most extreme withdrawal of Being (SvG 60, 101). Heidegger therefore contrasts metaphysical-scientific-technological explanation, calculation, and research with a certain reflection. This reflection does not secure for itself a being upon which it chances from its ground, but rather asks about Being and its sense, and it lets the manner in which Being and ground belong together become problematic. This reflection requires a transformed man. It no longer requires the man who—as *animal rationale*, the self-securing organism—wants "to live by means of atoms" (as stated in a popular book with a preface by Nobel Prizewinner Otto Hahn and a foreword by the Defense Minister of the Federal Republic of Germany, cf. SvG 198), but rather the man who as a mortal is given over to Being and its truth by his being-toward-death.

156

The reflection asks whether the manner in which Being and ground separately receive their essence is something ultimate which is not to be questioned further. Does the equation, "Being is constant presencing and therefore ground," itself have a ground? The Being which grounds, insofar as it is simply the ground, cannot have for its part another ground. Ground stays away from Being as ground; as ground it "is" groundless, the abyss (SvG 93). May being-the-ground for its part be thought of in terms of constantly presencing Being? The word ground means—in expressions such as "sea-bottom," "from the bottom of one's heart,"— "that, to which we go down, to which we return, insofar as the ground is that upon which something rests, that upon which something depends, from which something follows" (SvG 162). The ground can also be the "natural ground," the fruitful soil which becomes that which it is over a long period of time. Such a ground could be meant when Heidegger thinks of Being as the abysmal ground in accordance with its truth and thereby in accordance with its there. If Being is thought of as abysmal ground, then the metaphysical determinations of Being and ground are left behind. The Nothing belongs to Being as the abysmal ground; it is, therefore, no longer the constant, completely positive presencing which "grounds" everything which is present and which itself, in accordance with its essence, counts as "explained" if it is grounded for its part in the most permanent of that which is present (SvG 119, 185). Being, to which the Nothing belongs, is "in essence finite" (WiM 40); it is in its truth, simultaneously the abysmal, unavailable, occurring both of revealing (grounding) and concealing (the withdrawing of a deliverable ground). When one experiences Being from its truth, one can no longer secure it as constant presencing and as a ground at one's disposal. Thus the metaphysical-technological reaching out for the ground is broken at the center of its essence. Technology may be able to produce and to secure some being; however, it cannot have at its disposal the fact that it itself is a destiny of truth regarding beings.

Heidegger can appeal to the mystical tradition when he thinks of the abysmal character, the "without why" of Being. In connection with verses of Angelus Silesius, and of Goethe as well, Heidegger differentiates between ground as "why" and ground as "because." The ground which answers the investigative question "Why?" is the deliverable, sufficient ground which belongs together with constantly present Being. In contrast to this ground as why stands the ground as because, the abysmal ground upon which the why-question, the grounding and the accounting for something, has no effect. The rose is—according to Angelus Silesius— *because* it is; it is without any why (SvG 68ff). "The because, which wards off every accounting for and every why, names the simple, plain lying-before that is without why, upon which everything depends, upon which everything rests" (SvG 208). In the because Heidegger still hears the old "the while" or "because" [*Dieweilen*], the staying [*Weilen*] and the enduring (thus he separates himself from the mystical tradition, insofar as the latter indeed experiences the abysmal character of Being, but scarcely the temporal and historical character of the truth of Being in it).

The ground thought in its other essence as "without why," as the

157

"because" and "the while," unlocks an "outer door" to the question about the sense of Being (SvG 205f). The sense or the truth of Being could be experienced as the "without why," the "because" and "while" of that abysmal play into which man is brought with his essence, mortal Dasein. Heraclitus spoke about this play in the first beginning of Western thinking when he called *"Aion"* [Greek, world period] a child who plays. "The 'Because' sinks in the play. The play is without 'why'. It plays, because it plays. It remains only play: The highest and most profound. However, this 'only' is everything, the one, the only" (SvG 188). If Being is thought of as this play, then it is thought of as "it itself" (PL 76), as underivable from any unchanging being, as incapable of any further grounding. Being is thought in its truth as the event of appropriation in which "nothing" happens (NII, 485), since the appropriative event is not simply an attribute of something, since it cannot be explained from a being to be established, and it itself is not actually substantialized with regard to "the" event. The "without why" of the truth of Being is because it is; this because is the whiling, a temporal and fateful breaking open of the truth suddenly and at any time, but not a "becoming" insofar as becoming is thought only as the opposite of constant Being.

158

Heidegger calls into question the manner in which Being and ground belong together in metaphysics—namely, as constant presencing and deliverable ground. He thinks another essence of Being and ground and thus brings the truth of Being itself up for discussion. If this truth is experienced as appropriative event, then the words "Being" and "ground" can no longer be adequate to this experience. They are returned to metaphysics, and in the future they will no longer be "basic" or central terms; instead they will simply be guidewords of Heidegger's own thinking, words which open an "outer door" but which cannot say what is actually to be said. If Heidegger returns these words to metaphysics after he has explained them, then it is not a matter of a mere change of words, but rather of a change in questioning and thinking, not least a change in approaching the question about identity, difference, and ground.

In the circle of *Sein und Zeit*, identity and difference are stratified in a number of ways so that the one difference (or identity) surpasses the other. The manifestness of beings (ontical truth) can be carried on to the expressly assumed revealing of the Being of beings (to ontological truth), and this revealing to the (fundamental-ontological) question about the sense of Being (cf. G 12ff). The sameness of Being and thinking (identity) is consequently different. According to a communication to Max Müller,[28] Heidegger wanted to distinguish the differences in his development of the third division of the first part of *Sein und Zeit* in the following manner:

159   a) the '*transcendental*' or ontological difference in the narrower sense:
the difference between a being and its being-ness.
b) the '*transcendentalness*' or ontological difference in the wider sense:
the difference between a being *and* its beingness from Being itself.
c) the '*transcendent*' or theological difference in the strict sense: the
difference between God and a being, beingness, and Being.

The question about identity and difference gives the impression as if the
one identity, or difference, could be grounded in the next as the condition
of its possibility. Not only is a being to be grounded (metaphysically-
ontologically) in its "Being," the beingness of a being, but this beingness
for its part is to be grounded (in terms of fundamental ontology) in the
question about the "Being" or "essence" of Being, Being itself or the sense
of Being. Indeed, this Being itself is to be related once more (theologically)
to an ultimate "transcendent one," one which goes beyond and grounds.
Thus the question can arise as to whether philosophy can offer God as this
last transcendent one or whether, as mere philosophy, it must stop at
Dasein.

Insofar as thinking within the sphere of influence of *Sein und Zeit*
understands itself as a grounding, something remarkable befalls it. It
attempts to secure identity and difference as well as transcendental
determinations such as "Being as being-the-ground" in a transcendence
which is specified as factical existence and thereby as temporal and
historical. However, thinking speaks about "the" Being, "the" difference,
"the" ground as if Being, difference, ground were not at all affected by
temporalness. The grounding of the transcendental determinations in
transcendence is understood as an attempt to obtain an "idea" of Being.
Transcendence itself is then also understood logically as the Idea of Ideas,
as the Platonic ἀγαθόν (SuZ 437, G 52ff, 40ff). If transcendence, that
which is authentically present in Dasein and in the transcendental horizon of the sense of Being, is ἀγαθόν, then Dasein and the sense of Being
are "ground" in accordance with the grounding essence of ἀγαθόν which
makes fit for service. In *Sein und Zeit*, the words "ground" and "sense" are
used synonymously: Being is the supporting ground of beings and thus its
sense and truth, "because 'ground' is accessible only as sense, even if it is
160 the abyss of senselessness." Yet as the ground of Being, the sense of Being
is nothing cryptic, but rather the Being or essence of Being, Being itself,
"insofar as it steps into the intelligibility of Dasein" (SuZ 35, 152). The
sense of Being and Dasein, which are really the same thing, are, strictly
taken, not only ground (as Being) but also the "ground of the ground"
(G 53). This ground is of course abysmal ground, and what the word
"Idea" is to name in the language of a thinking which experiences the
ground of ground as abysmal would still have to be clarified. In any case

the thinking which wants to show the temporalness of the sense of Being gets entangled in concepts like idea and ἀγαθόν. Such concepts arise from a thinking that has forgotten the temporalness of the sense of Being in favor of the presupposition that Being is constant presencing and in this sense ground. The thinking of *Sein und Zeit* can become entangled in these concepts because it as well—as *fundamental* ontology—is still bent upon wanting-to-ground. Because this wanting-to-ground disguises the temporal and the abysmal character of the truth of Being, Heidegger again gave up analyzing the difference and the grounding of the one in the other as he intended to carry it through in the third division of *Sein und Zeit*; such tasks are "not experienced but only speculatively erected," and "still 'ontotheological'." This statement not only ventures to assert something about God," an assertion which is not really made in the experience of 'essential thinking';"[29] in fact, its whole approach to the question is inappropriate.

The decisive insight which issues from wanting-to-ground is that "the" Being of beings as a whole does not exist; consequently, there is also not "the" difference, "the" identity. Being arises out of a truth which is the appropriative event. It presents itself in that it holds itself back so that it is not "the" Being, not constant presencing and thus not deliverable ground. The question about the "essence" (the "idea") of Being is inappropriate for the simple reason that it stems from a view that we have a "grasp" of Being—in the sense that we could comprehend and encompass "the" Being whereas beings show themselves historically in the light of their Being only at a given time. The thinking which still puts the question of *essence* to Being is also inappropriate, insofar as it does not expressly rid itself of the presupposition that essence is without exception *constant* presencing. When the question of essence in modern times is formulated **161** as the question about the conditions of the possibility for the actuality of the actual (whether it be in Kant's transcendental or Hegel's absolute sense), then it is manifest how much essence is deliverable ground and how, by means of the question of essence, everything which is not at one's disposal is screened out. If the question about the "essence of ground" is raised, then something paradoxical happens: Being thought as Being-the-ground is represented from its essence or its Being-the-ground so that ground is no longer ground, and essence is no longer essence in the traditional sense. The "Being" (the idea) of Being, the ground of ground, is thought as abyss. Consequently, wanting-to-ground is broken down. It becomes evident that one can no longer ask about a why, about the possibility of the truth of Being, since every questioning about possibilities already moves within this truth (*Die Überwindung der Metaphysik*). Only when one sees through grounding as a way of metaphysical thinking will the way become free to experience the truth of Being as history at a given time which is not at one's disposal.

Only slowly did Heidegger's thinking relinquish its wanting-to-ground. Experiencing the thrownness of the grounding projection had to be deepened to experiencing the abysmal character of the truth of Being. The leap became the "guiding attunement" of thinking when it was recognized that there is "never a direct progression which goes in the same direction and again employs the leading question applied to Being [*Seyn*]" from the leading question (about Being as the beingness of a being) to the basic question (about Being itself or the truth of Being). Rather there is only "a leap—that is, the necessity of *another* beginning" (*Beiträge*). The leading metaphysical question about the Being of beings cannot be applied to itself since it is already inappropriate. It has forgotten the "abysmal ground" upon which it stands—the truth of Being—and therefore takes Being as constant presencing and deliverable ground. The "going back to the ground of metaphysics" becomes the leap. This is the "hazardous venture of initially forging ahead into the region of the history of Being." This "most daring element in the advance of seminal thinking" appears in the "guise of the most reckless"; nonetheless, it is attuned in that awe which belongs to the insistence of the still pending nature of the truth of Being which always is denied us as well.

162   The leap of thinking adapts itself to the occurring of the truth of Being which is not at one's disposal; thus the thrownness and abysmal natures of being-there [*Da-sein*] are first brought to their truth by a thinking which takes the leap as its guiding attunement. "The *leap* (the thrown projection) is the accomplishment of the projection of the truth of Being [*Seyn*] in the sense of inserting into the open so that the one who projects experiences himself as thrown—that is, he is appropriated by means of Being" (*Beiträge*).

From a thinking which finds its guiding attunement in the leap, Heidegger, in the lecture about the principle of ground, criticizes the early work *Vom Wesen des Grundes* for a "false thoroughness" (SvG 48). This treatise attempts to ground even the being-the-ground in its "essence," to outdo what is thought metaphysically by means of what is thought in a higher way. Thus, however, this treatise ignores the unthought which supports everything that is thought in the principle of ground. The treatise is not yet reflective enough to "experience" the "empowering of the mighty principle of ground" (SvG 48). This empowering is the belonging together of Being and ground as that appropriative event out of which Being and ground grant their essences to one another. Heidegger tries to experience this in that he no longer presents the ground in terms of its essence, but rather pays heed to the empowering as the unthought in what is thought in the principle of ground. With this the question about the essence of ground is not simply dropped; rather it just reaches its "appropriate region" (SvG 92). Essence is now thought verbally and thinking, "in terms of the history of Being," notes expressly that "the" Being, "the" difference, and "the" ground do not exist; instead there is Being, difference, and ground in epochal characterizations (SvG 176, ID 63ff). "Essence," thought verbally, is experienced as closely bound up with the occurrence of language, as the dominance of a word or principle. The basic words and principles are historical because the facts about which they speak are historical, are "way" (SvG 153ff, 159ff, 94).

The principle of ground says something about every being. It speaks about the Being of beings, but without directly bringing up for discussion the holding sway of this Being which is different in each case. There is, therefore, no basis in what is thought and directly said for the experience of this holding sway (SvG 95). It is the leap into what has been previously forgotten which, as what is unthought, supports in a concealed way everything that is thought. What has already been thought provides a "hint" about this unthought since the Being of beings is thought in it even if the dominance of Being, the truth of Being, is not (SvG 129). The thinking which accomplishes the leap is a discussion or an emplacing; it inquires into what is unthought in that which has been thought. It thus experiences tradition, namely, as handing itself down to what has remained unthought (SvG 83ff, 42ff). The thinking which in emplacing [*Er-örtern*] is handed over to what is unthought in that which was previously thought is transported, by means of the unthought, from the abode of the previous thought to another abode (SvG 94f, 106). What was previously unthought, the truth of Being, comes to language in this abode. Until the thinking ahead into the truth of Being has been "transformed" from this truth to another Saying, a "leap" from what was previously thought to the unthought therein is needed (SvG 159).

163

THE TRANSFORMATION OF THINKING

If thinking is to interrogate not merely beings about their Being, but rather Being itself regarding its truth, then it must be transformed. It may not raise the question about beings as such and as a whole in such a way, as metaphysical thinking does, that the question about the truth of Being itself cannot arise at all. The transformation demanded by thinking is an ever-increasing struggle to revise one's own approach in such a way that thinking becomes free to experience the truth of Being itself. How this transformation occurs in Heidegger's thinking and how Heidegger again and again revises his own approach upon the way of his thinking is to be shown in what follows.

At the beginning of his way of thinking, Heidegger, starting with the problems of logic and language, raises the question about how Being preserves unity in the multiplicity of its modes of articulation. To be able to develop this question, Heidegger reaches back to metaphysics, the Western doctrine of Being. Having taken his bearings from the highest summits attained by metaphysics in the age of the Greeks, the Middle Ages, and in modern times, Heidegger opposes the modern "cursory breadth" and "the lifestyle which superficially runs its course" in order to re-emphasize the structure of spiritual life extending into the transcendent. His concern is not with a spelling out of reality but rather with a *"breakthrough* into the true reality and the real truth" (*Die Kategorien und Bedeutungslehre des Duns Scotus* 240, 236).

164

Heidegger found the single thought which he had to think in the question about true reality and the really true, about beings in the openness of Being and the openness of Being in beings. In his first works, however, he had not yet developed this thinking into the question which determines his path of thinking. Heidegger does ask the metaphysical question about reality and truth or Being and truth, but he does not yet develop the question about the truth of Being itself. It is therefore not surprising that Heidegger still speaks the language of metaphysics and to a large extent appropriates the concepts of his time. For him, "existence" and "Dasein" mean "reality" in the metaphysical sense. For example, he still takes the concept of mood or attunement in the customary, pejorative sense and he does not yet recognize the basic phenomenon of attunement in its significance. This is evident when in his dissertation (53), Heidegger affirms that "even in philosophy" one must hold "that research free of moods and value judgements is possible." A language which Heidegger later avoids like a shallow swamp still provides the leading concepts: value, cultural value, life value, world view, strong personal experience, subject, and so forth.

With complete consistency, Heidegger refers to his own philosophizing in the sense of metaphysics as a doctrine of categories. "A theory of categories" means addressing beings as beings, determining beings in terms of their Being and articulating Being in the multiplicity of its modes. In *modern* metaphysics this addressing of beings as beings is subordinated explicitly to the court of reason. Metaphysics becomes "critical"; that is, its questioning goes back to reason as the possibility of exhibiting beings as beings, and as the illumination and delimitation of scientific reason, it is "logic" or "theory of science." Heidegger retains this critical turn, and at the beginning of his *Habilitations* lecture, *Der Zeitbegriff in der Geschichtswissenschaft,* he expands upon it. He states that in the metaphysical impulse awakened in philosophy, will to power expresses itself; nonethe-

less the critical consciousness in modern science and philosophy is too
vigorously alive for philosophy to be able to master culture "with unjus-
tified and badly founded claims to power"; consequently the
epistemological-logical questions remained pressing. Later Heidegger
showed that a metaphysics which is a theory of categories and, as
"critical" metaphysics, is logic and a theory of science, travels the course
of metaphysics without the essence of metaphysics having become problematic for it (K 65ff, NI, 527ff, II, 71ff).

Where Heidegger attempted to grasp the history of thought about value
in his first works, he later exhibited the presupposition of this approach as
well. Thought about value is a specifically modern thought. In it Being as
the condition for the possibility of beings has become the arithmetical sign
with which even history is to be mastered. Nietzsche is the genuinely
consistent "philosopher of value." The neo-Kantian philosophy of value
preserved and indeed still handed down "a trace of genuine knowledge
about the essence of philosophy and of philosophical questioning in
opposition to the forward thrust of the natural sciences of 'psychology'
and 'biology', the allegedly authentic and sole 'philosophy'." "Nonetheless, this attitude, 'traditional' in a good sense, still denied to 'value
philosophy' the opportunity to think over the thought about value in its
metaphysical essence, that is, actually to take nihilism seriously. It was
believed that one could escape nihilism by returning to Kantian philosophy, but this only made way for nihilism and abandoned the peering into
the abyss which such nihilism conceals" (NII, 48, 98, 99).

The appropriated traditional and contemporary ways of thought are
not decisive for Heidegger's path of thinking. What is decisive is the
question which he could hear from out of them: How should one think the
unity from which the multiplicity of the meanings of Being can be
articulated? This question was fundamentally transformed when in
Heidegger's thinking the experience of history was freed from the metaphysical approach which distorts history in its primordiality, that is, when
history was finally experienced as the forgotten background of metaphysical thinking. If metaphysics thinks Being in terms of constant presence,
that is, in terms of presentness, then, it thinks it within a horizon to which
time and history belong. If one raises the question about *Sein und Zeit*, then
one no longer asks about the Being of beings and the multiplicity of the
modes of the meaning of Being solely in a universal ontology or doctrine of
categories; instead, in the first place, one asks "in a fundamental-
ontological manner" about the sense of Being, about the ground of the
manifold expressibility of Being, and about the how, the temporalness of
this ground.

For ten years Heidegger methodologically grasped ontology as well as fundamental ontology as "phenomenology." The temporalness of the sense of Being and its accomplishment in Dasein is to be encountered when "destruction" joins "phenomenological seeing." Destruction is supposed to clear away what in the heritage of our thought disguises an experience of the sense of Being and its temporalness. "But this destruction, like 'phenomenology' and all hermeneutical-transcendental questioning, is not yet thought in terms of the history of Being" (NII, 415). Phenomenological research appears as evidence of a hidden ultimate, and destruction appears as penetration to this hidden ultimate, as a dismantling of the distorting tradition, but not as submitting to the history of the truth of Being. Thus, phenomenological research and destruction cover up the experience of the temporalness of the sense of Being, toward which they, of course, are supposed to lead.

To be sure, the phenomenological seeing seeks to bring into view the phenomena and also the phenomenal, Being itself, in every phenomenon, but like every "metaphysical" thinking born of the Greeks, it is not free to inquire about the essential origin of appearing and Being, the truth of Being itself (Sp 134f). Heidegger therefore gives up phenomenology, but only in order to bring up for discussion the concealed essence of the phenomenological, the experience of the truth of Being. The essence of the phenomenological is to be thought in terms of a λόγος, a saying, in which what appears and comes to the fore, the phenomenon, is made to appear from itself, to show itself openly. At the same time, however, the essence of the already presupposed truth of Being as unconcealment does not remain unthought (VA 213).[30]

167   Heidegger sought to discuss the essence of the phenomenological already within the sphere of influence of *Sein und Zeit*. He grasped phenomenology as "hermeneutical" and grounded the phenomenological letting-be-seen in the understanding of factical existence. Heidegger clearly differentiated hermeneutical phenomenology from every hermeneutic that has to do merely with the sciences of the spirit. In Heidegger's sense, hermeneutics means that Dasein in its hermeneutical accomplishment, the understanding of Being, permits the sense of Being to manifest itself and from this Dasein understands not only the being which it is but also beings which it is not (SuZ 37). In spite of this the impression remained that the understanding belonging to hermeneutical phenomenology could indeed do justice to the phenomena of history's region of Being, but not for the phenomena of those regions in which the nonhistorical occurs, e.g., invariable nature, the mathematically "ideal," or the archetypes of art which are rooted in the natural depths of the soul.

Since it was not yet clear in the published part of *Sein und Zeit* how the "hermeneutical relation"—the relation of existence to the sense of

Being—was to be thought, one took hermeneutical phenomenology as an intimate contact of the understanding of Being in man, as a historical-anthropological absolutizing of the Being of finite-historical man. *Sein und Zeit* appeared as a hermeneutical theory which represents the understanding of Being with respect to its essence (temporality and the hermeneutical circle) and thus critically secures it as *fundamentum inconcussum veritatis*. According to Heidegger's later experience, the attempt of a Dasein which understands Being to represent its own essence and to secure it as the ground of further questioning, in other words, the "critical" reflexion of understanding upon itself, keeps Dasein from subordinating itself to the history of truth and from having the abysmal truth of Being become manifest. Not even the discourse about the hermeneutical "relation" is capable of saying what is actually to be said: the fact that the essence of man is being-*used* for the occurrence of the truth of Being, for the carrying out of the appropriative event. Heidegger, therefore, also gave up the title "hermeneutics," but only so that the essential matter to be thought in what is hermeneutical could be expressed in the question about language. The latter, as the primordial record [*Ur-kunde*], requires man for that "errand" which ("hermeneutically") brings tidings from the appropriative event of the truth of Being (Sp 104f, 125ff, 153ff).

That one finds the "primary" sense of hermeneutic in the analytic of **168** Dasein shows to what extent *Sein und Zeit* stands in danger of establishing human understanding as the foundation of truth which is to be secured critically in a modern metaphysical manner. As a being among all beings, Dasein is distinguished in that it understands Being; it is the "exemplary" being which must be taken into view first of all if the question about Being is to be unfolded. Nonetheless the "securing" of this exemplary being remains only the "point of departure" for the "authentic analytic" which, as the analytic of Dasein, illuminates the projection of the sense of Being (SuZ 37f, 235). Dasein is, as tradition says, the "soul," which in a certain manner "is" every being, since the former understands the latter in its Being (SuZ 14). In addition, Dasein is also beyond itself; it is, therefore, "transcendence." Nonetheless Heidegger does not think of transcendence in specifically modern fashion, in terms of consciousness for which Being has become objectivity and thereby the representability of objects. The transcendence of Dasein is thought rather as the opening and the holding open of that "*transcendens* pure and simple" which is Being. In this other than modern sense, hermeneutical phenomenology is "transcendental knowledge" (SuZ 38).

The determination of Being as *transcendens* summarizes how the essence of Being has made itself clear for man up to this point. However, this introductory and retrospective determination of Being is only the beginning for a thinking ahead toward the truth of Being (PL 83). This thinking ahead first occurs when the transcendence of Dasein becomes problematic, when the mode of Dasein's transcendence is conceived as existence. Metaphysical thinking about transcendence was sharpened by means of Christian theology. For example, Zwingli determined man's transcending as a "looking up to God and his word," and Kierkegaard spoke of existence as a relation which relates itself to God in that it relates itself to itself (SuZ 49, 12). Nonetheless, the finiteness and temporality of existence are still conceived here from the relation and contrast to God. In contrast, Heidegger first of all excludes man's possible relation to God and defines existence from itself as finite and temporal so that it becomes factical existence.

169   . Is the concept of existence sufficient if Dasein is to be conceived as There [*Da*] and thereby as the abode of the truth of Being? As Heidegger shows in his reflection upon metaphysics as the history of Being (NII 399ff), the concept of existence belongs in the modern age and thereby indeed to metaphysics. That this concept could play so large a role in the last one hundred fifty years presupposes that the truth of Being was forgotten, that Being determined itself by accentuating the that-it-is in contrast to what-it-is, and that ἐνέργεια became *actualitas* which in turn recently became the reality of subjectivity. With absolute subjectivity, whose Being is willing, Schelling differentiated that which is only the "ground of existence" in the sense of groundwork and basis from that which is "authentic," that is, existence. Kierkegaard narrowed this metaphysical-speculative concept of existence to the anthropological realm on the basis of a Christian but specifically subjectivistic passion for the salvation of the soul. Only man "exists"; his existing is faith, an adhering to the reality of the real.

When Heidegger used the concept of existence in *Sein und Zeit*—"temporarily" as he later emphasized—he thereby took a decisive step upon the way of his thought; he thought the understanding of Being as finite and temporal. But this step was only *one* step as he was under way in questioning about the truth of Being (NII, 473ff). For Heidegger, existence was never something final or self-evident; for this reason Heidegger could never admit that his thinking could properly be characterized as "existential philosophy." For him, an existential philosophy—insofar as it is not merely the stillborn of philosophical journalism—can be nothing but an offspring of modern subjectivism. To be sure, the early work of Karl Jaspers regarding the *Psychologie der Weltschauungen* was a significant impetus for the young Heidegger. Yet farther along his path, Jaspers, instead of taking hold of the problem of laying the foundation of metaphysics, did in his *Philosophie* of 1932 precisely what Heidegger wanted to avoid: he simply presupposed the modern metaphysical attitude. Jaspers legitimizes science's thinking in terms of a world view as world orienta- tion, contrasts this with the different "illumination"of existence, and then still seeks the "metaphysical" relationship to another ground, to "tran- **170** scendence." Heidegger has nothing more to do with such a philosophy, and he even expressed this, for example, in a letter to Jean Wahl, who in 1937 put Jaspers and Heidegger together as "existential philosophers" inspired by Kierkegaard. Since Jaspers for the same reason[31] clearly said that Heidegger's thinking and his own had *essentially* nothing in common, the nonsensical chatter about the one existential philosophy as the ex- pression of our time actually could have been omitted.

The concept of existence has become the conceptual fashion of the day. To be sure, we ought not forget that the summons to "existing" called man back to himself, but despite this, one cannot dismiss the question as to whether this summons does not belong in that subjectivism which determines the final phase of metaphysics. Does one not move insensibly in this subjectivism if one believes that one must make up to the cry for existence by discussing "existentiell" philosophizing, the philosophy of existence, existence-theology, the existentiell or existential study of litera- ture, and so forth? Existential philosophy experienced its most extreme culmination in French existentialism. J. P. Sartre, the main representative of this existentialism, was decisively stimulated by Heidegger's early publications. After all, does not *Sein und Zeit* in fact call man "Dasein" because it assumes that the essential determination of man could not be accomplished by "citing a material what" because it finds the "essence" of man in existence, but not in an essence [*Essenz*] (SuZ 12, 42)? Does man as existence not make himself into what he is as essence? Sartre believed that Heidegger could be understood in this sense, but he thereby missed Heidegger's authentic tendency. Heidegger therefore drew a sharp line of demarcation between existentialism and his own thinking. *Sein und Zeit* does not set existence over essence, but tries rather to approach Dasein as the There, as the region of the truth of Being. Only in this region can the claim of a metaphysical statement about the priority of essence over existence or the claim of the antimetaphysical reversal of this statement be settled. For Heidegger above all, the essence of man is not that freedom which extricates itself from solid being and posits itself upon itself, but **171** rather freedom as the carrying out of the free or open, of the truth, into which beings desire to enter. The "projection" of existence is not *project* as a positing which represents, not the accomplishment of subjectivity, but rather, as thrown and historical, in each case a submitting oneself to the occurring of the truth of Being (PL 68ff, 79f).

Heidegger can differentiate himself from existence-philosophers and existentialists so decisively only because he began his questioning differently than they did from the start, because he took up metaphysics as a problem in order to be able to overcome it and its outcome in subjectivity at its source. For Heidegger, this overcoming was a long path. To be sure, *Sein und Zeit* already considers Dasein in terms of questioning about the sense of Being so that Heidegger could later interpret Dasein as the There of Being, existence as the ecstatic indwelling in the truth of Being, and resolute existence as receptiveness for this truth (WiM 14f, PL 74ff, *Gelassenheit* 61). Yet in *Sein und Zeit* existence is still not yet what it should authentically be. If it were, the step from Dasein's temporality to the temporalness of the sense of Being would have to have been successful. *Sein und Zeit* would not have had to fail. Resoluteness, for example, is indeed in *Sein und Zeit* not thought of as the representing and willing of what is permanent; nevertheless it is thought of as a willing, namely as the wanting-to-have-a-conscience in which Dasein chooses itself and thus appropriates its nullity or "guilt." The willing of metaphysics, the grasp for permanent ground, is already broken down, but the overcoming will first still lead through the most extreme decisions in favor of this willing. The "choice" of self in the "boldness" of "anxiety," in which Dasein even in inescapability and powerlessness still tries to assert its power, will become the self-assertion in the face of the "Nothing." Thinking is "to develop its highest defiance" in face of the superior power of fate—just like Prometheus, about whom Heidegger therefore spoke as the "first philosopher" in his rector's address of 1933. Even in *power*lessness willing still remains as the willing of power. If the attempting to maintain oneself in one's essence is "self-assertion," then knowledge of the essential is a willing (E 16; Hw 55). Heidegger must first appropriate the modern way of thinking about knowing (Dasein) as willing before he can reflect upon the fact that this essence of knowing and of Dasein cannot leave the truth of Being into what is unique to its essence (to be thought verbally). If this reflection is accomplished, then knowing, by means of a not willing, must prepare for a thinking which is neither a willing nor only the mere opposition to thinking as willing, a not willing, but rather a thinking which gains its essence by being addressed and called by the truth of Being (*Gelassenheit* 31ff). If one thinks of the essence of thinking and Dasein in this manner, then what is simply more authentically brought into the discussion is what was already experienced in *Sein und Zeit*, toward which *Sein und Zeit* was under way: in *Sein und Zeit*, wanting-to-have-a-conscience is conceived as understanding a *call* (SuZ 288).

It is always necessary to see the way which Heidegger has gone. At the same it is time-wrong to assert an undifferentiated sameness or a merely

172

superficial difference between Heidegger's early and later thinking or else to take particular points along Heidegger's way of thought and play them off against one another. Whoever wants to do this can of course easily bring Heidegger's early and later statements into apparent opposition. For example, the mineness and authenticity of individualized existence in *Sein und Zeit* is extracted from the inauthenticity of the one.[32] In this way it is to be shown that all of "care" belongs to Dasein as the There. It should in no way be said that authenticity is determined by how far an individual would draw back upon himself or to what extent "Dasein" feels affected by and moves in what is called its "existence." It is rather to be shown that authenticity is determined by the extent to which the truth of beings is simply taken over from what is handed down or else taken up and primordially appropriated from the occurring truth of Being. Authenticity is determined by being appropriated into the truth of Being; it is therefore totally unimportant whether the individual draws back upon himself and whether or not he feels affected by his "existence." Therefore, Heidegger can later say (as Nietzsche said about himself) that essential thinkers have "no choice" (NI, 37); individuation and the decision for oneself only hinder being appropriated into the truth of Being (NII, 482). The truth of Being is a region where there is "nothing to be responsible for," where everything is in perfect order, even if there was "no one" who found the word there, precisely because this region is responsible for itself and vouches for itself, but is not at man's disposal even though it needs man's essence for itself (*Gelassenheit* 49). Strictly taken, these formulations run counter to those of *Sein und Zeit* and yet maintain the course toward the truth of Being as *Sein und Zeit* has entered upon it.

173

Along this course "existence" is transformed into "ek-sistence." The existence which in its resoluteness attempts to grasp the sense of Being as an ultimate foundation experiences its powerlessness and "guilt." Thus it is the "placeholder of the Nothing." It keeps the place free for the totally Other, for what is the Nothing to beings, for Being itself which is not at one's disposal, which cannot be make available like beings. The Nothing, however, is first of all the "undeveloped" essence of Being (WiM 46). If one experiences Being in its complete truth, then one must think the Nothing as the refusal (Hw 104), as the abyss in the truth of Being. If existence watches over the refusal and concealment as the vital heart, as the secret of truth, then it becomes ek-sistence, the earnest [*inständigen*] standing out [*ausstehen*] of this truth. The "placeholder of Nothing" becomes the "shepherd of Being." The truth of being is the shelter which preserves and tends to everything in the truth, which allows beings to be beings and thus also permits man to be man. This shelter "needs" man as the shepherd who takes the shelter into his care, but who does not have it at his disposal—to whom the shelter can be entrusted without becoming his property (Hw 321; PL 75, 115).

If existence becomes ek-sistence, then the focal point in the sameness of Being and thinking will shift from existence to the occurring truth which is not at one's disposal. What was thought earlier will therefore be re-thought. Dasein's attunement, for example, will no longer be understood in terms of the changing moods of man (SuZ 134ff), but rather in terms of the "voice of Being" which, by means of its claim, will always destine thinking to the carrying out of its truth about beings. Thus it will attune it to its epochal uniqueness (*Was ist das—die Philosophie?* 35ff). Attunement is no longer the existential of an existential analytic, but rather a manner of governing the truth of Being and consequently the situating of ek-sistence through this truth. The distinctiveness which anxiety receives among moods is no longer "systematically" grounded in the fact that it, and "only" it, experiences the Nothing (WiM 31, 37); rather it is regarded in terms of the history of Being. Essential anxiety endures nihilism as the destiny of Being and attunes one to the terror of the abyss (WiM 12, 46). As the rector's address of 1933 puts it, if God is dead, "the perseverance of the Greeks in the face of beings, which initially was one of wonder, must be transformed into the completely uncovered exposure to the concealed and uncertain, that is, into that which is questionable." Thinking comes into a new attunement, and it is attuned in each epoch. Greek thinking, for example, abides in astonishment in face of beings, and modern metaphysics leads from doubt to certainty (*Was ist das—die Philosophie?* 37ff). The end of metaphysics is experienced in anxiety. If the Nothing experienced in anxiety shows itself as the veil of Being, then anxiety becomes the awe with regard to the attunement of the "thinking about the origin" which has "come home" (EH 124). Awe is no longer a mere modification of fear (cf. SuZ 142), but rather corresponds to the Greek αἰδώς, which is essentially in "awe" of the gods. It goes together with the releasement which can let beings be beings from the openness for the truth of Being even in the complete domination of the technological mastery of beings.

If existence becomes ek-sistence, then not only is what was thought earlier thought in another way; it is also won back in a new way which, for *Sein und Zeit*, remained an insufficiently developed problem. For example, this work attempts to press forward beyond an explication of the tempo-rality and the historicality of Dasein to the temporalness of the sense of Being, that is, starting from a familiar being, man as Dasein, to think ahead to the unthought and the unknown. But this attempt failed. If the sense of the truth of Being is now experienced as the occurring appropria-

174

tive event which has always occurred and can occur abruptly, then from this experience Dasein also comes into a more primordially experienced essence. Dasein becomes the "abode of the insightful moment" of the truth of Being. Thus the questions which once remained open about the connection between moment and situation, between time and space, and truth and world, are displayed in a new light.

If existence is thought as ek-sistence, then the "primary" sense of attempting to bring the sense or the truth of Being up for discussion can no longer be existential analysis. The essential characteristics of the truth of Being can no longer be grasped as "existentials." They can no longer be named in terms of what, when compared to the truth of Being, would have to be called secondary if a reckoning up between the same of the truth of Being and ek-sistence were possible. **175**

Once the concept of existence has played out its controlling role, the concept of transcendence will also fall. It is surrendered to metaphysics, particularly to modern metaphysics (SvG 132ff, VA 74). The question will now read as follows: how could transcendence, the stepping beyond beings to Being, become descendance in the modern age, the stepping back of subjectivity into itself (*Zur Seinsfrage* 18)? Even the concept of "transcendental horizon" is now left behind (SuZ 39). As Heidegger interprets it (*Gelassenheit* 38ff, 50f), one thinks of the ascent beyond objects in the transcendental of the transcendental horizon, in the horizon of the field of vision which encompasses the outlook (the Being of beings as idea or as the condition for a possibility), and in this way reaches beyond appearance. However, the transcendental horizon is that side of the truth of Being which is turned toward us and thus apparently at our disposal. The concealment which belongs to the unconcealment of Being appears to transcendental knowledge as an empty nothing (as the X of the thing in itself). If this concealment is thought as the innermost core of truth, then the truth of Being can no longer be grasped as transcendental horizon. Of course it can also no longer be grasped as "the sense of Being," since sense is thought primarily in terms of projection and understanding, and thus in terms of the power of subjectivity (SuZ 151ff). Certainly "sense of Being" and "truth of Being" say the same thing (WiM 18), but not without distinction; rather, they do so in the way that Parmenides and Kant say the same identity of thinking and Being. As a *philosophical* term, the word sense belongs to the modern philosophy of subjectivity, the circle of Diltheyian hermeneutics, Neo-Kantianism, and neo-Hegelianism. For this reason, sense as a philosophical term cannot speak of truth as **176** unconcealment even if a root meaning of the word sense may also point directly to what Heidegger thinks of as belonging to the "sense of Being," to the way, course, and direction.

Sein und Zeit wants to prepare an ultimate *ground* for the doctrine of Being; consequently, this work is not only existential analytic but also *fundamental* ontology. It thereby remains unclear how existential analytic and fundamental ontology belong together. Must one seek fundamental ontology, as it says on page 13 of this work, in the existential analytic because this founds all ontologies and even the question about the sense of Being itself? Or, as it says on the same page, does this analytic cling to the "previous working out" of the question about the sense of Being? The published portion of the analytic only prepares the "ground" for reaching the answer to the question about the sense of Being (SuZ 17). Is it or is it not the case that this answer is fundamental ontology or even existential analytic? The book on Kant says that fundamental ontology lays the finitude of the understanding of Being as the ground of metaphysics; thus it is the "first step" of a metaphysics of Dasein (209). Nonetheless, Heidegger later says that his procedure in *Sein und Zeit* is called fundamental ontology because it tries to arrive at the sense of Being, and thus at the truth of Being as the ground of metaphysics (WiM 21, PL 109f).

Before we set Dasein and the sense of Being off against each other as the one and the other ground, we must ask how one is to think of Dasein in general, whether as the being "man" or as the abode of the truth of Being as it occurs in man. The end of *Sein und Zeit* repeats the thesis that phenomenological ontology springs from existence and returns back to it; however, it says that this thesis should not pass for dogma, "but rather as the formulation of the still 'enshrouded' fundamental problem. Can ontology be founded *ontologically* or does it also require an *ontical* foundation for this; and *which* being must take over the function of founding?" *Sein und Zeit* allows no doubt that Dasein must take over the role of founding, because it is "distinguished" from among all beings by its *understanding* of Being. As existence, Dasein is, therefore, set apart from every being. Yet even this presentation of Dasein's distinctiveness is placed into question at the conclusion of *Sein und Zeit*: "What so clearly appears as the difference between the Being of existing Dasein in contrast to the Being of beings that do not have the character of Dasein (reality, for example) is still only the *point of departure* for the ontological problematic, and it is nothing by which philosophy can be reassured" (SuZ 436f).

To be sure, man is distinguished from other beings in that he has the understanding of Being; nonetheless, this talk of the "distinctiveness" of man remains misleading. It makes it appear as though the understanding of Being is a property of the being "man." After all, not only man but in their own way other beings as well stand in Being as the truth regarding them. If one asks about Being and the truth of Being, then one must expressly include every being in the question. In this sense, Heidegger asks: Why is there anything at all rather than nothing? If one expressly includes every being in the question, then the fundamental ontology which seeks to secure existence as the foundation of the doctrine of being becomes "metaphysics." Nonetheless, in this, the "fundamental question" of metaphysics (WiM 42), thinking not only "metaphysically" goes beyond beings toward their Being, but the why of every being and thus the sense of Being is placed into question.

In his first works, Heidegger had taken up the term "metaphysics" in a positive manner, but then the spirit of phenomenological research forced him to reject metaphysics and its "constructions." In *Sein und Zeit* Heidegger still placed the term "metaphysics" in quotation marks; ironically he turned against the contemporary endeavors to reaffirm "metaphysics" (2, 21, 22). Nonetheless, the attempt to ground anew the doctrine of Being had to lead necessarily to an examination of metaphysics. Heidegger did not simply reaffirm metaphysics but asked—in his inaugural speech at Freiburg—about its essence. He did not interpret Kant—in line with the then novel direction in Kantian interpretation—from the metaphysical content of his thinking as a metaphysician, but rather in his examination of Kant he wanted to develop the *problem* of metaphysics. The question of Being of metaphysics was driven back upon the more primordial question from where the question of Being could even be raised (K 203). This "from where," the ground of metaphysics, is Dasein. Yet Dasein is not **178** simply man, but rather the There of the openness of beings as it occurs in man. Like every being, man is what he is only "on the basis of the Dasein in him." The metaphysics which is taken up as a problem is the "metaphysics of Dasein," the metaphysics to be grounded anew not merely "metaphysics about Dasein" but the metaphysics which fatefully occurs "as Dasein." Using Kant's terminology, Heidegger also calls it the "metaphysics of metaphysics" (K 207f). If metaphysics grounds beings in Being, metaphysics asks of metaphysics, what grounds Being as Being? In a pedagogically intended, provisional difference, to be sure, it differentiates the metaphysical question about the Being of beings as the guiding question from the basic question about the truth of Being itself. The basic question is not simply shifted ahead of the guiding question; rather, in the questioning of the basic question, a transformation of the guiding question occurs. What now becomes a *problem* is what the "as such" and the "as a whole" in the question about beings as such and as a whole can genuinely mean.

Is Dasein or the truth of Being now the ground of metaphysics that is to be sought in the asking? Heidegger thought the understanding of Being as the ground of being human; he thought this ground as abysmal and thus took it as the point of departure for the grounding of Being (NI, 577f).

Being is in its truth "ground," but nonetheless a ground from which for its part, the ground is left out, ground as "abyss." The ground as abyss is at the same time "non-ground." It covers and buries its own grounding, and only as abyss and non-ground is it "primordial ground" (*Beiträge*). For a time, Heidegger also spoke about the "finitude" of the understanding of Being and of Being itself (K 197ff, WiM 40). Nonetheless, this concept of finitude has its dangers. It misleads thinking into looking for an infinitude as the necessary presupposition for finitude and thereby into taking infinitude as well as finitude each as beings (K 222). "The discussion about the 'finitude' of Being remains both a diverting and inadequate name for its abysmal character" (recapitulations of the Nietzsche course *Der Wille zur Macht als Erkenntnis*). If thinking preserves the abysmal character of the truth of Being (the concealing contained in it), it can then

179   once more positively appropriate the discussion about the infinite. Infinitude then does not mean what is simply the opposite of the finite, but rather the intimate, no longer unwieldy togetherness of the finite ("Hölderlins Erde und Himmel" 25). If one thinks Dasein and Being itself as abysmal, then one can no longer contrast them with one another as two different, self-sufficient grounds; the one is not without the other. Indeed the regress into the "ground" of metaphysics appears to arrive at the "categorical question," namely, whether Being, as it shows itself in the difference between Being and beings, is to be grounded in accordance with its truth in the nature of man and thus in the transcendence and existence of Dasein, or whether the nature of man is grounded in the difference between Being and beings. However, if one asks the question in this way, then what is to be genuinely sought in questioning, that is, what is grounding and ground in general, would miss the mark (NII, 243). Wanting to ground misses the abysmal, fateful sameness of Being and Dasein, whether it establishes Being as the last *subjectum* in the metaphysics of subjec*ticity* [Subjek*tität*] or as the transcendence of the finite or absolute subject in the modern metaphysics of subjec*tivity*. Reflecting upon the essence of ground leads thinking to attempt to give up wanting-to-ground and to experience in a "leap" the sameness of Being and Dasein in accordance with its present "how."

Sein und Zeit remained incomplete not because of some external circumstances but because its point of departure carried within it the necessity of failure. On the one hand the thinking of *Sein und Zeit* was under way to the truth of Being; on the other hand, however, it sought to experience the truth of Being metaphysically as it can never be experienced, as the ultimate foundation, as the ground to be delivered up for the doctrine of Being. Indeed *Sein und Zeit* begins with the question as to what it means that, starting with Greek thinking, Being has been understood in terms of presence and thereby in terms of presentness. Yet *Sein und Zeit* does not stop at this question and does not put up with the history in which Being has shown itself to thinking as presence. Instead, *Sein und Zeit* sets out upon a circuitous route; it first secures the existence which understands Being and represents historicality as the "essence" of this existence. Consequently, *Sein und Zeit* was not only subjectivistically and anthropologically misunderstood because it arose from previous thinking, but "against its will" this work itself fell into the danger of "becoming only a **180** new strengthening of subjectivity" (NII, 194f). Because *Sein und Zeit* had not yet sufficiently extricated itself from metaphysical, representational thinking and the modern tendency to begin from subjectivity as the foundation to be secured first, it was unable to find its way back to its question about Being and presence, Being and time, from the detour upon which it had set out. The transition from the analysis of Dasein based upon temporality to the unfolding of the temporalness of the sense of Being itself was not successful. Heidegger already failed in his attempt to think the unity of the ecstases of temporality, and thus to reach the jumping off point for exhibiting the temporalness of the sense of Being. In the essay *Vom Wesen des Grundes* he therefore tried to make the "transcendental horizon" of the sense of Being visible for the first time independent of the problem of "temporality." However, even this essay, by overtaking ontical truth by means of ontological truth, got bogged down in that wanting-to-ground which misses the unity of systematic and historical thinking; consequently it is unable to experience the temporal and historical nature of the truth of Being. "The crisis," as it says in the *Beiträge*, "could not be mastered by means of merely thinking along in the established direction of questioning —instead one had to venture the manifold leap into the essence of Being itself which simultaneously demanded a more primordial introduction to history." One had to raise the question about the essence of truth, but this question had to be transformed into the question about the truth of essence, about the unconcealment of Being. Since Being comes to presence for us from the errancy of a metaphysics "which has forgotten Being," one had to raise the question about the essence of metaphysics. For its part, this question had to become the question as to how thinking can place itself into the essence of metaphysics, the essence to be thought verbally, and how it can draw back the unthought in metaphysics by a thinking characterized by the history of Being. Thinking had to give up the delusion of a metaphysics by metaphysics in favor of the "transitional" thinking imbued with the history of Being.

The transition accomplished by thinking in terms of the history of Being is the setting up of one's abode [*Einkehr*] in the truth of Being. But transition and the setting up of an abode are not the turning from one thing to another, for example, the replacement of the ground "existence" by the ground **181**

"Being."[33] Instead, one experiences in the transition the sameness of Being itself and Dasein in another way in that thinking sets up an abode in the unthought of what has already been thought. In a turning it turns itself against itself and uncovers the "ungrounded" in the "grounding" of itself (NI, 24). In this sense *Sein und Zeit* already accomplishes a turning. The analysis of the understanding of Being in terms of temporality, in terms of which the doctrine of Being is grounded, is in turn to be grounded in the ungrounded of the temporal sense of Being. If one speaks of a turn already in *Sein und Zeit*, then one may not overlook the fact that the actually accomplished turn was never realized and indeed was not even realizable in the way planned in *Sein und Zeit*, as the "systematic," grounding transition from existence to the sense of Being. The circle in which the understanding of the Being of existence and the sense of Being are combined can be traversed only if thinking gives up metaphysics' wanting-to-ground and its production of grounds, only if it experiences ground in its other essence as abyss (NI, 654). Thinking can turn only if the truth of Being, which had turned away in its primordial essence, lets this turning away be experienced and thereby points to its primordiality.

The turning as Being's setting up an abode in its truth presupposes the turning as the turning away of Being from its truth. When Being determined itself "as Being" (as constant presence), it concealed its truth; it remained in view only as the *openness* of beings, but not as concealing and closing (Hw 310). The Greeks, who grounded metaphysics and that means the Western truth about beings, were fascinated by Being as the openness of beings and consequently had to forget with a certain necessity the truth of Being: that Being is at once laying open and concealing. This forgetting is not to be thought as if the Greeks had hit upon the nonhuman beings, the "world," and had therefore forgotten the genuinely human, temporal existence and thereby the sense of Being as well. This course of thought (cf. SuZ 25)—suggested by the Christian admonition toward "inwardness" and corresponding to the popular representation of the "objective" thought of the Greeks—is not essential for Heidegger's way of thought. What alone is essential is the suggestion that the Being of beings was forced upon Greek thinking with such power that it was taken as what is permanent and in this sense as what lies-in-view. The constant "present-at-hand-ness" of Being—with reference to Greek thinking Heidegger later speaks only about "presence" or "presencing"—is not the external and the "worldly" which lies in view, since it can in fact be realized in the "mental," for instance, in mathematical symmetries or in an ever unchanging prototype. If the vanishing of Being shows itself in nihilism, then thinking can be reminded that self-withdrawing and holding-itself-back belongs to Being. Even though one thinks of with-drawal and concealing, one can experience Being in its *truth*. Thus the turning becomes possible as "turning the oblivion of Being into caring-for its essence" (VA 182). The turning is thereby the winding in which that circle is traced where Dasein and the sense of Being are combined. Just as the skier executes his turn because he wants to remain upon the way and wants neither to plunge into the abyss nor get lost, so it is with Heidegger. His thinking turns against itself in face of the abyss of nihilism so that it can keep to the way toward the truth of Being. The turning is an overcoming of the turning away, according to the existential analysis an overcoming of Dasein's turning away from its authenticity (SuZ 184), and according to the history of Being, of Being's turning away from its truth. This turning is that setting up of an abode in the truth of Being only in that it overcomes the turning away which has already occurred.

If Being sets up an abode in its truth, then the "oblivion of Being" seems once and for all to be eliminated. In truth, however, the decisive experience is that the forgetting of the truth of Being is not something which could at some time be annulled for good. Taken positively, it rather belongs to the carrying out of the truth of Being, namely, as the knowledge of errancy as the enabling of history, as the knowing, even eloquent silence of the abysmal character and concealment in primordial unconcealment. As protecting of the abiding abysmal character, the turning furnishes no ultimate grounding. Consequently it is not the turning in an absolute sense but rather the turning which is entrusted to us. If the turning takes the forgetting of the truth of Being as a preserving of the mystery of this truth, it remains situated by metaphysics which precisely in its oblivion of **183** Being is the "history of the mystery in the promise of Being itself" (NII, 370). This talk of "mystery" must also be properly understood. It should not be understood as if Heidegger believed that one could exhibit and lay open once and for all what is unthought and concealed in metaphysics. When Feuerbach calls speculative theology the secret of theology and anthropology the secret of speculative philosophy, he believes to have definite knowledge about theology and speculative philosophy. When Marx calls the *Phänomenologie des Geistes* the secret of Hegelian philosophy, he believes that he knows what the essence of Hegelian and every philosophy is—it is, according to his view, the labor whose essence is thought in the *Phänomenologie des Geistes*.[34] Neither Feuerbach nor Marx knows a mystery in the genuine sense, since a mystery is in truth only a mystery if it is the *abiding* mystery which never entirely reveals itself, yet from time to time grants an openness. Heidegger thinks the truth of Being is this abiding mystery. When he calls it "appropriative event," he does not throw into relief a constant essence, its ultimate being-the-ground. Instead, he seeks to articulate the experience of this truth which is possible for *us today*. The experience of intrinsically historical truth cannot leap out of the historical "essence" of truth; it cannot itself want to be unhistorical.

A thinking which accomplishes the turning and thus protects the mystery in the truth of Being can no longer be understood in terms of the grounding metaphysics. Metaphysical grounding comes toward Being only as the truth of beings, and, as onto-theo-logy, cuts itself off from the way toward the truth of Being. Obviously a thinking from out of the truth of Being can no longer claim to be "ontology." For the later Heidegger, ontology is merely a feature of ontotheological metaphysics. Above all this thinking can no longer be understood as "fundamental ontology." "As long as this thinking continues to characterize itself as fundamental ontology, this designation will cause it to get in its own way and obscure the way" (WiM 21). The term fundamental ontology makes it appear as **184** if the thinking of the truth of Being were still a kind of ontology, of course not just as the grounding of beings in Being but also as the grounding of Being in the "Being" of Being. The same goes for the phrase "metaphysics of metaphysics" (Hw 243), which Heidegger therefore gives back to modern metaphysics (NII, 244, 370). The question, "why is there anything at all?", which was taken up as the basic question of metaphysics, proves to be a merely transitional question. When properly thought, this question can assist one in experiencing the abysmal ground-like occurrence of truth, but as a question it is already unsuccessful, since in asking about *ground as why* it bypasses the abysmal truth of Being. Consequently all answers in its sphere must fall short (NII, 374; cf. already SuZ 202). Because Heidegger took up this question, because he made use of terms and phrases such as fundamental ontology, metaphysics of metaphysics, and regress into the ground of metaphysics, and because he distinguished between the basic question and the guiding question, he preserved the connection with metaphysics. To be sure, he also made it appear as if the authentically "foundational" granting of truth would be realized for the first time in a new grounding of metaphysics, in going back from Being as the truth of beings to the "Being" or the essence of Being itself. Yet a reflection upon the essence of ground shows that a thinking which intends to be more foundational than metaphysics gets in its own way and is, therefore, an illusion.

At first Heidegger held onto the term philosophy (cf. "Beiträge zur *Philosophie*") in order to leave it behind by reflecting upon what is said in it. Philosophy arose when familiarity with the Being which governs, the Φιλεῖν τὸ σοφόν, had already been lost and was now to be won back within a humanistic-metaphysical thinking (*Was ist das—die Philosophie?*

20ff, PL 47ff). A "philosophy of philosophy" (cf. *Was ist das—die Philosophie* 17f; Hw 92) can no longer tempt that thinking which has seen through the delusion of the "metaphysics of metaphysics." In the philosophy of philosophy a specific type of knowledge is examined. Philosophy understands itself as the *conceptual* portrayal of a world and life view, and thus as the "expression" of historical life. It is grounded in historical life and its possibilities for world views.[35] If Heidegger can no longer characterize his thinking as philosophy, then he can certainly no longer characterize it as **185** science. First Heidegger tried to lay the ground of science with a "science of Being as such, of its possibilities and derivatives" (SuZ 230), and consequently to have science exist on the basis of metaphysics (WiM 40f). The tendency of scientific knowledge to realize itself in a mere "making-present" was undone, and knowledge was tied to full temporality and to Dasein's wanting-to-have-a-conscience (SuZ 363). According to an early lecture, the task of philosophy is to throw "torches" into scientific work. *Sein und Zeit* found the authentic movement of the sciences in the testing of basic concepts and in their crises of foundations (SuZ 9). Later Heidegger laid stress on the tendency in scientific work to take over untested the posited foundations. Thus he now had to contrast the wanting-to-have-a-conscience, thought as "reflection" in terms of the history of Being, with the "lack of reflection" of the sciences (Hw 69ff, VA 45ff); for his own thinking, he had to abandon "the unsuitable focus upon science and research" (PL 110).

However one may feel about the terms metaphysics, philosophy, science—what is decisive is that the question about the truth of Being is not understood in the traditional manner as a metaphysical question. If one says that Heidegger thinks Being as appropriative event or, less clearly expressed, Being as time, as history, and if one then places this specification "Being as appropriative event" at the level of the metaphysical presupposition that Being is constant presencing, then one misunderstands everything. Heidegger does not replace the metaphysical determination of Being with another one. He asks instead how Being can be understood as Being at all, that is, he asks about what is concealed by the "as" in the usage "Being as Being," about the truth of Being itself.

If the equation of Being and constant presence becomes problematic and if one therefore asks expressly about the truth of Being itself, one does not then deny that within certain regions of beings the Being of beings can by all means be constant presencing. For example, the condition for the symmetry of a mathematical equivalence has the character of constant presence—it makes it possible for us always to return to the symmetry of **186** the equation. (The problems of "natural law," of prototypes or "archtypes," and of a "universal metaphysics," for example, are connected to the completely legitimate question as to whether Being is not constant presencing within limited regions.) One should annul only the hypostatization of constantly presencing Being as the only Being. A thesis that the Being of beings is no* constant presencing, but is rather as a rule temporality in the sense of transitoriness could be proven false by the demonstrable Being, for example, of mathematical objectivities. Heidegger, of course, never asserted such a thesis.[36] He only denied that the Being of beings has the character of constant presence in all cases, and asked whence the Being of beings is determined in general. To comprehend the so-called merely "present-at-hand" as it occurs, for example, in a pure manner through mathematics is a thoroughly "legitimate task"; nonetheless knowledge should not go astray in this task; it should not want to equate knowledge in general with the manner of knowledge belonging to the exact sciences (SuZ 153).

To be sure, thinking should also not simply contrast itself with the mode of knowledge of exact sciences and orient itself mainly to non-exact sciences or to the nonscientific, hermeneutical-historical experiences. When Heidegger speaks about a "history" of Being or about the truth of Being as the "appropriative event," then we must strictly differentiate what is here called "history" and "event" from that which is usually called history, namely from history as that region of beings, which, for example, is distinguished from nature. What nature and history are in their Being can be thought adequately only by experiencing the truth of Being itself. The experience of this truth must certainly prove successful in its questioning the Being of the different regions of beings; otherwise thinking from the truth of Being would itself remain abstract in that sense which Hegel meant when he criticized Schelling's philosophy of identity as abstract.

At first Heidegger speaks about the truth of Being as if it were "Being itself," but then he differentiates this Being as "Being [*Seyn*]" from Being [*Sein*] as the mere beingness of beings. Thus around 1936 he can speak of "Being [*Seyn*] as appropriative event." Now when the truth of Being has been brought up for discussion as appropriative event, it loses the name of Being; the word "Being" [*Sein*] is given back to metaphysics which thinks the Being of beings in Being and all of a sudden takes it as the permanent (NII, 336, 354f, 389f). Being thought of as the Being of beings can now be thought of only "from out" of the appropriative event of truth as what authentically presences in Being—but not "from out" of the appropriative event as a super-Being or supreme being. Thus the appearance that "appropriative event" is a transcendental determination of Being in the sense of metaphysics is lost (E 14, Sp 260 footnote). If the basic word in

187

Heidegger's later thinking is no longer "Being" but "truth," if the question which is developed is meant for the structural fitting-together of the most primordial truth, does Heidegger then not leave behind the question of Being as a penultimate question? Far from abandoning the question, he first brings it into that region where it can be settled. Truth as unconcealment is nothing other than Being, above all nothing "over" Being but rather Being itself, that which presences in Being (presencing as unconcealment).

With the question about Being and time Heidegger came upon *his* way toward the truth of Being. Thought as the step upon Heidegger's way of thinking, *Sein und Zeit* is therefore neither an "ideal" nor a "program," "but rather the self-preparatory beginning of the presencing of Being [*Seyn*] itself." It is the beginning of not what *we* devise "but what compels *us*, provided that we have become ripe for it, into a thinking which neither yields a theory, occasions a 'moral' activity, nor secures 'existence'. Rather it is something which 'only' grounds the truth as the field of play of time and space in which beings can again come to be, that is, can become the preservation of Being [*Seyn*]." " 'Time' was to be made possible to experience as the 'ecstatic' field of play of the truth of Being [*Seyn*]. The carrying away [*Ent-rückung*] into what has been cleared was to ground the clearing itself as that which is open and in which Being gathers itself in its essence. One cannot point out such an essence as something present-at-hand; its essencing must be awaited like a thrust. What remains foremost is to be able to wait in this clearing until the hints come. Thinking no longer has the favor of the 'system'—it is historical in the particular sense **188** that Being [*Seyn*] itself as appropriative event first of all sustains every history and therefore can never be calculated. The historical preparedness for the truth of Being [*Seyn*] takes the place of systematization and deduction. This first requires that truth itself, even from its scarcely heard essence, must create the fundamental characteristics of its abode (Dasein), and the subject of man must be transformed into the builder and guardian of this abode. The accomplishment of this preparation for our history is the sole concern in the question of Being. All 'contents' and 'opinions' and 'ways' in particular with reference to the first attempt of *Sein und Zeit* are accidental and can vanish" (*Beiträge*).

Heidegger tried to settle the question of Being when he thought metaphysics as a critical doctrine of categories or logic, phenomenology as hermeneutic phenomenology, and then metaphysics as the metaphysics of Dasein. His attempt continued when he took up phenomenology and metaphysics as possibilities of a way, but nonetheless changed them along the way and returned them to a more primordial questioning. Heidegger finally gave up all claims of entering into existing philosophical possibilities and ways. He sought to eliminate the misunderstanding that what would now be thought would be only what had always been thought under similar terms (PL 110). Heidegger permitted his own path to remain "nameless" (Sp 121) so as not to allow his own question to be distorted by an inadequate approach and in order to be able to retrieve in "another beginning" that which in Western thinking lies closest to its source.

8

THE OTHER BEGINNING

By overcoming the approach of metaphysical thinking, Heidegger tries to retrieve the forgotten ground of metaphysics. This ground is experienced as the abysmal Because [*Weil*] and whiling [*Dieweilen*] and thereby as the enduring seminality from which thinking is as it is. Since the seminality of this seminal element has been forgotten and buried, "another beginning" must set it free again. In this other beginning, thinking supposes not only that the truth of Being is temporal and historical, but furthermore that the experience of the truth of Being is itself a historical accommodation to it. The question thus arises whence this experience comes historically, where it has its essential origin, and where in the Western tradition the truth of Being was most likely preserved.

The young Heidegger starts from the metaphysical, above all from the Aristotelian theory of Being, and impelled by Christian theology he asks if the forgotten ground of metaphysics is not the temporal and historical character of the truth of Being. It was possible for the attempt "at an interpretation of the Augustinian—that is, Graeco-Christian—anthropology with regard to the basic foundations arrived at in Aristotle's ontology" to be a path to the analysis of *Sein und Zeit* (SuZ 199 note). By formalizing the theological motives which Kierkegaard had allowed to become effective again, by appropriating Dilthey's historical understanding of life, and by examining the new Kantian grounding of metaphysics, Heidegger wishes to bring the problem of metaphysics to a head. But when Nietzsche enters this process, the experience of tradition is transformed in a fundamental way.

Kant can now no longer acknowledge the problem of metaphysics. To be sure, Kant distinguishes himself by establishing the finitude of the transcendental I; but he does not think any further about the how of transcendence, something which later Idealism, however, does in its own way. Kant is not aware of what is specifically modern in his metaphysics. If in modern metaphysics the imagination becomes the enabling ground of knowledge, then man "fantasizes"; his representation imagines Being into being, the "objective," but this $\varphi\alpha\nu\tau\alpha\sigma\iota\alpha$ no longer occurs, as it does in Greek thinking, within primordial unconcealment, the coming-to-appearance of what presences out of itself (Hw 98). Modern metaphysics disguises the truth of Being; Kant's thinking is only a step in the course of this metaphysics which brings matters to a head precisely there—in Nietzsche—where it takes its most extreme step.

According to Heidegger's later experience, Dilthey also swims in the stream of a "metaphysics" which does not reach the decisive stage for him. He brings modern historical thinking to self-consciousness. Yet this is a thinking which in the modern metaphysical manner seeks to establish what is true as what is permanent and certain. It thus covers up the truth as the origin which bursts open ever again and is not at one's disposal; thus it is precisely what it no longer intends to be, metaphysics as the truth merely about beings. In this way, historical thinking is unsuccessful in grasping genuine historicality and even becomes fixed in the unhistorical; that is, the objectifying historical methods are removed from the claim of tradition and thus destroy genuine handing down.[37] The most extreme refining and differentiation of historical methods, therefore, accompany barbarous domination of an entirely unhistorical thinking which simply proclaims its claims to truth. History finally plunges into its own perplexity, historicism, in that it realizes that every historical cognition has for its part a historical location. Since this insight relativizes historical establishing and securing, it severely disrupts them (cf. VA 80). In 1917 Spengler believed in *Der Untergang des Abendlands* [*The Decline of the West*] to have discovered for the first time that every culture and age have their own world view. This seemed to be a revelation; but it was so only "for the crowd of those who are unfamiliar with actual thinking and its rich

191   history" (NI, 360). Above all, "discoveries" like these impede the decisive question: If every thinking has a definite "location," must one then not ask whether this locations is not to be thought as the There in Dasein and thereby as the place of the truth of Being? Beings, as research seeks them, ought not to be posited self-evidently in terms of what is permanent and ascertainable; rather, one must develop anew the question about the truth of Being. Yet this question remains foreign to historicism as is every other "metaphysical" thinking which proceeds from beings and returns via permanent Being to beings as determinable (NI, 365, 380f). Since Dilthey conforms to the anthropological-historical point of departure and endpoint of metaphysics, but does not reach the decisive stage, his thinking as well cannot contribute what is decisive to the question about the truth of Being as the "ground," the seminal element of our history (Hw 92).

Why does Kierkegaard and the Christian theology renewed by him no longer provide the essential impetus? Kierkegaard's opposition to Hegel is a counterposition which lives off the opponent and appropriates his conceptualization. Because Kierkegaard remains within "metaphysics" in this manner, he has "not the least relation" to the question about the essence of Being (WhD 129). He takes over metaphysical conceptualization without questioning it from top to bottom; nonetheless, in this conceptualization he says something entirely different from metaphysics. He is not a thinker at all, but rather a "religious writer" (Hw 230). As Kierkegaard approached Hegel, so Pascal had already approached Descartes: Pascal declared Descartes' efforts to be useless and sought what is essential in man in an entirely different dimension, without questioning in terms of its own ground the dimension which had been opened by metaphysics and the Cartesian transformation of this metaphysics (NII, 187). Kierkegaard as well as Pascal point to a possibility of Western humanity in which Heidegger now sees some harm; the metaphysical foundation of our history is accepted, but then by means of a "religious" decision one springs out of this history into a counterposition which does not experience this history in accord with its seminality, and thus remains determined by the non-essence of this history. Heidegger sees his opponent in a Christianity which is lived in this way, just as in a "liberalism" which **192** transforms culture and civilization into a substitute god, and in the "total world view" in which man shuts himself up in himself and in his willing (e.g., through the fascistic call to a "folk" which no longer even exists as a community in truth).

Because Nietzsche pushes the metaphysical-anthropological attitude to extremes, just as he foregoes half measures like the flight into a religious counterposition, he—and no longer Kierkegaard—brings matters to a head.[38] If Nietzsche properly expresses the logic of metaphysical thinking in the statement, "God is dead," then a faith which remains within the metaphysical experience of truth—and even if it is only a counterposition—can arrive only at an illusory god. If in such belief one still believes in the Christian God and takes his world as the standard, then this is similar to "that process by which the appearance of a star extinguished for millennia still shines; nonetheless, this shining remains a mere 'illusion' " (NII, 33). The Christian faith, as a result of the amalgamation with metaphysics which knows only the truth about beings and not the truth of Being, has disguised the claim out of which it lives. Indeed, it has itself promoted the non-essence of metaphysics. Self-certainty was prepared through concentration upon the certainty of salvation, and the subjectivism of modern times was co-formed by the theory of justification. For example, Kierkegaard's religious authorship reduced the concept of existence to the anthropological, etc. Heidegger no longer formalizes the expressions of Christian theology—as he still did in *Sein und Zeit*—in terms of their ontologically fundamental-ontological implications, but rather asks about their metaphysical conditionality.

For Heidegger, the entire Judeo-Christian tradition is indeed no longer

a primordial claim; rather, it is perceived in its derived, perverted form
and set at a distance. This means that the prophets of the Judeo-Christian
faith did not say (like Hölderlin) the word of the holy which grounds in
advance; rather, "immediately before that they spoke of the God upon
whom the security of deliverance into heavenly happiness relies" (EH
108).[39] As Heidegger now suggests, the believers of the Christian-Jewish
193   religion presuppose the one God because they wanted to withdraw from
the respective history which is not at their disposal. The monotheism of
this religion was therefore able to link up with the similarly motivated
metaphysical ontotheology. According to Nietzsche, the God of the theology which arises in this way is the "blunder" of a humanity which makes
up a God for itself according to its own base requirements for security (NI
321f). "Sin" and "repentance" as the relation to the eternal, to the
constantly presencing willing of the redeeming, otherworldly God, are
just as "metaphysical" as Nietzsche's willing of the eternal return; they
are, however, the willing of powerlessness rather than of power (WhD 44).
One's own will is relinquished in favor of the divine will, but one still
thinks about a will which wills its self-permanence and which consequently does not give rise to history, the appropriative event (cf. *Gelassenheit* 35f, 60). Heidegger thinks that faith in creation belongs, as a "moral,"
anthropomorphizing explanation of the "world," alongside the Platonic
representation of the activity of a Demiurge (NI, 350). If the world is
explained by the act of the creator, then beings will always be known in
terms of their Being, namely, as "created." Consequently, the question
about the sense of Being can no longer arise since the faith in creation
which explains everything prevents thoughtful questioning (NII, 131f,
58f; E 5f).

Heidegger turned to thoughtful questioning. Nonetheless, the thinking
of *Sein und Zeit* still appropriates the historical thinking of the Christian
faith as an impetus. To be sure, the experiences of faith, e.g., the experience of sinfulness, are excluded from every possible philosophical knowledge; yet faith remains a possible answer to the questions referred to by
thinking. *Sein und Zeit* is to sketch out questions for theology as well (SuZ
180, 306 note). At the time of the Nietzsche lectures, thinking and faith
were moved so far from one another that the possibility of a relation
between them is hardly visible anymore. Heidegger refers (WiM 20) to
the statement of the apostle Paul: God permitted the wisdom of the
world—that which the Greeks sought—to become foolishness (I Cor.I,
20).[40] In a 1953 discussion about thinking and believing, philosophy and
theology, Heidegger said: philosophy carries on only the sort of thinking
194   that man is capable of on his own; where man is addressed by revelation,
thinking ceases. "The Christian experience is something so completely

different that it has no need at all to compete with philosophy. If theology continues to maintain that philosophy is foolishness, then the mysteriousness of revelation is far better preserved. Therefore, the ways part in the ultimate decision."[41] The first Nietzsche lecture in fact made the following remark about Plato's Republic: "The free self-grounding of the historical Dasein subordinates itself to the jurisdiction of knowledge—and not of faith insofar as one understands the latter as including a divine testimony of truth empowered by revelation." (NI, 194). Heidegger, to be sure, does not seek knowledge which stands on its own; he does not want to be a "sage," but only one who points out and shows the way (VA 7). Heidegger pursues a questioning which holds itself open for the claim of the divine. Must not this questioning then consider the Christian possibility of faith also as a possibility? Does Heidegger not question in such a way that the answer of the Christian faith is a possible one for him? Does the Christian answer not annul history as discussion and as the movement that always questions further? In *Sein und Zeit*, Heidegger still speaks about a "believing questioning" and refers to Luther (SuZ 10). In the aforementioned conversation of 1953, he holds the opinion that for Luther there was no question with respect to the "claim," since in the letter to the Romans he heard God's word from the outset. Does not questioning and further questioning, historical openness, permanently belong to the "believing" to which thinking, as it was understood by the later Heidegger, can establish a relation? Can the Christian message still be a possible claim for this thinking? Doubtless it can be so, since it is so. The flaw, the absence of the divine as Heidegger experiences it, is "not nothing, but rather it is the presence of the concealed fullness still to be appropriated, the fullness of what has been and of the presencing so gathered, of the divine in Greek culture, in the prophetic Jewish culture, and in the preaching of Jesus. This no-longer is intrinsically a not-yet of the veiled arrival of its inexhaustible essence" (VA 183; cf. also Sp 96). The decisive question, however, is *how*, that is, from what preliminary understanding is the Christian faith understood here. In other words, which questioning marks out the space in which the claim of the divine can then be heard.

For Heidegger, the experience which determines everything is that **195** what the Jews, Christians, and Greeks have considered divine is that which has been; only through the experience that "God is dead" can there again be a future (NII, 29), but which seminal, thoughtful questioning directs man into this future? One does not find the seminal element of thinking in metaphysics, for it is enslaved by its non-essence, and the god of its ontotheology is not the "divine God" (ID 51, 70f). For Heidegger, the seminal element is also not the occurrence of truth manifested in Jewish-biblical belief; this belief is referred to its primordiality without further reflection. For Heidegger, the seminal element is also no longer the Christian faith, because Heidegger begins from the experience (and this is the "theology" in his "philosophy") that Christian theology has not preserved what was entrusted to it as being holy. However, pre-metaphysical Greek thinking, as Heidegger surmises, could have at least established a clue to the seminal, the abysmal ground of Western history, to the truth of Being itself. Heidegger sees this seminal thinking of the Greeks in the vicinity of that claim of what is holy as it was put into effect in the Greek temples. Art, which puts truth to work, rather than philosophy and science, could have established the primordial essence of truth. Greek tragedy brought to language what became form in Greek buildings and sculpture. According to Heidegger's experience, however, Hölderlin brought back its saying in a changed form for our time. Consequently Hölderlin's poetic saying becomes the decisive impetus for Heidegger's thinking. Because Hölderlin found the way to his unique saying, "the knowledge of the truth of Greek culture, Christianity, and the East" was transformed in general (EH 86, note).

THE FIRST BEGINNING OF THINKING

Sein und Zeit already contains significant references to Parmenides and Heraclitus, to their questioning about Being (14, 212), perception of Being (25f, 171), truth (219, 222f), and world (100). Nonetheless this work is still thought out in terms of his examination of the Platonic-Aristotelian question of Being and the Aristotelian theory about logos. The way that Christian faith experiences history provided an essential impetus for this examination. Heidegger's examination of the earliest Greek thinking became decisive for him only when he developed the question as to what extent the truth of Being is forgotten in Platonic thinking, and when Nietzsche's phrase about the death of God caused the Western tradition to be seen in a new light. In the summer semester of 1932, Heidegger lectured on the "Beginning of Philosophy." In the course *Einführung in die Metaphysik*, offered in 1935, it says that the greatest aspect of a great matter is always the beginning, and that this was also true of Western thinking. Whoever takes up the question of Being of this thinking "must return to its beginning" (12, 75). In this lecture course, Heidegger goes back to the thinking of Parmenides and Heraclitus in order to be able to undo the metaphysical difference between Being and appearance, Being and becoming, Being and thinking, and the restriction of Being to constant presence which accompanies it. Plato's theory of truth is examined in terms of that which sinks into oblivion within it. Aristotle's thinking is sounded upon a *"dying echo* of the great beginning of Greek philosophy and of Western philosophy" (*Vom Wesen und Begriff der φύσις* 288).

In later, only partially published works, Heidegger, from out of the need for "another beginning," tried to win back the first beginning of Western thinking in its seminality. According to Heidegger's experience of the matter of thinking, the seminal aspect of this beginning must be truth as unconcealment. Does not the Greek language already give a hint to this seminal aspect when it speaks about truth as ἀλήθεια, about truth as unconcealment (PL 32, VA 259)? To be sure, truth then loses the relation to concealment, because concealing conceals itself and the forgetting of this concealing is for its part forgotten (VA 263f). Still, as Heidegger suggests for consideration, perhaps the relation of unconcealment to concealing was not expressly brought to language in Greek only "because this language itself comes from this relation." Not only the word ἀλήθεια, but words like λανθάνω and αἰδώς as well are conceived from the reciprocal relation between revealing and concealing (VA 261f, 228).   **197**

The Greeks experience the Being of beings as the presencing by which everything which presences comes into the unconcealed. Being determines the unconcealment of beings, but thereby allows the relation of unconcealment to concealment to sink into oblivion. Thus it keeps its truth (to be revealing and concealing at the same time) to itself. This keeping-to-itself, the "epoch" of Being, destines the West to that world-historical epoch which is the errancy of the oblivion of Being: a shaping of the truth about beings and a forgetting of the essence of this truth. Errancy belongs to the epochal essence of history in which the one is always forgotten in favor of the other. Errancy can, therefore, never simply be pushed aside. It first of all enables history as the relation from destiny to destiny and along with it the dialogue between one historical thinking and another (Hw 310ff). If the errancy of metaphysics reaches its limit today (Hw 343) and if, thereby, the destiny of truth which directed Western history in its essence draws to a close, then by means of a dialogue with the Western dawn, an "eschatology of Being" must seek to wrest from this dawn that seminal element which may be capable of setting free another beginning, "another destining of Being" (Hw 301f, 309). Heidegger consequently asks whether this seminal aspect does not become apparent in the first preserved saying of Western thinking, in the saying of Anaximander, that is, whether at least a clue to the truth of Being does not manifest itself there.

Heidegger leaves it open whether Anaximander, as tradition would have one believe, already used the phrase τὰ ἐόντα—even if ἐόν does not become the fundamental word of thinking until Parmenides (Hw 323 ff). However it may be, Anaximander thinks the Being of beings in accord with the matter. However, as Heidegger tries to make evident with a passage from Homer, for the Greeks "Being" means presencing into unconcealment. That which presences, according to Anaximander's saying, is added to the interstice between a twofold absencing, between coming to be and passing away. If what in each case presences persists in its presencing, it then takes itself out of its "transitional" period; it makes a pompous exhibition of itself in its obstinancy of wanting to persist; it insists upon the permanence of enduring. Far from this obstinancy stands that accommodation in which the one being allows space and a space of time to another. This accommodation occurs in accordance with the basic feature in presencing, the χρεών. This is the usage [*Brauch*] in which Being (presencing) as unconcealment needs the being (that which presences) and joins it to the specific nature of its presence. Insofar as Anaximander thinks usage as the basic character of Being, he says something about the truth of Being itself. But neither with him nor anywhere else in Greek thinking does one find an attempt to develop the being-present and the not-being-present of what presences in terms of its essential origin, the temporal playing field of the truth of Being.

What Anaximander experiences as "usage"—Being in accordance with its essence and its truth—Heraclitus thinks as Φύσις. This is "that which never perishes," the opening up and holding sway, a self-revealing which remains sheltered in self-concealing. Self-concealing is no mere self-closing, but rather a sheltering which preserves for revealing ever anew the essential possibilities of opening up (VA 271). Φύσις is the unconcealment which reveals that which presences into presencing but thereby hides the revealment in the mystery of concealment. Men and gods belong to this unconcealment in a special way. They are not only brought to light by it; they are also those "inconspicuous ones who in their own way jointly bring forth clearing as they preserve and hand it down in its enduring" (VA 279).

Heraclitus thinks the unconcealments as Φύσις but also as πῦρ—fire, Φρόνιμον—that which meditates, ἁρμονία—the interstice, Φιλία—the reciprocal inclination, πόλεμος and ἔρις—confrontation and struggle in which gods and men struggle for their essence, ἕν—the one unifying all (VA 272ff). He thinks unconcealment in its sameness with λόγος (VA 220f). The λέγειν in λόγος is a placing and a gleaning; the placing is a placing together, bringing-together-into-lying-before and having-lie-before; it is, therefore, a gleaning as gathering and preserving. As a flash of lightning suddenly gathers everything that presences into the light of presencing, so does the λόγος gather everything into one (VA 222).

This λόγος may not be taken as the hypostatization of a specific feature of man's essence; however, man's λέγειν may also not be thought as a merely subsequent correspondence to a λόγος in itself. Thinking must rather find its way to that "simple center" from which the λέγειν of man and the λέγειν of λόγος attain the origin of their essence (VA 225). This center is that wherein the matter of Western thinking, the Being of beings, occurs, the truth of Being. This truth as λόγος appropriates the λέγειν of man in that it adapts this λέγειν for itself. As soon as Being in its truth was addressed as λόγος, would one not have had to experience language there as a way to preserve and safeguard the truth of Being? Language then would have been understood not only in terms of making known and signifying but also as "saying," as the "gleaning place," as the "gathering having-lie-before of what presences in its presence" (VA 212, 228). The Greeks may have dwelt in this essence of language but they did not think it. To be sure, the essence of language and thereby of logic flashed in the light of Being itself when Heraclitus thought the word λόγος as the word about Being. "But the flash suddenly died out. No one grasped its ray and the nearness of what it illuminated. We will not see this lightning flash until we place ourselves in the tempest of Being . . . " (VA 229).

In this tempest the metaphysical essence of Being and thereby the essence of man as well would have to become questionable, and the name "Being" would have to become a "provisional word" (VA 213, 229). Yet are not these questions about the "essence" of man and indeed about the "essence" of Being beside the point, unimportant, when measured against the need of today's world? Heidegger reminds us of the principle of Heraclitus: "Boldness needs to be extinguished before conflagration." Is this what is most necessary, to engage immediately in the conflagrations which lay waste to the earth and threaten still greater devastation? Or is it that we should seek to extinguish boldness which presumes lordship over all beings, but which goes wrong about the mode of acting because it is not acquainted with Being itself, its truth, and the primordial "preserve" of this truth (VA 226)?

Heraclitus thought the "bold thought," that is, that concealment belongs to the unconcealment of Being. Parmenides left what is thought in this thought to remain unthought, but nonetheless experienced it (VA 255). Parmenides expresses the primordial essence of thinking and of Being. Thinking is a having-lie-before (λέγειν) and a taking-into-care **200** (voεῖν); Being is presence, coming-forward into unconcealment and thus a lying-before, a resting in a lingering to which the concealed suddenness of the constantly possible absence in concealment belongs (WhD 142ff). Along with his essence, thinking, man is used for Being; in this being-used, the sameness of thinking and Being occur. In the *Einführung in die Metaphysik*, Heidegger thinks the occurring of this sameness as the counter-maneuverability in which the holding sway of Being uses man for its openness, in which man shatters upon overpowering Being in the violent act which risks the mastery of Being (123f, 129, 133). The cryptic remark in which Parmenides calls Being and thinking the "same" later becomes Heidegger's way upon which thinking "does not go beyond what Parmenides thought but rather only back into what must be thought more originally" (VA 249). In this puzzling phrase, "the same," the unfolding of the truth of Being is, if not said, then at least present in silence. For its part, thinking always brings along Being as the truth of beings in that it is "needfully used" for the settlement of that twofold in which Being and beings can be distinguished, in which Being (presence) can first appear and beings (that which presences) can become evident.

Yet Heidegger asks from where is thinking summoned to allow beings to lie before in their Being and to take this into care? Truth as unconcealment is what does the bidding; it is the bidding goddess which calls from the preface of Parmenides' didactic poem. "Hearing her saying, Parmenides says what he thought. At the same time, he allows that wherein the essence of ἀλήθεια rests to remain in what is unsaid. The sense of divinity of the goddess, ἀλήθεια, also remains unthought" (VA 247f). If this bidding is that of a goddess, can one even ponder the bidding which called not only the thinking of Parmenides but also that of the entire West upon its way? Can the divine be questioned any further? In any case, Heidegger believes that the bidding is the genuine matter for thinking; in no case is it that element in history which must be shoved aside as unintelligible and obscure, as what one tends to call "fate." "It is so little the case that bidding as granting is unintelligible and foreign to thinking that it rather **201** remains precisely the matter to be genuinely thought; as such it waits upon a thinking which accords with it" (WhD 103). Still, Parmenides names μοῖρα, that apportioning and granting which brings Being and thinking into its essence, only in a subordinate clause (VA 251f). Parmenides does not consider the essence of Being any further. Being concealingly shelters its truth by making itself the most thoughtworthy of thinking. Parmenides could have nonetheless experienced this concealing sheltering, since he does say that truth yields to the everyday discourse of the mortals which is capable of naming only familiar beings (VA 255).

The Greeks think Being as presence, as coming forth into unconcealment. Still the relation of unconcealment to concealing and of presence to absence is experienced in the earliest Greek thinking only as that which is considered no further and is forgotten immediately by later Greek thinking. Unconcealment is taken as pure revealedness; Being can therefore be thought as *constant* presence. In order to assure Being's constancy, the Nothing is excluded from Being. Becoming is thrust into the region of that which does not genuinely exist, and with it goes appearance, repeated shining forth. Unconcealment is no longer this shining forth which at the same time withdraws itself and conceals itself into itself, but rather the pure and constant clearing, the idea. In fact, the theory of ideas was possible only because the truth had been thought as unconcealment. Nonetheless this theory of ideas represses concealing as a decisive essential feature of unconcealment. The structure of unconcealment therefore collapses (Hw 341f; VA 252; NI 212; E 145f).

Heidegger seeks to regain the seminal essence of truth. He supposes that this seminality most nearly attained linguistic expression at the beginning of thinking (Hw 336). He thereby presupposes that the bidding under which the earliest Greek thinking stood and the bidding of later Western thinking are the same (WhD 105). What is said about every greatness also applies to the greatness of Western thinking: "All greatness can have only a great beginning. Indeed its beginning is always its greatest feature" (E 12). To be sure, the earliest Greek thinking is seminal certainly not because it is historically first but rather because it laid the ground for the occurrence of truth in the West. This ground is—as abysmal ground, as while and whiling—the enduring seminality which determines everything. Going back to the earliest Greek thinking is, therefore, neither a return to the past nor a renaissance of antiquity, but rather a going back into the ground of our world, the "grounding" of this "ground," and thus another beginning. By means of the conversation with Greek thinkers and their language our thinking strikes "roots into the ground of our historical Dasein"; it recovers the seminal element which endures but which was soon covered over (VA 47).

202

What the earliest Greek thinkers have thought is certainly difficult to communicate. These thinkers in no way speak to us from their own unique element. The testimonies from their thinking which remain handed down to us are only pieces and fragments. Furthermore, these no longer stand in their original context but come down to us only in the contexts of other subsequent thinkers and mostly through the doxology of the Aristotelian school. From the outset early Greek thinking is handed down in the contexts of later thinking and then interpreted by this thinking as "pre-Aristotelian" (Hegel), "pre-Platonic" (Nietzsche), or "pre-Socratic" (Diels). It is finally related to modern scholarship and natural science and consequently understood first as a primitive type of natural philosophy and then in a countermovement to this interpretation, as "rational theology." In any case the beginning of Greek thinking is understood by a thinking which, according to Heidegger's experience, did not preserve the seminality of the beginning but disguised it.

A thinking that wants to bring the fragments of the earliest Greek thinking to language again must discuss the tradition and the previous interpretation of these fragments and point out the limitation of their presuppositions (cf. VA 231ff, 257ff). In this discussion one not only tests the presuppositions of the other but also "submits" what is one's own "for discussion" (WhD 110). There is no presuppositionless and absolutely valid interpretation, and if we address it without presuppositions and purposes, history gives no answer. We always have to bring along the decisive questions; consequently, we can again bring to language what was thought earlier only from our respective standpoint.

203   Heidegger's particular presupposition is that the earliest Greek thinking provides at least a clue to what remained covered up in metaphysical thinking, the truth of Being as unconcealment. Heidegger believes that one can exhibit this clue. To be sure, his concern is not to exhibit merely something present-at-hand or to provide the "historically correct" interpretation; it is rather to *wrest* from original Greek thinking the matter which is in accordance with the most seminal aspect of thinking. Heidegger's interpretation thus becomes "dialogue." However, dialogue is never dialogue if one only keeps talking to the other or merely speaks ill of his discourse. It is a conversation between two speakers only if the one directs the other to what is unthought without presenting this unthought as another opinion. One seeks to point out that it is the unthought of what was thought by another, that it is what must be thought in terms of the matter. Heidegger seeks what is Greek about the Greeks not for their sake "nor even merely for a clearer dialogue, but solely with reference to what would like to be brought to language in such dialogue, supposing that it comes to language from itself" (Hw 310). By means of dialogue thinking itself is to find its way toward itself, to allow what is seminal in Western thinking—whether it may now be experienced in the earliest Greek thinking or not—to again be seminal. With his references to Anaximander, Heraclitus, and Parmenides, Heidegger does not intend to contribute to historical research which yields what is objectively demonstrable; he would rather like to point to an event, to the event of the other beginning (VA 261).

Heidegger leaves it open as to whether or not what is seminal to thinking in accordance with the matter has entered the historically provable field of presentation at all, for example, in the case of Heraclitus (VA 279). The exertion with which Heidegger concentrates upon the experience of the matter enters his interpretation as the "violence" which casts behind itself everything customary and wrests away from the other what he genuinely was supposed to have thought (E 134). This excess in the performance of the task of thinking the beginning of Western thinking from another beginning asserts itself in formulations like the following: Anaximander's χρεών "probably" names a clue for what remains to be thought in the word "usage" [*Brauch*] (Hw 340); the task of sheltering

Being in the essence of language "prepares" itself when the word λόγος   **204**
becomes the name of Being in Heraclitus (VA 228). Certainly a thinking
is all the more in danger "of straying past what was once thought" the
more it devotes itself to the matter alone. Nonetheless, in spite of everything doubtful in its interpretation, such thinking could think, in this turn
toward the matter, the same matter as early thinking (Hw 341)—not what
is equivalent but rather what is different in itself but still the same,
the *historical* matter. If there is no relationship from one destining to
another without errancy and thus no history without errancy, then
precisely this passing by in going astray is what is to be genuinely grasped
(Hw 311). The somewhat "erroneous" Kantian interpretation of the
Platonic theory of ideas belongs to the historically influenced development
of this theory. The early Greek thinking to which Heidegger devotes
himself therefore remains for the dialogue what is "continually worthy of
thought" precisely because it "preserves" in itself "the possibility of a
transformation of the destining"; consequently, finitely limited, "mortal"
thinking allows itself to find itself respectively through dialogue (VA 256).

Breaking through the customary interpretation of the earliest Greek
thinking, Heidegger put a new question to this thinking and thus transformed the dialogue about this thinking. Does Heidegger receive an
answer to his question? Is the earliest Greek thinking by means of his
questioning brought to language so that all traditional fragments become
eloquent, so that what Heidegger experiences as the seminality of thinking
which supports everything is allowed to become audible in their speaking?
Or does Heidegger's interpretation cover up what the Greek phrases and
statements say from themselves? Within the Greek saying, does the word
ἀλήθεια mean unconcealment as Heidegger thinks it? To be sure, this
word has a privative formation. Still, since the word λήθη is determined
exclusively by the medium λήθεσθαί or λανθάνεσθαι and since early
Greek testimonies do not relate the word ἀλήθεια to this medium but
rather to λήθειν and therefore to hiding, to concealing, does it not oppose
λήθη merely indirectly? Does ἀλήθεια (related to concealing and hiding)
not originally concern the relationship of one who knows to one who does
not know so that in Homer it is related to the *verba dicendi* and is not yet the
unconcealment presupposed by all speaking to the other and about
things?[42] Is it not the case that Anaximander's Apeiron is so little the use   **205**
which ordains this one world in accordance with its essence that it is
rather the possibility of infinitely many worlds? Is Heidegger's interpretation of the handed down fragment, the so-called "saying" of Anaximander, compatible with what has otherwise been handed down regarding
Anaximander's thinking? Does not Anaximander's attempt to determine
the structure of the world in terms of number already point to the

Pythagorean thesis that the essence of things is number—consequently to a thesis which Heidegger tries to drive out of seminal thinking?[43] Does Heidegger still follow the orientation of thinking from Parmenides when he specifies, as the bidding of this thinking, the unconcealment in which the ways toward Being, toward Nothing, and toward appearance still belong together? Is the movement of this thinking not rather determined by thinking of Being as free of negativity and thus as permanent, by excluding the path toward Nothing and by devaluating the path of appearance?

If it is the case that the question which Heidegger puts to the earliest Greek thinkers did not bring to language what these thinkers say in terms of its unique element, there is always still the question as to whether Heidegger's search for the truth of Being does not have an essential right. Aside from whether or not Heidegger "correctly" interprets the early Greek thinkers, one must still ask how he brings the matter of his own thinking to language in dialogue with them. One should in no way remove this dialogue from the context of questioning to which it belongs. If the dialogue immediately inquires into correct and incorrect interpretive results, then its unique alignment to the *other* beginning is already misplaced. Only after this dialogue is carried out can one and must one ask whether early Greek thinking points to what Heidegger supposes to be the seminal element of Western thinking.

If one believes that one is able to show that what Heidegger seeks in early Greek thinking—the truth of Being as unconcealment—is not thought about there, then for the first time one arrives at the genuine question: where is the beginning, the historical arrival of the thinking which Heidegger attempts? Can one at all justify the thesis that the beginning must always be the greatest aspect of a great thing and contain **206** all later aspects in itself? Compared to the earliest Greek thinking, is not the Socratic question about what is good already a new beginning? Or is this question thought more primordially in the Heraclitean reflection upon the ἦθος (PI 104ff)? Does not thinking also make a new beginning when the historical understanding of the Judeo-Christian faith becomes its impetus? To be sure, the Christian experience of λόγος is, for example, "worlds apart" from that of Heraclitus; nonetheless, the New Testament "presentation" of λόγος is not simply the Philonic one (E 103). Rather, what Heidegger carries into Heraclitus' theory of the logos could have come to language in the Christian logos speculation, Being in its truth as destining and thus as language.

It is essential for Heidegger's relation to the early Greek thinkers that he understands these thinkers in terms of their neighborliness with the poets. *Einführung in die Metaphysik* draws on the poetic saying of Sophocles in order to understand the thinking of Parmenides. Heidegger later illustrates the "it may need . . ." of Parmenides with a remembrance of Hölderlin's poetic saying (E 110ff; WhD 116ff). According to Heidegger's experience, early Greek thinking and poetizing correspond to one another in that both are "poetic" in their essence, they grant and preserve the historically occurring truth of Being (Hw 303,63f).[44] To be sure, Heidegger brings thinking and poetizing into proximity only to be able to hold apart decisively the mythical saying of the poets and thoughtful questioning: "Philosophy does not spring from myth. It arises only from thinking in thinking" (Hw 325). Heidegger nevertheless resists the now common thesis that myth (which the poets say) has been destroyed by logos (as the philosophers convey it). According to Heidegger's conception, the opposition between thinking and poetizing cannot be formulated this way; myth was destroyed not by logos but rather by the god's self-withdrawal; in this way myth fell out of its primordial essence. Logos turned against myth only when both of them had lost their original essence (WhD 7). According to Heidegger's experience, seminal thinking and seminal poetizing, each in their own way, are open to primordial truth. How this truth shows **207** its seminal essence in art and poetry remains to be asked.

THE SEMINALITY OF ART

The treatise, *Der Ursprung des Kunstwerkes*, provides no "philosophy of art." "The reflection upon what *art* is, is entirely and decisively determined only by the question about *Being*" (*Der Ursprung des Kunstwerkes*, Reclam-Ausgabe 99; supplement from 1956). The reflection asks how the truth about a being (Being) in its essence, how the truth of Being itself is to be thought. "What is truth itself such that it occurs at times as art?" (Hw 28, 46). In the reflection upon art one experiences the truth as appropriative event. With this new experience of truth the experience of the structural fitting together of truth is also transformed. One now no longer thinks only "world" as the framework, but rather the togetherness of world and earth. This concept of the earth conceals within it the decisive step which Heidegger took along his way of thinking when he thought about art.

Sein und Zeit is on the way toward putting an end to the world-forgetfulness of Western ontology. This work thinks Dasein as being-in-the-world without reaching the step of unfolding the sense of Being, the transcendental horizon for the determination of Being as Being, as world. Perhaps the world is still not yet thought primordially enough for its sameness with the sense of Being to be able to come to light. We experience the source of the insufficiency of *Sein und Zeit*'s concept of world when we ask from which phenomenal regions Heidegger develops this concept.

Heidegger takes his point of departure from the ontological structure of "environmental" beings, πράγματα, "equipment." In no way does he intend to identify the ontical context of useful things, of equipment, with the world, but he believes that the structure of equipment has, for a *first characterization* of the phenomenon of world, the privilege of forming a transition "to the analysis of this phenomenon and of preparing the transcendental problem of the world" (G 36 note). Nonetheless, does the environmental being not also cover up the world in its primordial essence? If the world is seen in terms of equipment, then it shows itself as **208** "environment," as the context of references and significance of the ready-to-hand; consequently, the conception of world as the totality of the present-at-hand is kept at a distance. The referential context is secured in the praxis of Dasein as the ultimate for-the-sake-of-which. Equipment, only insofar as it is properly equipment, that is, "serviceable," is absorbed in the project which the will projects in the ultimate for-the-sake-of. Having-to-do with equipment is supposed to function smoothly, although it can also present an unusable being; that is, the ready-to-hand is sometimes unable to be ready-to-hand and can even obstruct concern. Equipment in this case is no longer absorbed in the referential context of the environment; nonetheless, precisely when the world is lacking, the world announces itself (SuZ 73ff). An analysis proceeding from equipment can certainly consider the lack of absorption of something into the context of significance as something negative. In doing so, however, it covers up an essential structural moment of the world, the letting-be-concealed, that sheltering which prevents a mere absorption of a being in the relations of significance. While thrownness and state-of-mind of understanding remain in the background, the for-the-sake-of in which world is grounded as environment is thought one-sidedly in terms of the understanding which projects significance (SuZ 86, 356). Thus the world does not show itself in its primordial essence. Therefore it cannot allow an encounter with it, for example, with nature experienced primordially. In world as environment, the forest becomes lumber, the mountain a stone quarry, the river water power, the wind "wind in the sails." Forest and mountain, river and wind are not experienced as those which also always withdraw themselves into an inexhaustible otherness and strangeness (SuZ 70). In addition, other beings such as the ring worn upon one's finger cannot be illuminated with respect to their Being through the analysis of equipment and its worldliness (SuZ 389).

The withdrawal belonging to the "worlding" [*Welten*] of the world is experienced in anxiety and in the wanting-to-have-a-conscience which takes its "guilt" upon itself. In the experience of the nothing, the world as world shows itself to anxiety. Everything within the world plunges into a "complete insignificance"; it takes on the character of "non-involvement" and *empty mercilessness.*" What calls in the call of conscience is Dasein in his uncanniness, being-in-the-world as "not-at-home," "the naked 'That' in the nothing of the world" (SuZ 187, 343, 276f). The analysis of anxiety and conscience shows once more the metaphysical motive of providing Being and its sense as an ultimate ground. It even manifests a modern characteristic; it speaks about the "naked" That in the nothing, and modern inquisitive thinking wants its object "naked" and unvarnished. Nonetheless, the metaphysical motive is bound up with the anti-metaphysical motive of allowing Being itself to be a Nothing which is not at one's disposal. To this there is added a motive stemming from Christian eschatological thinking: history and its worlds are oriented to an ultimate which, compared to all that is demonstrable within the world, is a "nothing."

209

Yet how can this experience of the world as world in terms of nothing and of complete insignificance be thought together with the analysis of world as environment or context of significance? To be sure, the analysis of the fundamental structures of Dasein in terms of their temporality once again brings about a decisive *turning toward* the concept of world. What world is is clarified by the horizonal schemata which belong to the temporal ecstases of existence, by the for-the-sake-of of futurity, by the in-face-of-which and at-which of the past as having been, and by the in-order-to of the present (SuZ 365)? Since, however, what authentically "worlds" in the world withdraws itself as a nothing, the falling tendency to understand the worldly in terms of the innerworldly is validated in the use of the concept of world. In the concept of world history (389,381) and in the concept of world time (422) the accent falls upon the innerworldly. Of course, the essay *Vom Wesen des Grundes* then tries to win back the primordiality of the concept of world.

Because that which authentically worlds in the world withdraws itself as a nothing while the nothing is not yet *unfolded* as the essence of Being, the essential aspect of the world stands as something other than the world either as environment or as context of significance. What worlds in the world and thereby the momentariness of wanting-to-have-a-conscience remain empty since its filling by what is merely environmental must be prevented. The insightful moment is *kairos*, and it is as sharp as the blade of a knife; in fact, this blade is so sharp that no "values" have their place upon it. Already in the "hermeneutic of facticity," attentiveness to the sense of accomplishment prevents a positive assessment of the sense of value. In *Sein und Zeit* the moment, as Plato said with Kierkegaard's approval, is an ἄτοπον. It is a nothing. To be sure, *Sein und Zeit* points to the "situation," but the unity of the insightful moment and situation can only be thought as the plunge out of the authenticity of the insightful moment into the inauthenticity of being hard-pressed by what occurs situationally. The insightful moment "is" only when Dasein *draws back* from the situation in order to be there in a "sober enrapture" for what occurs in the situation (SuZ 328, 338). Dasein is not yet thought as the *abode* of the insightful moment for the truth.

It is striking that in *Sein und Zeit* the present is swallowed up by the future (as having been) and thus receives no positive determination. While the temporal ecstasis of the future is richly determined by existence, projection, anticipating death, resolvedness, and that of the past by facticity, thrownness, guilt, repetition, the present remains—at least in its authenticity as the insightful moment—empty (even as it is in a certain Christian and, above all, gnostic experience of time). Of course, the motive working under cover to keep the moment empty entangles the analysis in contradiction. In the fundamental analysis, state-of-mind, understanding, and discourse are exhibited as basic structures of Dasein. These structures can occur both in their authentic mode (for example, state-of-mind as anxiety) and in their inauthentic mode (for example, state-of-mind as fear). In the progression of the analytic (SuZ 231) state-of-mind (facticity), understanding (existence) and *falling* are suddenly declared to be the constitutive moments of Dasein. Falling, which as the possible modification of state-of-mind, understanding, and discourse in no way stands on a level with these structural moments, presses forward and displaces discourse, or at least forces it away. Yet this occurs because in *Sein und Zeit* the insightful moment which remains empty permits no authentic discourse, that is, no authentic articulation.[45] Consequently, in that chapter which analyzes the basic structures of Dasein in terms of temporality, *discourse* ultimately is not coordinated with the present—this would have corresponded to the original beginning—but *falling* is. The present comes into play only in accordance with its inauthenticity. Furthermore, since the call of conscience gives Dasein to understand only the naked That in the nothing, there is no conversation between Daseins about what is authentically essential. The being-with of one with the other, of the one epoch with the other, can therefore not be positively thought in *Sein und Zeit* because Dasein is not yet that which in each case is proper to the abode of the insightful moment, because Nothing is still a naked That but not the veil of Being itself which is experienced differently in each case.

In *Sein und Zeit*, truth is the discoveredness of beings. The discovering of the being which becomes discovered and thus becomes "true" occurs primordially within the environment's relations of significance. Yet truth as the discoveredness of beings and the discovering activity of Dasein is grounded in a more primordial truth, the disclosedness of Dasein. If this disclosedness opens itself in resoluteness, then the authentic worlding in the world lights up as nothing compared to everything discoverable and all significance. In *Sein und Zeit* the world is at one time the structural fitting-together of the truth as environment but then more primordially as the nothing with respect to everything environmental. Now how is the experience of truth and its structural fitting-together transformed when thinking considers how truth occurs at times in art?

The origin of the work of art is the truth as it occurs primordially; in that originating which always breaks open, the truth about beings as a whole is transformed in ancient Greece, in the Middle Ages, and at the beginning of modern times. Art traces other ways to let truth occur in that it "sets" truth "to work." It brings forth a specific being which previously did not exist and which afterwards will be no more. This being places beings in general into the open in such a way that it alone "first clears the openness of the open into which it comes forth" (Hw 50). The work opens the truth and preserves it in unique openness. Truth is the open place which the work of art in beings as a whole breaks open, that clearing in which nonhuman as well as human beings can first be the beings which they are. Yet this clearing happens only on the basis of concealment. Art places a being into its openness in that, at the same time, it places it back into the inexhaustibility in which a being hides itself. Art shows how a being which presences in unconcealment maintains an "opposition of presence"; to the extent that it is unconcealed, it is also concealed. In the unconcealment the concealment holds sway not only as the non-essence, **212** the self-refusal of truth, but also as the counter-essence of the disguise in which the one being disguises the other and beings generally disguise Being. Amidst the familiar and common, art wrenches open the space for the uncanny and thus lets every clearing and revealing shatter on the concealment. Truth as it occurs at times as art is unconcealment. Nothing belongs to it as that which holds sway, as concealment and "veil," as the heart and the mystery of unconcealment.

A Greek temple, for example, shows how the structural fitting-together of this truth is to be thought (Hw 30ff). The temple stands in the midst of the fissured valley of rock. It encloses the figure of the god and in this sheltering lets the god stand out through the open colonnade into the region thus marked off as a sacred region. If the god presences, then "world" clears itself in its reflected splendor; the temple unites and gathers "the unity of those courses and relations in which birth and death,

harm and blessing, triumph and humiliation, perseverance and decline"
win for the essence of man the form of its destiny. The temple opens world
in which the stone and the beast, man and god are first capable of being
what they are and as they are. The temple sets up world, but in doing so it
establishes the earth. It lets it be seen as the rising which conceals itself
back in itself. The temple rests upon foundational rock and in this resting
forces out from the rock "the obscurity of its bearing which is massive and
yet compressed to nothing." The edifice withstands the storm and for the
first time shows the violence of the storm. The being steps into the
openness of the world, but it can enter into the world and show itself as
that which it is only because it arises from that which in the arising
conceals itself in itself and which consequently never merely "arises" in
the open of the world. The work of art keeps the earth in the open of the
world, thereby allowing the earth to be earth, the arising which conceals
itself in itself and its inexhaustibility.

The structure of the truth as unconcealment is the togetherness of world
and earth. World is the articulation of the open, the clearing, earth the
articulation of the self-closing, of the concealment as the sheltering. World
is never without earth. It is not simply the clearing, but rather the clearing
which comes forth from concealment. Earth is not earth without world. It
is not the utterly closed up, but rather the self-closing and concealing
which holds itself into the openness and shelters this in itself. World is
grounded upon earth, earth cuts through world. The with-and-against-
one another of earth and world is "strife"; nonetheless this strife is only
insofar as truth occurs as the original strife of clearing and concealment.
The work of art kindles this strife and lets this strife attain its movement
from the work's unique resting in itself (Hw 37f, 44).

The artwork's resting in itself which gathers the movement of truth and,
thereby, the work-character of the work into itself all should be understood only from themselves but not as a mere addition to what is
apparently known in the artwork as "material." Heidegger begins his
essay by asking whether we know at all what this material, the thingly and
equipmental aspects in the work, is, what a thing and a piece of equipment are at all. A painting of Van Gogh first lets us experience what a pair
of shoes are. Only on the basis of the primordial truth as it occurs, for
example, in art, can we know about being-a-thing or being-equipment.
The natural-scientific experience of things is not the mode of truth upon
which all other experience of truth must be built—if it were, for example,
beauty would be explained as an addition of an aesthetic value to an
already familiar thingly, equipmental "matter." The natural-scientific
experience of things is rather an abstraction which ignores the primordiality with which the truth (e.g., in art) occurs. Even the praxis which

moves in a context of equipment and thereby in the world as environment does not attain the primordial essence of truth and its structural fitting-together. In the context of equipment, that from which equipment is made appears as mere "material." This material is used up. It vanishes in its serviceability. The stone, for example, disappears when the stone ax is made from it, and the wood vanishes in the building. In contrast, the work of art does not vanish in some serviceability. It does not—like equipment—get absorbed in the relations of significance; rather it stands and rests in itself. In it, it becomes expressly evident "that such work is at all rather than not at all" (Hw 53). The work constantly throws the event-fulness of its that-it-is and how-it-is before itself and around itself. Thus it lets truth be experienced as the unconcealment which rests in its abysmal That and How. Yet the work of art also shows that things are not consumed in their serviceability as equipment and in their environmentality; in any case they still stand in the way even if they are of no use. The truth of things is grounded not only in significance, the projected sense through which the will of an ultimate For-the-sake-of makes every thing usable; it is based just as much on drawing-back-of-itself-into-itself and on self-sheltering in the proper unfathomability. Because the world was understood in *Sein und Zeit* in terms of the environmental context of significance, the side of concealment in the structural fitting-together of truth is named (in the essay on the work of art) by a counter-word to the word "world," that is, by the word "earth." **214**

Nonetheless, *Sein und Zeit* lets the world be seen as more than environment. The analysis of anxiety and of wanting-to-have-a-conscience also shows that what genuinely worlds in the world is the Nothing—that which is Nothing in relation to everything discoverable and significant. If truth is now thought as unconcealment and its structural fitting-together as the strife between world *and earth*, then the Nothing is no longer—as in *Sein und Zeit*—an empty and "naked" Nothing; it is rather the self-withdrawing and the concealing as what accords and shelters inexhaustibility. Insightful momentousness as letting-oneself-go into the Nothing is now no longer seen merely as "becoming free from the idols which everyone has and toward which one is accustomed to slink away" (WiM 42). The truth which rests in the Nothing of all existing grounds as in its mystery can become the expanse for what is totally other than man and nonetheless needs man, the space of the holy (cf. PL 85f, 102f, 114). To be sure, man seeks more than the laying open of things; he asks not merely about truth, but rather about truth as what is holy and unholy, about whether beings rest in their truth or dwindle into an empty negativity. He asks about the holy as that which grants wholeness and, therefore, as the divine. If the holy shows itself in the region of a truth which is not at man's disposal, then man tries to find security not in the idolatrous, but rather in the divine. The holy shows itself to finite, historical man but never unheralded and therefore not as the "naked" Nothing. Instead it shows itself by

215   historically gathering itself respectively into the form of a god. Man does not have an "understanding" by which he is equal to God (onto-theologically thought) and by which he could therefore solve the mystery of truth. He is rather the "mortal" who remains directed to the fact that truth always grants itself as what brings wholeness in the shining forth of the god. Even the fate of god's failure to appear is also a way in which the world (from out of its belongingness to the earth) "worlds" (Hw 34).

Art is, as Heidegger summarizes it once more at the end of his essay, "a becoming and occurring of truth" (Hw 59ff). It lets the truth about beings occur as primordial unconcealment, it sets up the world, brings forth the earth, and is thus the origin which grounds history. It is "poetic" in its essence; that is, it grants or founds. Granting is a gift and an abundance; what is granted can never be read off from the present-at-hand or from what is at one's disposal. Truth occurs from out of the Nothing toward what is present-at-hand and ordinary. Granting is a grounding; it draws from below the closed ground from that wherein Dasein is already thrown as historical. If the granting is called "creative" [*schöpferisch*], then this creative aspect is not to be thought as the highly gifted achievement of the tyrannical subject, but as drawing [*Schöpfen*] from the spring, as projecting what is already thrown toward one. Finally, granting is a beginning. It has the suddenness of what we call a beginning even though one must prepare for this suddenness over a long time, even though it has surpassed everything futural and already contains the end concealed in itself. Does the poetic-granting essence of art not show itself above all in that art which brings the totality of beings into its truth?

HÖLDERLIN AND THE OTHER BEGINNING

According to Heidegger's experience, the tragic poets of Greece have preserved in their saying the essential aspect of the fine arts of the Greeks which was set to work in the temples. But if Greek poetry lets truth occur

216   in its primordiality, must it not then be an impetus for Heidegger's question about truth? Nonetheless, what once occurred in the Greek tragedies—the nearness of the divine in poetic saying (Sp 219)—is today no longer. If truth and the holy, the region for the appearing of the divine, are temporal, "the appropriative event," then the divine which has been cannot be simply asserted as present today. The gods who fled, as

Hölderlin says in his poem *Germanien*, have had their times. Once their days have grown dim, then their temples and figures also sink away.

> Only as from a funeral pyre henceforth a golden smoke,
> the legend of it drifts and glimmers on around our
>   doubting heads
> and no one knows what's happening to him.[i.]

The day of the gods which was cannot be called back, but indeed another day of a new revelation of the divine can be awaited. Hölderlin hopes that *Germanien* will be the land of this other day of the gods. Demigods—according to Hölderlin's *Der Rhein*—would then have to take upon themselves the Between between the gods and men, and the poets have to grant this Between.

In the winter semester of 1934–35, Heidegger lectured about Hölderlin's Hymns, *Germanien* and *Der Rhein*. For Heidegger, Hölderlin became the poet who waits in the time of the gods who have fled, who waits for the new gift of the divine. Hölderlin's poetic saying became the basis for a thinking which seeks to experience the truth of Being. Kierkegaard had pointed to this truth in that he had let man be seen in his temporal-finite essence, as "existence." By means of his completion of metaphysics, Nietzsche had brought thinking to a decision as to whether it was to forget finally the truth of Being or to ask about it anew. Kierkegaard, Nietzsche, Hölderlin—these are the ones who have taken the need of our age upon themselves, who have suffered the uprooting most profoundly. Thus it is no accident that they were prematurely taken from the light of day (*Beiträge*). Heidegger seeks to develop through thought what they experienced in the shattering. According to Heidegger's experience, Hölderlin came earlier than Kierkegaard and Nietzsche, but he nonetheless reached farthest into the future. He let the truth be seen as the holy, as the element of the divine, and this in a time, as **217** Nietzsche expressed it, in which God has been killed!

This godlessness, as it emerges at the end of the modern age, must be experienced in accordance with its origin if Hölderlin's word is able to be heard. This godlessness is not simply the loss of the old god, especially if one nonetheless always still appeals to this god in the most unrecognizable forms (as moral code, as the happiness of the most . . .). "The godlessness experienced from the history of Being [*Seyn*] arises from the

i. All quotations from Hölderlin are either quoted from or based upon *Hölderlin: Poems and Fragments*, translated by Michael Hamburger (Cambridge, England: Cambridge University Press, 1966).

flight destined through the abandonment of the Being of beings (that is, by the power of willing to will), from the flight in face of the need of needlessness. The world age of willing to will is needless because one fails to experience Being as the dispensation of the appropriative event into its truth, the overcoming into the beginning and the consequent grounding of the essence of man which can be determined only from the truth of Being." Needlessness is in truth the highest need; it prevents man from being addressed by the divine because it does not allow the other beginning to prevail in which the truth of Being shows itself as unconcealment and thus as the temporal-field-of-play for the holy. "Godlessness fills up the space-of-time of an appearing of a kingdom of gods whose gods are still undecided. This godlessness arises not from man's mere lack of faith or from a moral incapacity. This godlessness is the history which has occurred in the history of Being [*Seyn*] itself." The thinking which experiences the self-refusal of the truth of Being as the occurring of this truth sees itself directed to Hölderlin's word. "Insofar as thinking (in terms of the history of Being) now saw itself thrown into godlessness in accordance with its first inadequately self-understood attempt (in *Sein und Zeit*), it can be said in retrospect that a naming of the divine and of that which pertains to the gods becomes destiny in order that there historically be a hold at which thoughtful confrontation preserves the originality of its questioning; in this way, the hold itself which never becomes a means to an end clarifies itself in its own poetic history." The thinking of *Sein und Zeit*, anthropologically, existentially, and theologically clumsily misunderstood and misused, was still powerless to resist the pressure of metaphysics. Thus it also

218   tried to make itself intelligible to itself in the region of metaphysics. "In the moment of throwing off the last metaphysical misinterpretations, that is, in the moment of the first, most extreme questionability of Being itself and of its truth (lecture on truth 1929–30), Hölderlin's word, already previously known like that of other poets, became a destiny" (*Das Ereignis*).

Should we actually expect that by his word Hölderlin begins a new age, that his word turns godlessness around? Is the naming of the divine in general, *theology*, then the affair of the poet? In his talk, *Hölderlin und das Wesen der Dichtung* (1936), Heidegger says that Hölderlin calls for a decision whether poetry is to be essential for us in the future or not. As a poet of poets, Hölderlin grants an essence of poetry which anticipates the coming historical time and is, in this sense, historical (EH 44). Poetry appears to be the "purest of all enterprises," a "game." Nonetheless, poetry taken essentially is language, and indeed not a common type of language, but the "primordial language" of a historical people which first enables language at all (40). In language man attests to his belongingness to the totality of beings so that in this testimony world first breaks forth as the respective openness of beings and is, in the circle of this openness, the possibility of decision, and consequently, history (34f). Language occurs as "conversation," as an agreement upon the one and the same which becomes manifest in word. The poets must grant this one and the same, "that which endures." Dasein, being-in-the-world, or the "dwelling" of man must be grounded poetically because it is itself poetic, something always to be grounded historically. Poetry, appearing to be mere play, takes over this grounding with all of its danger (41f). It is the verbal granting of Being which brings a being into its Being or its truth, things into their essence, and thus allows world and history to be. But the world opens itself only if the gods place the mortals under their claim and if the poet in answer to this claim names the gods (37). The poet is bound to the "intimations" of the gods; he stands *between* this beckoning and the saying in which a people is always already mindful of its belongingness to beings as a whole. The poet is thrown out into this Between in order to obtain with difficulty the truth in behalf of his people (42ff). Yet the time whose poet Hölderlin is, is the "time of the gods who have fled *and* of the god who is to come" (44).

219

Heidegger finds the "purest poetry of the essence of poetry" in the poem *Wie wenn am Feiertage* . . . (47ff). This poem says that the poet is a poet when he responds to nature. "Nature" is Hölderlin's provisional word for what is "older than the ages." This continually once and future seminal element is truth as unconcealment which grants to everything that is the hale of lingering; thus, what is holy is that which grants the healing and the hale (61). Hölderlin's saying is of consequence for the holy; still, the poet cannot name the holy immediately, and the holy does not grant itself to the poet immediately. The holy gathers itself into a beam of light, the god, and encounters man in this manner. Only if the god is "directed" toward man can the poet name the holy. Reciprocally the god requires the poetic naming in order that it can gather the holy into itself. The holy is "beyond the gods"—not a distinct region above the gods but rather that in which the gods and the mortals can first of all be what they are (66f, 58). The poet of that poetry whose essence Hölderlin poetizes should never lose himself in the possession of the *one* God since his essential stand is not grounded in the "conception of God," but rather through what is "holy" in the "sphere" which is beyond the gods (67). For this reason, Hölderlin belongs to another beginning because he experiences poetizing as the naming of what is holy. What is holy grounds this other beginning (73f).

Truth experienced as the holy brings forth the "ground" of the coming historical Dasein, the enduring seminal element of another history. If the divine addresses man from out of the region of the holy, then truth accords to him a new being-at-home, the homeland as the "nearness" of Being itself (PL 84f), as an abode of truth. Yet as Hölderlin says in the poem *Heimkunft* (EH 9ff), only the one who seeks it from not-at-homeness is conveyed to the at-home-ness of the homeland. Hölderlin's homecoming into the at-home from being not-at-home is such that indeed the holy appears in the heralds who bring greetings, but the god which gathers everything upon itself remains distant.

220   However, since the missing god brings greetings in the nearness of the divine heralds, its lack is no mere deficiency. For that reason, Hölderlin's "people of the land" should neither strive to make a god for themselves "by means of stratagems" nor condescend to calling merely upon a customary god. The care of the poet is of importance for only one thing: "Fearlessly to remain close to the absence of god in face of the appearance of godlessness," until "the seminal word is granted" from the nearness to the missing god, the word which names the sublime.

In the course entitled *Hölderlins Hymnen* (summer semester, 1942), Heidegger tries to show how Hölderlin's homecoming occurs, how the coming into homecoming is to be thought. In his relationship to Hölderlin, Heidegger proceeds from the poetic hymns. According to his experience, the poetry about Hyperion and Empedocles still belong to Hölderlin's wanderings; they are not yet the homecoming (EH 121). In the aforementioned course, Heidegger turns to that hymn which speaks of the Ister. To be sure, he does not intend to interpret this hymn but only to provide "observations": indications, signs for attentiveness, points for reflection. The reflection concerns the river but also what distinguishes the Ister from the other rivers. For Hölderlin, the Ister ("Ister" is the Greek name for the Danube) is genuinely the river of *homeland*. For Heidegger as well, the upper Donau valley in the vicinity of Beuron which Hölderlin celebrates is the land of origin and homeland.

The Ister hymn begins by referring to a "now" and a "here": "Now come, fire!," "Yet here we want to build." They who here call "now" are themselves those who are called by the approaching fire. They are called to the "vocation of poet." They come from the Indus, from where Bacchus comes, whose priests are the poets. The now which these appointed ones call is nothing that can be dated historically. It is *datum* as a given and as gift. It is what is transmitted, that about which it is already decided in what has been. It is appropriative event. The here which is mentioned is the here toward a there. Those who call come there from Indus and Alpheus and want to build here on the Ister which "dwells in fairness." The river "is" respectively the dwelling place which reigns over the sojourn of man upon the earth. The dwelling place is claimed by man as his own, yet that which is claimed requires appropriation. One must come to know the dwelling place by means of journeying.

The journeying seeks to gain the earth as the "ground" of being at-home. For Hölderlin the earth is not the creation of a creator nor the "vale of tears" as a mere passage to the beyond; furthermore, it is not the "earthy side" which attains its character by disavowing the beyond and by remaining stretched out in the metaphysical distinction between this sensuous world and the other world of the transcendental. For Hölderlin, the earth is a "goddess," and the river which makes the earth capable of cultivation lets the earth become the homeland in that it dwells and permits dwelling. It thus shows the essence of dwelling place and journeying. It is the dwelling of journeying and the journeying of dwelling. "The river is the dwelling of journeying because it determines the 'there' [dort] and the 'clearing' [Da] where the becoming at-home is established, yet from where, as becoming at-home, it also takes its point of departure." The river possesses a place itself; it *is* its dwelling place. For this reason it is said of the Ister that "in beauty it dwells. . . ." "Yet the river now is just as essentially the journeying of the dwelling place. The essence of the place in which becoming at-home has its point of departure and finds its entrance is such that it wanders. The essence of this wandering is the river." Still, the place is not the mere succession and accidental juxtaposition of the there and here; "the former place remains preserved in the subsequent one, and the subsequent one has already determined the former."

The unity of dwelling place and journeying appears to be the unity of space and time. Abode is a place in space and wandering a sequence of steps in time. What space and time are appears to be known in a metaphysical-scientific way. Nonetheless, perhaps metaphysics and science think space and time in terms of what is in space and in time. Yet, if this is the case, then they never arrive at the essence of space and time itself; it is true then that "The unity of dwelling place and journeying cannot be grasped in terms of 'space' and 'time' since the space familiar to us and the time to which we are accustomed are themselves derivatives of a region which first allows every openness to arise from itself because it is that which clears (the appropriating which clears)."

The river is the unity of dwelling place and journeying; thus it is that clearing appropriating from which all that is finds its essence. The rivers, as Hölderlin poetizes them, are not occurrences of nature nor parts of the landscape; they are also not men or gods and surely in no way "symbols" for human life. The rivers run their course—according to the poem *Stimme des Volkes*—untroubled by human wisdom; thus in their course they announce what is called in Hölderlin's *Anmerkungen zum Oedipus* the

221

222

"*frightful*, how God and man join together and the power of nature (the holy) and of man's innermost nature boundlessly become one in ire." The river allows man to become at-home in the passage through the strange and the not-at-home and thus reveals the essential ground of man's historicality—certainly not "of man in general" or "universal humanity" but of Western man.

The becoming at-home in passing through the strange bears the historicality of history and is, therefore, the fundamental truth of history. This becoming at-home is Hölderlin's single concern. For the sake of becoming at-home Hölderlin carries on a dialogue with strange poets; for example, translations of Pindar and Sophocles go together with Hölderlin's poetic hymns. The strange or unfamiliar to which Hölderlin turns is not something arbitrary, but rather the seminal element of one's own which has been, Greek culture. Yet this culture is neither taken as "classic antiquity," as the measure and model of the fulfillment of mankind, nor does Hölderlin strive for a renaissance nor want to return "romantically" to the Greeks. Hölderlin rather permits Greek culture as foreign to come in its essential opposition toward what is one's own; by means of the "difference which joins together" he seeks to come from the foreign to what is one's own.

In Hölderlins poetic hymns there is above all a reminiscence of the first chorus of Sophocles' Antigone, and this is not accidental. This choral song speaks about the essence of man; Hölderlin's river hymns speak about dwelling place and journeying, about becoming at-home, and consequently about the historicality and the essence of man. "Historicality is the distinction of that humanity whose poets are Sophocles and Hölderlin; in Greek culture something seminal has occurred and the seminal alone grounds history. The reminiscence of the first chorus song in Hölderlin's poetic hymns from Sophocles' tragedy, *Antigone*, is a historical-poetic necessity within the history in which the being-at-home and not-being-at-home of Western mankind is decided." In order to be able to hear better Hölderlin's poetic hymns, Heidegger explains the first chorus song of *Antigone*. Insofar as we recall this Sophoclean poetry, we are thinking through the care of Hölderlin's poetic hymn in its seminal form.

At the beginning, the song (cf. also E 112 ff) refers to the basic word of *Antigone*, indeed, of Greek tragedy in general "and thereby the basic word of Greek culture," Tò δεινόν, the uncanny. As the not-at-home the uncanny is blocked from its own essence; it does not attain at-homeness, yet it remains determined precisely by the at-homeness. Man is the most uncanny among things uncanny. He journeys everywhere and achieves a great deal, but still he remains without a way out. He comes to nothing and since he cannot restrain death, he evades it and therefore remains

223

precisely in his pursuit of beings dislodged from Being. Within beings he is the "singular catastrophe"—the reversal which turns him away from Being and his own proper essence, "so that for him at-homeness becomes the empty going astray which he fills up with his agitation." What is catastrophical in the essence of man ought not be debased as "sin." There is no sin at all in Greek culture but only in Christianity where it occurs alongside faith. The one side of the catastrophical, the turning away, should also not be grasped as the merely negative. "In the historical moment, since the one side is devalued in the counterturning of Being towards the lesser and the inferior, Greek culture falls away from the course of its essence, and the decline is decided. The mark of this change is the philosophy of Plato." It is also insufficient to think the negative positively and to bring it under the absolute as Hegel, Schelling, and Nietzsche attempt to do, for they remain determined precisely by the Platonic-Christian devaluation of the negative. To begin with, this negative can be called the malevolent; this would then be thought as a characteristic in Being itself.

Sophocles brings the countermovement of the uncanniest to linguistic expression: "Towering high above the abodes, deprived of abodes." Man can dwell among beings; he has an abode among beings because Being **224** opens itself for him and gathers him in for its openness. This abode is the polis. What the polis is should certainly not be thought in terms of what today is experienced as the "political." Today in the realization of man the political is one matter among others. Even the "priority of the political" and the "totality of the political" (as it was demanded by National Socialism at the time of Heidegger's lecture course) mean something entirely different than the essence of the polis. The demand for the priority of the political arises from the recent consciousness which wants to master history with its plans, and the unquestioned character of the political belongs to this assertion about the totality of the political. In contrast to this, the polis is the abode of the truth which grants itself; it is, therefore, the region of what is worthy of question and thereby of the appropriate or inappropriate. Yet this abode itself has the basic feature of pressing toward surmounting and thus of dragging into ruin. Beings play their appearance against man who attempts too much in the abode of essence and thereby becomes the one without an abode. He is as the most uncanny the one who is not-at-home.

The final verses of the song point to this uncanny element of the hearth, that is, according to the Greek experience of the "homestead of being at home," of "Being itself, in whose light and brightness, glow and warmth, every being has gathered itself already." In the tragedy Creon is still indeed the outcast, but not the "inoffensive" Antigone. Or even Antigone?

Against the advice of Ismene, Antigone takes up into her essence that "against which one exerts oneself in vain"—that which is sent, the destiny itself. Antigone offers—as she says in the opening dialogue with her sister—a dangerously difficult counsel: "to take up into one's own essence the uncanny which appears here and now." Still, is the banishment of Antigone of no consequence because she takes the uncanny upon herself? The closing verses of the choral song have their own uncanniness in that they hint at differentiating between an authentic and an inauthentic being-not-at-home and being-uncanny. The entire tragedy is nothing but this differentiation: "Being-not-at-home can go forth into mere arrogance toward beings in order to force from the latter an escape and an abode respectively. Yet this arrogance towards beings and among beings is only **225** what it is from out of the forgottenness of the hearth, of Being. Being-not-at-home, however, can also break this forgottenness through 'remembrance' of Being and from belongingness to the hearth."

In that conversation with Creon which follows the choral song, Antigone herself tells to whom she belongs. She knows that she is greeted by "Being," that is, by "hearth" as the ground of all at-homeness: "Not merely some present moment nor only on some yesterday, but this constantly presences and no one knows from where it appears of old." What Antigone characterizes is neither the blood relationship with the brother nor is it the dead, but rather what first gives necessity to the distinction of the dead and the priority of blood. "The determining which determines Antigone in her Being is beyond the higher and the lower gods. Yet, it is at the same time what thoroughly attunes man as man. The determining element is also not merely a human ordinance capable of nothing regarding the decree of the gods and which only properly falls under what holds sway even over the gods. The determining element never allows itself to be met somewhere as something merely posited; nonetheless it has already appeared to all without anyone being able to name a being from which it has arisen. Consequently, the essence of Antigone belongs to the unconcealed." Antigone is *authentically* the most uncanny. She is therefore not excluded from the refusal of the hearth because she stood outside of the uncanny but rather because she takes upon herself the not-being-at-home as a having-to-become-at-home in Being. Antigone appropriates death and the Nothing into her essence because knowing herself as belonging to Being, she does not merely dawdle about among beings. Becoming-at-home in Being, she is therefore one who is not-at-home among beings. "Antigone herself *is* the poem of becoming-at-home in not-being-at-home." This becoming-at-home in being-not-at-home is most worthy of poetry because it is authentically the most poetic, history as "the risk" of distinguishing between the unauthentic and the authentic being-not-at-home and as the decision for authentic being-at-home.

The choral song of Sophocles and of Hölderlin's river hymns poetize the same thing, becoming-at-home. Yet they do not poetize the identical, since the Greeks and Germans are historical in different ways, that is, they must become at-home in different ways. Hölderlin struggled to grasp the **226** difference between Greek and German poetry. In the letters to Böhlendorf in which Hölderlin speaks of this difference, it is not a matter of mere rules of art but rather of poetry, that is, of how it is determined by what is to be poetized, the becoming-at-home. Becoming-at-home, as Hölderlin knows, achieves at-homeness only by going through the not-at-home. "The law of being-at-home as a becoming-at-home consists of the fact that historical man at the beginning of his history is not versed in the at-home; what is more he must become not-at-home toward the latter in order to learn by departing from the home-like towards the strange about the appropriation of what is one's own. He first becomes at home only in the return from the strange." Hölderlin expressly referred to this law in the fragment: "The spirit is of course not at home in the beginning . . ." (cf. EH 85ff). If, for the Greeks, what is proper to them is the fire from heaven, and what is strange is the clarity of presentation, then it is the reverse for the Germans. The German poet must therefore journey to the South and fetch fire from heaven because only in this way can he make what is proper, the clarity of presentation, his own. If the Germans could learn to make use of what is their own freely, they could perhaps one day surpass the Greeks in that which is foreign to them, in the fire from heaven. It could be, as Heidegger says alluding to Hölderlin's poem, *Der Gang aufs Land*, and to the drafts of it, "that a 'guest house' is built and a foundation is established for the gods to which the temples of the Greeks no longer measure up" (*Hölderlins Hymnen*).

The hymn to the Ister says that the Ister, the river of the homeland, invited Hercules as a guest. In the third Olympian Ode (fragments of which were translated by Hölderlin) Pindar already says that Hercules brought the olive leaves to Olympus "from the Ister's shaded springs." To be sure Hölderlin does not bring Hercules and the Ister together because Pindar does since he thinks another relation between the two than Pindar does, a relation "which for the Greek poet was no necessity and therefore also not possible." "The presence of the guest in the home-like abode says that even and precisely in the abode of the at-home, the journeying, even if transformed, still presences and remains as determinative. The guest, that is, the Greek poet of the heavenly fire, is the presence of the not-at-home in **227** the at-home. The guest turns the home-like thinking into a constant remembrance of the journeying into the unfamiliar (the 'colony'). The

appropriation of what is proper or one's own occurs only as the confrontation and the hospitable dialogue with the unfamiliar. To-be-the-abode, to
be the essential place of the at-home, is the journeying into what is not
immediately granted to one's own essence but which must be acquired by
journeying through it. Yet the journeying is at the same time and necessarily abode, a relationship which thinks forward to the at-home. . . ."

The Ister flows toward the East, but it always looks as if it arrives from
the East; it looks as if it "flows almost backwards." The river lingers about
the source in such a way that it leaves it only with difficulty—"not because
it remains only in the at-home, obstinately clinging only to this, but rather
because at the source it already has invited the not-at-home into the
at-home and is urged into the at-home by the not-at-home. The Ister *is*
that river at which the unfamiliar, as a guest, is present already at the
source in whose currents the dialogue of one's own and the unfamiliar
constantly speak." The river of the homeland, the upper Danube, is
named by the un-homelike name: "Ister" was the name of the *lower*
Danube for the Greeks. The Ister has an entirely different essence than the
Rhine. The Rhine exalts and leaps; indeed, in the hymn to the Rhine,
Hölderlin does not shrink from the phrase about the "raving of the
demigod." The Rhine originally turned toward the East soon alters its
course and vanishes into the distance. The Ister, on the contrary, hangs
suspended "all too patiently" there in the mountains where it is worth-
while to be young; it is "grieved." Still, its sorrow is the holy sorrow, the
knowledge of the necessity of lingering at the source.

The Ister fulfills the law of historicality: it is in an abode and a
journeying. It remains at the source in that it flows forth and invites the
unfamiliar to itself as a guest as it becomes at-home from the not-at-home.
In this way, the Ister grounds the poetic dwelling of man. Yet its essence is
thereby the essence of that poet who must poetize the poet, who must
poetically grant the poetic dwelling of man. The river is not a "symbol"
for the poet; rather the poet and the river of the homeland are one on the
basis of their essence to be "demigods." The tenth stanza of the hymn to
the Rhine—the inner axis upon which the structure of the whole turns—
begins with the phrase, "Now I think of demigods." What does this
"now" mean? It means at this time I sing the spirit of the river, at this
time, according to *Wie wenn am Feiertage* the holy is my word, at this time—
according to the hymn to the Ister—the fire comes. The holy which comes
allows dwelling as the authentically poetic dwelling. The rivers and the
poets are what they are by means of this holy. They are oriented toward
the holy which is beyond the gods. Communicating the holy and the
divine to men, they are demigods—standing between gods and man.

As demigods, the rivers and the poets—according to the hymn to the

228

Ister—fructify the land. They prepare the ground for the hearth of the house of history, and they open the space of time within which a belong-ingness to the hearth and a homeland are possible. The rivers fructify in that they are "towards language," a "sign." Language—the showing of that which shows itself by itself—is the essence of the sign. The river, the poet, the demigod: they are the sign. The sign is "used" to keep in mind sun and moon and the change of day and night and in order that the divinities feel warmly together. According to the eighth stanza of the hymn to the Rhine, an other who must patiently bear his incomparability with the gods must indeed vicariously feel for the gods since the divinities feel nothing by themselves. This other allots to man the share in the divine and, standing between them, distributes the holy with the gods and man without apportioning or dismembering the holy. "This communication happens in that this other points to the holy, names it, and *is* itself the sign which the divinities need. Then the 'feeling' and the 'keeping in mind' is the mode of man. Man is man in that he is in such and such a frame of mind respectively; in such being in a frame of mind the totality of beings as such shows itself and manifests itself. Yet the sign bears everything primordially in mind in such a way that in naming the holy, it permits the divine to show itself; it permits the holy to show itself as the fire which the poet ignites (cf. also WhD 6ff).

If the truth shows itself as the holy, then homecoming occurs. Yet homecoming is not yet a remaining at the origin, the dwelling in one's own. Speaking about remaining in the flowing forth, about the being-at-home which has the unfamiliar as a guest, the Ister hymn says: "There could be much to say about this." From this much to be said the poem says "remembrance" of some matters (EH 76). It shows how the poet who comes home thinks about the leaving which has occurred and how he permits what has been to arrive as the futural element to be developed in remembrance. The care of the poet now is to found expressly the enduring in the at-home. In the founding the origin is founded in its own essential ground so that—as the source—it goes back into its own ground in arising and flowing and thus imparts the enduring as the enduring seminal element. The holy is what approaches as it withdraws, what has been and endures futurally, what must be secured in its enduring by means of a poetic founding. The festival to which the gods come as guests and at which that true element upon which men can depend occurs is grounded in the distance of its nearness. The festival sent by the holy is the origin of history. The poet grounds history when, by naming the holy, he founds that enduring upon which a historical humanity dwells as its "ground" (EH 137ff; cf. also VA 187ff).

The truth as appropriative event and as the While of the shining forth of

229

the holy, and destiny as the mediating center bring man and the god, earth, and world (the "sky") into the intimacy of their togetherness. They are the enduring seminal element of our history. Nonetheless this seminal element has not been grounded thoughtfully. It has remained "spared," but has thereby prepared itself for drawing near and by means of its drawing near brings our history to another beginning. Hölderlin is one for whom the way to the church is "not paved"; yet he remains upon the way and in the journeying, and his later song comes from the neighborhood of the church tower "blossoming in lovely azure with the metal roof." Thus he awaits this drawing near as the return of the "spiritual Greece." Hölderlin's later poetical project, *Griechenland*, which speaks of such matters, is interpreted by Heidegger in 1959 and 1960 in the lecture entitled *Hölderlins Erde und Himmel*. Now, after the byway of the Germans led to the decline, the discussion can no longer be about the "German" as the proper element which Hölderlin shows. Yet Heidegger expects that Hölderlin would like to let the seminality of the Western element be seen in every decline and danger. Western history could thus open itself by its seminality to the "few other great beginnings" which have occurred upon this earth and which first allow the earth to be "earth," the region of a possible becoming at-home (*Hölderlins Erde und Himmel* 27, 36).

230

That which is Greek shows its seminal character in this other beginning. What is genuinely Greek is now no longer the metaphysical as it was founded by Plato and Aristotle and which has since molded the West over millennia. What is Greek is also no longer determined by the figure of Socrates which, for example, was brought into view by Kierkegaard, but which also distorted the Greek dawn for him. The genuinely Greek is now that which preceded Plato and Socrates, which was perhaps still preserved by the earliest Greek thinkers and which speaks in every case from the temples and the tragedies. It is the experience of the truth, the un-concealment, which is not at one's disposal and which occurs respectively, which as the holy always gathers itself suddenly in the claim of the god. Greek *philosophy* has disavowed this experience of truth and god in favor of an allegedly truer truth and a more divine god. Nonetheless, Heidegger disavows this disavowal. According to his experience something has come into work and to expression in Greek art and poetry whose primordiality has not been made secure in the philosophy established by the Greeks. By means of Greek tragedy, Hegel already in his early philosophy allowed something to manifest itself which his later philosophy no longer saw as sharply, the conflict in the divine.[46] In his writing about the *Geburt der Tragödie*, the young Nietzsche, under the cowl of the learned, with the bad manners of the Wagnerian and the dialectical clumsiness of the German (as he later said), expressed his authentic experience, the experience of the world as tragic Dionysian-Apollonian play. By means of tragedy, Heidegger allows himself to say not only something about the essence of the metaphysical absolute or of the "world," but something still more seminal, and earlier, that is, the essence (to be thought verbally) of truth and of the holy. It is Hölderlin who experienced tragedy in this primordiality as an occurrence of a truth and of a god which respectively draws man into it and which consequently prevents all "metaphysical" attempts ultimately to constitute and establish god or a corresponding "absolute." Hölderlin above all gave prominence to tragedy in that it **231** plays a part in a time of reversal (and one would do well to ask from where this motif genuinely comes to interpretation). Heidegger strengthens this motif further so that he considers Sophocles together with Hölderlin as the "poet of historicality."

To be sure the "old holy theaters" always remain something other for us, Greek; they are not one's own. Nonetheless, Hölderlin, in the hymns which arose together with his translations of Sophocles, is the poet of the coming time, that is, the poet of that transition in which the divine is what has been, but consequently what will be as well. The hymns are songs of festivity and celebration; that is, what they are is determined by festival and by celebration, by the wedding festival of gods and men which Hölderlin thinks of as the While, as the true which *occurs appropriatively.*

Truth as appropriative event, as the While of the holy, is for Heidegger the enduring seminal element of Western history. Still, what is Western has become European and thus determines the history of our planet. What is European is characterized by what distorts and covers up the seminal, by the metaphysical-scientific-technical having beings at one's disposal. The task which falls to a thinking that maintains itself in the neighborhood of Hölderlin's poetry is to make the seminal visible again in the metaphysical-technical world, to "re-tune" our accustomed thinking to the unaccustomed, thinking experience of the seminal (cf. *Hölderlins Erde und Himmel*). "There must first be the thinker in order that the word of one who poetizes is perceptible" (EH 29).

The first concern of thinking must be that we do not reach too short when we turn toward Hölderlin's poetry, that we do not miss the seminal element of this poetry because we think of its essence in terms of the well-known metaphysical essence of art. How art is art is determined from the world in the manner in which the totality of beings is opened and man is installed in this openness. Since for two thousand years Western man's experience of the world has been metaphysical, the essence of art is also determined by the basic metaphysical difference between the sensuous and the non-sensuous. The sensuous, non-real beings have value as a copy of the non-sensuous, real beings; the non-sensible and transcendental **232** have value as the model for the sensuous. Art is sense representation, literally, symbol, the representation of a meaningful non-sensible in something sensuous—in figure, sound, stone. For Plato, and for Hegel in a different way, the merely symbolic element of art is devalued in favor of that pure appearing of the idea as it happens for thinking. When Nietzsche reverses this devaluation of the beautiful and of art, he nonetheless remains within the metaphysical beginning; that is, even the "realism" which takes the non-sensuous back into the sensuous as the illusion which life must create for itself is still "metaphysical," that is, guided by the difference between the sensuous and the non-sensuous.[47]

Hölderlin's poetry does not belong to this metaphysical essence of art. Hölderlin's poetic saying becomes fruitful in that it is a naming, "a singular determining which cannot be assigned directly to other poetry and other poets. The historical Being of the poetry of Goethe and Schiller is such that it neither must be nor can be a naming even though Goethe and Schiller are historically contemporary with Hölderlin" (*Hölderlins Hymnen*). Hölderlin himself speaks of naming in the sixth and seventh stanzas of *Germanien* as well as in the hymn *Am Quell der Donau* where the naming goes beyond the naming of the gods to the naming of Nature, that is, the holy. Naming always draws the named up into its essence; it nominates what is named to what it is. Hölderlin does not poetize *about* the river; rather, his naming brings the river into its essence for the first time by founding the primordial truth. Hölderlin's poems about rivers are not symbols; they do not build a non-sensible meaning upon an already well-known sensible one. The river is not securely known beforehand because it is known as chemically analyzable water, as the geographically describable watercourse, or as the bearer of aesthetic values which must be ascertained for tourist advertisements (cf. EH 20f). Rather, the river is experienced *as* river when Hölderlin poetizes it, and only within such a primordial, poetic-historical experience of the river's essence can there be—as an abstraction from this experience—chemical analysis, geographical description, and the ascertainment of aesthetic values (cf. EH 20f). Naming as the poetic-historical Saying manifests the primordial truth which remains the insurpassably seminal element for all metaphysical-scientific thinking. For this reason this Saying also cannot be grasped adequately from the metaphysical standpoint of thought. Because Hölderlin's river poetry is a naming, it is not a symbol, "and therein lies the farther-reaching assertion that this poetic art is not metaphysical. To the extent that art exists in the strict Western notion only as metaphysical art, Hölderlin's poetry is, if it is not metaphysical, also no longer 'art'. The essence of art and metaphysics are not sufficient to lend this poetry the essential space appropriate for it" (*Hölderlins Hymnen*).

A thinking more primordial than the metaphysical must let the essence of Hölderlin's poetry become visible. "The historical determination of philosophy," as it says in the *Beiträge*, "reaches its summit in knowing that one must create the hearing for Hölderlin's word." Heidegger first of all puts aside his own attempts at thinking so as to be able to build that "vestibule" in which Hölderlin's singularity can become visible and his word audible. In this attempt, in the dialogue with Hölderlin, Heidegger's thinking is transformed and he gains another language for himself. Hölderlin's sayings such as, "long is the time, yet the true appropriatively occurs," speak penetratingly into Heidegger's thinking and grant him the basic words of his Saying. Through the reflections upon art and poetry, the entire standpoint of the question is transformed. *Because Hölderlin was*, Heidegger as a thinker can express the following opinion: Being [*Seyn*] is the striving coming-to-pass which primordially gathers what has appropriatively occurred (the Dasein of man) and what has been refused (the god) in the abyss of its Between; in this clearing world and earth contest the belongingness of their essence to the space of time in which the true comes toward a preserving, which in such preserving finds itself as the 'being' ['*Seiende*'] toward the simplicity of its essence in Being [*Seyn*] (the appropriative event) (*Beiträge*). That Hölderlin's poetic saying becomes the reverberation for Heidegger's thinking certainly does not mean that Heidegger's thinking itself would become poetic saying or the mere interpretation of the poetic *mythologia* and *theologia*. The relation to Hölderlin makes Heidegger's thinking "mythological" no more than the relation to Kierkegaard makes *Sein und Zeit* "theological" or the relation to Nietzsche makes the overcoming of metaphysics approximate Nietzsche's metaphysics. Above all, some other word about the holy is not simply to be replaced by Hölderlin's word. Entirely apart from the fact that Hölderlin's poetic word is no quotable mythology, a thoughtful relation to Hölderlin can take up his experiences only as *questioning*. Thus Heidegger asks—supported by Hölderlin's poetic saying—how the truth of Being occurs and manifests itself as the holy, how the holy gathers itself in the claim of a god, and what is meant in general when we speak about God and about gods.

234

Heidegger carries the opinion and the lead which Hölderlin's poetic saying gives as he questions thoughtfully in constant discussion with earlier thought. The thoughtful discussion about God is not theology nor is it itself a naming of the divine. It is rather an exhibition of how the seminal element of thinking can be experienced. This seminal element, the unconcealment which shows itself as the holy, grants itself in such a way that it always gathers itself into the claim of something compelling and divine which is never to be grasped immediately. The talk about the earth is no foreign "mythical" or indeed "gnostic" sound in the region of thinking; rather, it becomes thoughtfully necessary if the structural elements of unconcealment are experienced in their primordiality. To the earth which conceals itself in its abysmal character there belongs the world as the open and the cleared. Thus in his later work Heidegger can call the world "sky." Even the concept "sky" is a word of a thinking which questions and, in any case, not a "metaphorical" one as, for example, the concept of the transcendental "horizon." If what belongs to the earth as the Open is no longer called "world" but rather "sky," then the totality of the structural fitting-together of the truth can again be called "world"; thus the restriction of the concept of world can be annulled. One must then sharply distinguish the concept of world in this wide sense from every metaphysical (world as the totality of beings) and every historical-anthropological world concept (world as the horizon of historical projections). This world—the fourfold of earth and sky, divinities and mortals—is nevertheless what phenomenology sought as the "natural world" and what

235 the metaphysics of metaphysics looked for as the "ground" of Western thought, the seminal element by which every thinking is what it is and how it is.

By means of Hölderlin's poetic saying thinking is directed to this seminal element. The turning toward Hölderlin and via Hölderlin to Greek tragedy is a decisive step upon Heidegger's way of thinking. To be sure it may be possible to demonstrate that some, indeed many particular aspects of Heidegger's interpretation of Hölderlin and Sophocles are contestable or simply incorrect. Yet this demonstration is not at issue here. Still, it could be that Heidegger, however he may have misinterpreted some particulars, still has allowed us to see with incomparable power what is essential in what addresses us from the poetry of Hölderlin and Sophocles; this would be similar to how Hölderlin's translations of Sophocles, in spite of their shortcomings and errors, make the word of Sophocles more eloquent than the other translations which do not escape what is usual and worn out in our language. In any case a critique of Heidegger's dialogue with Hölderlin would be truly "critical" only if it took into account that in this dialogue Western history in its entirety is to be decided upon. The critique would thus become the differentiation of one's own experience of history from that of Heidegger. It would thereby be not only a delimiting and a circumscribing of Heidegger's experience but above all and first of all self-criticism, the demarcation of and the limiting to what is one's own. In the turn toward Hölderlin as in the reflection on art and in the dialogue with the earliest Greek thinkers, there was never anything else at stake for Heidegger than this limiting to what is one's own, the freeing toward what is one's own.

9

THE FREEING TOWARD WHAT IS ONE'S OWN

Whoever seeks to bring back in "another beginning" the forgotten "seminal" element of Western history, the element which has never genuinely been a beginning, becomes, as Hölderlin knew from experience, a stranger to his own time (Hw 88f). Under the domination of man who makes himself master over every being and thereby forgets Being and its truth, the earth has become the "unworld of *error*," the "straying star." Thus those who preserve truth and world in their seminal character, the "shepherds," dwell "invisibly and outside of the wasteland of the devastated earth which is still of use only for establishing man's domination" (VA 97f). Those who think seminally travel away from the streets and courses of the technical world upon "field paths" and "timber tracks." In reality even these ways have already been paved as streets and the following is true: "Today the authentic thinking which explores the primordial lore of Being still lives only on 'reservations' (perhaps because it, in accordance with its origin, is as ancient as the Indians are in their fashion.)" (*Aufzeichnungen aus der Werkstatt*). The danger is that the reservation as it is still permitted today as the region of thinking remains a *mere* reservation, an artificially maintained and properly established park for hours of diversion and distraction. The crucial danger nonetheless comes from thinking itself: Does it not degenerate into a retrospective romanticism if it tries to preserve the vanishing tradition by going back to its covered primordiality? Does it not create illusions for itself, does it not flee in face of the actual into a futureless byway when it opposes today with something "more seminal." Can thinking do justice at all to that which is today? As it already says in the *Beiträge*, "romanticism has not yet been brought to an end. It once more attempts a *transfiguration* of beings, but a transfiguration which is concerned only to be a reaction against the general explanation and calculation of beings or to be something in addition to such procedures." If we do not want to assist such romanticism, then we should not take the "shepherd of Being" as a romantic figure nor generate a backwoods-like discussion from the expression "timber track."

Today one can successfully travel a "timber track," a way which suddenly leads to the untravelled, only if one travels over and ponders again and again the streets along which the perfected workaday world moves and if one thereby—if this abstruse image may be permitted here once—comes to a point "where a timber track branches off" (cf. *Zur Seinsfrage* 12f). The "outside" and "byway" to which this way leads is also in truth the concealed essential center of the technological world, the truth which—as the seminal and foundational element of unconcealment—precedes every openness of beings and which carries toward man the possibility of a new becoming-at-home with its alignment with the structural fitting-together of the world. In the experience of truth and world, Heidegger's thinking frees itself from all the errancy of the metaphysical tradition and for what is one's own; however, it can free itself because truth and world are the open space, the freeing of and the surrender to the proper element of a particularly historical being-at-home. What is proper or one's own is not what one seeks and obstinately asserts against reality in a romantic flight toward the past or in imagining an illusory future. It is rather what, as forgotten and misplaced, supports what is "real." One can find it, therefore, only through an "insight into what is."

By reflecting upon Nietzsche's "metaphysics," Heidegger first insightfully penetrated what exists today and what will be in the near future. Since Nietzsche's day, we actually had to experience what Nietzsche saw coming and suspected obscurely. The devastation of the earth about which Nietzsche spoke to still deaf ears has become evident to all. The question remains whether what Nietzsche opposed to this devastation is the way out into the open space or is itself still a devastation. If this question is legitimate regarding Nietzsche, it is also legitimate with respect to the attempts to proclaim in Nietzsche's concepts "total mobilization" and "total war" as the predominant state of the world today, and then to seek the way out of the nihilism of this condition in which man becomes the victim of his own machinations (cf. Heidegger's examination of Ernst Jünger: *Zur Seinsfrage*).

238

In an independent reflection Heidegger asks about what exists today, about what manifests itself and thus announces the necessity of a decision about history. In this reflection he questions the science which is today so entwined with life that life is possible only as scientific and no longer as direct and natural. Technology is considered according to the different ways in which it is actualized—in the shaping of consciousness through modern media technology as well as in the automation of the production process, in the unharnessing of atomic energy as well as in the manufacturing of corpses in the extermination camps. This reflection asks about the place that poetry has in today's world or how the painting of, for example, a Paul Klee, provides an answer to the demand through the tide of the world. Nonetheless, I cannot address all of these questions here; I must confine myself to what is fundamental and how it is discussed in the lectures which Heidegger gave in 1949 in Bremen under the title, *Einblick in das, was ist.*

The insight into what is should not remain the mere procedure of man who, wanting to know himself, investigates his situation. In this insight, the important matter is that the "lightning flash" which unites man with the occurrence of unconcealment catches fire. The manner of the appropriative occurrence of truth which, according to Heidegger's experience, today precisely calls for a decision because it is radically distorted by the technological "world," is the structural articulation of the world as the fourfold of earth and sky, divinities and mortals. The second section of this chapter seeks to gain a perspective upon how this "fourfold" is to be thought.

INSIGHT INTO WHAT IS

In the series of lectures, *Einblick in das, was ist*, Heidegger proceeds from what appears to be the simplest and self-evident matter, the "thing" (VA 163ff; cf. 1D 75). He thus takes up a question which was already a guiding one in *Sein und Zeit*. There the merely presented "present-at-hand" thing was distinguished from what stands in a context of significance, from that with which we are occupied as "equipment." In the lecture series, *Der Ursprung des Kunstwerkes*, Heidegger took his point of departure from the question about the thingliness of that concrete something of the work of art, something which is regarded as the "substructure" upon which aesthetic values are erected. The philosophical tradition thinks this thing as the bearer of properties, as the unity of a sensory manifold, as the synthesis of matter and form. Yet, as Heidegger shows, one cannot think the equipmental character of equipment nor the work character of the art work from these approaches. After Heidegger had brought equipment and work into view, he had to ask again about that primordial thingness from which one has to think of the different ways in which a thing, a being as a being, can be at all.

If we reflect upon the thingness of the thing, then we must—as the lecture *Das Ding* shows—proceed from the fact that today everything that is, every thing, is threatened by annihilation: atom bombs can extinguish life on earth. More terrifying still than this bursting apart of everything is that today everything melts together into a homogeneous lack of difference. Film, radio, television, commerce which overcomes distances, all appear to bring everything that is equally near and yet do not bring what

239

we call the "thing" in a distinctive sense any nearer. Things rather become empty, null, and meaningless in their abundance; in this sense they are "annihilated." Is the annihilation of the thing merely a contemporary phenomenon, or is it the case, asks Heidegger, that the experience of the thing in its primordiality has as yet never been thoughtfully grounded? From the perspective upon which Plato entered, the thing was thought from the self-manifesting appearance in terms of the "idea," and thereby considered merely as that which "stands over against the producer as what is to be produced." Thingness was experienced as a standing-toward [*Herstand*], whereby the process of standing-toward in what stands-toward was twofold: "on the one hand, the standing-toward in the sense of being derived from . . ., whether this be a self-generation or a being-produced; on the other, standing-toward in the sense of what is brought forth as standing into the unconcealment of what already pre-

240   sences" (VA 166). In the modern age standing-toward became the object [*Gegenstand*] which was no longer thought in terms of coming forth into unconcealment but rather in terms of standing over against presenting. If science presents the thing as an object, for example, the jug filled with wine, then it reduces everything experienceable to the quantitative and measurable; in this methodological abstraction it thus sacrifices the primordiality of the thing. The knowledge of science is certainly compelling; nonetheless, that which compels, when it is thought in terms of the primordial experience of the thing, endures in the compulsion "to sacrifice the jug filled with wine and to set in its place a hollow space which liquid fills up. Science turns the jug-thing into something null in that it does not admit of things as the real which sets standards" (VA 168).

If we want to experience the thing in its primordiality, e.g., the jug as jug, then we should not physically reduce the jug's holding capacity to an arbitrary emptiness for an arbitrary fluid or still more abstractly for a specific aggregation of matter. We have to start asking in a different way about how the jug contains. The jug contains in that it takes up what is poured in and retains what is poured in. The taking up and the saving is determined by the pouring out, by the bestowing of the outpouring. The jug gives water and grants wine. In the water there lingers the spring, and in the spring the rock and the dark slumber of the earth as well as the rain and dew of the sky. In the wine there abides the earth's nourishing element and the sun. The jug grants the draught for the thirst of the mortals and enlivens their good fellowship. Yet it also bestows the outpouring, the libation, which is dedicated to the gods and which gratifies the celebration of the festival to the sublime. The jug gathers earth and sky, the gods and the mortals. Thus it is "thing": it appropriates "world" as the fourfold of earth and sky, divine and mortal, in that it retains the fourfold in its actuality and thus brings the four into their own.

The gathering essense of the thing still echoes in the word "thing" since this word belongs in the vicinity of the Old High German word, "thing," which signifies gathering. The Roman word for thing, the word *res*, also means that which approaches us. The neo-Latin *cosa*, *chose*, goes back to *causa*, a word which in its original meaning means that question at issue, **241** the matter to be settled. Yet these tracks to the gathering essence of the thing were already disguised when the essence of the thing was determined by thought in Greek fashion, and by the Latin *ens*, that is, by being as what presences in the sense of what is produced and presented (VA 174).

The gathering and staying of the thing is a drawing near which does not level out to a complete lack of distance but rather maintains the distance. If the thing gathers world, it then concerns us. It conditions us. We men are not those who have beings at our disposal to merely use them up and exploit them. We are, rather, called by the thing which stays the world into the play of the world. "We are—in the strict sense of the word—the gathered. We have left every presumption of something unconditioned behind." (VA 179) As the mortals, we are drawn into the play of the world from out of which the "thinging," the gathering of the thing occurs. The gathering of the thing is the bringing near of the world which brings everything into its own, its essence, in that it allows the world to be what is distant, what is not at one's disposal. World and thing have their essence only apart from each other (from out of the difference, which is what the appropriative event carries out; cf. Sp 17ff).

When Heidegger speaks of things he mentions jug and bench, footbridge and plow, but also tree and pond, brook and mountain, heron and roe deer, horse and bull, as well as mirror and clasp, book and picture, crown and cross (VA 181). In the Darmstadt lecture of 1951, *Bauen Wohnen Denken* (VA 145ff), he distinguishes between growing things and those which do not grow but which must instead be expressly erected. Within the latter, Heidegger, given the theme of the lecture, stresses those which clear a space and are therefore "sites," those which are built. In the lecture series, *Einblick in das, was ist*, Heidegger does not develop these differences (which would be carried still further), but rather proceeds at once in the necessary limitation to what is basic to the question of whether today there are still things at all. The lectures, *Das Ge-stell*, *Die Gefahr*, and *Die Kehre*, develop this question. The thoughts of these lectures are repeated in abridged form in the 1953 lecture, *Die Frage nach der Technik*.

Does today's technological world still allow things, that is, does this

242 world still allow room for the world as the fourfold of earth and sky, gods and mortals? If we want to question in this way, we must then ask about the essence of technology. We usually try to represent technology's essence by means of an instrumental-anthropological determination: technology appears as a means to the end and thereby as the activity of man since man sets goals and prepares a means for himself (*instrumentum*) in order to achieve his goal. Causality reigns where goals are pursued and means are used. Causality is primordially thought—in the thinking of Plato and Aristotle—as the interplay of different ways of occasioning. Occasioning lets what is not yet presencing to come into presence and is, therefore, a bringing-forth. To be sure, bringing forth, $\pi o i \eta \sigma \iota \varsigma$, is for the Greeks not only the manufacturing of the workman and the artist but also the bursting open of $\Phi \acute{v} \sigma \iota \varsigma$. What presences in this bursting forth has the awakening of the bringing forth, for example, the bursting forth of the blossoms in blossoming in themselves and not—as what is brought forth by craft and art—in another (in the worker or artist). The bringing forth brings to a shining forth, "it brings out of concealment and forth into the unconcealment. Bringing forth comes only insofar as the concealed comes into the unconcealed. This arriving is based upon and flourishes in what we call the revealing" (VA 19). Only in the region of truth as unconcealment is there bringing-forth-from, occasioning, causality, means and end; as a bringing-forth-from, technology belongs in the region of truth. Even the word $\tau \acute{\epsilon} \chi \nu \eta$ requires this strange thought from us: the Greeks think as a way of revealing the $\tau \acute{\epsilon} \chi \nu \eta$ of manual activity as well as that of art and of knowing one's way about. "It reveals that which does not bring-itself-forth by itself and does not yet lie before, what can therefore appear and sometimes be omitted in this way and sometimes in another" (VA, 21).

Still, it is not the fact that man generally uses equipment as a means which presses hard upon us when we ask about technology, but rather the fact that equipment utilization has risen to that degree and distinctiveness which differentiate modern technology from all previous use of equipment. Nonetheless even modern technology is an entirely specific manner of revealing: "The revealing which permeates modern technology is characterized by ordering in the sense of challenging forth" (VA 24). Formative **243** activity does not yet "order" the soil, does not yet challenge it forth but rather gives itself and its activity over to the earth and to the cultivation of its powers of growth. It is otherwise with the modern food industry. It sets upon the air for the delivery of nitrogen and draws the old "cultivation of the soil" into the arranging which challenges forth. A windmill is still left to the wafting of the wind, and the old wooden bridge is still built into the stream and the valley. In contrast the modern hydroelectric plant rechannels the river into the interlocking system of the ordering of electrical energy: the Rhine is now what it is in terms of the essence of the power plant; it is now the supplier of hydraulic pressure. How different is the essence of the Rhine in Hölderlin's hymn! To be sure, the river today also appears to remain the river of the countryside; still, as such it is "nothing other than the object of sightseeing, the object arranged by the tourist industry which has set up a vacation industry there" (VA 23f). The ordering becomes all-encompassing; nothing remains which could escape it. All regions are drawn into it, for example, even the "beauty" of the "scenery." God himself can be presented and delivered over in the light of causality as *causa sui* and thus be robbed of his essence (VA 34). Ordering first encounters nature as the main storehouse of the energy supply; such ordering therefore first manifests itself in the rise of modern exact natural sciences. It does not, however, confine itself to nature. Modern technology is also not a mere *employment* of the exact natural science. If one ascertains such to be the case, then this discovery remains insufficient even if one adds that physics, as experimental, is directed for its part to technical apparatus and thereby to the advancement of the construction of apparatus. Modern physics is not a forerunner merely of technology but rather of the *essence* of technology, the setting upon which challenges forth. The setting upon which challenges forth already holds sway in physics as pure theory and therefore directs this theory to the ordering of the experiment. To be sure, modern natural science begins in the seventeenth century while machine technology first occurs in the eighteenth century. "But that which is chronologically later, modern technology, is, with respect to the essence which holds sway in it, historically earlier" (VA 21f, 29f).

That which is shows itself to the setting upon which challenges forth and to the ordering as "stock or reserve on hand." Everywhere it is ordered to stand in position and indeed to stand in order to be itself available for further ordering. That which is so ordered has its own standing. We call it the "reserve on hand" (VA 24). The word "reserve" is thought as the name for the revealedness in which beings manifest themselves as reserve. The reserve is no longer objects; rather, the objects which still maintain a certain vis-à-vis toward man in his capacity for presentation vanish into objectlessness when they become reserve. The airliner on the runway, thought in its truth, is no longer an object. In its truth it is revealed only as the reserve which is to secure the possibility of transportation. It is used in the context of ordering in such a way that it loses every kind of independence (24f). Even in modern physics the object vanishes. Classical physics still believed that one could determine, that is, to project unambiguously, every state of movement of the spatial body at any time at once according to location as well as with respect to the quantity of motion. Atomic physics can "determine" a state of movement

244

"basically only either with respect to location or with respect to the quantity of motion." Its projection, no longer unambiguous and complete in the sense of classical physics, is rather of a statistical nature. Since the object is determined either according to location or according to the quantity of motion, it loses concrete presentability. Thus it loses its objectness and in its revealedness becomes reserve (59 ff).

Where beings are mere reserve and where revealing is a setting upon and ordering of the reserve, there unconcealedness holds sway as enframing. "Enframing means the gathering of that setting upon which sets upon man, that is, challenges him forth to reveal what is real in the manner of ordering it as reserve" (28). The enframing is what presences in technology and is itself nothing technological; it is the essence of technology.

Enframing—the manner of revealing which holds sway in technology and the world, the structural fitting-together of the primordially experienced truth—are the same, namely, ways in which unconcealment occurs. They are indeed not identical but rather even as the same utterly opposed to one another. In the enframing of technology the Being of beings is presentability and deliverability, the disposability of the reserve; what presences in Being, the respective occurring of the unconcealedness which is not at one's disposal, remains forgotten. In enframing, Being withdraws from the truth of its essence, holds world back, and hands beings over to neglect. World (in the genuine sense of the word) is, in contrast, the preserve of the essence of Being, the structural fitting-together of unconcealment and the preserving of the being as "thing." To be sure, the holding sway of the world is experienced only upon a way of errancy, from its other if it is thought from the Being of beings, from the presence of the presencing. World appears to subordinate itself to Being while Being as the openness of beings nonetheless only presences from its essence, from unconcealment and the world. In metaphysics, Being ossifies into constant presence which finally becomes reserve's disposition to being ordered. The negativity of Being is experienced in nihilism. If metaphysics and nihilism are to be overcome, then the essence of Being must be experienced from out of unconcealment and world; its ossification into constant presence must therefore be dissolved. "When world first occurs expressly, Being passes out of sight, but along with it the Nothing also vanishes into worlding" (*Einblick in das, was ist*).

Today technology has become a danger for mankind. Nonetheless, the threat does not come primarily from the possibly fatal activity of its machines and apparatus. It comes rather from its essence which has been long in preparation, enframing, and it concerns not only this or that man of this generation, but rather the essence of man (VA 36). A root of the word "danger" contains the meaning, "to entrap," and in fact, entrap-

245

ment, the setting upon which challenges forth in the enframing of technology, is *the* danger. Each destiny of revealing carries the inherent danger that man goes astray in the unconcealed and misinterprets it. Enframing, this destiny of the revealing that predominates today, is nevertheless the highest danger: Being lets its essence (unconcealment and world) sink into oblivion as it turns away from and against this essence since it appears as the reserve's disposition for being ordered. Thus Being also deprives man of his essence, for the latter indeed has his essence only insofar as he is used for the appropriative event of unconcealment and world. Enframing gives man the possibility of elevating himself into the form of the lord of the earth; at the same time he himself stands constantly in the danger of becoming used up as the mere reserve of ordering—to be more "material," the "work material" of the work place or even the "patient material" of a clinic. To be sure, man is never mere reserve; nonetheless, he is what is challenged forth in that setting upon which challenges forth, which posits being as reserve. Where all revealing is an ordering, man certainly does not experience the fact that he himself is claimed by enframing when he carries on the ordering. In the face of clamorous technology he experiences nothing of the essence of technology. He appears, as Heisenberg said, to encounter only himself, while it is precisely himself and his essence to be used for the appropriative event of unconcealment that he no longer encounters (35). The unconcealment which holds sway as enframing disguises the essence of man and its own essence insofar as it lets revealing be only as a challenging forth and a setting upon; yet even enframing cannot be experienced according to its essence through challenging forth and setting upon. Enframing also disguises all other ways that unconcealment can hold sway when it lets revealing be an ordering. Claimed by enframing without experiencing this claim according to its limited validity, man moves "continually at the brink of the possibility of pursuing and carrying on only what is revealed in ordering and of taking every standard from such ordering. Because of this, the other possibility is closed, namely, the possibility that man admit himself earlier and constantly in a more original way into the essence of the unconcealed and in its unconcealment to let himself experience as his essence the needed belongingness to revealing" (33f).

What is most dangerous in this danger is the fact that it awakens the appearance of the lack of danger and of need and thus conceals itself as the danger which it is. Only if enframing is exeperienced as that mode of revealing in which unconcealment disguises itself is the danger manifest *as danger*. The danger shows itself then as that turning in which Being turns away from its essence and thus prevents man from coming into his essence. If the danger *exists* in this way, then there grows—according to

246

Hölderlin's phrase—that which saves; there grows that which draws one back into the forgotten essence and thus brings this essence to shine forth for the first time. In the danger there is manifested the possibility of that turning in which the oblivion of the essence of Being changes course. This oblivion is not simply set aside but rather exeperienced as an indication that the holding back of itself and the remaining forgotten, the self-concealing, belongs to revealing and thereby to the essence of truth and world. Technology is experienced as a constellation of revealing *and concealing* and thereby as a specific mode of unconcealment, as a destiny of unconcealment (41).

That which saves does not stand outside of technology but is rather rooted in and flourishes in its essence (37). Man never attains that which saves as long as he pursues technology only blindly or else damns it as the work of the devil. He does so only when he takes up an abode in its essence. Technology itself, experienced in its essence, opens the passage into the unconcealment which preserves Being in its essence and which places itself out into the world as its structural fitting-together. In the experience of the essence of technology, the latter is discerned and recognized as a specific mode of revealing. It is limited in its own way to allow revealing to occur in order that it no longer obstructs other ways of revealing and the essence of unconcealedness itself. As Heidegger explained in other places, man achieves releasement to use technical appliances and apparatus without taking technical setting upon and ordering as the sole mode of revealing. He becomes open for the mystery, for concealment as the heart of unconcealment, and thereby free for the bursting open of the world (cf. *Gelassenheit*). The "insight" does not bind man ultimately to that which is valid today as real. If this insight discerns that which is as the danger, then it becomes the "lightning flashing in" which draws man into the precipitous holding sway of unconcealment, which brings man before the breaking open of the structural fitting-together of unconcealment, of world as the fourfold of earth and sky, gods and mortals.

THE WORLD AS FOURFOLD

The insight into what is liberates Heidegger's thinking into the world as the proper element. Heidegger himself states how this world is to be thought: it is the fourfold of earth and sky, gods and mortals. The earth "yields when it is cultivated, bears fruit and nourishes, fosters waters and stones, plants and animals." The sky "is the path of the sun, the course of the moon, the brightness of the stars, the seasons of the year, the light and twilight of the day, the darkness and brightness of the night, the favor and the dreariness of the weather, the movement of the clouds and the bluing depth of the aether." The divine ones "are the beckoning messengers of the godhead. From the concealed holding sway of the messengers, God appears in his essence which witholds him from any comparison with what presences." The mortals "are the men, who are called the mortals because they can die. Death means, to be capable of death as death." Death, as the shrine of what is Nothing, shelters the presencing element of Being in itself, and is thus the mountain shelter [Ge-birg] of Being. The mortals are "mortals" when they are present in the mountain shelter of Being, are the "the presencing relation toward Being as Being" (VA 176f). Earth as well as sky, the gods as well as mortals are never by themselves, but rather only together with the others; they are only in the onefold, the dance and round dance of the four, the play of the world.

When Heidegger thinks the world as the fourfold, he is reflecting on the oldest thoughts. Man, still at home in the mythical experience of the world, experienced the world as the marriage of earth and sky, and he saw himself as the mortal under the claim of God. Even Plato touches on the thought—in his own fashion—that the world is order as the togetherness of heaven and sky, gods and men (cf. Gorgias 507–508), and other testimony could easily be brought forward, for example, from Chinese literature. Heidegger himself builds the bridge from his thinking about the world to the mythical world experience of Hölderlin. There can be no doubt that Hölderlin's poetry was, for him, the decisive impetus for thinking the world as the fourfold of gods and mortals, earth and sky.

Perhaps it is time to draw the oldest wisdom of myth into thinking. If thinking is to venture this attempt, then in an independent approach it must unfold the question about what it is that myth, whose wisdom is pre-seminal, names for thinking. Thinking can never simply take over answers if it does not want to give itself up as thinking. If we ask about the world, the knowledge of what earth and sky is will certainly dissolve in our hands. Why does Heidegger call the earth that which yields under cultivation? Why does he give it a special nearness to natural beings? Why do sun, moon, the weather, the stars, which announce the time to man, and even the tides stand for the sky? The earth is not what lies at man's **249** feet, the sky not what is above his head, for earth and sky are not beings at all but rather "regions of the world." What Heidegger says in a short lecture about earth and sky may provide a first hint to what is to be thought, but perhaps scanty allusions disguise more than unfold what is to be thought. When Heidegger calls man the mortal one, must he not then surely know who man is? Yet, he says in another place that if we would not fool ourselves any longer, none of us would know who we are (Gelassenheit 37). Concerning the divine, he indeed says that he who has experienced theology, not only of faith but also of philosophy, from a mature tradition, today prefers to be silent about God in the region of thinking (ID 51). If this is so, then what can talk about the divine mean?

No hint can directly tell us how the world as the fourfold is to be conceived. Yet, perhaps we ourselves can enter upon the way toward the experience of world if we heed how Heidegger came to this experience. He achieved it upon a way that begins with the question about Being. Being is the openness of beings; a being comes into its Being when it is taken expressly as that which it is. If a being is taken *as* a being, then a rift arises in it; its closed resting-in-itself is torn open and being is differentiated from itself. The rift tears open the difference between Being and beings; it establishes that Between through which beings arrive in the openness of Being. Moreover, the thinking which takes beings as beings is used for this openness. The Between allows Being first of all to be the Being of beings; it is what comes to presence in beings as its "ground" and truth. Heidegger asks how this Between, the truth of Being, authentically presences. He thus experiences it as the simultaneity of revealing and concealing, as the appropriative event of unconcealment.

Heidegger thinks of unconcealment in many ways. Unconcealment is the open air of the clearing whose clearing remains preserved in a veiling and concealing (VA 275ff). The clearing is the nearness which draws near, in that it preserves the distance in itself (the nearness, cf. Sp 211). It is the dimension of all dimensions, the opened Between for every measure (VA, 195f); it is region which as "that-which-regions" [*Gegnet*] lets beings occur in their openness (*Gelassenheit* 40ff). As region, unconcealment is the most primordial movement, the way itself (*Tao*, as Laotse says), that movement which first opens all ways of "thinking," of acting, of speaking (Sp 197f). The movement comes from the rest, which is not to be conceived as rigid motionlessness, but rather as a resting in itself which gathers all movement in itself and releases it from itself (Sp 213, SvG 143f). As "stillness" the rest calms that which is in the withinness of its resting in itself (Sp 29ff, 141ff, 213ff).

Among the names for what holds sway as unconcealment, one name is the decisive one, world. This name refers to the structural fitting-together in which unconcealment is formed. What holds sway in the world is consequently the revealing self-concealing of unconcealment, an occurring. When we say that the uncolcealment "is," we are certainly speaking obscurely. Being and its essence, the unconcealment and the world, "are" not in the way that a being "is," since they are indeed not one being among other beings. For this reason Heidegger says: they "come to presence" or "hold sway," and the "presencing" is thereby to be conceived as that appropriative event which is concealed in presence. Since

250

concealment belongs as enduring revealing in the occurring of unconcealment, this occurrence should not be conceived as a teleological process in
which concealment—at least as the ultimate goal—would be annulled in
favor of revealedness. Heidegger calls an occurring in which revealing and
concealing are inseparably interwoven "destiny."

In destiny the essence of time holds sway. The time which is meant here
is surely not legible from beings within time. It is, as it says in *Sein und Zeit*,
the "temporality" which belongs to the transcendental horizon of the
sense of Being; it is the manner in which unconcealment occurs. This time
was not adequately discussed in the metaphysical tradition; the Being of
beings was conceived in terms of presence and the present. This tradition
did not question the temporal horizon which stands behind presence and
the present. Instead, time itself was understood in terms of presence and
the present, and consequently conceived as a succession of presencing and
present or non-presencing and not-present (past or future now-points).
One of the ecstases of time, the present, was given greater weight than the
other ecstases, and was established as the basic character of time; the
other ecstases were even thought in terms of it. Heidegger tries to break
this supremacy of the present: he thinks of time as the contemporaneity of
having been, present [*Gegenwart*], and future, or, as he also says, having
been, presence, and waiting over-against [*Gegen-wart*] (Sp 213). Contemporaneity is the interplay of the three dimensions; the interplay is something like a fourth dimension, which—if one may even count here at all
—is in truth the first and seminal aspect from which the others stem. The
three dimensions are all equally essential; they do not endure the prepon-
derance of one dimension (the present). The past as having been, which
departs in that it remains, and the future, which arrives in that it is still
outstanding, should not be thought of in terms of the constancy of the
present, that is, as what is not yet present. The present is not at all what is
permanent since the past and future could also be thought of as its
negation; rather, the present (as the moment) is attained only if past and
future play into one another. Contemporaneity cannot be represented as
the in-itself of time; it is, rather, experienced in the differentiation which
joins together, the differentiation which differentiates itself from what has
been, which permits the future to arrive, and thus accommodates itself to
the moment of what is proper. When Heidegger thinks time as contemporaneity, he does not then step toward an atemporal "eternal" present over
the time which has always departed to the inaccessible past and is still
outstanding as future. On the contrary, he definitively cuts off this way.
Eternity, experienced from contemporaneity, is in the uniquely occurring
moment; it has the freedom to withdraw with this moment in order to
return as the transformed and that which transforms (not the "same").

251

Time as contemporaneity holds sway along with the space that is to be conceived in that primordial sense in which it is not the placing before-, next to-, and beyond-another, but rather that which first of all opens the separateness of placing; it "makes room." Time as contemporaneity and place in this sense form the temporal field of play, the agitated region of

252 unconcealment, which opens itself as destiny by drawing itself back into its concealing. Time as the measurable series of time-points, space as the measurable separateness first appear when—as it has happened from Aristotle's physics on—the concealing and self-withdrawing are covered over in favor of the measurable present [*Präsent*], and this apart from the primordial play of the temporal field of play (cf. WhD 40ff). The space posited in calculation, however, does not exhaust the essence of the temporal field of play: on its basis one cannot experience, for example, the nearness and farness of God or the over-against-one-another of God and man. If space and time are posited *only* in terms of what is calculable, then the world as the temporal field of play will be destroyed (Sp 208ff). If, on the other hand, space and time are interpreted in terms of the temporal field of play, then this interpretation does not intend "to show the previous knowledge of space and time as 'false'"; on the contrary, this knowledge will first of all be "inserted into the definitely limited region of its correctness and it will be made clear that space and time are in essence as inexhaustible as Being itself" (*Beiträge*).

Unconcealment is arranged as the destiny of the temporal field of play in the fitting-together of the world, in that it posits itself before the fourfold of earth and sky, gods and mortals. As the one basic characteristic of unconcealment, concealing appears as the earth which goes forth only as it conceals itself. The other basic characteristic, revealing, is expressly discerned by the sky which stands over the earth beyond man's disposal, thereby raising the earth into the open. World is the strife between earth and sky—strife as the intrinsic belonging together in which the one cannot be without the other. Yet world is never a world "in itself" and thus "for" anyone, but rather occurs as the openness of beings in man. Along with his essence, man is used for the occurring of unconcealment—used nonetheless as the mortal to whom the holding sway of truth and world is given only when it gathers itself into the claim of that which is entirely other, the divine.

The world as the fourfold of earth and sky, gods and mortals, is not based upon a "ground" external to it. It can also not be explained by drawing out from the fourfold itself one of its structural moments as that which grounds everything. The concealing revealing which holds sway in the world remains an abysmal or groundless grounding for which no

253 ultimate ground can be secured. The world is, therefore, the play in which every grounding sinks (SvG 188).[48] It is the fourfold as a "mirror-play" in which each—the gods as well as the mortals, earth as well as sky—mirrors the essence of the others and thus is reflected back into what is proper to it. Mirroring is not to be conceived Platonically as portraying a copy but rather as the veiling which clears, which, as appropriative occurring, brings one into what is proper, one's own. The mirroring is a clearing only on the basis of concealing; it is, therefore, occurring as destiny. The unity, which as the onefold of the quadrature [*Vierung*] holds the four together, is not rigid identity but rather lively dance (VA 178f). The unity of the four is the intimacy of an "infinite relation." The infinity to be thought of here is not the endless, but rather the movement of the world which releases from itself and takes back into itself everything finite, and is itself neither something finite nor the mere opposite of the finite. World-infinity is also not the fullness-of-self, a supreme being which grounds everything, but rather *abysmal* grounding, the *concealing* revealing, and consequently appropriative event. "In-finite means that the ends and sides, the regions of the relationship, do not stand detached, one sidedly alone, but rather freed from one-sidedness and finitude; they belong together in-finitely in the relationship which 'permeates' and holds them together from the center" (*Hölderlins Erde und Himmel*). As the infinite relationship of earth and sky, gods and mortals, and thereby as the appropriative event, the world brings into its own that which is. In the experience of the world there occurs that entering into one's own in which one's own is *as* one's own—as the historically unique, because historically destined, as occurrence. On the basis of the enduring not-at-home and therefore inaccessible, world historically grants the being-at-home in one's own; it grants what is one's own as "homeland."

How does world claim for beings, releasing them to themselves, what is their own? How does world shelter beings in unconcealment? This sheltering does not happen in such a way that a self-sufficient being and a self-sufficient unconcealment would be brought together. Rather, truth and world shelter themselves in beings when beings shelter themselves in them. World grants "things" in that things linger with and gather world. At a time in which truth and world hold themselves back, and every being appears to dissolve into an empty nothing, Heidegger first tries merely to lead the way to the essence of truth and world. He disregards the **254** multiplicity of beings; he asks about the courses upon which truth and world shelteringly conceal themselves in beings so that he can travel the narrow path to the experience of truth and world. But if truth holds sway only in that it shelters itself in beings, then the reverse way must also be possible, that is, to show how beings in their multiplicity are sheltered in the world. Upon this way, the concern for the "universal theory of categories" and for "the ontological ordering of beings" is taken up in a transformed way as questioning the "steps" upon which beings are sheltered in truth and its structural fitting-together, the world. Nonetheless, when we question in this manner, we question in the direction opposite to that which Heidegger's questioning specifies. "But whether," as stated in the *Beiträge*, "a man can master both, who may know and decide? That is to say, can he master the standing out of the appeal of the appropriative event as refusing and the performing of the transition to grounding the freedom of beings in themselves—to renewing the world from saving the earth? Thus, there indeed remain those who burn themselves out in such history and its grounding, always separated from one another—the peaks of the most isolated mountains." Yet perhaps a consequence of Heidegger's thinking, which starts out differently than Heidegger does, can still at least awaken the question as to what Heidegger considers to be in need of thought.

If we ask about the steps upon which beings are sheltered in truth and world, then we apparently repeat the Platonic and neo-Platonic idealistic question about stratifying beings from those which do not genuinely exist up to those which exist in a pre-eminent sense. If, however, the world is the appropriative event in which every ground sinks away, the stationary endpoint is lacking toward which the stratification is directed and by which the necessity of its advance could be grounded. If truth and world are the destiny not at one's disposal, then the outline of the openness into which beings place themselves is a respectively historical joining together but not an ordering exempt from time. How does Heidegger unfold this joining together, how do beings separate themselves into the multiplicity of its "regions" for his world experience? How does Heidegger's thinking carry along questions about the dead, about living nature, about man and God?

To be sure, *Sein und Zeit* does not expressly ask about nature; nonetheless, the work forestalls the opinion that nature is to be equated with present-at-hand or ready-to-hand natural thingness. The nature which "surrounds" us, "the phenomenon 'nature' as in the sense of romanticism's concept of nature," is distinguished from "nature" as the object of the natural sciences. The essay, *Vom Wesen des Grundes*, refers to this distinction between natural thingness and "nature in a more primordial sense" and says that in *Sein und Zeit* nature "is lacking" because it cannot be encountered either in the sphere of the world as it surrounds us or in general as something *to which* we *relate*. "Nature is primordially manifest in Dasein in that the latter as the attuned being with a state-of-mind exists *in the midst of* beings. Since, however, state-of-mind belongs to the essence of

255

Dasein, the analytic of Dasein provides the basis for unfolding the problem of nature (SvZ 211, 65; G 36 note). If Dasein's state-of-mind as being-in-the-world is conceived as the structural moment, earth, in the there [*Da*] of Being, of the world as the structural fitting-together of truth, then one must put the question about nature in terms of the question about the earth. This is how it happens in the *Beiträge* where Heidegger recalls that nature was first φύσις, the abode of the gods, and then the opposite of grace, but that today it is only the object of technology. Everything is used up; at best, the "countryside" still remains as a place for recreation. Heidegger consequently asks why the earth does not defend itself against this destruction? "Who gives rise to that strife in which it finds what is open to it, in which it shuts itself up and is earth?" The earth is only earth from its strife with the sky (the "world," as it is still called in the *Beiträge*), a strife with which man must struggle. If one posits nature not only in terms of what is constantly disposable in it, but also thinks of its openness as the strife between self-concealing earth and sky which, as that which stands out and is not at one's disposal, always raises the self-concealing earth into the open, then nature becomes "earth." "Earth is in a respect *more primordial* than nature—because it is historically related."

If physics posits nature as object and as reserve, then what is posited by physics is "indeed nature itself, but still inevitably only nature as the region of objects whose objectivity is first of all determined by the handling of physics and expressly set up in it." From the outset, physics disregards a multiplicity of characteristics which appear in nature; consequently, what it grasps is only "*one* mode," "*one* way," in which nature manifests itself. "Even if the region of the objects of physics is unified and closed in itself, this objectivity can never encompass the fullness of nature's essence." Physics cannot decide by its own means what it neglects when it posits nature as object and reserve. When it is posited by physics, does nature not withdraw itself (as Goethe supposed) in the concealed fullness of its essence? This question is the matter of a reflection which seeks to explain the ways of revealing, according to the character of their revealing concealment, and thus as different courses of unconcealment (VA 61ff). If one recalls that nature is concealed in that it shows a definite manner of unconcealment to the research of physics, then what is disclosed by physics can no longer appear to be an ultimate, secure "in itself" upon which other properties, "aesthetic values," for example, would have to be attached as additions.

If nature is revealed in that it simultaneously conceals itself, then it cannot be simply the constituted product of a subject nor the mere object

256

and reserve of technology. Unconcealment, as it breaks forth *in man*, of course presupposes the experience of nature in its going forth and self-closing. On the other hand, man must nonetheless recognize the nature which withdraws itself into its strangeness as presupposing his own existence. The fact that Dasein is supported by something non-Daseinly, natural, and therefore other, oppresses man above all in the closeness which he possesses as a result of his corporeality to merely living things.

Already in *Sein und Zeit* there are some allusions to the problematic of life. It says that the ontology of Dasein precedes the ontology of life (247). In reality nature certainly precedes man; it is earlier than the latter and can be without him—in truth, however, it "is" not at all, since there is an "is" only where there is also a saying of the is. When *Sein und Zeit* speaks of the priority of the ontology of Dasein, it refers—corresponding to the transcendental-philosophical approach—to the ordering of truth and knowledge; the man who knows precedes the knowledge of nature, and the opening of this truth precedes being-in-the-truth. "In the ordering of **257** possible comprehension and interpretation, biology as the 'science of life' is founded in the ontology of Dasein, even if not exclusively in it. Life is a specific way of Being, but essentially it is only accessible in Dasein. The ontology of life is realized in the manner of a privative interpretation; it determines what must be so that something like a merely living being can be" (49f). In light of these statements, one must ask whether we approach life if we rob Dasein of certain determinations in the way of privation or indeed of "reductive privation" (194) so that only a merely living being remains. Is life a privation of Dasein in the sense in which the closedness of ensnared Dasein "deprives" (184) the disclosedness of authentic Dasein? Certainly not; in such a privative procedure, the intrinsic specificity of the mode of Being called "life" would get lost. The interpretation of life as privation is so to the extent that it indeed presupposes a clarification of what "Being," "Dasein," "reality" and so forth mean. Life itself in no way is to be comprehended in the privative interpretation as a privation of Dasein. Man indeed is not to be established as the *telos* of nature; this would presuppose that all roads lead to him, that the entire fullness of nature is preserved in him, and that life is a merely living creature as a robbed, reduced Dasein. For this reason, in the first sketchy pronouncements which have been cited on the problematic of life, Heidegger says: biology could "not" be founded "exclusively" in the ontology of Dasein.

The *Beiträge* present hints for such a privative interpretation of life. Life, which is to become "the other counter-sound" of Dasein, is grasped as the "incipient opening of a being towards it" in which the self still remains preserved. What is alive is in a "dizziness," and in this dizziness all stimulation and excitability are realized. It shows different levels of a "darkening": "The *darkening* and the essence of *instinct*; the *preservation* of the self and the *priority of the 'genus'* which knows no 'particular individual' as having a self; the darkening and the *worldlessness. . .*" Even in the letter on humanism, Heidegger interprets life by setting it into relief against Dasein. Organisms, he says, are not in need of Being; they do not endure the truth of Being nor preserve the presencing of its Being. Consequently, they have no world (nor "environment" but only "surroundings"); they therefore also lack language, the saying-of-the-is. Nonetheless, this privative interpretation should not present animals ultimately in terms of Dasein, but rather should lead us before the abyss which separates us from the animals to whom we are still related through our bodies. "Of all beings, it is probably most difficult for us to think the essence of a living thing, on the one hand most closely related to us, and on the other still separated by an abyss from our exsisting essence" (PL 69f). **258**

The interpretation of life which starts out from Dasein is not to encourage an anthropological explanation, but rather to shunt anthropology aside as far as possible by making it clear that *we* are always that which understands, and that our self-understanding is in play even where we confront something unintelligible and strange. For Heidegger, the mechanistic clarification of life is no escape from anthropomorphism, since it remains unsuitable to life, even if it may be able to illuminate some of its essential characteristics. In the mechanistic interpretation, the organism is conceived in terms of creatures as man makes them; the organism is contrasted with these creatures in that it is determined as that which produces itself. Heidegger finds an expression for this conception precisely in the fact that life is grasped as an organism in terms of an organizer (cf. *Vom Wesen und Begriff der Φύσις* 143f; organon is originally equipment, but because this word was used above all to refer to the organs of the body, the organism as a living thing could be distinguished from a mere mechanism). The mechanistic explanation does not reach the essence of life, and the anthropological interpretation is not capable of leading to the fullness of life's essence. The animal which appears so near to us remains abysmally strange because beings open themselves to it without even expressly enduring unconcealment. The animal's going out toward the open remains closed and bound in itself in an equally strange and fascinating manner. Self-revealing and self-concealing are united in the animal in such a manner that our human interpretation can scarcely find a way, as soon as it avoids the mechanistic explanation of the animal's essence (feasible at any time), as decisively as it does the anthropological interpretation (VA 274).

Man is different from both dead and living nature. Man is one being among other beings; consequently, one can also consider him in terms of **259** his specificity and difference compared to other beings. Yet man is also not merely a being like other beings, but rather the place at which Being, truth, and world occur so that beings can appear as beings. Because of this, being human is not thought of adequately enough if man as a specific being is differentiated from other beings by means of a specific difference, for example, as *animal rationale* from other living creatures. From the beginning of his way of thought, Heidegger insists that one must differentiate between man and the other beings in another way, namely, by differentiating between what has understanding of Being and what does not. In the *Brief über den Humanismus* he puts his finger precisely upon this point (PL 5ff).

For Heidegger, the genuine theme is not man as a being distinguished from other beings and manifesting a multifaceted determination. The theme is rather man as that one whose essence is used in such a way that beings can step into their Being, that Being can occur and, as unconcealment, can align itself into the structural fitting-together of the world. In Heidegger's thinking, one finds, for example, only a few hints as to whether and how man can be conceived as the unity of body, soul, and spirit. If Heidegger takes up this questioning, then for him it transforms itself into questioning how the unconcealment of Being is experienced if man is thus determined as he is determined. Being is posited in terms of a constant presence if spirit (reason) supplies the guiding thread for the interpretation of beings. This metaphysical interpretation is upended when (in Nietzsche) the body becomes the guiding thread. Furthermore, Heidegger asks about the orderings of community and society only to direct the view upon Being and its truth. What is said about the One in *Sein und Zeit* yields no contribution to social philosophy; rather, it indicates that for the man whose thinking is levelled down to self-evident matters of the One, beings in accordance with their Being must be that which is securely established so that the question about the truth of Being cannot come forward (PL 59). To be sure, Heidegger portrays in detail some ways in which man (as an artist or technician, for example) maintains himself in history; nevertheless, this does not occur in order to distinguish history's region of Being from that of nature and to unfold its possibilities, but rather "solely" to attain in general the experience of the truth of Being. When Heidegger consequently thinks of man as the abode, the there or clearing of Being, and applies it all to transform man into this, his essence, then the questions about the unity of body, soul, and spirit of man, and about the orderings of society and history are not thereby set aside; indeed, what is to be found is precisely the ground upon which these questions must be raised.

Man spans the widest oscillation of Dasein when he takes over death as

260

his own. He gives Dasein over to its inescapable abysmal character, and consequently lets it be the abode-of-the-moment for the unconcealment whose occurrence cannot be brought back to any final ground. To be sure, the essence of death can also be disguised; a "dying" experienced as mere extinction disfigures death, just as a metaphysical interpretation does which takes it as a mere passage to a secured "eternal" life. However, in death experienced essentially, man arrives at that by which he is sustained in his essence, that seminal element which takes back all that is into itself. Thus it is that which endures, the occurring of unconcealment and world, by which all that is finds its way into its Being or essence. Death appropriates man for the appropriative event of truth and world and thus transforms him into his essence to belong as the "mortal" in the fourfold of earth and sky, God and mortals.

As the mortal, man stands before the gods. The world to which he belongs is the Between between him and the gods, the appropriative event which conveys gods and mortals to one another. Truth and world do not give themselves suddenly to man, but are rather always gathered into a highest claim which creates a compellingness. If this claim establishes being-at-home or permits being-not-at-home to be experienced as such, then it is the claim of the healing [Heil] which grants or the healing which withdraws, of the holy in its arrival or turning away. In what is holy, the divine preserves itself as the healing which grants and the healing which withdraws. This divine always shows itself as the claim, as God or the gods.

261

From the beginning, the question of God stands over Heidegger's path of thinking. This way begins with a metaphysical approach which, because it goes back to God as the ultimate ground, consequently ends up as speculative theology. Heidegger opposes this metaphysical theology in the courses which he held after the First World War. The god that metaphysics tries to comprehend, catch hold of, and lay at the basis of thinking is not the living god of faith nor the god of freedom and of history. *Sein und Zeit* is no longer grounded upon a speculative theology; rather, it wants to drive out radically the remains of Christian theology from philosophy (SuZ 299). Yet the relation of man to God is thereby not to be denied; on the contrary, room must be made for a renewed theology in Luther's sense (SuZ 10). In the 1927 lecture, *Phänomenologie und Theologie*, Heidegger rejects every attempt to reduce the Christian character of the Christian faith to a universal religious-philosophical principle, a religious *a priori*, or an imminent spiritual value: God gives testimony for belief in the crucified Christ in his historicality. A revelation which is history cannot be universally and judiciously produced, nor can it be grounded in a universal principle; it is a *positum*, something put forward which is to be taken upon oneself and which can be opposed in thought by a questioning which remains open.[49] The possibility of a thinking forward to the essence of God is left open in *Sein und Zeit* (cf. the note in SuZ 427). The unpublished part of *Sein und Zeit* was to delimit the ontological difference from the theological one.

In the years after *Sein und Zeit*, Nietzsche's experience of the death of God became decisive for Heidegger. Whatever Nietzsche may have meant with the phrase about God's death, for Heidegger God himself is not dead, but rather the god as experienced in metaphysically determined Western history. As Heidegger writes in *Aufzeichnungen aus der Werkstatt*, "Let us not forget too soon Nietzsche's phrase [WW XIII, p. 75] from the year 1886: 'The refutation of God—actually, only the moral god is refuted'. For reflective thinking, this says that the god thought as value and as the highest value is no god; consequently God is not dead, for his divinity lives. It is even nearer to thinking than to faith, provided that divinity as presencing receives its origin from the truth of Being, and provided that Being as the appropriatively occurring beginning 'is' something other than the ground and cause of beings." The "moral god" is the mistake of a humanity which denies itself and life (NI 321f). If this humanity is overcome, then this mistake, the moral god, will also be refuted. When Heidegger thinks of the moral god as the metaphysical god, then on the one hand he limits Nietzsche's discussion about God to the metaphysical experience of God and on the other gives the critique of the moral-metaphysical god an entirely new profundity. Thinking becomes metaphysics, and God comes into this metaphysics when the primordial essence of unconcealment is forgotten and when Being is secured as constant presence and grounded in an ultimate ground and highest value. Metaphysical thinking needs God as the ultimate ground and highest worth, but as such he is not experienced in his genuine essence. Thinking can find its way toward the genuine essence of God only if it—in an overcoming of metaphysics—reaches toward the seminal essence of truth. Only if thinking gives up the metaphysical god does it become free for the "divine god" (ID 70f). Heidegger can raise anew the question of God because, according to his experience, only the metaphysically conceived essence of God is refuted and not the divinity of God. Hölderlin, who transforms and retrieves the pre-metaphysical experience of God in the Greek tragedies, can guarantee the possibility of a *theology* which, even in a time when God withdraws himself, knows itself to be placed under the claim of the divine.

Heidegger's *Beiträge zur Philosophie* ends, and necessarily so, with the question about God. In these notes, Being is conceived as itself, as the appropriative event of unconcealment. Unconcealment gathers itself in such a way that a claim which determines and transforms all, a divine claim, can speak and encounter man in such unconcealment. "To be used by the gods—to be shattered by this elevation—we must inquire into the essence of Being [*Seyn*] *as such* in the direction of this concealed element. Still, we cannot then explain Being as what is apparently subsequent; we must rather grasp it as the origin which first of all *separates* [*ent-scheidet*] and   **263** *appropriates* [*er-eignet*] gods and men." The man who is transformed into Dasein and thus knows himself as used for the occurring of unconcealment stands "at the disposal of the gods." "At 'the disposal of the gods': this means to stand far away and without, that is, outside the familiarity of 'beings' and their interpretations, and to belong to the most distant ones for whom the flight of the gods in their farthest withdrawal remains what is closest." Being as the appropriative event of unconcealment conveys God to man by appropriating man for God. Thus Being, in the daring of the immediate word, is named "the trembling of the gods— (foreboding the decision of the gods about their god)." Since the decision about whether and how God addresses man can never be pronounced by man, and since the thinking forward toward the truth of Being must let this decision remain undecided, Heidegger speaks in an indefinite way not only about "God" but also about "the gods." He denies Being to the gods although God should no more be thought of as "non-being" as "being" [*seiend*]. Being is denied to God so that he is not conceived—as in metaphysical thinking—as the most pre-eminently existing being and thus disguised in his genuinely divine essence. "To begin with, refusing Being to 'the gods' means only that Being does not stand 'beyond' the gods; but the latter also do not stand 'beyond' Being. Still, 'the gods' do stand in need of Being [*Seyn*]—and this saying already thinks of the essence of 'the' Being. 'The gods' do not need Being as their possession wherein they find a stand. 'The gods' need Being so that through this— which does not belong to them—they can nonetheless belong to themselves. Being is that which is used by the gods; it is their need, and the needfulness of Being names its presencing, which is needed by the 'gods' but is never caused or conditioned. The fact that 'the gods' need Being throws them into the abyss (freedom) and expresses the refusal of every grounding and proving."

If the divine is experienced in terms of the appropriative event of unconcealment, then the essence (to be understood verbally) of the divine is raised to its ultimate and highest element—man who experiences God in the appropriative event of unconcealment is the "future one" for the   **264** "passing by of the last god." The god who here is called the last god is not an end in the sense of a ceasing. The fact that he is experienced in his finality is rather the beginning of futural history. The "last god" is also not simply another god compared with the gods that have been; rather, he gathers these others into the final and highest essence of the divine. Man is most likely to experience how he is the "last one" when he himself endures death's finality and extremity. What is last appropriates into the appropriative event, whose seminality has overtaken everything later, because it permits no reckoning and counting. The god experienced from the appropriative event as the last god is only "passing by." He is not to be brought to a standstill and secured as the ground which grounds everything. He has "his *essencing* in the beckoning, in the onset and staying away of the arrival as well as in the flight of the gods which have been and in their concealed transformation . . . In such presencing of the beckoning, Being itself comes to its *ripeness*. Ripeness is a readiness to become a fruit and a bestowing; herein the *last end* comes to presence—the *essential end* demanded from the beginning and not brought to it from without. The innermost finiteness of Being reveals itself in the beckoning of the last god." Nonetheless, Being and its essence, that appropriative event of concealment, is not itself God even if it is the element which God needs to appear. "The appropriative event and its joining together in the abysmal character of the space of time is the net in which the last god ensnared himself in order to rend it and have it end in its uniqueness—godly and singular and the strangest of all beings."

The divine which is experienced from out of the appropriative event of unconcealment can no longer be posited and established as the ground which grounds everything. It withdraws into groundlessness. It appears only occasionally in destiny and thereby remains what is other to what is human. Historicality belongs to its essence insofar as the former is conceived in terms of the revealing-concealing appropriative occurring. If the divine is experienced in this way, then one should not forget the idea that even a claim of the divine has its time; if it was "true" for that one time, then it does not have to ground the unconcealment of another space of time. Gods as well can "die. The most fearful jubilation must be the dying of a god." Here "dying" does not mean an end in empty nothingness, but rather is something which takes oneself back into uniqueness and matchlessness. "Death" is thought of as the highest testimony for Being and the appropriative occurring of its truth. Since man is capable of enduring death expressly as death and thus of becoming united to the appropriative event itself, he "surpasses" the gods insofar as they are gathered entirely in the boundaries of a historical claim. For man, the overshadowing of the gods is the going under into the abysmal character of the truth of Being; nonetheless, in becoming overshadowed, the gods remain higher than man. If time and history are experienced from the appropriative occurring of unconcealment, then God should no longer be

265

conceived as without time and history, as standing beyond time and history. He can only be investigated in terms of the tragic movement of history, in terms of the moment. As Heidegger says in a course on Nietzsche, perhaps it exists there at all only as the thing to be questioned, as that which is called upon: "It remains to be seen whether God is more divine when he is questioned, or when he is certain and, when as certain, he can be, as it were, set aside as the need arises in order to be brought back as needed" (NI, 321ff).

If the divine shows itself only in the respective, historical claim, how can it then still be thought of in its "unity"? Is the "eternity" of God representable as "infinite temporality" (SuZ 427, note)? May the fullness of the divine be brought together in the thought of the "last" god, or does this combination leap over the historical experience of the divine? Does not the thought of the "last god," of the God of gods, remain unthinkable, since although the historical "essence" (to be understood verbally) of the divine as the last and highest unfolding of essence is thought of in it, it is then perhaps no longer thought of in a historical manner? Before these questions could be answered, one would have to ask more precisely how the "lastness" of the "last god," his "*going* by," is to be conceived. In his later works, Heidegger himself withdrew the discussion about the "passing by of the last god" as he had developed it in the *Beiträge*. He then spoke more guardedly about "the divine ones," the "beckoning messengers of the godhead" from whose concealed holding sway God appears in his essence (VA 177). Heidegger (with Hölderlin) also calls the gods "angels." The angels are the messengers who place man under the claim of the holy and divine; in this way they always silence the abysmal happening of unconcealment in being-whole.[50] As these messengers, the divine ones belong to the world, to the structural fitting-together of unconcealment.[51]

The question of God arises when one asks how a binding claim can gather the occurrence of truth and world to itself. Such a question is necessary for a thinking which asks about the joining-together of truth and world. Thinking recognizes that its task is to hold open the region for a divine claim which grants wholeness; indeed, it tries to reopen this region. However, starting from itself it is never capable of deciding whether, and how, such a claim speaks to and encounters man, for the thinking to which the question of God necessarily belongs does not itself "theologically" or "mythologically" answer an actual claim.[52]

Right from the beginning of its way, Heidegger's thinking carries along with it the question of God. This thinking follows the course of the Western experience of God and must therefore pass through Nietzsche's experience of the death of God. So that it can finally swing onto its own

266

way, it must travel the farthest roundabout ways; for example, it must still try to think about the modern will to create as "preparing to be ready for the gods," although this creating and willing will no longer even allow such readiness to come forth (cf. NI, 254). That which is contemporary, which appears as a new beginning and is in truth the destruction of the seminal occurring of unconcealment and world, lies as a snare upon the way. The questioning about God must be kept alive in a time of most extreme confusion; for this very reason, the pertinent phrase of the chorus from *Oedipus Rex* stands over the way of this questioning: "Yet the godhead of the gods goes astray" (*Das Ereignis*). Thinking must in itself clear away what interrupts preparing to be ready for the gods; like Oedipus, it must bring to light with a singular, ruthless passion for knowledge the concealed failure which lies upon its own, the Western way. Thinking is consequently summoned onto a tragic way, into that downfall which is not empty annihilation but which rather enters the occurrence of unconcealment. It is the entrance into an occurrence which realizes itself by distinguishing and appropriating God and man, earth 267 and sky in their toward-one-another, and which thus takes its place with regard to the structural fitting-together of the world. If thinking becomes free for this occurrence, then it can no longer reckon way and errancy, the nearness and the farness of the divine, in terms of "good" and "bad" times, or even in terms of human fortune and misfortune. The closing verse from the "last poetry of the last poet in the seminal Greek culture," from Sophocles' *Oedipus at Colonnus*, stands over such thinking as well (cf. WiM 51):

> So desist now and awaken
>   the lamentation never more.
> In every direction what has appropriatively
>   occurred
> keeps to itself and preserves a decision of
>   fulfillment.

10

THE QUESTION OF SAYING

The world as the fourfold of earth and sky, gods and mortals is not an in-itself which would stand over against man, but is rather the occurrence of the unconcealment of beings in man. As the "mortal," man belongs in this occurrence; he along with his essence is used for it without this occurrence coming to be at his disposal. Heidegger calls the essence of man Da-sein, but he calls it "thinking" as well. The thinking meant here belongs to the remembrance which in all changes of history remains thankfully mindful of the exhortation which occurred, and which grasps it as something transformative and futural. In his essence, man is the "remembrance" of Being, that is, of the unconcealment which takes its place with regard to the fourfold of the world (cf. *Zur Seinsfrage* 31). According to myth, memory—or "the [feminine [*die*]] memory," the *Μνημοσύνη*—is the daughter of earth and sky. As the bride of Zeus, memory becomes the mother of the muses; she thus bestows all Saying and thereby permits the gods and mortals to be together (WhD 6ff, 87ff).

The thinking which belongs to remembrance is not some "theoretical" activity separated from praxis, but rather the primordial way to preserve truth and to inhabit world. Thinking is what authentically presences, not only in the political act, but also in the work of art and in the speaking of the poet and the thinker. Among the ways of expressly preserving truth, language is certainly distinctive; the other ways of the occurrence of truth and world cannot be without it (cf. Hw 60ff). The question about language is not added to the question about truth and world as another inquiry; rather, it is the question about truth and world formulated with respect to how truth is expressly brought forward and preserved and how world is inhabited. This question, the question about Saying, is to be the aim of our further reflection. First we will show how Heidegger understands his way toward language to be sustained by the way which the occurring of truth and world takes to arrive at human speech. We will then examine in a second section which manner of Saying is suitable for a thinking as Heidegger attempts it.

THE WAY TOWARD LANGUAGE

The question as to how Being and language belong together, how logic and language are necessary in order that the *ens* can be a *verum*, was asked early at the beginning of Heidegger's path of thinking. In an overview, "Neuere Forschungen über Logik," which appeared in 1912, Heidegger writes: "What is logic? Even here we stand before a problem whose solution will remain reserved for the future" (466). In his dissertation, Heidegger joins in waging the struggle against psychologism in logic; yet he also insists—and this insistence is even more valid today than previously—that the theory of judgement of mathematical logic (especially Russell's) be subjected to a *philosophical* test. "What would be shown is how its formal character keeps it from the living problems of the sense of judgement, its structure, and meaning of knowledge" (97 note; cf. also SuZ 159). What is put into question is not the imminent perfection of logic, but rather its sense of what it in general accomplishes. In the *Habilitationsschrift* Heidegger carries on the question, "What is logic?" to the question: "What is language?" Here he also raises the question of *essence*. The demand to pay attention to the "genetic development of language" is rejected with the remark that psychological-historical investigations do not belong to the philosophy of language. "The latter has to seek its problems in an entirely new dimension. It is responsible for setting forth the ultimate *theoretical* foundations which lie at the basis of language" (163). At this point, history is still forced from the region of essence, since the *verum* is thought of as interchangeable with an *ens* conceived self-evidently as a constant presence. In his early work, Heidegger does not disturb the metaphysical presupposition that history indeed establishes Being (as "value"), but Being itself stands beyond all history; for this reason, he does not ask how traditional logic and the language experienced in terms of it are limited by the problem raised by history experienced in its essence.

270   To be sure, Heidegger had already taken up this question, if not in a genuinely philosophical manner, when he considered the relationship of Being and language. "At that time," as he himself writes, "I was especially intrigued by the question regarding the relation between the word of Holy Scripture and theological-speculative thinking. It was, if you will, the same relation as that between language and Being, but only concealed and inaccessible to me, so that on many detours and byways I looked in vain for a guiding thread" (Sp 96, 91f). If speculative thinking is related to the word of Holy Scripture, then it must develop a claim which is historical in itself. "Historical" certainly does not mean: "to establish historically." The claim is not a present-at-hand "Being," standing and establishing in rigid permanence, but rather an occurrence which is not closed, the way which leads into an open future. In this claim, truth acknowledges itself in that it holds itself back; it remains a mystery which points toward a future revelation. The claim as the claim of wholeness calls for a decision; it leads the believer into that truth in which the believer—as the Gospel of John says—has his future stay, the house in which he dwells (John 8, 31f). The claim bestows a new Being, but it does so historically and for a time (thought of in the Christian manner, for the time until the second coming of Christ, until the other fulfillment). Speculative thinking tries to develop this Being as the Being of beings. In this attempt, however, the inherited thinking of Being must still shatter, since here Being is not constant presence, but rather the appropriative event which announces itself in that it withdraws itself. If language is related to this Being, the historical claim, then it can no longer be conceived "metaphysically" from a *verum* which is interchangeable with a constant presence.

If thinking introduces the problematic of time and history into the problem of Being, if it asks about "Being and time," then the phenomena to be analyzed can no longer be comprehended by traditional logic. In *Sein und Zeit*, Heidegger says that the breakdown of traditional logic can "not be surprising when one considers that it has its foundation in a still crude ontology of the present-at-hand. Because of this, it is not made fundamentally more flexible by means of many corrections and amplifications. These reforms of logic oriented toward the 'sciences of the spirit' only aggravate the ontological confusion" (129). The theme of Heidegger's early reflection on Aristotle is, among others, the "ontological" interpretation of traditional logic and, consequently, its relegation to its limited sphere (even the horizon of the hermeneutical phenomenology of *Sein und Zeit* is still determined by his examination of Aristotle, cf. SuZ 32ff). In the ontological interpretation, traditional logic appears as a "logic of the present-at-hand." It allows one to think logically about only those aspects of objects which can always be brought before thinking as constantly present-at-hand; consequently, it does not allow time and history into Being itself. By contrast, the λόγος, which Heidegger's hermeneutical phenomenology follows, explicates the self-understanding of a being whose Being is transformed when it interprets itself, and thus grasps its Being or essence as a historical-temporal *potentiality*-for-Being. The hermeneutical λόγος shelters the existential-hermeneutical As which permits something to be taken *as* something within and for praxis; it does not level this "As" down to the merely apophantic "As" which allows something to be presented theoretically in terms of what is present-at-hand in it (SuZ 157ff, 361f).

271

In *Sein und Zeit,* Heidegger gains a new approach for the problematic of logic and language; he understands these in terms of discourse, that is, discourse as articulating the understanding state-of-mind and, therefore, ultimately historical-temporal being-in-the-world. Consequently, language becomes the articulation of the world which is always bursting open. Heidegger also requires that the grammar that seeks its foundation in the logic of the statement, and so in the ontology of the present-at-hand, be established on new foundations (165f). He demands a logic other than the traditional one, but in *Sein und Zeit* he does not develop the problem of this other, "hermeneutical" logic.[53] Nevertheless, *Sein und Zeit* does show the hermeneutical λόγος at work.

This λόγος does not work with "categories," the determinations of the "what" of the present-at-hand, but with existentials, the determinations of that being which is never to be comprehended as a "what," but rather thought of as a "who" (SuZ 44f). Existentials have a formal-indicating character. Although formality is striven for, the form of the desired formality is still not abstractable from the content. It is not an empty husk, but always springs toward concrete substantial fulfillment. The latter does not come to fill an empty form from outside; it is rather the case that the formally *indicating* thinking has always come to meet this fulfillment. To be sure, such fulfillment is not yet co-posited; it remains in the air and is not at all derivable through the thinking which merely gives formal indications. Heidegger therefore distinguishes between the "existential" interpretation of Dasein in terms of its "formal" structures and the "existentiell" decision in which Dasein seizes its respective concrete possibilities and obligations (SuZ 12, 312f). The "existential" analysis is not simply neutral or even indifferent with respect to the gain and loss of existence. Insofar as the analysis announces authenticity as a possibility of existence, it summons one forth into this possibility which it must have already experienced. The formally indicating thinking is already in the existentiell decision to the extent that it asks about its possibility; still, the decision itself is withheld. This thinking (which can be indicated only inadequately by means of rethinking the form-content schema) initiates one into the occurrence of truth, but it gives only an indication of truth and not yet the concrete fulfillment of truth. Still, its questioning as sounding out has a tendency to awaken. The evocative and provocative character which belongs to many of Heidegger's performances must be understood from this sounding out.[54]

The existential analysis is to do justice to the movement of history and the underivability of its decisions. Still, the difficulty does not lie merely in gaining and preserving openness for history. The decisive difficulty appears first of all when one asks whether the questioning thinking which

272

sounds out is not itself historically determined from the beginning. This question indicates in general the problematic of *Sein und Zeit*: Can a "hermeneutic" extract itself from the course which the occurrence of truth carves out in order to develop itself "methodologically" and thus to give the occurrence of truth a *fundamentum inconcussum*? Does not the analytic of the understanding of Being itself already stand under a destiny of the unconcealment of Being? Is not the entire approach (which begins with the subject as existence) determined by the way which the occurrence of **273** truth has gone in the West? When Heidegger put these questions to himself (in the "turning" of his thinking), he removed the question of Saying from the hermeneutical-existential approach. By this time, he developed the question as to how the manner of Saying in Western thinking is determined in terms of how Being has accommodated itself to its truth.

Even with this new approach, Heidegger proceeds from the fundamental experience that the traditional, logical manner of thinking is insufficient for the question about Being which is necessary today. If nothing is intended for Being, if thinking prepares to experience Being in its truth as the appropriative event not at one's disposal, then "the fate of the domination of 'logic' within philosophy" is decided: "The idea of 'logic' itself dissolves in the whirl of a more primordial questioning" (WiM 36f). The questioning mentioned here is more primordial than the metaphysical questioning about Being because it turns the forgotten truth of Being into a problem. The idea of "logic," which is undone in this questioning, is the self-evident character of the domination, indeed, of the sole domination of "logical" thinking in philosophy. The "more primordial" question polemically opposes the opinion that traditional logic is supposed to be able to exhaust the possibilities of thinking, but it does not call into question the limited material right of logic. In its first steps this questioning is a "vortex"—a breakthrough to a new approach, but is not yet the clearness and calm of that which has found its way to itself. In this vortex, the more primordial questioning cannot yet initiate logic into its limited right; nonetheless, it fundamentally admits that logic is one, even if *only* one, "particular" mode of interpretating thinking (WiM 47, E 92).

When Heidegger speaks of the idea of "logic," he encloses the word "logic" in quotation marks. His question about logic, and above all even the polemic against today's "corporate business" of logistics, sociology, and psychology (WhD 10), in no way concerns traditional formal logic and its advance in logistics within its limited, pertinent right; it has to do with the amateurish excessive demand upon the capabilities of logic and logistics.[55] In the "vortex" of his questioning, Heidegger pushes himself away from the traditional logic only because he seeks a λóγος which will   **274** make possible for thinking what formal logic cannot accomplish, to correspond to unconcealment as a fateful, transforming happening. The question about "logic" questions that language in which thinking can correspond to this unconcealment. Thus, Heidegger can say that "the transformation of logic into the question about the *essence* of language" is concealed behind the term "logic" (WhD 100).

In order to find the λόγος of a language in which thinking is capable of corresponding to the occurrence of unconcealedness, Heidegger asks: How did it happen that thinking believed that it had to be one-sidedly oriented to logic? Under what sort of metaphysical pressure did logic stand in general, in what metaphysical maelstrom did the tendency to take the logical way as the only strict way of thinking come to dominate? Heidegger does not ask about logic's historical development. Rather, he asks what metaphysical decisions must have occurred so that all speaking could be brought into line with logic. How did it happen that in philosophically exact speaking, the concept was based upon the category, the statement upon judgement, and sentence construction upon the conclusion, so that ultimately Kant could develop the basic categories in his transcendental logic from the forms of judgement, and Hegel could grasp metaphysics as "logic" (cf. E 91 ff; WhD 99 ff)? What does it signify that logic today has become world-historically efficacious in its transformation into "dialectic" (cf. *Grundsätze des Denkens*)? The "ontological" interpretation of logic, as Heidegger set out this task in his first work, becomes a matter of the "history of Being." Heidegger tries to show, for example, that for Aristotle the principle of contradiction is a principle of Being, but that this principle, in accordance with the change in the Western conception of truth, in Nietzsche's work had to become an "imperative," to which thinking is either subordinate or not. For Heidegger, what characterizes the metaphysical mode of Saying throughout is the fact that Saying takes something as something according to its permanence, so that it can always return to what is permanent. From the beginning, the λέγειν in Western thought is having-beings-lie-before in the unvariability of their Being, and only because thinking received its *essence* from this having-lie-before could logic begin to dominate thought with its inflections (cf. WhD 99ff).

275

The destiny of Western thought is that Being appears as constant presence, that beings are displayed in terms of their permanence, and that thinking is experienced from having-lie-before and thereby falls under logic's dominion. For Heidegger, however, this destiny is not self-evident and unquestionable. In his questioning, he goes back to the temporal horizon from which Being is understood as presence; consequently, he also goes back to that primordial λόγος which is leaped over by traditional logic as a proper mode of Saying valid within its limits. Since for Heidegger the historical origin is at the same time the origin of essence (E 94), he tries to reach the primordial λóγος by examining the earliest Greek philosophy. Heidegger first of all disregards the later interpretations of thinking (for example, even Aristotle's interpretation), so that what comes later will not distort his view for the seminal element in earliest Greek thinking. The interpretations of Heraclitus' work from the essay *Logos* (VA 207ff) repeat the decisive thoughts from the logic course of 1944. In a 1934 lecture entitled *Logik*, Heidegger first attempted to comprehend the essence of language by reflecting on λóγος—at a time when the nearness and farness between thinking and poetic saying had become decisive for him (cf. Sp 93f).

If thinking experiences Being in its essence as the appropriative event of unconcealment, and thereby as presence and absence at the same time, which λóγος does it follow? This thinking can no longer conform to logic, since it no longer posits beings as something permanent to which one can always return. It also may not intend to strive after a super-logic, since this super-logic, the "dialectic," is understood only in terms of traditional logic (and it may be because of this that dialectic, as Hegel pursues it, demands rather than excludes contradiction). Finally, the thinking of the truth of Being may not turn aside into what is un-logical, flee logic powerlessly and take refuge in a pseudo-poetic saying. Above all, this thinking cannot proclaim what is illogical since even this is understood only in terms of logic, in terms of simple opposition to it. The thinking of the truth of Being   **276** must be understood from its own proper matter. Its task is to correspond to the presence as well as the absence in Being, to the revealing as well as the concealing, to come from the revealment which has already occurred and to take up lodging in what is concealed—not in order finally to set aside concealment, but to tend to it as that which always shelters the revealment in its inexhaustibility. The thinking of the truth of Being has its basic character in that silence which lets concealment expressly be concealment. Thinking does not discuss one thing in order to be silent about what one in a strict manner cannot discuss; rather, its silence is eloquent, its discourse is silent; that is, it gives revealment back to concealment. Silence is a making silent of concealment as the mystery which shelters everything. The "logic" of the thinking of the truth of Being is making silent, "Sigetics" [*Sigetik*]. "Silence is the prudent lawfulness of making silent (σιγᾶν). Silence is the 'logic' of philosophy insofar as it asks the basic question from another beginning. It seeks the *truth of the essencing* of Being [*Seyn*]—and this truth is the beckoning-suggestive concealment (the mystery) of the appropriative event" (*Beiträge*; cf. also N I, 471f).

Sigetics (the name is meant only for those who need titles and classifica-
tions everywhere) points toward the essence of language; whoever develops Sigetics as the "logic" of the truth of Being is "on the way towards
language." Under this title, Heidegger gathers together the lectures and
essays from the years 1950–59 which are to bring the essence of language
to experience. The lecture, *Die Sprache*, intends to present the essence of
language through what is purely spoken in one of Trakl's poems. The
Gespräch von der Sprache gathers all those thought-motifs which determined
Heidegger's way into the question about language: the question about
Being in metaphysics and the overturning of metaphysics, the impetus
which came from that which is biblical, the transformation of phenomenology into hermeneutical phenomenology, and the nearness to poetic
saying. For help in bringing thinking before the question about language
and Being, Heidegger's additional talks call upon Stefan George's later
experience: "There is no thing where the word breaks off." The last
lecture, *Der Weg zur Sprache*, draws together the experiences from being on
277   the way to language in order to help thinking into the decisive experience.

In his lecture, Heidegger begins with the fact that in traditional
reflection upon language, language appears as a linguistic statement. As
the different Western names for language already show, language is
understood as tongue, as dialect, as the activity of the speech organs.
Language is conceived in terms of human speech as a being which has the
character of the sign and which is the bearer of "meanings." According to
Aristotle, the written letters point to the vocal sounds, the sounds to the
dispositions of the soul, and the latter to those matters affecting them. In
Hellenism, showing is understood in terms of the sign as an "instrument"
sprung from convention, "an instrument for a designating which adjusts
and directs the representing of one object to another" (Sp 244f).[56] The
consideration of language beginning in this way "peaks" in Wilhelm von
Humboldt's reflection on language. Humboldt understands language as
the "work of the mind to make articulated sound capable of expressing
thought"; he thus understands language as an activity of mankind which
in its development forms different historical world-perspectives and languages as well. "Humboldt's way to language is oriented toward man and
leads through language to something else, the grounding and portraying
of the spiritual development of mankind." Language is explained by going
back to the activity of man; thus, it is indeed grasped in its essence, but
only in that, "as it itself, it is taken in hand by something else" (249f).

Heidegger does not intend to escape from language by trying to explain
it in terms of something else (this something else is still communicated
linguistically!). Rather, Heidegger would like to bring language *as language*
into the discussion. To this end he takes his point of departure from

speaking. He thinks of speaking (together with silence) as Saying, Saying in accordance with the primordial sense of the word as "showing, having-appear, having-be-seen, and having-be-heard" (252). From speaking as Saying, language appears as the saying [*Sage*], while the saying in turn appears as the index which has presencing and being-absent appear and fade away; it has them show themselves and withdraw. Yet Heidegger neither understands showing and the index in terms of the sign posited by man (as Western reflections on language usually do), nor does he intend to make available an existing ground for language, since seeking after the grounding could miss the essence of language in its questioning. Instead, Heidegger asks what is "active" in showing, and what determines the "active element." Heidegger finds "being appropriate" as that which is active in Saying and showing. This befitting "establishes what presences, and what is absent, in its particular proper element out of which the latter appears before the former and lingers in its own fashion." The befitting which brings all that is to itself "is," even in its establishing, the act of occurring [*Ereignen*] and thus belongs to the appropriative event [*Ereignis*] (258).

278

Man is "used" for the appropriative event. He gains his essence from what promises itself to him in the Saying which occurs appropriatively (out of the truth as unconcealment), in that he comes to meet the Saying with what is proper to him. In the response which man gives to the word of the saying, he brings the soundless saying into the sounding of the word (260). His speaking rests as being in accordance with heeding the promise of the saying; man can attend to the saying only because he belongs to it in his essence (254f). His Saying is a being-told [*Sich-sagen-lassen*]; thus it is never man that speaks, but language alone, although language does so only in that it uses man for itself. The "way towards language" is, genuinely thought, not something that *man* accomplishes. This way lies rather in that movement in which language as the Saying, as the index, comes to be spoken in man's speech.

How does language come to be spoken today? Today, since every being is thrown into the setting upon and ordering of technology, language has become "information" which informs one about beings and thus places them at man's disposal. Language is formalized so that it can serve technologically-calculating man as information. When the formalized languages repeatedly refer back to the "natural language" because they need to be able to come to language themselves, then the indispensable "natural language" is still acknowledged only as something provisional. But perhaps Φύσις can appear—if the insight into that which is becomes the lightning flash of truth—in the nature of "natural language," and language can enter the discussion as the gathering of the going out which

279

goes back in itself, as λόγος (262 ff, 257, 185, 215, 237). The most ancient, soon forgotten essential coining of language—as λόγος (cf. VA 212f, 228f)—would again be spoken. Language would enter the discussion in that way in which it has remained unthought in Western thinking, as the most proper manner of gathering the going out which goes back in itself, of the appropriative occurring of unconcealment. Heidegger experiences his effort to allow the essence of language to be expressed as a twofold attempt. It first tries to let the forgotten, historical origin of the Western experience of language to be genuinely the origin for the first time. It then tries to bring the primordial Western experience of language together with the experience of language of the other great traditions in a "conversation about language" (as Heidegger conducts it with a man from Japan, cf. Sp 83ff). As Saying, as index, and thereby in the manner of appropriative occurring, language comes to man's speaking only if this speaking is capable of making the "essence" of language silent—if it makes no assertion about language as something present-at-hand but experiences "from language" its essence as historically promising itself. We can experience the essence of language repeatedly, but we do not know it if knowing means "to have seen something, looking it over, in the entirety of its essence." We catch a glimpse of language only to the extent that we are looked upon by it, appropriated into it (Sp 265f).

If language is expressed as the saying, then it is experienced as the "house of Being" (PL 60, 111f, 116). Being lets beings be as beings; in its essence, it is the open space of that clearing which, as simultaneously presence and absence, repeatedly frees beings into what is peculiar to their essence. Language as saying and index holds sway throughout and fits together the open space of this clearing "into which every presence and absence appears and must announce itself" (Sp 257). Language is thus the guardianship to which presence and absence are each entrusted and thereby the "house" in which beings can find their way into their essence without Being having to be changed into the rigid permanence of mere presence. As the house of Being, language gathers the occurrence of unconcealment. This unconcealment, which through the veil of Nothing preserves Being as what is not at one's disposal, is, when thought in its **280**   alignment to a structural fitting-together, the world. Thus, as the saying which manifests, language is the "clearing-concealing, veiling bestowal of the world" (Sp 200). Language holds the four world regions—the divine ones and the mortals, earth and sky—apart in their opposition (214f). It itself has its source in this opposition: "If the gods call the earth, and in the call a world resounds so that the call begins to sound as the Da-sein of man, then language is—as something historical—the word which grounds history" (*Beiträge*). The spoken word of speaking, in terms of which language is usually represented, must also be conceived in terms of the separation of the fourfold of the world. In the sounding, the structural moment "earth" is announced; consequently, sounding belongs necessarily to the essence of language (Sp 208). In the spoken word, that movement of the world-play which Heidegger calls the "pealing of stillness" is refracted, the soundless appropriative occurring which settles everything into its proper element and thus allows the world to burst forth (30, 262).

THE TOPOLOGY OF BEING

There are many ways in which language speaks. Poetic thinking, for example, stands next to thoughtful speaking, and perhaps this proximity is not something arbitrary. Thinking could still nonetheless find its essence by contrasting its speaking to poetic speaking. Heidegger suggests that we would be prepared for a decisive change in our relation to language if we experienced the fact that thinking and poetizing belong to one another—that they belong to one another in that Saying in which man accommodates himself to the appropriative event (cf. Sp 267).

Thinking and poetizing are close in that they remain differentiated from one another by their own characteristic kind of saying. Heidegger announces the difference when he says with formular conciseness: "The thinker says Being. The poet names what is holy" (WiM 51). The poet experiences unconcealment as that which grants being-at-home and being-whole—as what is holy. Nonetheless, what the poet does—to give an immediate response to the claim of what is holy, to "name" that which is holy and divine—the thinker cannot pretend to do. He says Being; that is, he examines the traditional Saying of the Being of beings in terms of the truth of Being and brings this truth as unconcealment, the structural articulation of unconcealment as world, to language. The poet prepares the arrival of the gods and thus founds that which endures; in naming what is holy, he can find his way toward that which is beyond all question, even though he may always remain exposed to the mistaken course between what is holy and unholy. Thinking, on the contrary, must renounce the immediate response to the claim of the holy; it nonetheless takes its stand in the necessity of evaluating what is questionable. Listening to the concealed promise, it initiates one into the occurrence of truth by means of a questioning. By venturing the experience of godlessness, it grounds the abyss of Being and brings forth, even as it is not-at-home in what is not-at-home, a new beginning. To be sure, this differentiation between poetizing and thinking is not that between two presentable objects; it is rather a historical—not a super-temporal, but a futuristically

281

necessary—difference, experienced by thinking as the self-differentiation over against what stands in oppressive closeness. As that which is differentiated, thinking and poetizing belong together in the thanks by which man, in taking leave from everything familiar, pledges himself to what remained unsaid, as what is to be said in the future, and is thus heedful to what is promised but concealed (cf. *Das Ereignis*).

The difference between poetizing and thinking leaves open the question as to how thinking is then to be characterized in terms of itself. How can the λόγος, which Heidegger's thinking follows, be grasped in accordance with its own proper way? Since this thinking does not intend to proceed arbitrarily, wherein does the binding force which it claims for itself lie? I would like to answer these questions by following some of Heidegger's suggestions and developing them somewhat arbitrarily, differentiating among explanation, elucidation, and emplacement in order to understand finally emplacing as the "topology of Being."

Thinking becomes explanation when beings become a network of cause and effect and in this sense become that which is "real." "We encounter beings as what is real in calculative activity, but also scientifically and in philosophizing with explanations and proofs. To this belongs also the assurance that something is inexplicable . . ." (PL 60). One being is led back to the other; beings are led back to their "Being" as to their ground. Beings are comprehended in terms of their ground, so that as something which is comprehended they come under the lordship of man. Nothing without ground—this is the great principle which explanatory thinking follows. The modern age brings this principle, and explanatory thinking along with it, to its complete development. In the nineteenth century, explanation becomes the sole method of the sciences; not only natural sciences, not only psychology, but even the genuine sciences of the spirit are ruled by explanation. Religion, for example, is led back in an enlightened, positivistic manner to psychological conditions, perhaps to man's fear, and is thus counted as having been explained. In a less crude explanation, it is taken back to the history of the soul, the history of individuals and peoples. Even poetizing, indeed philosophy itself, is explained as an expression of the spirit of a people or a world view. "Extension" or "consciousness" is each the ultimate by which explanation arrives, whether or not consciousness is conceived as historical spirit. The reference to the two Cartesian substances suggests that one ask whether the metaphysical reaching out for an ultimate ground does not ultimately stand behind explanation. Heidegger interprets metaphysics as an explanation—that is, of beings in terms of their Being, and of Being in terms of a supreme being.

282

If metaphysics is interpreted as this explanation, as onto-theo-logy, then ontological grounding is thereby not simply to be branded as ontic explanation—as if it has not been metaphysical thinking's endeavor precisely to contrast itself with ontic explanation! Yet one has to ask whether ontological grounding within metaphysics has been differentiated from such explaining so that it precluded every misunderstanding. In general, must not ontological grounding—as "grounding"—come close to ontic explanation? According to Heidegger's conception, the ontological grounding of metaphysics cannot adequately be differentiated from ontic explanation as long as Being is not thought of as itself, according to its truth. In his reflection upon metaphysics, Heidegger tries to show that thinking, as soon as it loses the element of the truth of Being, must become the technology of an explanation in terms of first causes (PL 58). However, Being, conceived as itself, avoids every explanation (NII, 485)—and Heidegger attempts precisely this, to think of Being itself without concern for the possibility of a grounding of Being in a being. Upon his way of thinking, Heidegger experiences Being as abyss [Ab-grund]; consequently, his thinking comes "into the groundless" "insofar as Being now can no longer be grounded upon a being and explained in terms of it" (SvG 185, 118f). Still, Dasein will not come before what is genuinely thoughtworthy until ontically explanatory thinking sees only groundlessness. Upon his way of thinking, Heidegger only slowly learned to avoid the ways upon which thinking remains concealed and infected by wanting to explain—as in his attempt at a fundamental ontology and at a metaphysics of metaphysics. Nonetheless, from the beginning, his polemical thrust was directed against explanation; thus the analytic of Dasein, begun as the founding of ontology, already distinguishes between "clarifying" the essence of Dasein's finitude and "every hurried 'explanation' of the ontical origin of the same" (G 54).

To ward off explanation: this was the innermost direction of phenomenology, that manner of philosophizing and researching, which decisively determined the beginning of Heidegger's thinking. For thinking it signified a release since at the beginning of our century, phenomenology and ontology confronted explanation and pointed out, for example, that still nothing is said about what is religious if religion is interpreted as an expression of a historical humanity and thereby explained by something else. Not to "explain" logic psychologistically, not to take religion and philosophy immediately as an expression of a people's spirit, but rather first of all to show everything in its own essence by means of an unprejudiced describing: this is the meaning of the demand, "To the things themselves." A thinking whose essential feature one can characterize as

283

"elucidation" is opposed to explanation. Elucidation then means: to show something in the clearness of its essence and to keep all hasty explanation at a distance.

The danger of elucidation is that the clarity of essence is again taken self-evidently as a constant, fixed presence in accord with the basic **284** tendency of metaphysical thinking and made to reside in a place beyond the heavens. Thus, a region of logical laws "in themselves," of values "in themselves," or "essentialities in themselves" is set up, or, in a recent turn, led back to a transcendental I which lies beyond any exhibitable I. Consequently, the problem arises as to how one can build a bridge from values in themselves, what is religious in itself, to the concrete history of ethical behavior and of faith.

Heidegger points out that no bridge needs to be built here at all. History and the essence of beings are not two banks foreign to one another. They can actually be separated as banks from one another only when the river of unconcealment flows between them. There is Being of the essence of beings only within the occurring of unconcealment which needs man in his historicality. Being should not be taken out of this region of occurring truth, and the character of constant presence should not be attributed to it as self-evident (even though the Being of beings may also have the character of constant presence in limited regions).

Heidegger first pointed to the region of truth which occurs as the presencing in Being in terms of man's intrinsically historical understanding of Being. In that he grasped phenomenology as hermeneutical; the word "understanding" became the leading word of his thinking. To be sure, hermeneutical phenomenology and its elucidation which understands do not escape an ambiguity; it continues to appear as if understanding in the historical sense is the self-understanding of a humanity put forward as the ground from which everything is to be explained. The leading word, "emplacement," characterizes perhaps more precisely a thinking which belongs to that unconcealment whose appropriative occurring always situates Being as the openness of beings and of our questioning about Being. The task of the thinking which emplaces is to preserve elucidating from hypostatizing the elucidated essence to a constant presence. The clarity of the essence must be experienced from the occurring unconcealment; elucidation must thereby always change into emplacement (cf. Sp 121).

Emplacement is the manner of saying which Heidegger follows, the **285** λόγος of his thinking, and indeed in a manifold sense. Emplacement means first of all to discuss what has already been thought of in terms of the unthought, to bring into the discussion what has remained unsaid in what is said. Emplacement gathers a hint about what is to be thought of from the way in which a matter has already come before thinking. For example, insofar as it has been revealed as presence, Being hints that one should think of the time horizon of presence, that one should raise the question about Being and time. In the hint, what is thought of refers to what is unthought and what is revealed alludes to what conceals itself. As the "tidings of the concealing which clears" (Sp 141), the hint initiates one into truth as the unconcealment which occurs and yet remains inexhaustible. The hint requires from thinking the "leap" by which thinking, in leaping away from everything customary, leaps toward what has remained unthought; thus, it leaves the abode of what has already been thought of in favor of another abode (Sp 138). This leap escapes arbitrariness only *then* when what is to be thought of, toward which thinking springs, is in truth the unthought of what has been thought, what is intended. If thinking follows the demand for a leap, then it is inserted into the tradition which hands over what is unthought to it and thus releases it toward the other, proper place (SvG 83). Emplacement is thereby less a doing of the thinking subject than a becoming emplaced through the tradition. "Emplacement" does not mean so much to discuss *something*, as to bring ourselves to the place of the "essence" of something—"gathering into the appropriative event" (Sp 12). The way upon which emplacing thinking travels accomplishes the way which unconcealment makes for itself in that appropriative event for which thinking is used.

If returning to the unthought of what has already been thought delivers what is to be thought, then the difference between history and systematics becomes invalid. If emplacing thinking turns toward the tradition, it does not intend to posit "historically" (before itself and toward itself) what has been thought as an independent, established past; rather, one is to meditate upon what has been thought of in order that it yield an un-thought remainder. Consequently, the interpretation of what is thought of becomes the dialogue in which "the speakers, by means of the conversa-tion, first of all reciprocally admit themselves into *the* abode and bring themselves to what each speaks about" (WhD 110). In this dialogue the other is *not* understood *better* than he understands himself, *but differently.* In its place, "within the limits apportioned to it," every thinking under-stands itself best (Sp 134), and yet from another place, something un-thought can appear in what has been thought of in it. To be sure, much that is thought of sinks back into what is unthought when one attempts to find what is unthought in what has been thought; thus one can talk only about understanding differently and not about understanding better. Understanding differently cannot understand the other directly (perhaps in terms of an absolute knowledge of a humanity to which nothing human

286

is to be foreign); rather, it must understand it from the place which the other occupies. Emplacement realizes itself in that it expressly pays heed to the place of the abode in which a thinking or poetizing gathers (Sp 37ff, 76ff). This abode opens itself to thinking, but only from the place which thinking itself occupies. The emplacement which distinguishes the one place from the other is, thereby, a setting-apart-from-one-another, a distinguishing of places.

In this setting-apart, refutation of the others is not at issue. Compared with the basic thoughts and principles of the history of truth, refutation, "in the sense of a proof of unjustifiability," makes no sense. "Every essential principle points back to a ground which does not permit itself to be brushed aside, but which rather demands only that it be grounded more fundamentally" (NI, 503). What metaphysical thinking's will to ground represents here as the "more fundamental grounding" is in its truth the emplacement which tries to hear something unsaid in what is said in order to place this said in its abode within the history of truth and to bring itself, by saying the unsaid remainder, to the other proper place. What has been thought of is taken back into the history of truth experienced *differently*, so that in the sameness of the history of truth, one abode of thinking is differentiated from the other. "All refutation in the field of essential thinking is foolish. The strife among the thinkers is the 'loving strife' of the matter itself. It helps them mutually to the simple belonging-ness to the same from which they find what is proper [*schicklich*] in the destiny [*Geschick*] of Being" (Pl 82). The question about the right and lack thereof of an emplacement questions the right and lack thereof of the standpoint which thinking occupies and from which it realizes the differ-ence compared with another abode. This standpoint—the there, or clear-ing of a respective openness of the totality of beings based upon concealment (cf. NI, 378ff)—is never established as utterly necessary, but always entrusted to the venture of the "leap." The setting-apart is the *decision* for one's own proper place (NII, 98).

Through this decision, emplacement becomes a speaking from the abode. The abode that is meant is not to be represented by many places side by side, but to be experienced as that wherein unconcealment gathers itself historically (the word "place" originally means that wherein some-thing converges, for example, the tip of the spear, cf. Sp 37). Speaking from the abode unfolds an intrinsically historical context of truth when an abode belongs upon the way which unconcealment, as the mutual occur-ring of revealing and concealing, clears for itself. This speaking knows about the being-under-way of truth and thereby about its limits imposed by a definite historical location of truth. The border of this abode is determined by how concealment releases a revealing, and the insurpassability of the border is grounded in the fact "that the thinker can never say what is unique to him. It must remain unsaid because the sayable word receives its determination from the unsayable" (NII, 484). Thinking lives by wrestling with the unsayable and by the fact that finally thinking can only make it silent. If "historical calculation" seeks the "inner boundary" of a thinker in the fact "that he is not yet acquainted with that strange something which contemporaries and successors take possession of as truth, and occasionally even only through his mediation" (NII, 485), then it has already suppressed the thoughtful nearness of concealment as the heart of truth and will misdirect thinking into presenting what is provable.

Speaking from the abode assumes the task before which "systematics" saw itself placed in recent philosophy. To be sure, this speaking can no longer bring forward a closed totality of essential insights; it must rather fit itself at its abode into the occurrence of unconcealment and thus put the "jointures" of thinking in place of the "system." This means the following: 1. As soon as the impossible, grasping the truth of Being in the developed fullness of its grounded essence, would be of concern—and this is always of concern in philosophy—nothing is left behind in *the rigor of the structural fitting-together* in the structure; 2. Here only *one* way to travel is permitted to be *at the disposal of* an individual as he resigns himself to overlooking the possibility of other and perhaps more essential ways; 3. The attempt must be clear about the fact that both joining and disposal remain a *dispensation* of Being [*Seyn*] itself, of the beckoning and withdrawal of its truth—that is, "something incapable of being gained by force" (*Beiträge*). The basic feature of emplacing thinking is not the determination of essence which sidetracks all questioning in a final answer, but rather the entrance into what remains open and questionable. This questioning is the piety of thinking, that is, the manner in which thinking joins to what is to be thought (VA 44). Questioning, however, should not become hardened and close itself off to the consolation of an answer; it is, rather, determined by what is promised to it as what is unsaid in what has already been said. It is therefore obvious that not the questioning, but rather hearing the promise is the genuine gesture of thinking (Sp 175f, 180). In the promise, what repeatedly joins or dispenses the openness of beings, the "essence" of things, promises itself. Since questioning does not ask about an ultimate ground, what is promised is not the ultimate answer, but rather what is promised historically. "The answer is only the very last step of the questioning itself, and an answer which dismissed questioning is nullified as an answer; capable of grounding no knowledge, it gives rise to and solidifies only mere opinion" (NI, 457f). The answer should not be dogmatized into one which closes off, nor should it

288

be loosened from the place in which it belongs. If emplacing thinking renounces the claim to be able to provide conclusive essential determinations everywhere, then it does not decline into an empiricism or positivism, but rather transforms the conception of what we call "essence."

Essence is usually thought as constant presence to whose rigid identity one can always return. While essence is universally valid and is in its universality valid for all men, this universality may even be seen upon the ways of finite human thinking only from definite perspectives; consequently it may not be fully attained. Nonetheless, Heidegger thinks the way as "itself" belonging "to the state of affairs" (SvG 94) and thus thinks **289** the essence as what comes to presence historically, as the moved and self-transforming essence. Even the historical essence is valid for many and, in this sense, "universal," but now universality is not what is intrinsically and always unchanging, eternal, and beyond time, but rather what is historically limited. The unity and sameness of the essence intrinsically contains the possibility of change. "The essential character of the essence, its inexhaustibility, is thereby affirmed along with its genuine selfhood and sameness; this is in sharp contrast to the empty sameness of the one and the same as which the unity of essence can be thought only so long as it is always taken only as the universal" (NI, 173f). The essence of poetry, for example, as Heidegger tries to experience it from Hölderlin's poetry, is futurally and in this sense historically valid, but not eternally valid in rigid identity beyond history. The decisive difficulty in Heidegger's thinking lies in the fact that the essence of Being as Heidegger attempts to bring it to language as unconcealment and world is not a super-temporal in-itself but rather what we can experience only because Western languages are historically determined by the Saying of is and because Western thought is historically formed by the question of Being; yet this can change (cf. E 40ff, 62).

As a speaking, emplacement remains determined by the abode of the abysmal character of the history of truth; consequently it cannot arrive at an ultimate basic insight and theory from which it could construct an encompassing system. Since emplacing thinking lacks the basic insight which grounds everything, it loses every right to want to ground, to legitimize or correct, either the poet's experience of the world or, for example, the world vision provided by physics and biology. Yet thinking can indeed discuss repeatedly the presuppositions which have entered into scientific work without having been thought any further. Emplacement indeed comprises the essence of that thinking which takes over in its own fashion the task before which metaphysics as the science of the first and last grounding once considered to be its own. By their own means, the

individual sciences cannot bring to light the presuppositions which slip
into their basic concepts and have entered into the basic approaches from
which scientific work is done. "Mathematics never allows what it is to be   **290**
constituted mathematically; philology never permits itself to be emplaced
philologically; what biology is can never be said biologically. The question
as to what a science is, *as a question*, is already no longer a *scientific* one."
The questioning of this question is the matter of the thinking which does
not impugn the justification and conclusiveness of what the sciences set
forth but discusses which presuppositions can ground the justification of
what is thought. This emplacing thinking is not "glued and added onto"
the sciences as if it were another region; it rather "lies concealed in the
innermost region of science itself," in what remains unthought in the
sciences yet thus precisely co-grounds them (NI, 372). Through emplacement, thinking shows its primordiality; it joins all Saying to that incomplete and inseparable occurrence of language which is the ultimate
presupposition for any manner of Saying and into which every manner of
Saying must be taken back since it arises from it, even if perhaps only in a
concealed fashion.

The thinking which emplaces attempts to set all revealedness back into
the unconcealedness which, as simultaneous revealing and concealing, is
way and destiny. For this thinking, the openness of a matter is not
"Being," that is, if Being is thought as constant presence and thus as the
revealedness before thought which has left behind every concealment.
This openness is always more than what it is since it "is" at all only
together with self-closing concealment. It is the "Nothing" of what is
permanent and at one's disposal, and it cannot be grasped by subordinating the matter as one type of constant and disposable generic universality.
Of itself, this openness "does not permit a definition in the scholastic sense
of traditional concept formation." It must be addressed in words which
bring revealing and concealing before thinking simultaneously and which,
as way-words [*Weg-worte*], direct thinking to what is unthought. What
way-words say "never permits itself to be drawn together and packed into
a definition. Such an intention would assume that it was able to grasp
everything in a representation which floats above the ages. Yet, thus
represented, what is temporal would be the historically limited realization
of the super-temporal content of the definition." To be sure, the realiza-   **291**
tion of super-temporal ideas and values in time is valid—according to the
Platonic differentiation of the sensuously changing from the super-
sensuous, changeless, true world—as the hallmark of history; nonetheless,
this presentation stems from history and "not from the experience of
history." If thinking refrains from wanting to grasp the truth by grasping

after super-temporal essentials, the truth which is appropriative event and, in this sense, history, then it omits what remains inadmissible in the matter; there is, therefore, no omission at all (SvG 153, 159f, 153).

Emplacing thinking reflects upon how a matter is historically expressed under different names. Yet, does not what is to be thought necessarily "drift apart in a chaotic dispersion" if it is discussed under different names rather than under an unambiguous concept? Heidegger responds: "Absolutely not; in what appears as a chaotic multiplicity of presentations, historically caught up and shoved together, a sameness and simplicity of the destiny of Being appears along with a genuine constancy of the history of thinking and what it has thought." The sameness to which Heidegger appeals is not identical with what is always the same and in this sense valid, but rather the "holding together in holding apart," the sameness which intrinsically contains a historical diversity, the "identity" which belongs to the appropriative event (SvG 153, 152). Emplacing thinking puts the names which speak historically back into the abode which they occupy "in the field of Western thought" and thus upon the course of unconcealment (SvG 25, 106). This course is opened to thinking only if thinking takes up its abode upon it. The basic words of the tradition are guide- and way-words which lead thinking to its own abode; the Saying of these words "does not merely illuminate a stretch of the way and its radius," but rather "makes a track and even prepares the way" (WhD 61). If thinking carries its word as response, in face of the hints of unconcealment, then the basic feature of the word itself is "hint"; the word beckons toward what is to be thought and initiates one into an occurrence of truth (Sp 114ff). The thinker has no other task at all than to let what is unheard and soundless in the appropriative event of unconcealment come to language from what is already a faint hint at his time, to attend to the decisive claim and to bring to word (SvG 86, 91, 47). Because he leaps away from what has already been thought and toward the abode of what is to be thought, the meaning of words and statements are transformed. Nonetheless, emplacement depends precisely upon this transformation; for it, the multiplicity in the meaning of the words is not inexactness to be avoided, but rather the diversity sought in the sameness of what belongs together historically. This diversity first of all enables an emplacement which breaks away from one abode, reaches toward another, and in this difference of abodes carries the sameness of the destiny in its diversity and historical otherness. The historically varied speaking of language is "arranged and directed through the historical destiny of Being" to which man corresponds through his thinking. "In each case the multiplicity of meaning is historical. It arises from the fact that we ourselves are respectively deemed fit, addressed, in the speaking of

the language in accord with the destiny of Being from the Being of beings"
(SvG 161).

Along his way of thinking, Heidegger attends ever more decisively to
the fact that the occurrence of truth is essentially an occurrence of
language, bound up with the historical speaking of language and its basic
words and principles. Already in *Sein und Zeit*, Heidegger attends to the
basic words of thoughtful Saying; for example, in illustrating the ancient
meaning of the word ἀλήθεια, he says: "Recourse to such illustrations
must guard against unbridled word-mysticism; it is in the end, however,
the business of philosophy to preserve the *power of the most elemental words* in
which Dasein expresses itself from being levelled to unintelligibility by the
common understanding which for its part functions as the source of
pseudo-problems" (220). Later, Heidegger bluntly calls thinking the
struggle for the word for beings as a whole, and the history of the West the
poetic and thoughtful struggle for this word which requires an "almost
inhuman loyalty" (NI, 492). Heidegger directs the thoughtful reflection
ever more decisively upon the basic words and principles in which a word
for beings as a whole is unfolded. Basic words are, for example, ἀλήθεια,
φύσις, λόγος, or will to power, eternal return, nihilism, superman, justice.   **293**
Leading principles are the principle of ground or Hölderlin's "poetically
man dwells." Distinctive grammatical forms, like the subject-predicate
relation in the sentence, a relation which sets the standard for our
thinking, pass over to these leading words and principles. The basic
words, principles, and forms of speaking respectively refer to an abode in
which the history of truth has gathered itself. A thinker like Leibniz
determines his place in the Western occurrence of truth by bringing the
principle of ground expressly to language as a basic principle of thinking
(SvG 47).

As guide- and way-words, the basic words of the tradition promise the
thinking which gathers itself in them the words in which this thinking
itself attempts to unfold the behest of truth. Heidegger sets out the word
ἀλήθεια as a basic word of the Greek Saying only because he finds in it
the hint to address truth in its primordiality as unconcealment. For our
part we understand the basic words of Heidegger's own speaking only if
we think along the way upon which they have emerged and which they
have taken into their speaking. For example, when Heidegger speaks
about the "enframing" of technology, then we may not with respect to this
word think about what immediately occurs to us from the accustomed and
usual meanings of the word. We must follow the occurrence of truth which
is to come to language in this word back to the opposition between φύσις
and θέσις; we must reflect upon how Kant brought θέσις to language
when he thought of Being as position and how this position finally

unfolded in modern science and technology as the context of a universally carried out representing and delivering, as enframing. Heidegger wants to capture this occurrence of truth in the word "enframing" without making technology contemptible as an unpleasant framework or a dead apparatus. This is evident when one notes that for a time he also thought of as enframing the establishment of truth in form occurring in the work of art (Hw 52; cf. also *Der Ursprung des Kunstwerkes*, Reklam edition 97f). A word happily found is nothing arbitrarily enacted but rather intrinsically preserves language's historical speaking in order to bring history, by means of its history, into the possibility of a decision and transformation.

294   Emplacement means to interrogate what has been thought regarding what is unthought in it, to allow the unthought to be expressed in word as the destined. Emplacement places what has already been thought back into its abode within the history of truth experienced in another way, submits itself in its own abode to the occurrence of truth, and in speaking from this place in the basic words of its Saying, unfolds a behest of truth. In this manifold sense, emplacement is topology and in accord with its highest possibility a "topology of Being"—that is, a topology of Being which, as itself, is experienced in its essence as the appropriative event of unconcealment and world (*Aus der Erfahrung des Denkens*, 23). Topology is the Saying ($\lambda\acute{o}\gamma o\varsigma$) of the abode ($\tau\acute{o}\pi o\varsigma$) in which truth as occurring unconcealment gathers itself.[57] The topology of Being is distinctive in that for the first time, it brings thinking in general into its emplacing, topological essence. This topology leads thinking to the abode of unconcealment; it allows Being itself as unconcealment, and consequently, as the way which produces abodes and which demands an emplacement, allows it to become the appropriative event.

That primordial thinking is itself emplacement is the result of an emplacement which remains open for further emplacements. Topological thinking is thereby not "legitimized" as an "absolute method." Topology is no method at all insofar as method transforms a matter into an object for a subject who, unbiased and detached, tries to grasp the matter as "object" and in methodological abstraction permits only that to count in the object to which one can constantly return. Truth as appropriative event is never an object for an unbiased subject, but rather the behest which repeatedly takes thinking into the claim and thus first opens the region in which objects can be grasped in methodological abstraction. In emplacement, thinking is indicated if it has brought about an experience. But to cause experiences does not mean to produce something or to take possession of it; it means, rather, that something meets us which disturbs and transforms us. "To experience means, according to the strict sense of the word: *Eundo assequi*; in going, to attain something underway, to achieve it by travelling upon the way." To effect experiences; this is the "method" in a more primordial sense of the word, the travelling of a way. Experience brings one upon a way upon which thinking renounces the one abode in favor of another because it seeks to correspond to what is still unthought (Sp 178, 159, 168f).

    295

If emplacement is not method in the usual sense of the word, it is in no way the "absolute" method compared to other methods of thinking. Yet emplacement must indeed prove itself repeatedly as that most primordial Saying which emplaces all other manners of Saying (including the modes of the occurrence of truth not genuinely linguistic) in terms of the presuppositions which bring these modes of the occurrence of truth into their unique character. Nonetheless, emplacement cannot claim to want to derive from itself once and for all the other ways of the occurrence of truth according to their necessity.

Emplacement must renounce the will to "legitimitize" itself. To want to legitimize itself here means to want to *prove* that truth is unconcealment, that it is the way which produces abodes, and that it requires emplacement. Thinking can bring about the experience of truth as the way and also prove this experience; still, the way of truth does not allow itself to be encompassed as a whole and thus to be presented and handed over for proving. If the way would be encompassed as whole, then it would no longer be way, since the way is, in the genuine sense of way, only way if it opens from a definite abode. The way "in itself" is not the way which is encompassed and presented as complete, but rather the way in its insurpassable being underway. Heidegger does not want to destroy the way as way by relating it to an ultimate goal or by bending it back into the circle of a self-subsistent absolute. The question as to where the occurrence of truth and language is grounded or whether it is indeed self-subsistent as *causa sui* is rejected since all wanting to prove and to ground remains inappropriate for truth as unconcealment (VA 134). No grounding is permitted to secure the fact that truth is as it is experienced; rather, occurrence of truth first of all opens the region in which the ground and the grounded can be differentiated. We can "only name" the appropriative event of truth "because it tolerates no discussion or argument; for it is the location of all abodes and temporal fields of play" (Sp 258). We can no longer "discuss" the appropriative event insofar as discussion means asking about a still unthought ground which grounds everything. But if we take the term discussion [*Erörterung*] in a more essential sense, then the occurrence of truth and language itself is the authentic emplacement, the way which produces abodes and which leads thinking from one abode to

    296

the other. As way, truth is the location of which there is none, and which is not representable because it "is" the giving of abodes, of the regions of clearing of the unconcealment.

Emplacing, topological thinking attempts something simple. It tries to use language in a meditative way. It calls attention to the fact that our speaking is determined by presuppositions which have remained unthought and asks, as the topology of Being, what we, Western man, really mean when we say "is." Topological thinking reflects upon the fact that we join ourselves to a definite abode in the occurrence of truth when we speak as we do; it yields what is proper not as the only true matter which alone correctly measured up to what is constantly true, but rather as it is left in the hands of further emplacement. At the conclusion of his letter to Ernest Jünger—that is, at the conclusion of an attempt to give topology to the topography that Jünger gives nihilism, to show the abode from which it is spoken—Heidegger provides a word which stems from Goethe but which should be properly claimed by topological thinking as the characterization of itself: "If anyone considers word and expression as holy testimonies and does not perhaps want to bring them, like coin or paper money, into rapid immediate circulation but rather wants to know them exchanged as true equivalents in spiritual trade and traffic, then one cannot blame him when he notes how normal expressions at which no one takes offense still exert a damaging influence, confuse opinions, distort concepts, and give entire domains a false direction" (*Zur Seinsfrage* 44).

The way of thinking of Martin Heidegger at which this presentation is aimed is itself a singular, great emplacement, not as some argumentative discussion, but as that decisive emplacement of Being which brings thinking into its emplacing essence for the first time. The essential steps of this emplacement were to be followed in this presentation. Because this emplacement has its essence in the fact that the step back into the unthought of what is thought is the step forward (cf. ID 45 ff), the presentation must also mirror this toward and from, the backwards and forwards. The question about history and time goes toward the question of Being; thus the question of Being is taken up anew as the question of Being and time. The question about Being and time must itself again be examined as to how it is imprinted by history; thus Being which is thought from the horizon of time can be experienced in its historical essence as the truth which withdraws itself in that it gives itself. At the level of this question about truth, the history of thinking which has already occurred must be renewed, metaphysics must be put to a decision, and the question about truth as unconcealedness must be preserved in the confrontation with the metaphysical tradition. This tradition must be examined regarding what is most primordial and most seminal in it in order that truth

297

show itself as the joining together of the world which, to be sure, can be explicated only in a historical, emplacing Saying.

As a mere introduction to Heidegger's thinking, this presentation does not develop the Saying of the place of the truth of Being, that is, how it might place itself before Heidegger as the task *today*; rather, it only leads toward it. If one wanted to portray the thinking toward which Heidegger travelled along his way of thinking as a topology of Being, one would have to show how Heidegger accents the prejudices of this thinking by reflecting upon the guiding words of Western thinking and how he above all brings the decisive prejudice to language, that Being was thought as constant presence and that substance therefore had to become finally the subject which establishes its own permanence. One would have to show in detail how Heidegger allows himself to be led by the guiding words of Western thinking to the basic words of his own thinking in order to bring what is unthought in what is thought to language as that which is destined and to be thought. This unthought is the horizon of time from which Being was thought in a concealed manner as the appropriative event of the unconcealment; this event aligns itself to the joining together of the world and is submitted for a decision precisely then, when it withdraws itself to the utmost on the enframing of technology. If the emplacement of the tradition, as Heidegger has conducted it, still occurs rather differently in the different abodes of his way of thinking, then this already shows that emplacement remains problematic in itself. It does not occur to be **298** described as a non-fragmented and complete appropriation of the tradition, not even then, when the one who describes observes that this emplacement is not a history of philosophy from Anaximander to Nietzsche but is rather carried out in order to enable a speaking from one's own abode. Speaking from one's own abode is only suggested in the works which Heidegger has published; thus, this speaking could in no way be the genuine theme of this presentation.

It is no accident that this introduction closes with the reflection upon the question of Saying. The fact that Heidegger, after he has travelled the way of his thinking for fifty years, tries to bring the question of Saying to a decision has its own necessity. A thinking which wants to move from the emplacement of the tradition to speaking from one's own abode must ask which language is appropriate to its speaking. "What is difficult" as Heidegger himself says, "lies in language. Our Western languages are in different ways languages of metaphysical thinking respectively. It remains open whether the essence of Western languages is intrinsically metaphysical and therefore utterly imprinted by onto-theo-logy, or whether these languages grant other possibilities of Saying and, simultaneously, of the not-Saying which says" (ID 72). Can the language in which beings and the Being of beings have been addressed be transformed in a way that thinking in it is capable of corresponding to the appropriative event of unconcealment and world? If language has transformed itself in the emplacement of the tradition, in listening to what is unthought in what is handed down, then the attempt can be made to allow this correspondence to come to language in this language. Heidegger has expressed the conviction that such an attempt need not miscarry in every case by placing Humboldt's quotation at the end of his book, *Unterwegs zur Sprache*—a quotation from that essay, *Über die Verschiedenheit des menschlichen Sprachbaues*, at which Wilhelm von Humboldt, as his brother writes, worked "alone in the nearness of a *grave*." Wilhelm von Humboldt says:

299

Without changing language in its sounds and still less in its forms and laws, *time* often introduces into it, by means of a growing development of ideas, an enhanced power of thought, and a more deeply penetrating capacity for sensibility, something it did not possess earlier. Another sense is then placed into the same housing, something different is offered under the same coinage, a course of ideas articulated in a different way is interpreted according to the same laws of combination. This is an enduring fruit of the *literature* of a people, but particularly of *poetry* and *philosophy*.

Appendix

[Translator's note: The following index is the author's own. To provide assistance to English-speaking readers, we have listed in brackets available English translations of the listed works. In many cases, however, the German work listed is a collection of essays, lectures, and talks, each of which has been translated into English and published at different times. For example, the collection of essays entitled *Vorträge und Aufsätze* has never been published in English as a complete work or in its original order, but each piece has appeared in English. When this has occurred, the German entry is followed first by the original German pagination of the given piece and then by reference to the English translation, itself often a portion of a larger English collection of Heidegger's essays.]

Martin Heidegger's writings were consulted in the subsequently listed editions. **316**
They have in part been referred to in the text of this book through the symbols placed in front of the title in the following list:

"Neuere Forschungen über Logik." In: *Literarische Rundschau für das katholische Deutschland.* Published by J. Sauer. 38. Jg. Freiburg im Breisgau, 1912. 465ff, 517ff, 565ff.

Die Lehre vom Urteil im Psychologismus. Ein kritisch-positiver Beitrag zur Logik. Leipzig, 1914.

Die Kategorien- und Bedeutungslehre des Duns Scotus. Max Niemeyer: Tübingen, 1916.

"Der Zeitbegriff in der Geschichtswissenschaft." In: *Zeitschrift für Philosophie und philosophische Kritik.* Band 161. Leipzig 1916. 173–188.

SuZ   *Sein und Zeit.* Siebente unveränderte Auflage. Max Niemeyer: Tübingen, 1953. [*Sein und Zeit* translated by John Macquarrie and Edward Robinson. New York: Harper & Row, 1962.]

Besprechung von: "E. Cassirer: Philosophie der symbolischen Formen. 2. Teil: Das mythische Denken." Berlin 1925. In: *Deutsche Literaturzeitung für Kritik der internationalen Wissenschaft.* Neue Folge. 5. Jg. Berlin 1928. 1000–1012.

G   *Vom Wesen des Grundes.* Vierte Auflage. Frankfurt 1955.

K   *Kant und das Problem der Metaphysik.* Zweite Auflage. Frankfurt 1951. [*Kant and the Problem of Metaphysics,* translated by James S. Churchill. Bloomington: Indiana University Press, 1968.]

WiM   *Was ist Metaphysik?* Siebte Auflage. Frankfurt, 1955. ["What is Metaphysics," translated by David Farrell Krell, in *Martin Heidegger: Basic Writings,* edited by David Farrell Krell. Harper and Row: New York, 1977, pp. 95–112.]

Die Selbstbehauptung der deutschen Universität. Vittorio Klostermann GmbH.: Frankfurt am Main, 1983.

VWW   *Vom Wesen der Wahrheit.* Dritte Auflage. Frankfurt, 1954. ["On the Essence of Truth," translated by John Sallis, in *Martin Heidegger: Basic Writings,* pp. 117–141.]

EH   *Erläuterungen zu Hölderlins Dichtung.* Zweite, vermehrte Auflage. **317**
Vittorio Klostermann: Frankfurt, 1951 [For a translation of pp. 7–30 of the German edition, see "Remembrance of the Poet,"

translated by Douglas Scott in *Existence and Being*, edited by Werner Brock, Chicago: Henry Regnery Co., 1949, pp. 243–269. And for a translation of pp. 31–46 of the German edition, see "Hölderlin and the Essence of Poetry," translated by Douglas Scott in *Existence and Being*, pp. 270–291.]

PL   *Platons Lehre von der Wahrheit. Mit einem Brief über den >Humanismus<.* Zweite Auflage. Francke: Bern 1954. ["Letter on Humanism," translated by Frank A. Capuzzi and J. Glenn Gray, in *Martin Heidegger: Basic Writings*, pp. 189–242.]

      Der Feldweg. Vittorio Klostermann: Frankfurt 1953. ["The Pathway," translated by Thomas F. O'Meara. *Listening*, II (Spring 1967), pp. 88–91.]

AED   *Aus der Erfahrung des Denkens.* Günther Neske: Pfullingen, 1954. ["The Thinker as Poet," in Martin Heidegger, *Poetry, Language, Thought*, translated by Albert Hofstadter, New York: Harper and Row, 1971, pp. 1–14.]

Hw   *Holzwege.* Vittorio Klostermann: Frankfurt, 1950.

      pp.   7–68, "The Origin of the Work of Art," in *Poetry, Language, Thought*, pp. 15–87.

      pp.   69–104, "The Age of the World Picture," in Martin Heidegger, *The Question Concerning Technology*, translated by William Lovitt. New York: Harper and Row, 1977, pp. 115–154.

      pp.   105–192, *Hegel's Concept of Experience.* New York: Harper and Row, 1970.

      pp.   193–247, "The World of Nietzsche: 'God is Dead'," in *The Question Concerning Technology*, pp. 53–112.

      pp.   248–295, "What Are Poets For?" in *Poetry, Language, Thought*, pp. 91–142.

      pp.   296–343, "The Anaximander Fragment," in Martin Heidegger, *Early Greek Thinking*, translated by David Farrell Krell and Frank Capuzzi. New York: Harper and Row, 1975, pp. 13–58.]

E   *Einführung in die Metaphysik.* Max Niemeyer: Tübingen, 1953. [*An Introduction to Metaphysics*, translated by Ralph Manheim. Garden City, New York: Doubleday Anchor Books, 1961.]

WhD   *Was Heisst Denken?* Max Niemeyer:Tübingen, 1954. [*What is Called Thinking?*, translated by Fred D. Wiech and J. Glenn Gray. Harper and Row: New York, 1968.]

VA   *Vorträge und Aufsätze.* Günther Neske: Pfullingen, 1954.

      Volume 1.

      pp.   5–36, "The Question Concerning Technology," in *The Question Concerning Technology*, pp. 3–35.

      pp.   37–62, "Science and Reflection," in *The Question Concerning Technology*, pp. 155–182.

      pp.   63–91, "Overcoming Metaphysics," in *The End of Philosophy*, translated by Joan Stambaugh. New York: Harper and Row, 1973.

      pp.   93–118, "Who is Nietzsche's Zarathustra?," translated by Bernd Magnus. *The Review of Metaphysics* XX (March, 1967), pp. 411–431.

Volume 2.
pp. 19–36, "Building Dwelling Thinking," in *Poetry, Language, Thought*, pp. 143–162.
pp. 37–59, "The Thing," in *Poetry, Language, Thought*, pp. 163–186.
pp. 61–78, " . . . Poetically Man Dwells . . .," in *Poetry, Language, Thought*, pp. 211–229.
Volume 3.
pp. 3–26, "Logos (Heraclitus, Fragment B 50)," in *Early Greek Thinking*, pp. 102–123.
pp. 27–52, "Moira (Parmenides VIII, 34–41)," in *Early Greek Thinking*, pp. 59–78.
pp. 53–78, "Aletheia (Heraclitus, Fragment B 16)," In *Early Greek Thinking*, pp. 102–123.
Was ist das—die Philosophie? Günther Neske: Pfullingen, 1956. [*What is Philosophy?*, translated by Jean T. Wilde and William Kluback. New Haven: College and University Press, 1958.]
Zur Seinsfrage. Vittorio Klostermann: Frankfurt, 1956. [*The Question of Being*, translated by Jean T. Wilde and William Kluback. New Haven: College and University Press, 1958.]

SvG   *Der Satz vom Grund.* Günther Neske: Pfulligen, 1957. [pp. 191–211, "The Principle of Ground," translated by Keith Hoeller. *Man and World*, VII (August, 1974), pp. 207–222.]

ID   *Identität und Differenz.* Günther Neske: Pfulligen 1957. [*Identity and Difference*, translated by Joan Stambaugh. New York: Harper and Row, 1969.]
Hebel—der Hausfreund. Günther Neske: Pfulligen 1957.
"Grundsätze des Denkens." In: *Jahrbuch für Psychologie und Psychotherapie.* 6. vol. Freiburg und München 1958. 33–41. ["Principles of Thinking" in Martin Heidegger, *The Piety of Thinking*, translated and edited by James G. Hart and John C. Maraldo. Bloomington: Indiana University Press, 1976.]
"Vom Wesen und Begriff der φύσις. Aristotles Physik b 1." In: *Il Pensiero.* Volume III. Milano-Varese, 1958. 129–156, 265–289.
"Antrittsrede vor der Heidelberger Akademie der Wissenschaften." In: *Wissenschaft und Weltbild.* 12. Jg. Wien 1959. 610f. ["Heidelberg Inaugural Address," translated by Hans Seigfried, *Man and World* (February, 1970), pp. 4–5.].
Gelassenheit. Günther Neske: Pfullingen, 1959. [*Discourse on Thinking*, translated by John M. Anderson and E. Hans Freund. New York: Harper and Row, 1966.]

Sp   *Unterwegs zur Sprache.* Pfulligen 1959.
[pp. 9–33, "Language," in *Poetry, Language, Thought*, pp. 189–210.
pp. 35ff, *On the Way to Language*, translated by Peter D. Hertz. New York: Harper and Row, 1971.]
"Aufzeichnungen aus der Werkstatt." In: *Neue Züricher Zeitung.* 27 September, 1959. Blatt 5.
Der Ursprung des Kunstwerkes (Reclams Universal-Bibliothek. Nr. 8446–47. Stuttgart 1960. [See translations listed above for *Holzwege.*]

318

"Hegel und die Griechen." In: *Die Gegenwart der Griechen im neueren Denken.* Festschrift für H.-G. Gadamer. Tübingen 1960. 43–57.

"Hölderlin's Erde und Himmel." In: *Hölderlin-Jahrbuch,* 1958 bis 1960. Tübingen 1960. 17–39.

Sprache und Heimat. In: *Hebel-Jahrbuch* 1960. 27–50.

NI,NII   Nietzsche. Zwei Bände. Günther Neske: Pfullingen, 1961. [NI, 9–10, 11–254, *Nietzsche. Vol. I: the Will to Power as Art,* translated by David Farrell Krell. New York: Harper and Row, 1979.

NII, 31–256, 335–398, *Nietzsche. Vol IV: Nihilism,* translated by Frank A. Capuzzi and edited by David Farrell Krell. New York: Harper and Row, 1982.

NII, 399–490, *The End of Philosophy,* translated by Joan Stambaugh. New York: Harper and Row, 1973.]

Die Frage noch dem Ding. Zu Kants Lehre von den transzendentalen Grundsätzen. Max Niemeyer Verlag: Tübingen, 1962. [*What is a Thing?* Translated by W. B. Barton Jr. and Vera Deutsch. Henry Regnery: Chicago, 1967.]

Kants These über das Sein. Vittorio Klostermann: Frankfurt, 1962. ["Kant's Thesis about Being." Translated by Ted Klein and William E. Pohl. *Southwestern Journal of Philosophy* 4 (1973): 7–33.]

In addition to Heidegger's published works, I have also consulted some few unpublished works—not to make full use of them, but rather to correct the distortion of the presentation as it arises when one characterizes the way of thinking only from the works published already. The early Freiburg lectures to which I refer in the text were known to me only from notes and indirect information for which, above all, I have Prof. Oskar Becker to thank. Other lectures and works were given to me for study by the author himself; I have quoted from the following:

Beiträge zur Philosophie [*Contributions to Philosophy*], 1936–38.

Die Uberwindung der Metaphysik [*The Overcoming of Metaphysics*], 1938–39.

Wiederholungen aus der Nietzsche Vorlesung "Der Wille zur Macht als Erkenntnis." [Recapitulation from the Nietzsche course, "The Will to Power as Knowledge", 1939.]

Das Ereignis [*The Appropriative Event*], 1941.

Hölderlins Hymnen [*Hölderlin's Hymns*]. Course from the summer semester, 1942.

Einblick in das, was ist [*Insight into That Which Is*]. Lectures first given in Bremen, 1949. [Of these four lectures, "The Thing" ("Das Ding"), "Enframing" ("Das Gestell"), "The Danger" (Die Gefahr"), and "The Turning" ("Die Kehre"), some form of all but "The Danger" is available in English. See *The Question Concerning Technology* pp. 3–49, and *Poetry, Language, Thought,* pp. 165–186.]

Notes

Chapter 1. Entrance into Metaphysics

1. Aristotle, in chapters 4,6 and 7 of *Metaphysik* (Met.) and in other places, cf. above all Met. E2. 106a 33–b2. In the summer semester of 1931 in a course entitled *Interpretationen aus der antiken Philosophie*, Heidegger dealt with Met. (the examination of δύναμις and ἐνέργεια); in the introduction, he analysed how Aristotle took over the task of unfolding the manifold expressibility of Being: Parmenides thought Being as the One, so Plato admitted the Nothing into Being; this taking over of the negative, nonexisting into beings signified the necessity of the unfolding of the One into the Many. Then Aristotle took a decisive step again in the gigantomachy about Being when he thought of the unity of Being as the unity of analogy and tried to exhibit necessity in the segmenting of multifaceted Being (cf. also SuZ 3). In a talk from 1955, Heidegger translated the sentence: Τὸ ὄν λέγεται Πολλαχῶς, from a transformed point of inquiry in the following manner: "Being-which-is comes to appear in a manifold way" (*Was ist das—die Philosophie?* 46).

2. Heidegger refers to the treatise *de modi significandi*, which was then still attributed to *Duns Scotus*. Later Martin Grabman showed that *Thomas of Enfurt* was the author.

3. In the *Habilitationsschrift* Heidegger promises searching investigations regarding the still open question about Being, value, and negation (237, note). He also calls attention to the fact that only by differentiating between the formation of value and the validity of value does the concept of a *philosophia perennis* allow itself to be established in a scientific-theoretical manner and does the solution of the problem of a scientific-theoretical consideration of Catholic theology allow itself to be taken in hand (240, note).

Chapter 2. Metaphysics and History

4. *Wilhelm Diltheys Gesammelte Schriften*. Volume 2. Leipzig and Berlin 1914 (1929). VI f.

5. *Wilhelm Diltheys Gesammelte Schriften*. Volume 1. 2nd Edition. Leipzig and Berlin 1923. 116.

6. The genesis of historicism can thus be described as the genesis of the sense for the individual, cf. Friedrich Meinecke: *Die Enstehung des Historismus*. 1936.

7. After the appearance of *Sein und Zeit*, Georg Misch undertook a first attempt to come to grips with Husserl and Heidegger from Dilthey. "Lebensphilosophie und Phänomenologie." In: *Philosophischer Anzeiger*. Year 3, Bonn, 1928–29. 267–368, 405–475; 4. Jg. (Vol.) Bonn 1929–30, 181–330. On the other hand, *Hans-Georg Gadamer*, in his philosophical hermeneutic *Wahrheit und Methode*, J. C. B. Mohr, Tübingen 1960, undertook to criticize the romantic hermeneutic, the science of history of the historical school, and the Diltheyian philosophy of life by means of Heidegger.

8. *Briefwechsel zwischen Wilhelm Dilthey und dem Grafen Paul Yorck von Wartenburg 1877–1897*. Halle 1923. 154, 158.

9. *Der Junge Dilthey. Ein Lebensbild in Briefen und Tagebüchern 1852–1870*. Edited by Clara Dilthey Misch. Leipzig and Berlin 1933. 140.

10. Cf. Wilhelm Kamlah: *Christentum und Geschichtlichkeit*. Second edition. Stuttgart and Köln 1951. 217ff. Kamlah's posing of the question is inspired by *Sein und Zeit*; nonetheless, in this book as well as in the later work, the issue for Kamlah is the differentiation of the "perceiving" ancients from the self-controlling reason of the modern age and thereby also a positive assimilation and critical mediation precisely of classical Greek thinking. Consequently the radical destruction of metaphysics as Heidegger attempts it is mitigated in favor of the perceiving reason of the ancients.

Chapter 3. Fundamental Ontology as the Grounding of Metaphysics

11. Because anxiety, which is essentially anxiety about death, becomes the decisive attunement for Heidegger, Otto Friedrich Bollnow, in his book *Das Wesen der Stimmungen*, first edition, 1941, reproaches the Heideggerian analysis of attunement as an "existential-philosophically" one-sided proceeding from depressed moods. An ontologizing of the investigation in the manner of a metaphysical ontology of essence approaches this one-sidedness. This critique nonetheless fails to recognize Heidegger's genuine concern even though Bollnow's concrete analyses remain of value. Cf. my essay, *Das Wesen der Stimmungen. Kritische Betrachtungen zum gleichnamigen Buch O. Fr. Bollnows*. In: *Zeitschrift für philosophische Forschung*. Volume 14. Meisenheim 1960. 272–284. In a manner similar to Bollnow's, Ludwig Binswanger attempted to correct Heidegger's approach in his book, **302** *Grundformen und Erkenntnis menschlichen Daseins*, first Edition, 1942. He has contrasted love to care which is an allegedly one-sided interpretation of human Dasein. Thus he does not understand care in the sense of the *formal* fundamental analysis of Dasein. Today Binswanger himself says quite correctly that in this book he "still completely misunderstood as anthropological theory the *a priori* explication of Dasein's care-structure." Nonetheless, "As contestable as my contrast between the essence of love and that of care is, the analysis of the pure essence of love appears justified to me even today . . ." ("Dank an Edmund Husserl." 70. In: *Edmund Husserl 1859–1959*. Phenomenologica 4. La Haye 1959). Heidegger himself, in the course entitled *Hölderlins Hymnen*, subordinates love as a specific way of the standing out of the truth of Being to being-toward-death: "The maintaining of the eccentric center of human Being, the 'central' and self-'centered' abode in what is eccentric, has its preliminary steps in love. The authentic sphere of standing in the eccentric center of life is death."

12. Thus one could attempt to understand Heidegger from Schelling and from the course of modern metaphysics in general. Cf. Walter Schulz: "Über den philosophiegeschichtlichen Ort Martin Heideggers." In: *Philosophische Rundschau*. Year 1, Tübingen 1953–54. 65–93, 211–232; *Die Vollendung des deutschen Idealismus in der Spätphilosophie Schellings*. Stuttgart 1955; *Der Gott der neutzeitlichen Metaphysik*. Pfullingen 1957.

Chapter 4. Phenomenology—Transcendental Philosophy—Metaphysics

13. Regarding state-of-mind and sensibility, cf. Ludwig Landgrebe: "Prinzipien der Lehre vom Empfinden" In: *Zeitschrift für Philosophische Forschung*. Volume 8. Meisenheim 1954. 195–209. Cf. also note 11.

14. Regarding this and the following, see Heidegger's letter to Husserl, Oct. 22, 1927, the various drafts of the *Encyclopedia Britannica* article, and Heidegger's notes about it in *Edmund Husserl: Phänomenólogische Psychologie*. Edited by Walter Biemel (*Husserliana Band IX*). The Hague 1962. 237ff, 517ff, 599ff, above all, 600, 610ff, 274, 602, 256, 517.

15. "Nachwort zu den Ideen," cf. *Jahrbuch für Philosophie und phänomenologische Forschung*. Volume 9. Halle 1930. 551.

16. Compare the quotes from Husserl's marginal notes to *Sein und Zeit* and to the book on Kant in Alwin Diemer: *Edmund Husserl*. Meisenheim 1956. 29ff, as well as Husserl's lecture of 1931: "Phänomenologie und Anthropologie" in *Philosophie und Phänomenologische Forschung*. Volume 2. 1941. 1–14.   **303**

17. The later work is beyond the scope of this presentation. There Husserl, among others, in a productive counterstroke also tried to make fruitful for his own thinking the objections which Heidegger brings forward. The meaning of this later work, but also the metaphysical precedents which remain unclarified in it, are discussed especially by philisophers who have in their own fashion travelled the way from Husserl to Heidegger. Compare Ludwig Landgrebe: *Philosophie der Gegenwart*. Enlarged edition. Berlin 1957. 34ff, 67ff, above all 73; Eugen Fink: "L'analyse intentionelle et la pensée spéculative" in: *Problèmes actuels de la Phénoménologie*. Paris 1952. 53–87; Eugen Fink: "Operative Begriffe in Husserls Phänomenologie" in: *Zeitschrift für philosophische Forschung*. Volume 11. Meisenheim 1957. 321–337. Compare also Max Müller: "Phänomenologie, Ontologie und Scholastik" in: *Existenzphilosophei im geistigen Leben der Gegenwart*. Second edition. Heidelberg 1958. 107–134.

18. Regarding the question whether Kant thinks from this root, compare finally Dieter Henrich: "Über die Einheit der Subjektivatät" in *Philosophische Rundschau*. Year 3. Tübingen 1955. 28–69.

Chapter 5. Going Back to the Ground of Metaphysics

19. Compare Hans von Soden: *Was ist Wahrheit? Vom geschichtlichen Begriff der Wahrheit*. Marburg 1927. Reprinted in *Urchristentum und Geschicthe*. Volume I. Tübingen 1951. 1–24.

20. The lecture "Vom Wesen der Wahrheit" was first given in 1930, finally formulated in 1940, and printed in 1943; consequently the printed text does not reproduce the lecture as it was originally given. The language of the printed text can in no way be the language of the 1930 lecture since a difference exists between the anxiety which stirs first the "daring" Dasein (WiM 37), and the releasement which admits itself into unconcealment and thereby also expressly allows concealment in unconcealment. The discussion in the 1930 lecture was not about this releasement but rather about Dasein's standing up against the concealment of beings as a whole, about a stand which shatters on the power of concealment. Nonetheless, the basic characteristics essential to us and the direction of the questioning have remained in the lecture; thus, with the given reservations we can find support in the printed text when we ask how Heidegger has advanced the way   **304** of his thinking beyond the position of "Was ist Metaphysik?" and "Vom Wesen des Grundes."

Chapter 6. Metaphysics as History

21. In his essay "Martin Heidegger und der Humanismus" in *Theologische Rundschau. Neue Folge 18/2*. 1950, Gerhard Krüger gives valuable isolated hints toward the interpretation of this ascent but still misses the fundamental direction of Heidegger's questioning.

22. Regarding Nietzsche's proofs for the eternal recurrence, compare Oskar Becker, "Nietzsche's Beweise für seine Lehre von der ewigen Wiederkunft" in *Blätter für deutsche Philosophie*. Volume 9. Berlin 1935–36. 368–387.

23. Heidegger notes that Schopenauer (and in his wake Nietzsche as well) had "misinterpreted" Kant's demand for a "disinterested" turn toward the beautiful as a demand for the "pure hovering in indifference." Schopenauer's aesthetics is not even to be compared from a distance with Hegel's aesthetics (NI, 127f). In contrast to this it must be pointed out that the radical subjectivizing of the aesthetics of genuis and the renewed transcendentalizing of man through the orientation to the "idea" became historically necessarily when the metaphysical teleological horizon, which still remained supportive for Kant, dwindled. The question is whether it is not of consequence that recent metaphysics flows out into a willing of Being (Nietzsche) and a willing of Nothing (Schopenauer); consequently Schopenauer's interpretation of art as a preparation for a last exhibition of willing—which is something quite different from a hovering in indifference!—is as metaphysically consequential in its way as is Nietzsche's interpretation of art as will to power. Only because of this could Schopenauer prophecy the guiding terms of modern aesthetics. Cf. my essay, "Schopenauer und das Wesen der Kunst" in *Zeitschrift für philosophische Forschung*. Volume 14. Meisenheim 1960. 353–389. One of the first questions for which Heidegger's "destruction" of the history of thinking becomes fruitful must always be whether the direct views about a thinker which Heidegger gives are in accord with the approach of Heidegger's thinking and his experience of the tradition as a whole.

24. The question remains whether beauty and art belong together at all for Platonism, whether Plato's discussion of art (in the *Republic*) and the discussion of the beautiful (in *Phaedrus*) must be strictly held apart.

Chapter 7. The Overcoming of Metaphysics

25. Schelling, *Sämtliche Werke*. 1856ff. Volume 3. 373.

26. *Wilhelm Diltheys Gesammelte Schriften*, I. Band 2. Auflage Leipzig and Berlin 1923. 388ff.

27. Arthur Schopenhauer, *Über die vierfache Wurzel des Satzes vom zureichenden Grunde*, sec. 4.

28. Max Müller: *Existenzphilosophie im geistigen Leben der Gegenwart*. Second expanded edition. Heidelberg 1958. 73.

29. Max Müller, 74.

30. In the "essence" of phenomenology experienced in this way, phenomenological seeing and destruction are one since it is not forgotten that the shining forth of Being (its coming-into-the-truth) belongs to the *history* of truth. The unity of the self-manifestation of Being and of history, and consequently the unity of the theory of categories, metaphysics, or logic on the one side and history on the other is the stimulating "idea" of the Hegelian *Phenomenology of Spirit*. The confrontation with *this* phenomenology became necessary for Heidegger when he—as Hegel had done in another way—tried to grasp Kant's transcendental dialectic as the ground of

the transcendental aesthetic, and logic in terms of the history of truth (K 221f). Heidegger published the attempt at an interpretation of the sense of Hegelian phenomenology in *Holzwege*, 105ff; still, in face of this interpretation, as in face of Heidegger's interpretation in general, one must ask whether it starts out in an even philologically accessible fashion. Cf. my essay, "Zur Deutung der Phänomenologie des Geistes" In *Hegel Studien*. Volume I. Bonn 1961. 255–294. In this essay, it is also briefly pointed out how thinkers like Marx and Dilthey already took up the "idea" of phenomenology, how Feuerbach and Chalybäus thought of the unity of metaphysics and history under the title "phenomenology."

31. The letters of Heidegger and Jaspers, *Bulletin de la Société francaise de Philosophie*. XXXVII. 1937. 161ff. Also see my essay, "Jean Wahl's Heidegger—Interpretations" In *Zeitschrift für philosophische Forschung*. Volume 12. Meisenheim 1958. 437–458.

32. It should be self-evident that the notorious difference between the individual and the One is no solution to the problem of the "objective spirit." Existence in the sense of *Sein und Zeit* is not at all to be established upon Kierkegaard's sense of the individual no matter how the related concepts may be able to mislead one to this opinion. Heidegger already opposed this opinion early on: "Mineness" is not differentiated in terms of an individualized I; my own self is rather neither I nor you, neither I nor we (G 38, E 22; NI, 275). It is certainly beyond doubt that Heidegger's questioning about community is some of the most unsatisfying questioning of his work. This must be said even when one considers that Heidegger never concretely worked out this question, that he dealt with it at all only with a "fundamental-ontological" intent (PL 58ff, 77f). This question is certainly not to be solved with the *coup de main* of an immediate introduction of the concept of *Volk* (cf. already SuZ 384, then EH).

306

33. Thus one indeed accounts for the "turning" which must certainly remain the strongest and most surprising matter for the age of the metaphysical-scientific-technical search for grounds. Cf. for example, Karl Löwith, *Heidegger. Denker in dürftiger Zeit*. Second expanded edition. Göttingen 1960. In his own work, Löwith began with his questioning anthropologically in order to come to the following thesis through a criticism of historical thinking guided by historical investigations: after the "death of God," thinking can find a ground only in the "world" which is ever the same. Löwith attributes to Heidegger a similar movement from man to the world (the historical world to be sure).

34. Ludwig Feuerbach: *Sämtliche Werke. Leipzig, 1846–66*. Volume 2. 244. Karl Marx, *Die Frühschriften*. Edited by S. Landshut. Stuttgart 1953. 251, 269.

35. *Wilhelm Diltheys Gesammelte Schriften*. Volume 8. Leipzig and Berlin 1931. 30.

36. Oskar Becker imputes this thesis to Heidegger's thinking and therefore posits a mantic phenomenology (foretelling the return of the same) alongside hermeneutical phenomenology, a para-existential philosophy alongside existential philosophy, a para-ontology (taking its point of departure from parousia, the constant presence of the idea) alongside ontology (which in Heidegger's sense thinks of Being as history). However much of Becker's interpretation of Heidegger's thinking may fall short—his critique is answered only when it is shown how Heidegger's seminal thinking can turn itself back toward comprehending the Being of beings and how it is thereby capable of positively evaluating Being which is "always" the same. Cf. Oskar Becker: "Mathematische Existenz" In: *Jahrbuch für Philosophie und phänomenologische Forschung*. Volume 8. Halle 1927. 439–809; *Grösse und Grenze der mathematischen Denkweise*. Freiburg und Munchen 1959;

Einführung in die Logistik, vorzüglich in den Modelkälkul. Meisenheim 1952. "Paraexis-
tenz: Menschliches Dasein und Dawesen" in: *Blätter für deutsche Philosophie.* Volume 17. Berlin 1943–44. 62–95); "Von der Hinfälligkeit des Schönen und der

307   Abenteuerlichkeit des Kunstlers" in: *Festschrift für E. Rothachker.* Edited by G.
Funke, Bonn 1958. 25–38; "Die Aktualität des pythagoreischen Gedankens" in:
Gegenwart der Griechen im neueren Denken. Festschrift für H. G. Gadamer. Tübingen 1960.
7–30.

Chapter 8. The Other Beginning

37. Gadamer, therefore (cf. note 7), in his ongoing discussion of the problem of
the sciences of the spirit, simply contrasts truth and method with one another.

38. It could indeed be the case that Kierkegaard's basic position and the
position of the theology in conformity to it is not a specifically Christian one, but
rather—expressed in traditional concepts—a "negative *natural* theology" (cf. Paul
Schütz, *Parousia. Hoffnung und Prophetie.* Heidelberg 1960; cf. also Wilhelm Anz,
Kierkegaard und der deutsche Idealism. Tübingen 1956). Like Nietzsche, Kierkegaard
could also—through the preconception for his religious authorship—drive metaphysics into its extremity. Metaphysics would then have two ways out: in the
de-powering of the subject, brought to completion in the unconditioned toward
absolute powerlessness (Kierkegaard) and in the empowering of the subject
toward absolute power (Nietzsche). Cf. Wolfgang Struve, "Die neuzeitliche
Philosophie der Subjektivität" (In *Symposion.* Volume I. 1949. 207–335, above all,
245). Thus like Nietzsche, Kierkegaard could become decisive not by formalizing
his religious assertions alone but rather by reflecting upon what is metaphysical in
the preconception from which Kierkegaard sets out. Heidegger certainly does not
think so: either Kierkegaard or Nietzsche is decisive for his dynamic thinking;
where Kierkegaard's religious assertions are formalized (in *Sein und Zeit*), Nietzsche's thinking is not essential; where Nietzsche has become decisive, there
Kierkegaard retreats.

39. Martin Buber remarks that he has nowhere in our time found such a
far-reaching misunderstanding of the prophets of Israel at such a high philosophical level as in this assertion. The prophets of Israel indeed immediately smash any
demand for security in the name of a god of the "historical demand." Cf. Martin
Buber, *Gottesfinsternis.* Zurich 1953. 87f.

40. Namely in that God saves men by means of the "folly" of the cross, men are

308   incapable of securing the relation to Him through wisdom. In an interpretation of
the Pauline principle, Heinrich Schlier observes with Heidegger that all Western
thinking stands under a historical "destiny." As a theologian Schlier concludes
from this that all searching after wisdom is an anachronism: faith in what is laid
forth in the kerygma (in the tidings) has taken the place of *sophia.* Cf. Heinrich
Schlier, "Kerygma und Sophia" In *Die Zeit der Kirche.* Freiburg 1956. 206–232.
In recent years, exegesis has above all explicated the gnostic background of the
Pauline expositions. Thus one had to ask whether Paul, as Heidegger insinuates,
directly opposed the Greek philosophical tradition at all in the quoted passage or
whether Corinthians had philosophical ambitions. Ulrich Wilckens (*Weisheit und
Torheit.* Tübingen 1959) shows that it was not the case. Paul directly opposes a
gnostic *sophia*-Christology and only indirectly opposes philosophy. While Schlier is
of the opinion that the kerygma is intrinsically dogmatic and that faith releases the
believers into a new being-wise, "*sophia*" remains, according to Wilckens, a

concept for Paul which can be applied to God alone. Cf. Wilckens' confrontation with Schlier, "Kreuz und Weisheit" in the journal *Kerygma und Dogma*. Year 3. 1957. 77ff.

41. Herman Noack, "Gespräch mit Martin Heidegger" In *Anstösse*. Published by the Evangelical Academy of Hofgeismar, I. 1954. 30ff, above all, 33.

42. Cf. H. Boeder, "Der Frühgriechische Wortgebrauch von Logos und Aletheia" In *Archiv für Begriffsgeschicthe*. Band 4. Bonn. 1959. 81ff. Cf. further Heidegger, *Hegel und die Griechen*. 55f.

43. Oskar Becker (cf. note 36), *Grösse und Grenze der mathematischen Denkweise*. 1ff., 161ff; *Die Actualität des pythagoreischen Gedankens*. 7ff.

44. Regarding the question as to whether the early Ionian thinkers do not already oppose the poetic naming of the divine, cf. Wilhelm Perpiet, "Vom Ursprung der Philosophie oder über eine spezifische Differenz von Denken und Dichten" in *Der Mensch und die Künste, Festschrift für H. Lützeler*. Düsseldorf 1962. 47–73.

45. The theologian Rudolph Bultmann proceeds in his existential interpretation of the New Testament from the fact that the New Testament message testifies only to the fact of revelation and reveals no content. In the hearing of this message "a distancing oneself from the world" occurs—the Christian not-being-of-this-world. Heidegger does not speak of such distancing in the "insightful moment"; he uses the term "distancing oneself from the world" more in relation to mathematical knowledge (SuZ 65, 112). To think the moment as not "worldly" is only a tendency in *Sein und Zeit* which counteracts other tendencies; above all it is one which Heidegger did not follow further down his way of thinking. Bultmann's existential interpretation can in general be placed only in relation to an existential analytic which, unlike that of *Sein und Zeit*, is not put into the service of the question about the truth of Being. Bultmann therefore could later produce an apparently seamless connection between the existential analysis and recent historicism (cf. Rudolph Bultmann: *Geschichte und Eschatologie*. Tübingen 1958). Yet the question is whether historicism and eschatological dualism provide the proper preliminary understanding for the interpretation of the New Testament.

309

46. Cf. Hegel's Jena essay on Natural Law (*Hegels Werke*. Volume I. Berlin 1832. 386ff).

47. The thesis that all Western art is metaphysical, is grounded in the Greek experience of the world, demands examination. Erich Auerbach (*Mimesis*. Second edition. Bern 1959) has shown in his attempt at a "topology," a determination of the abode of European literature, that the "realism" of historical existence as it dominates poetry today is rooted in the presentation of the passion of Christ which would not have been possible at all within Greek and ancient literature. The symbolic thought of the medieval "figural" and "typological" allegories is to be strictly separated from that of ancient allegories. In the Middle Ages the image is an analogy in an order of salvation *history* (for example, Jerusalem is the "pre-figurement" for the Christian Church, etc.); thus medieval figurative thought in no way means only a "referential corresponding within the order of *creation*" (NI, 506). Heidegger would ask whether the realism and perspectivism into which Auerbach sees European literature flowing does not belong to that "negligence" which characterizes the end of the metaphysically grounded age (NI 359ff.). F. Gogarten gives the *theological* antitheses to existentiell realism in his extensive discussion of "Mimesis": *Zeitschrift für Theologie und Kirche*, 51, Jg. 1954. 270–360.

Chapter 9. The Freeing Toward One's Own

48. Eugen Fink centers his thinking around the "world-play." Fink—trusted student of Husserl in his last years—begins with the concept of world of Husserl's later philosophy, but criticizes Husserl's interpretation of man's relation to the world as the infinite being of the transcendental subject; as a result, Husserl subjectivizes the concept of world and does not pay sufficient attention to man's finitude. Heidegger overcame this "subjectivism" (at least in his later work) and established the finitude of man. Like Heidegger in the years after *Sein und Zeit*, Fink also seeks to rediscover the thinking about the world in the earliest Greek thought. He assesses the ontotheology of metaphysics as the disfigurement of world thinking. Because of this, he sharply distinguishes between the world thinking of the Ionians and the ontology of the Eleatics which forgot the world (*Nachdenkliches zur ontologischen Frühgeschichte von Raum-Zeit-Bewegung*. Den Haag 1957). Fink wants to think through the *cosmological* horizon of the question of Being as it has been raised by Heidegger. He criticizes the "transcendental-philosophically abstract" approach of *Sein und Zeit*. In this work, world is related to man and is united to him as an existential. It is not asked how nonhuman being is in the world and "how mankind along with its existential constitution of 'being-in-the-world' is itself *in* the world as universe" (*Spiel als Weltsymbol*. Stuttgart 1960. 53). As justified as this critique of Heidegger's early work may be (it is indeed, as Fink notes, Heidegger's self-criticism), Fink's cosmological turn nonetheless contains the danger that the "transcendental" raising of the question (which Heidegger established within the turn toward the historical) is abandoned in favor of a speculative-dogmatic thinking of the world in itself. Guide-words which Heidegger intends in a "transcendental" sense, in terms of the history of Being, receive an entirely different meaning from Fink. The "way" is thought as a movement in beings, as the ascent of Being from lower to higher being. The "leap" becomes the "spring into the movement of the ascent of Being itself" (*Sein, Wahrheit, Welt. Vor-Fragen zum Problem des Phänomen-Begriffs*. Den Haag 1958. 38). Through his cosmological turn Fink can take up romantic-idealistic thought more positively than Heidegger does and, for example, criticize the way in which Heidegger attributes to Nietzsche the metaphysics to be overcome (*Nietzsches Philosophie*, Stuttgart 1960, 186ff). The question is whether Fink adequately follows Heidegger's allusion to groundlessness and concealment and thus to the fatefulness in the occurring of Being, truth, and world. If Fink evidently comes up short regarding this aspect of Heidegger's thinking, it is all the more noteworthy that Fink criticizes Heidegger for thinking being-in-the-world as being-in-the-truth, but being-in-the-truth one-sidedly in terms of language as revealing and clearing. Indeed concealment for Heidegger lies at the basis of revealment, but concealment belongs to Being "rather like shadows to light and not like lightless abysmal night" ("Welt und Geschichte" In *Husserl und das Denken der Neuzeit*. Den Haag 1959. 143–159, above all, 157).

49. Cf. Heinz-Horst Schreys report on Heidegger's lecture from 1927, "Phäno-menologie und Theologie": "Die Bedeutung der Philosophie Martin Heidegger für die Theologie" In *Martin Heideggers Einfluss auf die Wissenschaften*. Bern 1949. 9–21, above all, 12. For example. Rudolph Bultmann tries to show how a preliminary thinking toward revelation which does not alter the fact that it is not at one's disposal is possible in "Der Begriff der Offenbarung im Neuen Testament" (published in 1929, reprinted in *Glauben und Verstehen, Gesammelte Aufsätze*. Band 3, Tübingen 1960).

310

311

50. René Char writes in the *Feuillets d'Hypnos* ("Aufzeichnungen aus dem Maquis 1943–44," translated by Paul Celan; cf. *René Char: Poésies/Dichtungen*. Frankfurt 1959. 124–125): "Agreement with the messenger [*dem Engel*], our primary concern. (The angel: This, the word spoken in the inner man by the highest silence, the meaning which supports no evaluation of any sort, keeps clear of every concession to the religious. The lungs-tuner which gilds the nourishing shoots of the impossible. If the blood knows, it knows nothing of heavenly things. The angel: The candle going down in the north of the heart)."

51. Consequently, the proofs of God's existence "would not be what is traditionally called "natural theology," but rather the attempts at an answer to the historical claim of the divine. In contrast to this, *theologia* would have to receive its validity from the Christian message as the decisive experience of the fact that the powers of the messenger—as it says in the margin of the gospel, in Jude's letter—have "abandoned their house," that they and the man who lets their power be powerful are left to their own power and thus have fallen out of the true life which always exists only as gift and task. This "fall" should certainly not be substantialized (as it happens in the gnosis); rather it must be understood historically (along with the new freedom as the Christian message claims to bring). Cf. Heinrich Schlier: *Mächte und Gewalten im Neuen Testament*. Freiburg -im-Breisgau 1958.

52. Heidegger's thinking appears to theology in a very different light. On the one side it is unmistakable that Heidegger's first work carries within it questions of speculative theology and that Heidegger took these questions farther along his way. Still, the course entitled *Der Satz vom Grund* (with its critique of the concept of *causa sui*) can be read as a contribution toward speculative theology. Above all, scholastically oriented philosophers and Catholic theologians seek to make this side in Heidegger's thinking fruitful for their questioning about Being and God. On the other side, Protestant theologians (like Bultmann and Gogarten in his later work) place Heidegger's critique of metaphysics and of all speculative theology into the foreground. In fact, the radically critical position toward the speculative theology of metaphysics is taken up in Heidegger's overcoming of metaphysics, and only from this critical position could Heidegger in *Sein und Zeit* refer to the theology renewed by Luther. The turn toward Nietzsche and Hölderlin, which Heidegger executed after *Sein und Zeit*, then had to face the question of whether Hölderlin's poetic-mythical *theology* preserves what is Christian or whether it takes a counter-position.

Recently, the central problem of the history of the Old Testament has been raised in (Protestant) theology. The relativization of the *context* of history, as Karl Barth worked it out under the impetus of Kierkegaard and as Bultmann did so with the help of Heidegger's early hermeneutic, is to be annulled (cf. *Offenbarung als Geschichte*, in conjunction with R. Rendtorff, U. Wilckens, T. Rendtorff. Edited by W. Pannenberg, Göttingen 1961). In the movement of these endeavors, the salvation history about which the Old Testament prophets speak has been equated with the history of clearing about which Heidegger speaks. In his essay "Heilgeschichte und Lichtungsgeschichte" (in *Evangelische Theologie*, 22 Jg. (vol.), 1962. 113–141), James M. Robinson writes: "One can consequently say that Heidegger, in principle (if not also in praxis), has prepared the way upon which Old Testament research, transcending the boundaries of its discipline, could achieve a central role in the theological and philosophical discussion of our day" (138). One cannot dismiss the question as to whether Heidegger's thinking (even if more indirectly) is co-determined by means of the tradition which begins with

312

the Old Testament, whether or not Heidegger himself considers this question to be of value. The simple equation of salvation history and the history of clearing shows only once more the perplexity of contemporary theology, and with this the lack of reflection with which what is thought is reinterpreted in order to be made serviceable for one's own purposes. Nonetheless, the decisive question remains whether Heidegger does not place himself against the Old Testament tradition (as the young Hegel had done in another way, and as Nietzsche had done in an entirely different way), because he turns toward Greek tragedy. The contrast **313** between Greek tragedy's conception of God and the Old Testament prophets' conception of God would first have to be brought into view before one could discuss appropriately what Heidegger does "in principle." Cf. note 39.

Chapter 10. The Question of Saying

53. Regarding the matter, cf. Hans Lipps: *Untersuchung zu einer hermeneutischen Logik*. Frankfurt-am-Main, 1938.

54. In *Sein und Zeit* Heidegger refers to the *Psychologie der Weltanschaungen* by Karl Jaspers as a work which manifests the possibilities of existential analyses as an "existential anthropology" (cf. SuZ 301, 249, 338; also K 188f). To be sure Heidegger has also had to criticize this early work of Jaspers (in an unprinted larger discussion). Jaspers does not show how man enters into world views and attitudes; the world views are brought forward like patients in a clinic. A theoretical comportment permeates the book. Heidegger demands the overcoming of the opposition of theory and praxis, "ontology" and existentiell decision by means of a more primordially seminal thinking; he does not, however, demand the continuing use of the opposition nor the obliteration of what is different and opposed in praxis, nor does he permit philosophy to become "existentiell." In his later works, Jaspers yielded to this demand. In his well-known discussion with Rudolf Bultmann, he indeed asserts that there is no "existential analysis either as scientific knowledge or as earnest appropriation." the existential analysis is, if it is philosophical, simultaneously existentiell.

55. For a long time, no bridge appeared possible between logical positivism and linguistic-analytical philosophy on the one side and Heidegger's thinking on the other. Heidegger himself demanded this bridging in his dissertation, but never accomplished it himself. He also demands the examination of logic, above all Russell, in the overview *Neuere Forschungen zur Logik*. What he says there (570) is as valid today as it was fifty years ago: "Mathematics and the mathematical handling of logical problems reach the limits where concepts and methods break down, and it is exactly there where the conditions of its possibility lie. It is of value to accomplish the work first sketched out here, and it will not be accomplished as quickly as the overcoming of psychologism." Attempts at the mediation between Heidegger's hermeneutical phenomenology and logical positivism (as, for example, Oskar Becker undertook in note 36 of the aforementioned work) seem to relate **314** what is entirely disparate. Rudolf Carnap's essay "Überwindung der Metaphysik durch logische Analyse der Sprache" in *Erkenntnis*. Edited by R. Carnap and H. Reichenbach. 2 Band, Leipzig 1931. 219–241, above all, 229ff, expresses an opposition incapable of foreseeing the possibility of a common concern. Heidegger's discussion of the dissolution of the idea of "logic" appears here not as an allusion to the necessity of reflecting upon the problem of logic and language, but rather as an indication of a flight in face of logic into a "metaphysics" which is

nothing but an expression of an attunement to life. Still, the problems themselves (above all the problem of the hierarchy of metalanguages) must lead the neo-positive and linguistic-analytical reflection upon logic and language which is radically carried out (for instance, in Wittgenstein's later work and in the semiotics of Charles Morris) to the possibility of confronting an attempt which tries to think the occurring of truth as the occurring of language. Cf. Karl Otto Apel, "Sprache und Wahrheit in der gegenwärtigen Situation der Philosophie. Eine Betrachtung anlässlich der Vollendung der neopositivischen Sprachphiloso-phie in der Semiatik von Charles Morris" in *Philosophische Rundschau*. 7 Jg. (vol.), Tübingen 1959. 161–184.

56. Johannes Lohmann has shown in detail how subjectivity prevails in Hellenism and forces a decisive transformation of the conception of truth. Cf. his various works in the periodical, *Lexis*, edited by him (1948ff).

57. If we note that Heidegger's thinking, after the shattering of *Sein und Zeit*, ever more decisively takes up the task of bringing up the proper concern for discussion by emplacing the basic words of Western thought, then we can give (what Heidegger himself did not do) still a second meaning to the term "topol-ogy": topology is a determination of abode, the Saying of the abode of truth as the collecting which places, as the gathering (*logos*) in the basic and guiding words (*topoi*) of thinking. It raises the question as to whether a first approach to this topology is not found in the topic which reaches from Aristotle and from Cicero to Vico and which has decisively left its mark (if not so much on metaphysics, then still) upon rhetoric, philology, jurisprudence, and theology. According to tradi-tional understanding, topical thinking does not yield the true which is inter-changeable with constantly present Being, but rather only the probable, the ἔνδοξα or *versimilia*. But of shining forth and self-concealing was to belong essentially to truth, and the truth was to be true-appearance [*Wahr-Schein*] in its primordiality, topical thinking could no longer be devalued because it conveys "only the probable." Cf. my discussion of the book *Der Satz vom Grund* (*Philosophis-cher Literaturanzeiger*, 11. Band, Stuttgart 1958. 241–251), as well as the work "Dichtungstheorie und Toposforschung" in *Jahrbuch für Aesthetik und allgemeine Kunstwissenschaft*, Band V. Köln 1960. 89–201, "Sein als Ereignis" In *Zeitschrift für philosophische Forschung*, 13 Band. Meisenheim 1959. 597–632, above all 629ff, "Metaphysik und Seinstopik bei Heidegger" In *Philosophisches Jahrbuch*, 70 Jg. Freiburg and München 1962. 118–137. Cf. further note 55 of the aforementioned essay by Karl Otto Apel.

315

In terms of recent "critical" philosophy, emplacing thinking would have to be characterized as meta-critical. Hamann, in his meta-critique of Kant, has lent currency to the fact that the highest and final purification of reason, the purifica-tion of language, could not be achieved; language is rather the organon and criterion of reason, yet language is historical. This account of language which was developed by Herder and Humboldt, and in another way by modern linguistics, would have to be thought along with the transcendental-philosophical approach, above all with Hegel's attempted potentiation of transcendental philosophy in the *Phenomenologie des Geistes* when he not only asked about the conditions of the possibility of the experience of objects, but in a preliminary way after the possible modes of experience in general.

Afterword to the Second Edition

Only in special cases can one rework a book published twenty years ago in a way that will once again bring it up to date. This problem becomes unsolvable when the theme of the work was a philosophical enterprise which had not yet achieved closure, which in addition had a manifold influence, and which had to and indeed still must come into view after decisive considerations. In this case, an afterword can justify the new edition by noting not only that the book is still in demand and is still being translated into various languages, but also that it follows a specific approach that has not been taken up again with the same consequences. This approach attempted to retrace the individual steps by which Heidegger upon the way of his own thinking examined the traditional ways of philosophy and tried to lead the philosophizing of our time toward its task. Discussion about a path of thinking understood in this sense avoids elucidating a developmental history on the basis of a guiding motif, orienting itself toward a specific goal, or even portraying it merely historically as a movement that is systematically, so to speak, without results. In the meantime, the "way of thinking" of other philosophers has become a matter for discussion. One asks whether merely a heuristic meaning should be ascribed to the way or whether philosophizing proceeds from the fact that its matter is not given at all without the way, that perhaps this matter in fact vanishes in the realization of a way which is without end and which manifests changing perspectives. Heidegger himself placed the motto, "Ways—not works," at the head of the collected edition of his works. He thereby claimed a plurality of ways for his thinking. In any case, the way or the ways of Heidegger concern the way or the ways of philosophy; Heidegger is a thinker of epochal significance.

Philosophers of epochal significance bring a new vision to intellectual endeavors which can then be taken up in ever new variations, which can be tested, refuted, circumscribed, and modified. Thus the Western history of thinking could be apprehended in its entirety as a series of footnotes to Plato. Did not Plato, by means of his theory of ideas, oblige thinking to grasp what is in accordance with its lawfulness and then to bring the forms of lawfulness into a hierarchical totality? Ammonios Sakkas lectured in Alexandria, and his pupil Plotinus went on to win the Roman public, hungry for education and salvation, over to "Neoplatonism" with his talks; thus another side of Platonic thinking came into play, the ascent of the soul beyond all diverse matters toward that which is divine or toward Being, truth, and the One. Consequently, the footnotes to Plato represent at the same time a quarrel about the question as to what the true

Plato genuinely is. As Plato's greatest pupil, Aristotle said what later became a proverb: *Plato amicus, magis amica veritas.* In his critique of Plato, perhaps Aristotle places the theory of ideas within an inappropriate perspective; in any case, this physician's son shows that life is activity and that here under the changing moon it is a self-reliant practical philosophy which must initiate man into his life. This practical and political philosophy may be weighed down with matters which we can scarcely understand—for example, with the notion that some human beings are slaves by nature and with the alignment of the human community to the polis at a time when Alexander (Aristotle's pupil) constructed a world empire. Yet after the *Nichomachean Ethics* moved into the foreground, Aristotle's work could become for one who philosophizes something like a homeland from which to begin. Two thousand years after Plato and Aristotle, Kant from another perspective played the philosophy of Aristotle as the work of analysis off against the Platonic-Neoplatonic rapture over the ascent of the soul and its participation in the divine. Kant tried to conform to the task of philosophy in a transformed constellation by means of a new vision; that is, he asked about the *a priori* elements in knowledge (or in rationally orientated praxis as well). There should not be only an analytic *a priori* and an *a posteriori*, but a synthetic *a priori* as well. Kant's vision may have foundered in that there is indeed a correspondence, for instance, between the substance-accident relation and certain judgements, but hardly the relation asserted by Kant between judgements and the basic concepts as a whole. The attempt to question further with Kant the *a priori* elements in knowledge remains uninfluenced by such criticism. It is another question whether by means of this attempt one can also take up the manner in which Fichte, Kant's protest notwithstanding, and then Schelling and Hegel took up the transcendental approach and—as Hegel formulated it—grasped the substance of classical philosophy as subject.

Along with and in opposition to Plato and Aristotle, Kant and Hegel, Heidegger tried to determine anew in the twentieth century, that is, in a time of world-historical catastrophes and radical transformations, what philosophy is and can be. The title of epochally significant, great philosopher cannot be denied Heidegger if the usual procedure so ardently suggested by those who would like to pose externally as the directors of a politics of research is employed, that is, if one counts the publications in which works of Heidegger appear in relevant places or are discussed (Heidegger, then, would certainly not yet have been a great philosopher when he wrote *Sein und Zeit*). Given such tallies, one can still speak in the learned reviews of an old academy of Husserl, Heidegger, and Sartre as the popular philosophical writers of our century. Yet in the case of Heidegger, one can validly assert that by means of *Sein und Zeit* he decisively altered the significant phenomenological philosophy of Husserl and Scheler, that due to Oskar Becker he brought along the way with him a philosophy of mathematics and through Bultmann a new theology, and that with new impetus he later, above all, decisively determined continental European philosophy. To be sure, in all of these effects the dispute about what was ultimately at issue in Heidegger's thinking remained. When Heidegger allowed a star to be placed upon his tombstone, one asks what word he used to address this star toward which he had wanted to travel. Nonetheless, the title *Sein und Zeit* was only a sign on the way. Heidegger believed that one could no longer follow the classical philosophy which addressed Being as substance and which related substances to a supreme, divine being beyond further examination. In the attempt of recent philosophy to constitute an ultimate, secure way of access to beings in self-consciousness, Heidegger saw only a reformulation of the first approach. Yet these approaches had become questionable through the discovery of the evolution of life and even more through experiencing the historicality of the human being. Heidegger was thus concerned not only about Being as the truth of beings and about its relation to time but also about the truth of Being itself as appropriative event and as the clearing for the self-concealing. Is it these words, "appropriative event" and "clearing," which walk alongside words like "idea," "substance," and "transcendental" and in two hundred or two thousand years will even be able to guide philosophical reflection? If we look upon Heidegger's work, we see that the guiding words not only replace one another, but that along the various stretches of the way they will also be determined in ever new and different ways.

Thus for the sake of our own and of future philosophizing, it is as necessary now as before to ask about the steps which Heidegger has taken upon the way or ways of his thinking. Yet with this new edition of my early attempt, I do not wish to evade the question as to how I would approach this attempt today. I would also like to respond to the question often asked as to whether I have justifiably allowed Heidegger's entanglement in politics to remain unconsidered. Finally, I feel that for proper use of the book, one must note that with its specific perspective the work belongs in a definite position vis-à-vis the effect of Heidegger's thinking.

I

In the fifties, when philosophy and theology again sought an alliance after the great catastrophe, Heidegger often told a story about his fellow countryman, Konrad Gröber (rector of the Constance seminary and city pastor, later archbishop of Freiburg). In 1907 after Heidegger transferred from the gymnasium in Constance to the one in Freiburg, Gröber gave him Franz Brentano's dissertation about the manifold meaning of being in Aristotle. Brentano's fledging work, supported by the outline *Vom Sein* by the Freiburg theologian Braig, became Heidegger's entrance into philosophy. In the *Gespräch von der Sprache* (Sp 92f), Heidegger refers a Japanese guest to the fourth stanza of Hölderlin's hymn to the Rhine which says that birth and the ray of light which meets the newborn enable more than need and breeding. Was the doctrine of the manifold sense of "Being" such a ray of light which remained decisive even in the need of the time and in the proliferation of philosophical schools? According to Heidegger's interpretation of Hölderlin, birth for the Rhine is birth from the earth. The ray of light is the flash into which the essence of the leading god, Zeus, gathers itself. Semele, who desires to see the god, is consumed in its flash, yet Dionysos is born from the ashes of the incinerated. *The Bacchae* of Euripides shows in the work of Dionysos what a cultural revolution is. Yet this god also assigns to the poets the task of presenting to the people the divine fire enveloped in song. By referring to Brentano's dissertation, Heidegger does not want to give the impression that in 1907 he already knew what he asked about later. Yet it is doubtless Heidegger's conviction that with the question about Being he contributed to an epochal revolutionary transformation.

It may be that the differences, such as those among that-it-is, what-it-is and being-true in the use of the "is" as a copula, were prefigured in existential assertion and in uses such as "It is the case that . . ." However, medieval Aristotelianism had loosened (even by its use of Latin) Greek thought from its linguistic roots and had tried to develop it conceptually. In the 1935 lecture course *Einführung in die Metaphysik*, Heidegger asked whether specific historical-linguistic presuppositions in Indo-European, and especially in the Greek language, had not led philosophy to find its first and last question in a question of Being and then, perhaps, to fail. Heidegger's allusions have since been supplemented, corrected, and carried on from the philosophical as well as from the linguistic side. Charles H. Kahn, for example, brought the multifaceted research to a representative result in his 1973 investigation, *The Verb Be in Ancient Greek*.[i] In his view the Greek language prepared the way for philosophy in an auspicious way. However, in the *Philosophische Rundschau* (Vol. 24, 1977, pp. 161–176), Ernst Tugendhat discussed Kahn's results critically. According to Tugendhat linguistic presuppositions upset and misled philosophy. He maintains that to accept thinking as being impressed by language is

i. Kahn, C. H. *The Verb Be in Ancient Greek*. Holland: Reidel Publishing Co., 1973.

indeed the most ominous counter-enlightenment, and that in our century only Neo-Scholasticism and then Heidegger determined and contaminated philosophizing with a talk of Being that was barely scrutinized. As a matter of fact, it must be asked whether in talk about Being or about an ultimate "there is" the speculative tradition is not united with a hermeneutic tendency in such a way that truth appears as an occurring or as an inescapable "destiny." Nevertheless, instead of characterizing discourse about Being positively or negatively with mythologizing images or with slogans of ideological struggle, one should establish exactly how Heidegger makes use of this discourse in the various steps of his way. He proceeds from medieval Aristotelianism in order to surpass it quickly. The orientation toward the "I am" is attained then only beyond a breach, but is then decisively transformed in discourse about Being as appropriative event and then once more in terms of the problem of nihilism. These notions are to be contrasted with one another and then distinguished in turn from Kant's transcendental logic or from a nominalistically constructed ontology.

As the son of a sacristan from Messkirch, Heidegger was destined to become a theologian. If the gymnasium student received Brentano's dissertation as a gift, then it was given with reference to his study of Catholic theology which began with an introduction to scholastic philosophy. When Heidegger gave up theology after four semesters, it was not due to a turning away from it (in an autobiographical statement, he accounts for his change of study by noting that a heart problem made him unfit for the difficult duties of a spiritual career). After the end of his course of study, Heidegger even took over the administration of philosophical instruction for Catholic theologians. His *Frühe Schriften* (collected in the meantime) show that he appropriated scholastic Aristotelianism in its entire breadth. The essay entitled "Das Realitätsproblem in der modernen Philosophie" uses Külpe's critical realism against the phenomenalism [*Konszientialismus*] which follows Hume and against that of Kant. Geyser's work also introduces "Aristotelian-scholastic philosophy which has always thought in a realistic manner." Heidegger's closest teachers also provided references which led him further along; Braig, still in the spirit of the Tübingen Catholic theological school, led him to Hegel's and Schelling's significance for theology, and Krebs led him to medieval mysticism by means of works still important today. Support could be found in Husserl for objectivism and the differentiation of regions of Being—for example, of what is real and of being-true as validity. The work concerning the problem of reality speaks against Kant and rejects Hegel in whose thinking Idealism attempts to do entirely too much. Neo-Kantianism then brought Kant and even Fichte ever nearer. In the work of Lask,

Heidegger found a bond between Husserl and his new teacher, Rickert, and thus between Aristotle and Kant. Knowledge is seen in terms of judgement, and the possible employment of the categories is extended to the universe of the thinkable. If categories are not only the form for sensory matter but they also relate to beings and to what is valid, then they become the form of form, and in the delimiting of validity they even become the form of the form of the form (as Heidegger says in his report, *Neuere Forschungen über Logik*).

However, the young Heidegger is also concerned with concrete theoretical questions of science. In the gymnasium at Freiburg, a teacher had introduced him to the more difficult tasks of mathematics; later he became interested in evolutionary theory. Thus when he left the theological faculty, he studied philosophy along with mathematics and natural science. Only at the end of his studies did teachers like Finke (and Vöge) awaken in him an understanding for history. His *Habilitationsschrift* mentions Dilthey along with Rickert and Simmel "in relation to the *characteristic right* of individualizing sciences." When he along with Dilthey refers to Dun Scotus, the *Doctor subtilis*, as "the sharpest mind of all scholastics," he is obviously quoting the essay regarding historical-developmental pantheism which corresponds to volume two of the *Gesammelte Schriften*. This appeared in 1914 as the first volume of the Dilthey edition (page 321 of course speaks of the "sharpest mind of all scholastics"). The *Habilitation* lecture with its motto from Meister Eckhart's sermon, *Consideravit domum*, takes Rickert's distinction between the validity of value (in time and history) and the "eternal" validity of value back into that metaphysical understanding of time and eternity as Plotinus had delineated it. A review of the book of Nikolai von Bubnoff regarding *Zeitlichheit und Zeitlosigkeit* does again attempt to tie together the temporal reality of sensible perception with the timelessness of abstract thinking by reaching back to the old cliché about the opposition between Heraclitus and Parmenides. Bergson, who in the year of Heidegger's birth had finally made such harmonizations obsolete with his essay on time and freedom, is also evaluated in Heidegger's dissertation as a one-sidedly oriented Heraclitean thinker.

The summary which Heidegger appended to his *Habilitationsschrift* not only grasped scholasticism and mysticism as complementary sides of the "medieval worldview," but it also referred to Novalis, Friedrich Schlegel, and Hegel's "system of a historical world view." In Easter of 1917, Heidegger gave as a gift (with a Greek motto from Plato's *Laws* 728 C) Hermann Süskind's book, *Christentum und Geschichte bei Schleiermacher* (1911). Following Troeltsch in a "free Christianity," this book made the absoluteness of Christianity, which was still asserted by Schleiermacher, into the highest form of truth given us, and in this way it entered into history. At the beginning of August, 1917, Heidegger gave a lecture to a private group about the problem of that which is religious in Schleiermacher (above all, in connection with the second of the *Reden über Religion*). These few testimonies show that those tendencies which are known to us, for example, from the circle around Franz Rosenzweig in Freiburg and Heidelberg, had reached Heidegger somewhat late. These were the tendencies to answer the ideas of 1800 in a creative manner with the ideas of 1900. (Heidegger owned Rosenzweig's edition of the "oldest systematic program" of 1917, but said that he could "never reconcile himself with the notion": "Text by Schelling, notes by Hegel.") As in Rosenzweig's circle, this attempt led Heidegger to distance himself from his own origin and above all led to the decisive breach with the Idealistic tradition. On January 9, 1919, Heidegger explained to his patron, the Freiburg theologian Krebs, why he could no longer be responsible for the philosophical instruction for Catholic theologians: "Epistemological insights encroaching upon the theory of historical knowledge have made the system of Catholicism problematic and unacceptable to me—but not Christianity and metaphysics (these, of course, in a new sense) . . ."

To be sure, this distancing from the theological origin signified a radicalization rather than a turning away from theology. Heidegger repeatedly emphasized the fact that the Second World War had confirmed what alert minds (the greatest importance then surely belonged to Dostoevsky) had made visible long ago, that is, that the guiding representations or "values" of the European tradition had become powerless. When Spengler spoke of the decline of the West, Heidegger sought to grasp this decline as such and thereby as a possible transition. Bergson, Dilthey, and Jaspers provided important stimuli for this attempt, but more decisive for Heidegger was the fact that at that time theology rediscovered the eschatology of primordial Christian religion; it thereby took leave both of a Platonizing Christianity in Schleiermacher's sense and of Ritschl's brand of Kantianism. It is not known what in particular Heidegger studied at that time—indeed the breakthrough to the eschatology of primordial Christianity covered a broad spectrum extending, for example, from Albert Schweitzer's trust in the historical tradition about Jesus to the form-historical method which pushed toward breaking up the historical reality of the New Testament tidings into the details of literary formation. (There were also the popular, sensational endeavors, such as Arthur Drews' pseudo-romantic *Christus Mythe* of 1909. In his later years, Heidegger still identified with a secure grasp a casually mentioned variety of adventist faith as an after-effect of Drews, i.e., the returning Christ as an Orion with outstretched arms on the tree of the cosmos, the Milky Way.) In his lecture course on phenomenology entitled *Grundprobleme der*

Phänomenologie, held in the winter of 1919–20, Heidegger began with the fact that the factical, historical life had been discovered in the primordially Christian religion. This discovery then had to make its way by violent eruptions against the infiltration of Greek conceptualization in Augustine and in the medieval mystics, in the young Luther and in Kierkegaard. Heidegger bases philosophy upon what religion discovered among the specific "mythological" representations which have become foreign to us, that the final or ultimate things manifest themselves to man in a moment which remains beyond our control. Yet, does not such a notion give up the philosophy oriented to substance and essence, or that which is in search of secure self-certainty?

Along with Oskar Becker, Heidegger had become one of Husserl's assistants, and the latter's phenomenology now appeared as the possibility of a radical new beginning which even left Neo-Kantianism behind. It has often been reported that according to Husserl, phenomenology at that time was to have consisted of Husserl himself and Heidegger; for example, in a large work about Aristotle, Heidegger wanted to explain his manner of philosophizing phenomenologically. At the same time, he enthusiastically took up Dilthey, and the friendship with Jaspers was solidified in an assimilation of the latter's *Psychologie der Weltanschauungen* in which Jaspers had not only alluded to Kierkegaard, but had also viewed human life as existence in terms of boundary situations. The phenomenology of life, as Heidegger spoke of it in his lectures at the time, appeared to have its only true rival in that dialectic which followed Hegel. Heidegger frequently explained his opinion that the withdrawn Hegel book, with which Julius Ebbinghaus had habilitated with Husserl in 1921, had done a better job at making Hegel's dialectic visible than the explication of the Hegelian system in Richard Kroner's book, *Von Kant bis Hegel*. As the son of that Hermann Ebbinghaus who had confronted and so sharply attacked Dilthey on the basis of psychology, Julius Ebbinghaus was the idea of his father in his otherness—this according to Driesch's formulation at that time when he was a Hegelian. In his dissertation at Heidelberg, he explained that the Kantian formulation of the problem of categories ultimately led to Fichte and Hegel, that is, to the reciprocal action between unity and multiplicity, the I and the not-I. This "dialectic" was set forth in a work about Hegel's development up to the Jena years, a work which was to be more philosophical than Dilthey's paraphrases. Yet at the book's printing, Ebbinghaus believed that he was on the wrong track when, for example, the ultimate grounding he used a category itself needed justification. (The well-known dissertation by Klaus Reich who, like Ebbinghaus, turned back to a strict Kantianism, arose from a seminar with Oskar Becker about the problematic particular and unlimited judgements.) In an autobiographical presentation, Ebbinghaus talks about his friendship with Heidegger: "He had received, I no longer know from whom or for what reason, the Erlangen edition of *Luther's* works as a prize or a gift—consequently, during our shared evenings we read for some time from *Luther's* reformation writings." (*Philosophie in Selbstdarstellungen*, edited by L. J. Pongratz, Volume III, Hamburg 1977, p. 33). From these readings there emerged a work, *Luther und Kant*, which Ebbinghaus published in 1927 in the Luther Yearbook. Like the philosopher, the reformer places man under one command, but Luther legitimizes the service of God from a revelation, historically rather than philosophically. Whether and how one is to bridge this hiatus between the philosophical and the historical remained Heidegger's question when he came to Marburg in 1923 and won the friendship of Rudolph Bultmann. Unlike Kierkegaard and Barth in his explanation of the letter to the Romans, both of whom presuppose a dialectic between the eternal and the temporal, Bultmann built New Testament theology anew from a present eschatology. Yet Heidegger felt increasingly compelled to hold theology in a methodological atheism far from philosophy, but without deciding the matter "existentielly." Heidegger was called to Marburg in order to advocate phenomenological philosophy alongside Aristotle and Medieval philosophy: instead of the planned book on Aristotle he published *Sein und Zeit* in 1927.

The phenomenology of life, which Heidegger lectured about in his early Freiburg courses, is presented *in nuce* also in his review of Jaspers which, in the meantime, has become generally available in the new edition of the anthology entitled *Wegmarken*. Life is factical; it must understand itself historically from its particular situation. Even if Bergson and Dilthey speak about this life and Jaspers develops it as existence by means of Kierkegaard and boundary situations, one cannot yet say that the philosophical mode of access has also been adequately worked out. Jaspers may even appear more as a moralist, but his access to existence could still be considered "aesthetic," that is, contemplative. At the end of his review, Heidegger especially emphasizes Kierkegaard's contribution to the discussion of method. Indirect communication, in which even a skeptic or aesthete can draw attention to the religious sphere, becomes the formal announcement, complete with "hermeneutical" concepts, which points to the existentiell realization of life; yet it keeps it outside itself (and this still never "aesthetically" mitigates this being-at-the-ready [*Auf-dem-Sprunge-sein*]; cf. this book, page 271f. refers to reinserted German pagination). One unjustifiably appeals too quickly to the principle: *Individuum est ineffabile*. In fact the concern is precisely in finding a way of addressing (*fari*) what is individuated. Here Heidegger believes that Husserl's phenomenology can make a contribution. According to Heidegger's opinion, Husserl freed the analysis of knowledge from the one-sided orientation to judgement (which even the young Heidegger had followed). He pointed to the pre-predicative (and enabled the post-predicative); consequently, in spite of the nonessential point of departure from logical or epistemological questions, he grasped intentionality as comportment-toward. If a sense of content, of performance, and of relation belong to life, then a phenomenology as a hermeneutic of this life must be a phenomenology of matter, of act, and correlation. Yet it may not overlook the fact that the mathematician can self-forgetfully lose himself in his matter by keeping within his specific sense of relation. However, the philosopher must bear in mind that for life seeking to find its origin, the sense of performance is arch-ontic [*archontisch*]. Here man is not a mere realization of a What in a coincidental That; his Being lies rather in a how-to-be which, as a being-in-time, temporalizes time and thus first opens itself in its That for a What. The lecture course in the summer of 1925, published under the title, *Prolegomena zur Geschichte des Zeitbegriffs*, reproaches Husserl for again misplacing the breakthrough of phenomenology contained in the *Logische Untersuchungen* by taking up in the *Ideen* the preju-dices of the Platonic-Cartesian tradition for the sake of his orientation toward science.

If Heidegger takes Husserl's phenomenology as a radical new begin-ning of philosophizing, he also transforms it right from the start. In looking back along his way, Heidegger held that "the self-manifesting phenomenon" had been thought more primordially by Aristotle and the Greeks in *Alethia* than by Husserl (*Zur Sache des Denkens*, Niemeyer, Tübingen 1969. p. 87). The young Heidegger wanted to exhibit his way of phenomenological philosophizing not in terms of Plato and Kant, but rather from Aristotle. Yet we should not imagine that Heidegger arrived at his question about Being through constant meditation about the doctrine of a multifaceted Being. Had the "phenomenological interpreta-tion of Aristotle" actually appeared in 1923 in Husserl's Yearbook, it would have had the following contents: "The first part (about 15 sheets) concerns Nichomachean Ethics Z, Metaphysics A.1.2., Physics A.8; the second part (about the same size) Metaphysics ZHO, *De motu an.*, *De anima*; the third part to appear later." (Hans-Georg Gadamer quotes this passage from a letter of Heidegger from that time: *Heideggers Wege*. 1983, p. 118.) In addition, *Sein und Zeit* (p. 225) and the foreword to *Heidegger* by W. J. Richardson (The Hague, Martenus Nijhoff, 1963), mention both the sixth book of the *Nichomachean Ethics* and the ninth book of *Metaphysics* as decisive texts. In addition a *logos* and a relation of truth are granted in the first place to situationally bound praxis. This situation was then honed into *Chairos* in Christian eschatology. (*Die Grundprobleme der Phänomenologie* of 1927 attributes the discovery of *Chairos* directly to the sixth book of the *Nichomachean Ethics*; nonetheless, this discovery had been concealed again in favor of determining time from the "now" in accordance with a specific ontological option; p. 409). The disputed conclusion of the ninth book of the *Metaphysics* thinks Being and truth in the breadth that Heidegger seeks it. If Aristotle's *hermeneutics* brings into relief the judgement of forms as of the request [*Bitte*] by attributing to it a relation to "true" and "false," then according to Heidegger's opinion since that time, this does not mean that truth itself is viewed in terms of judgement (the *Rhetoric* also exhibits the disclosing power of moods). However, Heidegger does differentiate the apophantic As of the judgement or statement by which something is taken as something—the table as brown—from a hermeneutical As by which a hammer, for example, is taken as being too heavy in a context of significance and reference such as the carpenter's workshop (or indeed, by which existing grasps itself as existence). Can one not interpret the differentiated As in terms of a differentiated temporalization; that is, can one not assign to the ecstasies of Dasein's temporalizing of itself far-reaching schemata such as this As; from the differentiated unified activity of these schemata can one not then make distinctive ways of Being intelligible such as being-present-at-hand, being-ready-to-hand, and existential Being? In the winter of 1925–26, Heidegger abruptly broke off his planned interpretation of Aristotle in his logic course and switched to an interpretation of Kant's doctrine of schematism, in which time-related schemata refer to the categories.

In the winter of 1927–28, Heidegger remarked retrospectively that some years ago—in connection with the course from 1925–26—when he read Kant against the background of Husserl's phenomenology (*Phänomenologische Interpretation von Kants Kritik der reinen Vernunft*: 1977. p. 431), it was as if scales had fallen from his eyes. Husserl had also treated immanent time-consciousness in a famous lecture course in the winter of 1904–05; there he distinguished impression from retention and both of these from protension. Heidegger believed that, like Kant, he could grasp these moments as apprehension, reproduction, and recognition, and thereby as moments of the imagination understood as the common root of sensibility and understanding. It appears that the three dimensions of time (present, past, and future) can be related to the three basic moments of Dasein (articulation, state-of-mind, understanding). Section 69 of *Sein und Seit* arranges the ecstasics in which Dasein stands out into the three dimensions of time toward far-reaching schemata like As, In-face-of-which, At-which, For-the-sake-of, and Toward-which. From the interplay of these schemata, the sense of Being is then to be analyzed into exemplary modes of Being. If the For-the-sake-of-which of the authentic future as an anticipation of death becomes a manageable and ensurable toward-this, then we fall from the world of the last things into the world of a workman who seeks to eke out a living by means of his work. The hermeneutical As of the worker is modified into the apophantic As of pure scientific research even if the Toward-which still loses its leading force, etc. The lecture course of summer, 1925, promises for the third division of *Sein und Zeit* another conceptual interpretation of time which is to lead to the differentiation of the Being of nature and history on the basis of differentiated temporalness. In the course of the following semester and in the working out of section 69 of *Sein und Zeit*, the doctrine of schemata advances into the foreground; it can now become the core for the third part of *Sein und Zeit*. At the beginning of *Die Grundprobleme der Phänomenologie* from the summer of 1927, Heidegger makes a marginal remark in which he calls this course "a new conception of the third division of the first part of *Sein und Zeit*." Since the course was not carried out according to plan, it in no way "realized"—as the afterword of the editor says—the "central thematic" of the mentioned third division; instead near its conclusion he presents the new development of this division only in embryonic form (p. 1, 472, 431 ff.). In the essay *Der Satz vom Grund*, the "temporal interpretation" has already been set aside for the time being. In his discussion with Cassirer, Heidegger not only won the approval of youth, but he also surely realized that a hasty grasp of the doctrine of schematism would not bring the *Kritik der reinen Vernunft* as a whole into view. Even Scheler had said (about the concept of schema of the biological doctrine of the environment) that recent mechanistic physics follows a schema, that is, a biologically relative *a priori* belonging to man who understands himself as *homo faber*. Could such schematizations of the view of the world actually be comprehended by the formalism of the schemata which Heidegger developed? The plan of the third division of *Sein und Zeit* had changed even during the working out of the book; the new conception was soon not only laid aside but given up completely.

The present book indeed correctly portrays Heidegger's way to *Sein und Zeit* to the extent that it shows that the entrance into metaphysics became problematic through the experience of history; that from this problematization, the question about Being and time was formed, and phenomenology, just as metaphysics was ultimately, was undercut by a hermeneutical approach. Yet this book also levels out the details of the important steps. For example, Dilthey's assimilation is viewed immediately in terms of the Dilthey-Yorck correspondence, although this correspondence did not appear until 1923. In addition, the early lecture course, but also *Sein und Zeit*, and even later remarks are brought into play for Augustine. Eschatological motives are mentioned as stimuli, but it is never shown what happened when Heidegger, the passionate Freiburg reader of Luther, encountered Bultmann in Marburg. In fact, I began with the fact that these early stimuli in the meantime led to elaborate theologies (not only to a theology in Bultmann's sense but also to the fact that a concrete concept of history was contrasted to this theology from the Old Testament; the biblical theology was confronted with the theology of Greek tragedy and of Hölderlin). I was not interested in first impulses, but rather in their elaborations. Nevertheless, present demand is that the earlier work not be mixed with the later. The present portrayal could above all lead to the misunderstanding that in Heidegger a relation to history travels *alongside* his entrance into metaphysics before these two ways merged into the question about Being and time. Yet the plan for his book on Aristotle can show precisely that that metaphysical teleology fell, that teleology in which the soul directs itself toward a transcendence, that is, to an "external" God which then allows distinct regions of Being—for example, reality and ideal Being or being true—to converge. Throughout the twenties, one finds in Heidegger the impulse of an "existence-philosophy" since he seeks to grasp the relation to Being or the transcendental dimension of origin as factical-historical life or existence. In conjunction with Kant, Husserl himself aids in emphasizing the unity in the multiplicity of Being in the new conception of the third division of *Sein und Zeit* and thereby in allowing phenomenology to ask again about metaphysics. The genealogy of Being striven for in *Sein und Zeit* keeps unity and multiplicity together by orienting the multiplicity toward a guiding mode of Being (*pros hen*) and trying to find this guiding mode from the exemplary Being of a distinctive being, Dasein. In the course on Aristotle from the summer of 1931, he gives up on this orientation to "analogy" because it covers over the openness of the history of Being. Heidegger now no longer finds the guiding meaning of Being in general with Brentano and the philosophy of substance in *ousia*, but rather in *energeia*. If the latter is no longer conceived of as *entelecheia*, then as being-at-work it can point along with appropriating (*dynamis*) to the appropriative event and be interpreted as the reverberation of an early experience of *physics*.

II

Can one portray Heidegger's later paths of thinking without taking into consideration Heidegger's political entanglement? I had wanted to learn from Heidegger. Since I had studied history and even law for a time, I looked for nothing from Heidegger in this sphere. I also found a good reason to omit political questions altogether. In conversation, Heidegger confessed his political error of 1933 and decisively put it at a distance. Still, it appeared that one could still learn that precisely the unprotected radicality of the questioning together with the rejection of everything that endures had been able to lead right into the noose of what is contemporary. Did not that pestilence against which thinking sought help have its origin in this thinking itself? With this question in mind, I along with Heidegger himself referred to Oedipus (p. 226f.). When I shared this thought with Heidegger in a conversation about his political entanglement, he (who always so bitterly rejected, for example, the wrongful accusations about his attitude toward Husserl) expressed the following opinion: If you comprehend it so—Yes! With that these things were settled for me, then. Today the question certainly appears to me indispensable, whether or not this answer contains a reclamation of tragic greatness, which in truth does not finish with what happened. Was it not through a definite orientation of his thinking that Heidegger fell—and not merely accidentally—into the proximity of National Socialism without ever truly emerging from this proximity? With Kierkegaard and with the young Luther he had tried to break through a thousand-year-old dissimulation. Then he followed Nietzsche who—already in *Die Geburt der Tragödie*—sought historical greatness and promordiality and as the transition to this took up the tragic downfall. (A parallel criticism of contempory issues of the times, which was developed from Marx, could ultimately link up with Heidegger's assessment, but in my opinion it had no genuine significance for Heidegger himself.) Yet did not the way in which tragic greatness was sought also provide room for National Socialism even if the *Nibelungen* loyalty was not confirmed? There were thoughts of leader and master race even in Carlyle, and various styles of Anti-Semitism as Anti-Capitalism can also be found in French Socialism (in this vein there arose in France references to the soil of the homeland). Only in Germany could such thoughts succeed in stabilizing a revolution and in letting loose the struggle for world domination. There the defeat of the First World War had not been assimilated, and one wanted to rectify this defeat and not become a small insignificant part in the newly arising world civilization with its manifold problems and its despised modernity.

The talks which Heidegger held as the rector of Freiburg together with individual testimony are unambiguous: they vow loyalty to Hitler as the leader, because he is seen as the savior of Germany; they see the truth of Being, which is the truth for a people, occurring in a National Socialist revolution; they demand Germany's withdrawal from the League of Nations, honor Schlageter as the new martyr in whom the primordial rock of the Black Forest gets its chance to speak, and so forth. To be sure, the conclusion already of Heidegger's rector's address requires that all leadership grant "individual strength" to those who follow, that all following carry within itself a resistance, and that the opposition be settled in battle. Soon the discourse is no longer about the leader as the law of the German people, but rather about Hölderlin and the gods of the people, the "new" gods of the Germans. Did not those near him have to believe that Heidegger moved from one extremity to another? Heidegger wrote to Jaspers on November 20, 1931, that after the "doubtful" success of *Sein und Zeit*, he drew back into the "role of a curator in a gallery," who takes care to see that "the few great works of the tradition have some measure of orderly illumination for the spectator who casually hastens by." Jaspers recounts the Freiburg rector's Heidelberg lecture of June, 1933, in his biography: "He demanded total transformation of the spiritual essence. The majority of professors now holding positions are not up to the task. In ten years, a new generation of more capable *docents* will be brought into play; then we would relinquish our positions to them . . ." Heinrich Buhr reports (*Erinnerung an Martin Heidegger*, edited by G. Neske, Verlag Neske, Pfullingen, 1977. p. 53f) that in 1933 Heidegger spoke at a National Socialist training school in Todtnauberg against the Christian "depreciation, contempt, and denial of the world." He also offered Buhr, a theologian, a promotion on condition that he decide "in favor of what is greater," for philosophy and against theology; yet by the end of 1935, Heidegger said: You are right. Stay with your theology!"

Testimonies such as this make it clear that Heidegger himself had entered into a crisis of thinking and willing. The crisis which he saw approaching in the time of world war had now arrived for him in its entirety. On the one hand, Heidegger discontinued using the approach of *Sein und Zeit* which had made him the most famous of German philosophers, or else transformed it decisively in order to be able to grasp the formative forces in the need of the time and in the historical transition. On the other hand, Heidegger vacillated between the moving back into solitude or the restricting himself to philosophical reflection and thus hoping for a revolutionary effect. Bound up with the question of Being was yet another question: How is Being as the openness of beings realized in something which is "holy" that gives life a hold in the religious dimension? It had already been said of Heidegger long ago that like a fox he sweeps away the traces behind him with his tail, but in truth Heidegger has repeatedly provided important clues. Consequently, in the 1969–70 publication of his lecture, *Phänomenologie und Theologie* from 1927–28, Heidegger referred to the two friends, Overbeck and Nietzsche. The theologian Overbeck, whom Heidegger had already quoted in the Marburg discussions, established "the world-denying expectation of the end as the basic feature of what is originally Christian; at the same time

Nietzsche referred to Hölderlin in the *Ersten unzeitgemässen Betrachtungen*. One should not overlook the fact that *Sein und Zeit* does not only offer the historicality of Dasein as the key to a new theology, but it also explains this historicality as fate and destiny (with concepts which can most easily be derived from Greek tragedy). In the years of crisis after the publication of *Sein und Zeit*, there was a growing impetus to push toward overcoming the opposition between the methodological atheism of a phenomenological philosophy and a "positive" theology; among the factors which became significant or significant again were Eckhart and Hölderlin, the Amsterdam van Gogh exhibition, Walter F. Otto's book about the gods of Greece, and Cassirer's allusion to the overwhelming element of what is holy in myth.

Every historical breakthrough can rapidly get entangled in compromises which falsify it; it can thereby produce results which are directly opposed to what was originally sought. For example, Luther's revolution had certainly not sought merely the union of some princes with the city and University of Wittenberg and the new established church. Heidegger's case is different and especially bizarre. It was precisely in the years of his deepest crisis that the National Socialist Revolution confronted him. Not only this revolution itself, but precisely those who wanted to oppose it misled Heidegger to an involvement. In *Erinnerung an Heidegger* (p. 199), Georg Picht points out that the situation at that time was very unclear. He notes, for example, that even Eugen Rosenstock-Huessy wanted to add to his book about European revolution a postscript in which the National Socialist revolution appeared as the attempt of the Germans "to realize the dream of Hölderlin."

In the meantime, Heidegger's rector's address, *Die Selbstbehauptung der deutschen Universität*, was published again along with reflections from the year 1945 entitled *Das Rektorat*, 1933–34 (Vittorio Klostermann, Frankfurt am Main, 1983; Karl A. Moehling's contribution, "Heidegger and the Nazis" in Thomas Sheehan's anthology, *Heidegger. The Man and the Thinker*, Chicago, Precedent Publishing Co., 1981. pp. 31–43, gives reliable information regarding access to other important documents and the necessary dates). Heidegger begins his rector's address of May 27, 1933, by presenting the rector as the "leader" ["*Führer*"] and the teachers and students at the university as the "followers." Yet the leaders themselves must be those who are led—led by the mandate which is once again giving a destiny to the German people. This people has emerged into its futural history; above all the students are "on the march" and seeking "leaders" who would by word and deed clarify their destination. The university, "from science and through science," takes "the leaders and keepers of the destiny of the German people up in its education and cultivation" (p. 14ff). Consequently, the specialized sciences must by means of philosophy again become a knowledge which, like Prometheus, arises against and examines beings in totality. After the death of God discussed by Nietzsche and after the breakdown of the "decrepit culture of illusion," the German people again seek "greatness" in that they compare themselves with the greatness of the Greeks; yet greatness is guaranteed only by a "spiritual world" in which the spirit preserves the "strength of blood and soil." Such greatness always remains endangered; even knowledge is handed over to the superior power of destiny and must ultimately fail in face of it (pp. 11, 13, 19, 14, 11). In the text of 1945, Heidegger says (as he does in texts concerning de-Nazification proceedings, the proposal for emeritus status, and in the *Spiegel* conversation) that the First World War revealed that the powers which once led had lost their strength. In *Totale Mobilmachungen* and in *Arbeiter* Ernst Jünger spelled out what now determined history. Active nihilism as the new coining of Nietzsche's will to power appeared as the planetary reality in communism as well as in fascisim and "world democracy." The rector's address joined hope that in this most extreme peril the Germans could find the way back to their Western vocation with the National Socialist Revolution. If the opponents of National Socialism had pushed for taking over the rectorate in order to avoid the worst, Heidegger himself believed that he could steer the movement in the right direction. Even in 1945, Heidegger thought that while speaking of guilt, one must also speak of the guilt of those who did not seek "in a secret bond"—as he did himself—"to refine and to temper" the movement which had gained power (p. 25f). Immediately after the rector's address, the minister of culture quite accurately said to Heidegger that the address represented only a "private National Socialism," omitted racial thinking, and rejected the idea of political science. For this reason what did not belong together had to become disassociated during Heidegger's resignation. Heidegger's thinking was pushed into a byway and did not precisely take shape (as Heidegger had hoped) "in a developing fitting together of a specific behavior, from which what is primordial could have arisen once again" (p. 30f, 38f).

His Hölderlin course during the winter semester of 1934–35 resolutely criticized racial thinking and the falsification of the spirit as well as the assumption of poetizing and thinking by totalitarian politics. Yet it also complained along with Hölderlin: "Yet they cannot use me," "I am alone" (p. 136f). This means that this revolution should also have been my hour, but it travels other ways. In its concluding remarks the rector's address spoke of the "splendor" and "greatness" of the awakening in which "the new and youngest strength of the people" reaches out beyond what has become old and has already decided that the German people want to fulfill their historical mandate. The lecture course, *Einführung in die Metaphysik* (Summer, 1935), speaks of the "inner truth and greatness of N.S." (or "this movement" according to the printed version). At least at this one, much discussed passage it may be shown that Heidegger's way is clearly marked out, even if one may use the present editions sometimes only with additional information. Heidegger clearly distinguishes (p. 152 of the 1953 edition) the actual outer appearance of National Socialism and especially that of its so-called philosophy, from its inner truth and greatness about which Heidegger believes he knows from his own return to metaphysics. By referring to the Freiburg inaugural address and the rector's address, Heidegger once more ties this regress to the fate of the university and science but thus also with the "spiritual fate of the West." Europe lies in the "pincers" between Russia and America where, instead of "greatness" manifesting itself, one finds the "same cheerless frenzy of unchained technology and of the groundless organization of normal men." Yet what remains if one opposes the falsification of spirit into the forces of production (in Marxism) and its falsification into the intelligible ordering and explanation of laws (in positivism) with only the "organizing control of the mass and race of a people" (that is, as it is done in true National Socialism, something which Heidegger could not say publicly at that time)? It speaks well for Heidegger that he did not read a passage in which he responds to his critic, Carnap: his philosophy manifests "the most extreme flattening and uprooting of the traditional theory of judgement under the guise of mathematical-scientific method"; it wants to hand over the fundamentals "to modern physics in which all relations to nature are destroyed." It is no accident that this kind of "philosophy" is both "internally and externally connected" with "Russian communism" and celebrates its triumph in America (cf. the 1953 edition, p. 28, 36, and the new 1983 edition, p. 228). Thus in his own way Heidegger throughout binds the approaches of philosophy with political tendencies.

The printed draft of the 1935 course explains the talk of the inner truth of N.S. in a bracketed addition about "the encounter between planet-determining technology and modern man." In the *Spiegel* interview, Heidegger once more asserted explicitly against the doubters that this parenthetical remark was in his manuscript, but that it had not been read. In this manner the round parentheses are in fact to be understood. Still, Heidegger had to have spoken in an unusually positive sense about "modern man" if his encounter with technology is supposed to be able to constitute the "inner" truth of National Socialism. Is perhaps National Socialism in its outward appearance meant here after all, a movement which is to belong with Americanism and Communism so that it could have an inner truth, namely, the consequence of a history of decadence and a certain historical necessity? Heidegger interprets it this way in the *Spiegel* interview, but this idea appears to belong instead to the later years; but then the bracketed remark would be a later addition. Did Heidegger allow himself to be misled in his later interpretations by means of an inconsistent editing procedure?

Without a doubt, Heidegger was confused about these matters. In 1972, for example, I had published a small work, *Philosophie und Politik bei Heidegger*. I was not interested in historical questions but merely in current ones. In the meantime, Heidegger had been drawn into a rehabilitation of practical philosophy. Political tendencies became manifest which revealed a repudiation of all existing structures, a tack similar to that which Heidegger had used against the Weimar Republic (even if it did shout "hurrah" standing on the other foot). To the extent that one bluntly demanded the political totalization which Heidegger had always rejected, it was believed that Heidegger could be finished off by means of historically questionable references to his activities of 1933. Along with the thanks for this work, Heidegger included an additional remark: "I have nowhere spoken about the 'National Socialist movement' " (cf. *Einführung in die Metaphysik*, p. 152) (Feb. 2, 1974). I passed along this correction in 1974 in the afterword to the second edition of my work, but then I received a copy of the correction proofs of Heidegger's lecture course in which N.S. is discussed (cf. *Erinnerung an Heidegger*, p. 49f). In 1953, Heidegger had obviously wanted to avoid the term "N.S." which had received its historical unambiguity after 1935. Later, by glancing through the printed draft of the lecture, he was misled about what he had actually said.

The new edition of the lecture course quotes a letter which Heidegger wrote to Jerusalem in 1968 as a clarification of the debated passage. Therein Heidegger defends himself against the fact that one always singles out the one sentence from page 152 and passes over the lecture course in its entirety. From the entire work it becomes evident "that my position towards National Socialism at that time was already unequivocally antagonistic. The listeners who understood this lecture, therefore, also grasped how the sentence was to be understood. Only the party informers who—as I knew—sat in my courses understood it otherwise, as they well should have. One had to throw these people a crumb here and there in order to preserve the freedom of teaching and discourse" (p. 233). In his 1945 reflections on his rectorate, Heidegger stresses that an informer enlightened him about this surveillance in the summer of 1937 (p. 41). However, the debated statement of 1935 appears to be no crumb for informers but rather the expression of Heidegger's innermost conviction—namely his disappointment over actual National Socialism. The new edition of the course leaves the debated passage in the form it took in the printed draft. By going back to the manuscript, the new edition can in many other places revise the parentheses to brackets (because the additions were written later), but the manuscript for precisely this disputed passage is missing. On the basis of the manuscript copy and the correction proofs of 1953, the editorial afterword reaches the opinion that in 1953 Heidegger first expunged a harsh polemic, then replaced "N. S." with "movement" and inserted the parenthetical additions. (In this edition the dealings with Heidegger's text are often downright unkind. For example, there remains a senseless rupture of the second strophe and the second counterstrophe in the first chorus from Antigone, although this rupture can only be a misprint. Which Greek text Heidegger used is not discussed, nor is how the translation which Heidegger lectured about in 1935 appeared, when the printed translation came about, how it compares to the translation in the Hölderlin lectures of 1942, etc.)

Regarding his political entanglements, Heidegger himself definitively said that they must be portrayed and rendered exactly as they happened. He himself has given an essentially correct account of the decisive motives. Thus one should not allow the details to become blurred. Whoever does not want merely to judge Heidegger but also to appropriate initiatives and to learn from him must realize that in the thirties, Heidegger himself placed the decision about the truth of Being as he sought it in a political context. One must also see this in terms of what one wishes never would have occurred. It can at least provide the impetus for doing everything to prevent something similar from happening again under changed circumstances. The essential matter is then surely not that Heidegger allowed himself to be carried away to an involvement in 1933 (and, for example, did not, for this or that reason, immediately retreat or even emigrate); it is rather how he stood—in accordance with an all too well-practiced German tradition—with respect to the political arena in general. In looking back upon his rectorate, Heidegger emphasizes his inexperience in practical affairs; he always spoke of the party system of the Weimar republic only with contempt. Yet, is it a privilege of the German professor to take up practical affairs without becoming qualified for them? Is there not lacking in Heidegger's renunciation of Weimar Parliamentarianism a minimum of a well-balanced orientation to the nature of political tendencies? Even here Heidegger is merely representative; that is, the German philosophers (and not only the Germans) had attempted to make their contribution to the First World War with talk of war, but had in the long run given up their tradition of political philosophy. The so-called cleansings were accepted as something incidental which would surely have no effect. Evil was indeed even adjudged philosophically as the "fury" which of necessity belonged to historical transitions. The *Beiträge zur Philosophie* also emphasize that the essential characteristic of nihilism is not coupled with the question as to whether or not churches and cloisters were destroyed, men were "mass-murdered," and "Christianity" could go its ways; it has to do, rather, with mixing all possible world views which merely organize the given religious tradition, community, race, and class and which do not first of all ask about a possible truth. Yet would not a philosopher have had the occasion to reflect upon whether there are human rights to be defended—a right to life, to freedom of belief, etc.?

Heidegger emphasized (and even Hannah Arendt repeated his view) that he allowed himself to be snatched only briefly from the quiet work on the pre-Socratics during a sabbatical into the political whirlpool. Nonetheless, it remains to be considered whether violence does not correspond to the political blindness in which philosophical motives are projected into the fragments of the pre-Socratics and in which the rector's address decreed that Nietzsche was the "last" German philosopher. If Heidegger finally spoke of National Socialism as truly a disparagement, then this expression also shows what Heidegger had hoped for himself in the revolution of 1933. Something can be disparaged only if it genuinely had a mandate. After Stalingrad and Auschwitz, Heidegger emphasized both in his Parmenides lectures (p. 114) and in his Heraclitus lectures (p. 108, 123, 180f, 201) that the Germans alone, with their distinctive relation to the Greeks, can set into motion a "world-historical" reflection and against the "small spiritedness of the modern world" can deliver the West from its beginning into its history. If it is a matter of "conquering" at all, then this people has already conquered insofar as it remains the people of poets and thinkers and does not fall victim to a dreadful aberration of its essence. Do not those guiding images which led Heidegger close to National Socialism protrude all the more glaringly the more Heidegger apprehends a disparagement in National Socialism? He who still spoke in such a manner in the last years of the war could hardly experience the end of the war as a deliverance. A text from this time as decisive as the one about the determination of nihilism by the history of Being reverberates with the experience of an extreme exposedness. Heidegger began to translate Laotse who is said to have emigrated over the mountains. In the little cottage book, *Aus der Erfahrung des Denkens*, thinking, like an invalid in the time of convalescence, seeks to orient itself to the simplest experiences. Heidegger had spoken of what is catastrophic in tragedy, but the actual catastrophe was more terrible than what was pondered. Just as tragedy allows that which can give future life a new and different sense to shine forth in the demise (of Antigone, for example), so Heidegger also seeks a new era in the appropriated demise. For him, National Socialism in the developed form of its totalitarianism became a prelude to a future danger which, when taken upon oneself, could harbor something that saves. Heidegger now tries to ponder this saving aspect—without questioning any further the traditional standards of philosophizing or even only of speaking.

I do not think that my book lacks the usual reference to Heidegger's political entanglement of 1933; still, Heidegger's way of thinking certainly presents itself otherwise if one notes how themes from the religious and political dimension penetrate his thinking. Heidegger's thinking is stirred in a breath-taking manner by what he experiences as historical transition and by what portrays itself to him in its concreteness in an entirely different manner every five years. I have referred to this sense of urgency. Nonetheless, I have presented Heidegger's ways since the crisis of 1929 in such a way that it yields something like a systematic result. The transformation of the question about the sense of Being into the question about truth and freedom leads him to go back into the ground of metaphysics; thus metaphysics, above all from Plato and Nietzsche, can be submitted for a decision. The core of the overcoming of metaphysics, the harmony of the appropriative event and carrying out as the reformulation of identity, difference, and ground, leads to the other beginning manifested by the pre-Socratic philosophers and by primordial poetry and art. The Bremen lectures, *Einblick in das, was ist,* must show the freeing toward what is proper or one's own by the articulation of the world in fourfold and enframing. Discussing the question of Saying links the formal announcement of the early hermeneutics with later "poetic" thinking. In this manner one may be able to learn from Heidegger. If one wants to approach Heidegger's thinking in all the diversity of its ways and its fateful pregnancy, one must break up the individual stations and peer more vigorously into their individuality. The *Beiträge zur Philosophie,* then, should not be put with the later considerations about identity and difference which tie into Hegel and thereby into the Neoplatonic tradition; one should not merely be careful in being led to the strange discourse of the Bremen lectures from Heidegger's earlier questioning.

If one sees in what order Heidegger's steps follow one another, then the question about truth and freedom appears as a transition: Heidegger had viewed schematism or the imagination together with the practical reason which subordinates itself to a law. Heidegger now clarifies this relation to Idealistic philosophy with courses about Fichte and Hegel's *Phenomenology,* and Schelling and Nietzsche tread more and more vigorously to Leibniz. When Heidegger interprets Plato's parable of the cave, in his course *Vom Wesen der Wahrheit,* from the winter of 1931–32 (not yet published), he does two things; on the one hand, he measures Plato by Heraclitus' discourse about the *physis* which likes to conceal itself, while on the other he connects this interpretation with an interpretation of the *Theaetatus*. Nonetheless, does not Plato's discourse about *pseudos* and falsehood permit one systematically to gain access to what Heidegger now calls the concealing which is in truth taken as unconcealment? Along with Dilthey and Nietzsche, Heidegger leads "metaphysics" back to the principle of ground (cf. p. 152 again, German pagination in margins of this work); still, Nietzsche rather than Dilthey now leads one to the overturning [*Verwindung*] of metaphysics because Nietzsche formulates the problematic of nihilism and binds the question about time to the question about eternity.

At the outset, it is not yet a matter of explaining Nietzsche; it is rather the case that Nietzsche provides the decisive hints. Heidegger also sees the pre-Socratics as thinkers in the tragic age of the Greeks; he experiences in the "most fundamental form both romanticism and homesickness" in the "step-by-step recovery of the ancient ground," in the excavation of the earliest Greek philosophers as "the best buried of all Greek temples" (as Nietzsche writes in the posthumous text, *Die deutsche Philosophie als Ganzes*). *Einführung in die Metaphysik* seeks to understand Anaximander, Parmenides, and Heraclitus from the first chorus of Sophocles' *Antigone*. It thereby begins with the uncanny which comes to meet us from out of everything and which must be gathered against the wind by the most uncanny aspect of our being human. This going against the wind becomes a tragic process in that it is precisely the great man who is *pantoporos/aporas* and *hypsipolis/apolis*; that is, experienced in all, yet inexperienced, a universal citizen without a city according to Hölderlin's translation. Heidegger eliminates the period which separates the two characterizations in the contemporary Greek text and which assigns them to different men, yet this violence follows that of Hölderlin (however, in his old text from 1555, Hölderlin could find a good reason for his interpretation. After *apolis* there does not follow *to mee kalon* but *to men kalon*; thus, the interpretation of what is beautiful as a tragic process appeared to solve textual difficulties). When Heidegger now unfolds the question of truth along the guidelines of art and poetry and develops ontological projections in philosophy and science in terms of history, he also puts back into history the former fitting-together of principles. The *Beiträge zur Philosophie*, through which the wind of Sils-Maria has blown, develops in a persistent historicalizing a thinking which tries to ground Dasein in the "leap" as the abode of insightful moment of the truth of Being.

This grounding of the temporal field of play of the truth of Being at the same time prepares the "future ones" for the "passing by" of the "last god" (cf. p. 144, 262ff, 251). Hölderlin had spoken of the "pastness" of all that is "divine"; Heidegger expressly grants to the divine its essence, that is, eternity as passing by and with this the relation to history and to the unique moment. Thus, the Greek gods now in their expressly experienced essence stand as those who have been; a future relation to another divinity appears possible. Heidegger combines the "greatness" of the beginning of thinking among the Greeks and the philosophical motifs from Leibniz, Schelling, and Nietzsche with his reflection on Hölderlin. In this way he can orient himself to the creation of the great creators, so that in his lecture course in the winter of 1934–35 (p. 52), he uses Hölderlin's saying about the ages of the creator (God) as talk about the ages of the creators (in whom the creating power of God also stirs again). Yet Heidegger had to realize the following: the work of great creators in Nietzsche's sense does not belong to this age, but rather usable reserve (material at anyone's disposal), not the "leader" in this or that sense, but the functionary of totalitarianism, not tragic "greatness," but the struggle for domination of the earth in the name of "philosophy," that is, of the perishing of philosophy in totalitarian world views. After the experience of this catastrophe and its political consequences, Heidegger re-entered public life at the end of 1949 with the Bremen lectures. By this time, the awakening through Hölderlin was far advanced in that Heidegger thought of a gathering of everything divine into its essence and thus into the finality of the "last" god (although the discovery of the *Friedensfeier* again widely publicized this motif). Heidegger now believed that one could show only among the simplest things how world gathers itself in a thing so that this thing can become the abode of that which is holy. The jug can therefore stand for such a "thing" precisely because—as Laotse and the "mystics" made clear—it is "empty," and with its emptiness it grasps and transforms the world (in the libation). Hölderlin's latest poems from the "time of madness" also become important and the echo which meets us from Trakl's way to decline transfers to them. Yet "thing" and "word" in this sense cannot be placed on the same level with the concept of "equipment" from *Sein und Zeit* nor even with that of "work" from the writings of the thirties.

Even in his last publications, Heidegger certainly developed new systematic motifs. For example, the truth of Being cannot be called history; therefore, one cannot speak of a history of Being in the usual sense of the word because history, distinguished ordinarily from nature and ideal Being, characterizes not the dimension of origin but rather one of the derivative regions. To think "essence" itself in accordance with its primary meaning as being historical is a paradox to the extent that the historical openness of the fullness of the determinations by Being is covered up. Consequently, a word like "appropriative event" can no longer be comprehended in terms of occurrence and history, but rather in terms of the identity which unites thinking and Being (whereby this unifying is thought not in terms of seeing ideas, but rather in terms of belonging and being used for a mission). Nonetheless, instead of publishing a later work, Heidegger withdrew again when the thread between his difficult language and time broke. He could identify with Cezanne because this painter, after his break with Zola, his one-time friend, had painted in deepest loneliness the simplest things (a mountain, for example) in such a way that along with the things, the expanse from which they come and into which they withdraw is also there as the dimension of what is holy. For those whom it concerned, the eighty-year-old thinker quoted a statement from Cezanne (*Zum Gedenken an Martin Heidegger*, Commemmorative Text of the City of the Messkirch. p. 24): "I work, with few results, and too far removed from what is generally intelligible."

III

Since 1959, I had Martin Heidegger's help in working out this book; the book is thus imprinted with how Heidegger at that time viewed the way of his thinking. With the letter on humanism, *Holzwege*, and the *Einführung in die Metaphysik*, Heidegger had provided an initial insight into the ways that he had taken in the thirties. Thus, together with his students (from whom he separated in the meantime) he had striven for an entirely new result. The edition of the Nietzsche lectures was made ready, and since I participated in the enterprise, I could also experience first hand how Heidegger failed in his attempt at illuminating in a longer introduction the way he traveled from 1930 to 1947. It was not by chance that he (who still wanted to present his thoughts coherently in a major work) had looked out for younger people who could assist him in his new endeavors (the death of Dorothea and Egon Vietta in 1959 had surely made remaining alone tangible). It is perhaps characteristic of Heidegger that it was precisely to an outsider such as myself, to one who never heard him give a public lecture, that he granted long conversations and insight into important manuscripts. I had studied at Bonn—above all with Oskar Becker who as a mathematician and scientist came to Husserl and thereby met Heidegger. In his own way Heinrich Schlier had represented the theological work of the Bultmannian school and the controversies surrounding it. Besides, this university provided an orientation to work in humanities.

I was able to discuss thoroughly the individual parts of my book with Heidegger as they were being formulated. Some of it was determined by his comments, for example, the final, deliberately simplified unfolding of the problem of methods in terms of distinguishing between explaining, elucidating, and emplacing. In these conversations, I was naturally concerned about writing nothing "false" with regard to history. After the appearance of the book, Heidegger again acknowledged the appropriateness of the portrayal (June 8, 1963): "The only error which has attracted my attention thus far occurs on page 95 where you write that I "have taken up an '. . . and not rather Nothing' into the question about why." Heidegger pointed out that this addition already occurred in the well-known remarks of Leibniz and Schelling; to be sure, there the "nothing" is written in small letters and for him the question has another sense (as the *Einleitung* to *Was ist Metaphysik* shows). He also said that some years ago in connection with his lecture course, *Der Satz vom Grund*, he tried to set forth his interpretation of the question. Though he was not pleased with it, perhaps he would occasionally try again. Yet, one must ask what such help and acknowledgement signified. (Heidegger also reviewed a list of his teaching activities; in spite of this, courses were mentioned in the catalogue which were never held, and courses held and not listed were omitted, so that even the announcements of the collected works for years contained errors.) Occasional differences in our conversations should have genuinely disconcerted me. For example, I spoke of the 1923 course entitled *Hermeneutik der Faktizität*, yet Heidegger maintained that this course was called "Ontologie des Daseins." When he saw my doubtful expression, he hurried some meters back from the desk of his study and picked up the course catalogue. The title read "Ontology" (nonetheless, the course itself—according to Becker's recollection and even the placard on the bulletin board—used the title "Hermeneutik der Faktizität"). The dialogue with the Japanese guest in *Unterwegs zur Sprache* discusses a course from the "year 1921," which at first appeared to bear the title "Ausdruck und Erscheinen." Yet the question then arises whether the title did not read "Ausdruck und Bedeutung" (as in the first of Husserl's *Logische Untersuchungen*). Obviously what is meant here is the course entitled *Phänomenologie der Anschauung und des Ausdrucks* from the summer of 1920 which, under the subtitle "Theorie der philosophischen Begriffsbildung" discussed the methodological direction of phenomenology from a critique of Natorp and Dilthey. Why had Heidegger not gotten up from his desk to consult the exact title for the written copy and printing of these expressions? Were the formulations to have been one of the few touches of irony regarding Heidegger, that is, the irony regarding the all-out pursuit of course notes? Heidegger surely does not affect the orientation of his own early phenomenology of life when he says that he declared himself against "experience" and "expression." Indeed, he even grants that he would "never have arrived upon the way of his thinking" without his theological origin; nonetheless, he ascribes his early courses to the "youthful boundings" in which one can "easily" become "unrighteous" (Sp 91, 96, 128ff.).

Today the number of titles in the literature about Heidegger is in the thousands. Regrettably there is still no trustworthy information about Heidegger's early courses based upon notes and the few preserved manuscripts. (In this uncertain situation, I now ask myself, for example, whether Heidegger in his lecture course—and not just in conversations— also drew upon the letter to the Corinthians along with the letter to the Galatians and the one to the Thessalonians, which he treated explicitly.) Heidegger patiently and generously endured the fact that I treated his early lectures like Hegel's *Jugendschriften* (and thus also dreamed of a future discovery of the most beautiful of what he had worked out). Yet Heidegger would never have gone so far as to say, as Becker had, that *Sein und Zeit* is no longer the original Heidegger since it renders its breakthrough only in a scholastically congealed form. Heidegger suggested the opposite conviction to me, that he found his way to the question of Being in 1922–23 or 1923. If the *Gesamtausgabe* takes up the work regarding his dissertation, *Habilitation*, and Jaspers' review only as strange foundlings and otherwise begins with the Marburg lectures, it is from the conviction that the work which counts begins in 1923. Yet in 1923, is the question about the Being of Dasein as temporality already actually bound up with the experience that Being as presence has been thought in a temporally inadequate manner as mere presence (cf. p. 46f of this work)? Was there not a stronger break in the winter of 1925–26? These questions become important if one doubts that the discussion of Being taken as presence is about "time." Do not presence and the present here include spatiality, even the relation to "reality"? Questions of this type lead back to Heidegger's examination of Aristotle, but I misrepresented exactly this exposition, since the later Heidegger oriented the discussion about Aristotle entirely to the question concerned with the relation of ontology and theology. I also heard from Oskar Becker about that unbounded radicality of a significant interpretative thrust about which Hans-Georg Gadamer also reported: *Phronesis* in the sixth book of the *Nichomachean Ethics* is conscience! At that time I responded to this in amazement: But this is surely false, Herr Professor! Becker, who always urged us toward exactness both in logic and in interpretations, merely replied: By no means! Right or wrong, this was the newest philosophy at that time.

This most recent philosophy was the phenomenology of the factical-historical life. Heidegger saw such an alienation from phenomenology's primordial sense in Husserl's Cartesianism that he alleged that he could not understand Husserl's later critique of *Sein und Zeit*. After the break which occurred with Heidegger's Inaugural Address, Husserl had hinted at this (hardly insightful) criticism in 1930 in the Afterword to the *Ideen* and repeated it in 1931 in a Berlin lecture. In a daily paper, one Heinrich Mühsam related that Arthur Liebert, who had introduced this lecture, had referred to the capacity crowd in the *Auditorium maximum* by saying that the circle of admirers of a philosopher could one day fill the Sports Palace. During his lifetime (even in the *Spiegel* interview), Heidegger bitterly maintained that Husserl settled his "public account" with Scheler and himself in Berlin (to where Heidegger twice declined a call) "before students" in the "Sports Palace"; this was, he said, how Erich Mühsam (the poet and anarchist who was later murdered) reported it in one of the "large Berlin papers." In old age Heidegger sought to prove with a plethora of anecdotes that Husserl never had a primordial experience of history, and if one still credited Husserl with such an experience, Heidegger then claimed that it was due to retroactive impulses from his own thinking, for example, in the reading of pages 229 ff. of *Wahrheit und Methode*. "In the meantime you will also have seen Gadamer's book. Some gross errors occurred in that which concerns the relation of my thinking to Husserl and which can be removed only through careful philological work. Landgrebe's 'edition' of *Erfahrung und Urteil* had a devastating effect" (Jan. 7, 1961). Yet when in 1921 already Husserl wrote about history in an important manuscript as the "great fact of absolute Being," was this an exceptional formulation, perhaps even a response to the demands of a radicalization of phenomenology as Heidegger had expressed it to him? Questions of this type only slowly become amenable for discussion; a colloquium which I organized in the Husserl Archive at Louvain about the phenomenology of time provided controversial contributions toward this end (cf. the paper in volumes 13 and 14 of *Phänomenologische Forschungen*, 1982 and 1983).

After Heidegger, in the letter on humanism, had attributed the realization of a turning to his thinking, his way of thinking was divided into a thinking before and after the turning. The discussion of the turning in the specific sense gained in discussing nihilism cannot be carried back into the hermeneutical circle which plays not only between the analytic of Dasein and the unfolding of the sense of Being, but also between phenomenological construction and destruction (cf. p. 181 of this work). As much as I tried especially to dismantle the inappropriate use of talk about the turning, my presentation in its entirety nonetheless still remained oriented to this discourse; this happened above all because in this "introduction" I did not dare put an unpublished work like *Beiträge zur Philosophie* in the center. (Since one can hardly discuss *Heidegger and hermeneutical theology* adequately without the *Beiträge*, I again described the course of thought of the *Beiträge* in context: *Verifikationen*, published by E. Jüngel, J. Wallman, W. Werbeck, 1982, pp. 475–498.) The *Beiträge* were for me Heidegger's major work; nonetheless, in the notes of my book I still awaited the announced mature work in which Heidegger (as in his actual principal work) wanted to present his thoughts in context. To be sure, Heidegger complained that while he had gathered all the basic thoughts, he still lacked the language—one cannot just poetize. In the years after the publication of the present book, Heidegger went in an unexpected direction. In 1962, after the lecture *Zeit und Sein* again scholastically congealed, he traveled to Greece for the first time, and by encountering the Greek landscape itself he claims to have gained the impetus for a new orientation. Not even in Parmenides is self-concealment as the heart of uncon- cealment or "clearing" withheld. Mallarmé's talk of the "great Homeric aberration" points at least to the fact that the Greek interpretation of language was "unpoetic" (see *Vier Seminare*, 1977, pp. 133, 74). Indeed, two decades after the working out of *Sein und Zeit*, the manuscript, *Der Weg: Der Gang durch "Sein und Zeit,"* had called the experience of Being as presence and as present (that is, as the clearing of time) the basic experience which had to be withheld because it could not be transformed into an appropriate thinking and Saying; yet Nietzsche's talk about the "recovery of the ancient ground" [*Boden*] was rejected as "nostalgia"; the "clear pain of the tear of the parting" had been required.

To be sure, neither this or that final step upon Heidegger's way of thinking can be the decisive one; his ways can provide only different impulses which force one to come to terms with them. I had wanted my presentation as an introduction to be consciously free of explanations, but in introductory remarks and by reference to specific literature, I nonethe- less intimated where I saw matters entirely differently or preferred other ways. As I worked on this book, O. Becker wrote the essay *Platonische Idee und Ontologische Differenz*, which also appeared in 1963 as the conclusion of the volume *Dasein und Dawesen*. The questions touched upon there were the objects of conversations with Heidegger (the finest philosophical conversations which have fallen to my lot and yet which were controver- sial from the beginning). Heidegger manifested such an interest in these matters that he sought out Becker for a discussion; thus it appeared for a moment as if a convergence would be possible. In any case I had planned a second part to my book which was to provide a systematic discussion (about the question of nature, about praxis and history, and above all about affect and virtue, about language, conversation, and poetry, and about the religious dimension). Simultaneously with this new edition, I am collecting works in an anthology, *Heidegger und die hermeneutische Philoso- phie* (Freiburg/München, 1983), which instructively places Heidegger's thinking in a larger context. Yet, regarding those systematic themes I realized that what I had in view could not at all be presented in direct connection with Heidegger. On April 17, 1964, in reference to the "growing interest" in this book, Heidegger himself wrote: "I think now would be the time to stop writing *about* Heidegger. A substantive discussion would be more important." Yet both are still necessary: to bring into view appropriately the impetus which can emanate from Heidegger's thinking and to wean oneself from these initiatives in order to travel one's own ways.

Index

[Translator's note: The following index of proper names and works includes references and suggestions for further readings which the author has supplied throughout the text. These works are cited in the text by means of the abbreviations which have been provided below in brackets after the title. Complete bibliographic information can be found in the Appendix (pp. 243–246). Indexing of references to *Sein und Zeit* have not been included, since their sheer number would prove to be an encumbrance rather than an aid to the reader.]

Alethia 268
Alexander 260
Anaximander xvi, 159ff.
Antigone 180ff., 279, 281
Apel, Karl-Otto x, xv, 257
Aquinas, Thomas, Saint 18
Arbeiter 275
Arendt, Hannah 279
Aristotle 9, 12, 14, 18, 29, 35, 38, 64, 89, 121, 153, 158, 196, 204, 219, 222ff., 247, 260, 262, 264, 266, 267ff., 285
Auerbach, Erich 253
Aufzeichnungen aus der Werkstatt 191, 212
Augustine 18, 26ff., 52, 92, 266, 270
Augustinus und der Neuplatonismus 26
Aus der Erfahrung des Denkens [AED] 2, 26, 238, 279
Aus einem Gespräch von der Sprache 3
Avenarius 53

The Bacchae 262
Barth, Karl 255, 267
Bauen Wohnen Denken 195
Baumgarten 124
Becker, Oskar x, xiii, xiv, xviii, 250, 251, 256, 261, 266, 283, 284, 285, 287
Beiträge zur Philosophie 105, 115ff., 130, 145, 151, 175, 189, 191, 204, 206ff., 212, 215, 223, 226, 233, 279, 280, 286
Bergson, Henri 264, 267
Binswanger, Ludwig 248
Boeder, H. 253
Bollnow, Otto F. 248
Braig, Karl 262, 263

Bremen lectures 280, 282
Brentano, Franz 9, 262, 263
Buber, Martin 252
Bubnoff, Niklai von 264
Buhr, Heinrich 273
Bultmann, Rudolph xvii, 253ff., 261, 267, 271
Brief über den Humanismus 82, 210

Carnap, Rudolf 256, 276
Cassirer, Ernst 63, 270, 274
Cavailles, Jean xviii
Celan, Paul xvii
Cezanne, Paul 283
Char, René 255
Christentum und Geschichte bei Schleiermacher 264
Christentum und Geschichtlichkeit 248
Christus Mythe 265

Der Denkweg von Charles Sanders Peirce x
Derrida, Jacques xviii
Descartes, René 38, 40, 65, 97, 101, 155
Die deutsche Philosophie als Ganzes 281
Dilthey, Wilhelm ixff., 6, 18ff., 23, 33, 47, 54, 55, 60, 61, 122, 141, 153, 154, 264, 265, 266, 267, 270, 281, 284
Das Ding 193
Dostoevsky, Feodor 265
Drews, Arthur 265
Driesch, Hans 266

Ebbinghaus, Herman 266
Ebbinghaus, Julius 266, 267
Eckhart, Meister E. 14, 264, 274

Einblick in das, was ist 193, 195, 198, 280
Einführung in die Metaphysik [E] 75, 119, 138, 150, 156, 158, 163ff., 180, 221ff., 231, 251, 262, 276, 277, 281, 283
Einführung in die Phänomenologie der Religion 24
Einleitung in die Geisteswissenschaften 20
Encyclopedea Britannica 59
Das Ereignis 216, 228
Erfahrung und Urteil 286
Erinnerung an Martin Heidegger 273, 274, 277
Erlanger, Joseph 267
Erläuterungen zu Hölderlins Dichtung [EH] 140, 156, 158, 176, 183ff., 251
Erste unzeitgemässe Betrachtungen 274

Feuerbach, Ludwig 147
Fichte, J. G. 56, 260, 263, 266, 280
Fink, Eugen 254
Finke 264
Die Frage nach dem Ding 40
Die Frage nach der Technik 195
Freud, Sigmund xv, xviii
Friedensfeier 282

Gadamer, Hans-Georg xii, xiv, 247, 253, 285, 286
Geburt der Tradgödie 123, 272
Die Gefahr 195
Gelassenheit 139, 141, 156, 200ff.
George, Stefan 224
Gesammelte Schriften (Dilthey) 18, 264
Gesamtausgabe (Heidegger) 285
Gespräch von der Sprache 224, 262
Das Ge-stell 195
Geyser, Joseph 263
Goethe, Johann Wolfgang v. 126, 188, 207, 240
Gogarten, F. 253
Gorgias 201
Gröber, Konrad 261, 262
Grundformen und Erkenntnis menschlichen Daseins 248
Grundprobleme der Phänomenologie 265, 268, 270
Grundsätze des Denkens 222

Habilitationsschrift (Heidegger) See *Die Kategorien und Bedeutungslehre des Duns Scotus*
Hahn, Otto 125
Hegel, G. W. F. ixff., 14, 18, 29f., 45, 56, 62, 93, 97, 101, 116, 121, 129, 147, 154, 163, 181, 186, 188, 222, 223, 257, 260, 263, 264, 265, 266, 280, 285
Hegels Idee einer Phänomenologie des Geistes xv
Heidegger. The Man and the Thinker 274
"Heidegger and the Nazis" 274
Heidegger und die hermeneutische Philosophie xiv, 287
Heidegger: Perspektiven zur Deutung seines Werks xiii
Heidelberg disputation 27
Heisenberg, Werner K. 118, 199
Henrich, Dieter 249
Heraclitus xvi, xviii, 104, 119, 121, 127, 158ff., 223, 264, 279, 281
Herder, J. G. 93, 257
Hermeneutik der Faktizität 284
Hermeneutische Philosophie xiv
"Hermeneutische und mantische Phänomenologie" xiii
Hitler, Adolf 272
Hölderlin, Friedrich xvii, 6, 18, 156, 158, 167, 174–191, 197, 200, 201, 212, 215, 234, 237, 262, 271, 273, 274, 275, 281, 282;
Am Quell der Donau – 188;
Anmerkungen zum Oedipus – 179; *Der Gang aufs Land* – 183; *Germanien* – 175, 188; *Griechenland* – 186; *Heimkunft* – 178; *Der Rhein* – 175, 184, 185; *Stimme des Volkes* – 179; *Wie wenn am Feiertage* – 177, 184
Hölderlin und das Wesen der Dichtung 176
"Hölderlins Erde und Himmel" 144, 186f., 205, 212
Hölderlins Hymnen 178, 183, 188, 248
Holzwege [HW] 97, 98, 105, 138ff., 146, 148f., 153, 159, 163ff., 171ff., 191, 217, 238, 283
Humboldt, Wilhelm von 224, 242, 257
Hume, David 124, 263

Husserl, Edmund ixff., 6, 11, 14f.,
    51–62, 249, 260, 261, 263, 264,
    266ff., 271, 272, 283, 285f.

*Ideen zu einer reinen Phänomenologie und
    phänomenologischen Philosophie* xi, 52,
    285
Identität und Differenz [ID] 117ff.,
    157, 193, 202, 212, 240f.
Interpretationen aus der antiken Philosophie
    247
*Investigations of the Essense of Human
    Freedom* 45

Jaspers, Karl ix, xi, 28, 84, 102, 136,
    137, 256, 265, 266, 267, 285
Jünger, Ernst 192, 240, 275

Kahn, Charles H. 262
Kamlah, Wilhelm 248
Kant, Immanuel xii, xiv, 12, 14, 15,
    35, 38, 51, 59–67, 97, 99, 100,
    116, 124, 129, 133, 141, 142, 143,
    153, 222, 237, 249, 250, 257, 260,
    263, 264, 268, 269, 271
Kant und das Problem der Metaphysik [K]
    59, 62ff., 133, 143f.
*Die Kategorien und Bedeutungslehre des
    Duns Scotus* 10, 12, 43, 52, 83, 132,
    218, 247, 264, 285
Die Kehre 195
Kierkegaard, Søren ix, 18, 24f., 31,
    47, 136, 137, 153ff., 170, 175,
    186, 251, 252, 255, 266, 267, 272
Kisiel, Theodore xviii
Kockelmans, Joseph xviii
Krebs, Hans A. 263, 265
Kritik der historischen Vernunft 21
Kritik der reinen Vernunft 62–67, 270
Kroner, Richard 266
Krüger, Gerhard 250
Kuhn, Thomas xviii
Külpe, Oswald 263

Landgrebe, L. ix, 248, 249, 286
Lao Tse xvi, 3, 202, 279, 282
Lask, Emil 14f., 263
Lautmann xviii
Die Lehre vom Urteil im Psychologismus
    9, 15

Leibniz, Gottfried Wilhelm 74, 89,
    97, 100, 116, 122, 123, 124f., 237,
    282, 284
Liebert, Albert 286
Lipps, Hans 256
Logische Untersuchungen 15, 51, 52,
    268, 284
Lohmann, Johannes 257
Lotze, Rudolf Hermann 42
Louvain 286
Löwith, Karl 251
Luther, Martin 11, 18, 24, 26f., 31,
    157, 266, 267, 271, 272
Luther und Kant 267

Mach, Ernst 53
*Major Problems in Contemporary
    European Philosophy* ix
Maliarme 287
Marx, Karl ix, xviii, 147, 272
Misch, Georg xii, 247
Moehling, Karl A. 274
Morris, Charles x, 257
Mühsam, Erich 286
Mühsam, Heinrich 286
Müller, Max 127

Natorp, P. 284
Neue Wissenschaft x
Neure Forschungen über Logik 218,
    264
Nichomachean Ethics 260, 268, 285
Nietzsche, Friedrich xi, xvi, xviii, 2,
    3, 5, 18, 29f., 79, 81, 82–113,
    119, 121, 123, 124, 133, 139,
    144, 154ff., 175, 181, 186,
    192, 210, 212, 215, 222, 250, 252,
    254, 272ff., 279ff., 287
Nietzsche (two volumes) [NI.NII] 1,
    2, 5, 82–113, 115, 120, 122, 123,
    133ff., 143ff., 148, 150, 154ff., 163,
    212, 215f., 229, 232ff., 237, 251
Noack, Herman 253

Oedipus at Colonnus 216
Oedipus Rex 216, 272
*Ontologie oder Hermeneutik der
    Faktizität* 19
Otto, Walter F. 274
Overbeck, Franz C. 273

Parmenides   xvi, 30, 38, 40, 60,
    104, 119, 121, 141, 158ff., 247, 264
    279, 281, 287
Pascal   58, 155
Paul (Apostle)   18, 24, 25, 27, 156,
    252
Peirce, Charles S.   xv, xix
Perpiet, Wilhelm   253
Phaedrus   94
*Phänomenologie der Anschauung
    und des Ausdrucks*   284
Phänomenologie des Geistes   147
Phänomenologie und Theologie   211, 273
Phänomenologische Forschungen   286
*Phänomenologische Interpretation von
    Kants Kritik der reinen Vernunft*   269
Phenomenology and the Natural Sciences
    xviii
Philosophie der symbolischen Formen   63
Philosophie und Politik bei Heidegger   277
Philosophische Rundschau   262
Philosophie in Selbstdarstellungen   267
Phronesis   285
Picht, Georg   274
Pindar   180
Plato   18, 34, 35, 64, 79ff., 92–105,
    110, 123, 128, 158, 170, 181, 188,
    194, 196, 201, 235, 247, 250, 259,
    260, 268, 280, 281
*Platonische Idee und Ontologische
    Differenz*   287
Platons Lehre von der Wahrheit [PL]   50,
    79ff., 118, 127, 137f., 140, 142,
    149, 152, 159, 173, 209f., 228f.,
    232, 251
Plotinus   259, 264
Pongratz, L. J.   267
Prolegomena zur Geschichte des Zeitbegriffs
    268
Psychologie der Weltanschauungen   xi,
    136, 266
Pythagoreans   166

Ranke, Leopold von   22
Reden über Religion   265
Reich, Klaus   266
Das Rektorat   274
Republic (Plato)   79, 94, 109
Rhetoric   269
Richardson, W. J.   268

Rickert, Heinrich   14, 19, 264
Ricoeur, Paul   xv
Ritschl, Albrecht B.   265
Ritter, Joachim   xiv
Robinson, James M.   255
Rosenstock-Huessy, Eugene   274
Rosenzweig, Franz   265
Russell   218, 256

Sakkas, Ammonios   259
Sartre, J. P.   ix, xii, 137, 260
Der Satz vom Grund [SvG]   122,
    131, 141, 170, 202, 205, 229,
    231, 236f., 255, 270, 284
Scheler, Max   ix, 55, 58, 59, 61, 261,
    270, 286
Schelling, Friedrich Wilhelm v.   45,
    56, 89, 116, 117, 136, 181, 260,
    263, 265, 280, 282, 284
Schiller, Friedrich von   188
Schlageter, A. L.   272
Schlegel, Friedrich   264
Schleiermacher, Friedrich   54, 264,
    265
Schlier, Heinrich   252, 255, 283
Schopenhauer, Arthur   124, 250
Schulz, Walter   248
Schütz, Paul   252
Schweitzer, Albert   265
Scotus, Duns   247, 264
*Die Selbstbehauptung der deutschen
    Universität*   83, 274
Sheehan, Thomas   274
Silesius, Angelus   126
Simmel, G.   264
Soden, Hans v.   249
Sophist   34, 79
Sophocles   xvii, 166, 180ff.
Spengler, Oswald   154
"Die Sprache"   224
"Sprache und Wahrheit in der
    gegenwärtigen Situation der
    Philosophie"   x, 257
Strauss, Leo   xix
Struve, Wolfgang   252
Süskind, Hermann   264

Theatatus   281
Totale Mobilmachung   275
Trakl, Georg   224, 282

Troeltsch, E. 264
Tugendhat, Ernst 262

*Uber die Verschiedenheit des
menschlichen Sprachbaues* 242
Die Uberwindung der Metaphysik 129
Der Untergang des Abendlands 154
Unterwegs zur Sprache [Sp] xvii, 5, 7,
9, 53, 54, 60, 135, 152, 157, 174,
195, 202ff., 223ff., 230ff., 236, 239,
242, 284
Der Ursprung des Kunstwerkes 167,
193, 238

The Verb Be in Ancient Greek 262
Vico, G. x, xvi
Vier Seminare 287
Vietta, Dorthea and Egon 283
Vöge 264
Vom Wesen der Wahrheit [VWW] 69,
75ff., 80, 249, 280
Vom Wesen des Grundes [G] 72, 74ff.,
120, 127, 130, 145, 168f., 206f., 249,
251
Vom Wesen und Begriff der Quois 159,
209
*Von der mannigfachen Bedeutung des
Seienden nach Aristoteles* 9
Von Kant bis Hegel 266
Vorträge und Aufsätze [VA] 4, 31, 105,
118, 121, 134, 141, 147, 149, 154,
157, 159ff., 185, 191, 193ff., 201f.,
205, 207, 209, 215, 223, 226, 233,
239

Wagner, Richard 93
Wahl, Jean 137
Wahrheit und Methode xii, 286
Was heisst Denken [WHD] 29, 105,
118ff., 155f., 161ff., 185, 204, 217,
221f., 231, 236
Was ist das—die Philosophie 140, 148f.
Was ist Metaphsik? [WiM] 2, 28, 60,
69, 70, 72, 74f., 118, 126, 138ff.,
148f., 156, 173, 216, 221, 227, 249,
284
*Der Weg: Der Gang durch "Sein und
Seit"* 287
Wegmarken 267
Der Weg zur Sprache 224
Das Wesen der Philosophie xii
Wilcken, Ulrich 252
Der Wille zur Macht als Erkenntnis 95,
144
Windelband, Wilhelm 19
Winkelmann, J. J. 93
Wissenschaft der Logik xii
Wittgenstein, Ludwig 257
Wolff, Christian 124

Yorck, Paul Count 21ff., 47, 58, 270

*Der Zeitbegriff in der
Geschichtswissenschaft* 19, 36, 132
Zola, Emil 283
Zum Gedenken an Martin Heidegger 283
Zur Sache des Denkens 268
Zur Seinsfrage 7, 105, 115, 118, 141,
192, 217, 240
Zwingli, Ulrich 136